POLITICAL PASSAGES

POLITICAL PASSAGES

*Journeys of Change
Through Two Decades
1968–1988*

JOHN H. BUNZEL

Editor

With an Introductory Essay by
EDWARD SHILS

THE FREE PRESS
A Division of Macmillan, Inc.
NEW YORK
Collier Macmillan Publishers
LONDON

The Free Press
A Division of Macmillan, Inc.
866 Third Avenue, New York, N.Y. 10022

Collier Macmillan Canada, Inc.

Printed in the United States of America

printing number
1 2 3 4 5 6 7 8 9 10

Library of Congress Cataloging-in-Publication Data

Political passages: journeys of change through two decades, 1968–1988
  / edited by John H. Bunzel; with an introductory essay by Edward
  Shils.
      p.   cm.
    Includes index.
    Contents: A virtucrat remembers / Joseph Epstein — Notes on a
  journey / Julius Lester — How I spent my summer vacation / Martha
  Bayles — The New Left / Jeffrey Herf — Liberal in the middle /
  John H. Bunzel — Looking backward / Peter Collier — Letter to a
  political friend / David Horowitz — On hanging up the old red flag
  / Ronald Radosh — Errand into the wilderness / Michael Novak — Why did
  you sign that ad? / James Finn — The wide and crooked path / Carol
  Iannone — Irish Catholic / Richard Rodriguez.
    ISBN 0-02-904921-0
    1. United States—Politics and government—1945- 2. Liberalism—
  United States—History—20th century.   I. Bunzel, John H.
  E839.5.P594   1988   88–297
  973.92—dc 19   CIP

Contents

Preface   vii

Contributors   xiii

Totalitarians and Antinomians
Edward Shils   1

1. A Virtucrat Remembers
Joseph Epstein   32

2. Notes of a Journey   *Julius Lester*   60

3. How I Spent My Summer Vacation
Martha Bayles   88

4. The New Left: Reflections and
Reconsiderations   *Jeffrey Herf*   106

5. Liberal in the Middle   *John H. Bunzel*   132

6. Looking Backward: Memories of the
Sixties Left   *Peter Collier*   162

7. Letter to a Political Friend:
On Being Totalitarian in America
David Horowitz   187

8. On Hanging Up the Old Red Flag
Ronald Radosh   213

9. Errand into the Wilderness
                    Michael Novak   239

10. Why Did You Sign That Ad?
                    James Finn   273

11. The Wide and Crooked Path
                    Carol Iannone   302

12. Irish Catholic   *Richard Rodriguez*   326

   Index   348

Preface

It has often been said that hope for the future is nourished on the liberal left because liberal and progressive forces have historically represented a "vision of change" in an imperfect world. A much more strident variation on this theme was part of the discordant sounds of the 1960s. The new radicals proclaimed, on the basis of their own experience, that they had discovered the "real" America, by which they meant (among many other things) the "reality" of power and violence that lurks behind the facade of our institutions, principles, and ideals. To put it in overly simple terms, they had reduced the complex organization of postindustrial American society to a world in which the heroes and villains were easily identified and morality was simple and direct. Their mission was to destroy—by confrontation and by any other means necessary—an immoral and corrupt system that they charged was based on private power and the raw motivation of capitalist greed and had turned the American people into innocent victims of a subtle but cruel manipulation.

In the late 1960s and early 1970s, however, many liberals and others on the left (including the New Left, as it was called) saw America's time-proven capacity to bring about significant political, economic, and social change pushed beyond the point they could tolerate. Their world of liberal democratic values was soon in a state of great disorder. The wellspring of open-mindedness and tolerance dried up, giving way to feelings that ranged from disillusionment to anger.

Many books and articles have been written about this critical period in our recent history, most of them either social and political analyses of the times or sympathetic accounts by those who remember "the sixties" as "an American revolution" (Black Panther Huey Newton has said, "The sixties were like an apocalypse") that sought to force upon the national conscience their answers to the hard questions of peace, racial justice, individual freedom, and open government. But so far as I know, there is no book that brings together different individuals—all of whom at the time were liberal, progressive, or far left in their politics—who look back on those turbulent years and describe, in first-person essays, the events and experiences that led each of them to embark upon a political journey and, after searching thought and reassessment, end up someplace else on the political spectrum.

In June 1981, I was invited by a chapter of the American Jewish Congress to give a talk on my own political journey to a weekend conference at Greenwood Lodge in Soquel, California. It was something I had never really talked about in public before. My topic was "The Odyssey of a Liberal," and I used the occasion to be both personal and reflective. My talk was personal because I had been more than an observer in the year of violence and upheaval at San Francisco State. I had been directly involved as a participant and identified by the student radicals as "a target." It was reflective because my analysis of what actually happened in 1968–1969 enabled me to talk about the influence of events and ideas on my "belief system" and behavior.

It was out of the intellectual challenge and excitement of that evening that the idea for this book was born.

What has been called "the state of mind of the convert" can only be captured by imaginative self-analysis of the sort that was undertaken in Richard Crossman's brilliant collection of essays *The God That Failed* (1949), in which six outstanding writers set down with candor and in penetrating detail why they were initially attracted to communism and joined the Communist Party, and then what caused them to lose their faith and leave the Party. And although it had been suggested to me that a similar book might do for the sixties generation what Arthur Koestler, Ignazio Silone, Richard Wright, André Gide, Louis Fischer, and Stephen Spender had done for theirs, I soon realized that *The God That Failed* was not a good model—not for the book I had in mind. I knew that themes discussed by individuals of the calibre of Koestler and Silone that work well the first time tend to be trite and stale the second time around.

This, then, is a book in which thoughtful men and women reflect on what the late sixties and early seventies—those feverish years of antiwar protest marches, civil rights demonstrations, urban riots, campus violence, and so forth—meant to them and how and why they were changed by what they lived through. Each has had a unique journey and writes about it in personal terms. Some discuss events in which they played an active role as radicals of the left and that fundamentally altered the way they look at the world. Others, never part of the left-wing militancy of the period, were still involved politically and, over time, found that many of their firmest beliefs and assumptions had been called into question by their own journeys. Several who were not directly involved politically, and who may not have moved very far from where they once were, were nonetheless deeply affected by what they saw and have thought deeply about it. The range of experiences that forms the basis of these twelve odysseys of change is as varied as the authors themselves:

· Joseph Epstein's essay is about his journey from not very far out on the left to his destination not very far out on the right, with its concomitant radical change of assumptions about how society is and ought to be organized. One of the chief lessons he learned from the sixties is that "the left is scarcely the repository of all political virtue; far from it."

· Julius Lester writes about his years of involvement in the civil rights movement in the 1960s, including his experiences in Mississippi, his association with Stokely Carmichael and the "new cry of black power," his three days with Fidel Castro in Cuba, and, finally, his reaction to the disturbing realization that the movement had quickly become "antidemocratic." His journey, while one of change, has also been "one of accepting myself as I am and things as they are."

· Martha Bayles takes us beyond the "hothouse" of leftist politics to the simmering heat of rural Georgia. With clear-eyed candor, she describes her "radicalization" at Harvard and the reasons why she chose, in the summer of 1969, to get away from all that. Her activist friends declared that there was nothing to learn by going south at a time when the civil rights movement was no longer making headlines. But fortunately, Ms. Bayles disagreed. Her essay reveals how very much she learned from the people, black and white, whom she met, and from the mistakes, large and small, that she made.

· Jeffrey Herf examines the causes and impact of the radicalization on the New Left in the late sixties and the political and moral misjudgments that accompanied it. He then turns to his own much slower path of deradicalization, return to scholarship, and renewed appreciation of a liberal society in the last decade and a half.

• John H. Bunzel was at San Francisco State in the late sixties, when attempts to take over the campus by force came from the inside and from the new brand of left-wing political moralists. He examines why so many liberal and moderate faculty members refused to stand up to the extremists of the left when they sought to impose their will by threats or coercion, and describes how his involvement in the campus turmoil affected his "liberal mode of sensibility."

• Peter Collier talks about his experiences in the sixties as an editor of the radical magazine *Ramparts* and as a revolutionist in Berkeley alongside Tom Hayden, Eldridge Cleaver, and others. It is not only a chronicle of growing up absurd on the left but also an insight into the process by which an individual who has stepped into "history" (as he sees it) gradually realizes the implications of his facile beliefs and, through a painful process, is forced to reevaluate and reject them.

• David Horowitz's essay, written in the form of a letter to a New Left friend about his father's death, deals with the nature of the radical left—how to be in the left is to live inside a beautiful but criminal idea; how socialism is a political road paved with good intentions that leads to human hell.

• Ronald Radosh, whose political roots were in the radicalism of an earlier era, considered himself a "revolutionary socialist" in the 1960s and discusses how "some of the myths and assumptions we believed fell apart," leading him to "hang up the old red flag."

• Michael Novak analyzes several of the ideas and intellectual tendencies that led him into sympathy with the left and the gradual rejection of which led him to think his way out. Better yet, he describes his struggle to replace an inadequate vision of history with a more trustworthy one.

• James Finn traces his political past through the post-Vietnam period to explain why he now takes political stands that surprise and disconcert the liberal Catholic community of which he was long a member in good standing.

• Carol Iannone was drawn to the salvific promise of the counter-culture but found only gods that cannot save. For example, she found that feminism, far from being a means to greater self-possession for women, is a form of self-evasion.

• Richard Rodriguez describes his Mexican-American family up-bringing and Irish-Catholic education (which took strongly) to explain why he was resistant to the sixties and rejected particularly the sixties protestant antiauthoritarianism.

As editor, I am indebted to a number of people. I owe special thanks to the authors themselves. They allowed me to hound them on a monthly basis for over a year so that they would get their essays to me by the agreed-upon date—and we made it to the finish line pretty much together and on time. (My publisher said it couldn't be done.) I am grateful to Edward Shils, a truly distinguished and respected social scientist, for his comprehensive introductory essay that compares the "totalitarian temptation which my own generation faced with the temptation of antinomian hatred of laws, rules, and institutions with which the generation of the 1960s and 1970s was confronted." I am grateful for the support of the Hoover Institution and, in particular, the interest of Thomas H. Henriksen, an associate director of the Institution, who monitored the progress of the book from its inception. I also wish to acknowledge the many kinds of tangible and intangible assistance of my secretary, Virginia Gurrola.

Michael Joyce, Executive Director of The Lynde and Harry Bradley Foundation, and R. Randolph Richardson, President of the Smith Richardson Foundation, Inc., were both instantly enthusiastic about the idea for the book when I first discussed it with them. Without their support it would have remained only an idea.

From my point of view, the best part of being able to work closely with Erwin A. Glikes, the President and Publisher of The Free Press, is that he has become a valued friend.

John H. Bunzel

Stanford, California
August 1987

Contributors

MARTHA BAYLES is a novelist and critic who writes a weekly column on television for the *Wall Street Journal*. Her fiction and essays have appeared in numerous publications. She is the author of a book, forthcoming from The Free Press, about the rise and decline of America's youth culture.

JOHN H. BUNZEL is a senior research fellow at the Hoover Institution at Stanford University. He was president of San Jose State University in the 1970s and served on the U.S. Commission on Civil Rights from 1983 to 1986.

PETER COLLIER is the author of a political novel, *Downriver* (1978). He has also written, with David Horowitz, biographies of the Rockefeller, Kennedy, and Ford families. He was awarded a fellowship by the National Endowment of the Arts in 1980 and lectured abroad the following year for the U.S. Information Agency. He is presently codirector of the Second Thoughts project of the National Forum Foundation in Washington.

JOSEPH EPSTEIN, editor of *The American Scholar,* teaches in the Department of English and at the Medill School of Journalism at Northwestern University. His most recent book, a collection of familiar essays, is *Once More Around the Block*.

JAMES FINN is editorial director of Freedom House and editor of *Freedom at Issue,* its bimonthly magazine. He writes frequently on the relation between politics, religion, and culture.

JEFFREY HERF teaches in the Strategy Department of the Naval War College in Newport, Rhode Island, and is a research associate at the Centers for European Studies and International Affairs at Harvard University. He is the author of *Reactionary Modernism: Technology, Culture and Politics in Weimar and the Third Reich* (1984) and is completing *Power and Interpretation in West Germany: Intellectuals, Politicians and the Euromissiles* with The Free Press.

DAVID HOROWITZ was a left-wing activist from 1948 to 1974. During the sixties he wrote several radical books, including *The Free World Colossus*, edited *Ramparts* magazine, and helped to organize the Vietnam Solidarity Campaign. He is presently codirector of the Second Thoughts project in Washington, D.C.

CAROL IANNONE is a writer, editor, and teacher who lives in New York City.

JULIUS LESTER teaches in the Department of Afro-American Studies and the Judaic and Near Eastern Studies Program at the University of Massachusetts at Amherst. He is also the author of fifteen books of nonfiction, fiction, and poetry.

MICHAEL NOVAK holds the George Frederick Jewett Chair in Religion and Public Policy at the American Enterprise Institute. His latest book is *Will It Liberate? Questions About Liberation Theology* (1986).

RONALD RADOSH is a professor of history at Queensborough Community College, and the Graduate Center, City University of New York. He is the author, with Joyce Milton, of *The Rosenberg File: A Search for the Truth* (1983) and *Prophets on the Right: Profiles of Conservative Critics of American Globalism* (1975). He writes frequently for *The New Republic* and reports on events in Central America that affect U.S. foreign policy.

RICHARD RODRIGUEZ is a writer and journalist who lives in San Francisco. He is the author of *Hunger of Memory* (1982) and the forthcoming *The Protestant Reformation*.

EDWARD SHILS is Professor of Social Thought and Sociology at the University of Chicago; Honorary Fellow of Peterhouse, Cambridge, and founder and editor of *Minerva*.

Totalitarians and Antinomians

Edward Shils

The generation of persons who are now in their forties and their early fifties is not the only one which has had to face the temptations of spurious ideals. Has there ever been a generation since the French Revolution which has not come into the presence of temptation by one body of fallacious ideals or another? In the present century, there has been a continuing series of temptations with all their deceptive allures. My own generation in its youth had its fill of temptations, slightly different from but closely related to the temptations faced by the generation which is contemplated in this book. Since I am several decades older than the writers invited by Professor Bunzel to participate in the present memorial of a damaging decade, I have thought that it might be interesting to compare the totalitarian temptation which my own generation faced with the temptation of antinomian hatred of laws, rules, and institutions with which the generation of the 1960s and 1970s was confronted and in each case to give a brief account of my own responses.

Of what did the totalitarian temptation consist? It offered the prospect of a society free of conflict and injustice, in which human beings would be rewarded because they were human beings without regard to superiority or inferiority, without regard to their ancestral religion or their ethnic derivation, and without regard to sexual characteristics. It would be a society in which there would be no power of some human beings over other human beings. The totalitarian

1

temptation offered all the benign qualities of a pacific anarchistic regime, in which there would be no conflict among human beings because there would be no private property and hence no conflicting interests in the acquisition and retention of private property. Since there would be no conflicts of interests among human beings, there would be no suppression of their aspirations. The totalitarian temptation offered the prospect of a society in which individuals could develop themselves in accordance with their own inclinations. It offered the realization of the anarchistic ideal contained in Marxism.

The totalitarian temptation also offered the prospect of plenitude. Scarcity it asserted was an artificial creation of the regime of private property; once that regime was overcome by the abolition of the private ownership of property in the means of production and was replaced by the "social ownership" of the means of production, scarcity would cease. According to the prospect held out by the totalitarian temptation, the wastefulness of the competitive market would cease once a systematic planning of the entire economic system was put into practice. Planning required a strong central authority which was antithetical to the fundamental anarchistic ideal of the totalitarian temptation.

There was a third and distinctive feature of the totalitarian temptation. This was the concentration of power and authority in the government and in the political party which dominated the government and which excluded all other parties from attempting to accede to power. This entailed a monopoly of the public expression of opinion on all problems thought to bear on politics. It meant that there could be no autonomous collectivities in the totalitarian society, other than the single party which ruled it.

A fourth feature of the totalitarian temptation was the importance attributed to the industrial working class, the real interests of which were allegedly pursued and protected by the totalitarian party.

The totalitarian temptation entered Western Europe and the United States as an emanation of the Russian revolution of October 1917. In the United States, it drew to itself in the 1920s very few persons. It gained a slight following among literary and artistic intellectuals. It was the arrogation to itself of the anarchistic ideal which attracted these intellectuals, who were a tiny, isolated aggregate in American society on the 1920s. The Communist Party of the United States became the voice of the totalitarian temptation. Before the 1930s, the Communist Party held itself aloof from the intellectuals who espoused the first, emancipationist ideal; its attachment was from the very beginning to the third and fourth articles of the totalitarian faith; it took the second ideal to its heart after the promulgation of the First Five-Year Plan in the Soviet Union in 1927.

American intellectuals in the nineteenth and early twentieth centuries had been apolitical and antipolitical, constitutional and collectivistic liberals, Darwinian and utilitarian individualistic liberals, traditionalist conservatives, anarchists, radical and populistic democrats, and scientistic collectivists. Very few of them imagined a totalitarian solution to what they conceived to be the problems of American and European societies. In the opening years of the fourth decade of this century, a pronounced change took place. Intellectuals embraced all of the four ideals which together made up the totalitarian temptation. Not all the sectors of the intellectual stratum responded in the same way. Literary and artistic intellectuals went furthest in their submission to the temptation. Academic intellectuals did not go as far; technological and scientific intellectuals and intellectuals in practical-intellectual professions yielded least to the totalitarian temptation. There were also marked differences in the responsiveness of the generations. Among literary and artistic intellectuals, it struck all generations. Among academics, the generation of students and younger teachers was the most drawn by the temptation. It was also very differentiated in its attractiveness in the various regions or localities of the country. Hollywood and Berkeley in the West, Madison in Wisconsin although more sparsely than in the two Western cities, and then Cambridge, Massachusetts, and New York City. New York City and Hollywood were the sites of the most animated surrender to the temptation.

I reached majority in the early 1930s when the temptation first began to gain ascendancy over the minds of a relatively large number of American intellectuals. I was therefore one of those who was exposed to it. How did I respond?

———— • ————

About a half dozen years ago, a black student in one of my seminars on intellectuals was interested in writing a paper on the handful of black academics in American universities before and after the Second World War. Since this gentleman had once been a graduate student in the political science department and had dropped out, I encouraged him because I thought the topic might become the subject of a dissertation. I thought that he might respond favorably to my suggestion that he write a serious paper on the small group at Howard University, the most eminent of whom were Abram Harris and Ralph Bunche. One day he came to my room and after about an hour of discussion in which I laid out the topic for him, he changed the subject. He began the new subject with excessive flattery about how much he and his classmates esteemed me and then he said, "They don't raise any questions about you, but I am trying to get behind you." I asked him just what he meant. He replied to the effect that since it was evident that I knew such a lot about Marx and Lenin and about the history of socialism and communism, he suspected that I had been a "lefty" in earlier years. He wanted to know the truth: had I been a communist or fellow traveler of the communists in the 1930s or after that? I said, "Now, we have been discussing black intellectuals for about an hour today, and we have often talked about them before; it is surely clear to you that I know far more about black intellectuals than you do. Do you infer from that that I was once a black man?" He replied only, "That is a very good point." The fact is that I was never a communist or a fellow traveler. Since the country was being stampeded by communists and fellow travelers from about 1930 when I was in my twenties, I will reflect briefly on why and how I withstood the crush.

My parents, who were self-respecting, industrious, and prudent persons, were not educated at all by contemporary standards. My father must have gone to a Talmud Torah in Russia for a few years. This was well behind him when he arrived in the United States sometime in the second half of the 1890s, at the age of seventeen. He was fortunate enough to find employment in a cigar factory very shortly after his arrival in Philadelphia. He remained a cigar maker for the rest of his working life. My mother was about six or seven when she came to Philadelphia; she attended a public school for about three years where she was apparently a very good pupil and much esteemed by her teachers. She had to leave school in order to contribute to the support of her widowed mother and her younger brothers; one older brother and several sisters were already at work in various branches of the garment industry.

Like most of the poor Jews recently arrived from Eastern Europe, they had a very high regard for education, although they had had very little of it themselves. My father was probably vaguely a socialist, at least in his sympathies, although he never belonged to any socialist party. He read the *Daily Forward* in Yiddish from time to time, but he was not much interested in politics. Politics were never discussed at home by my parents or their friends and relatives. My one uncle, on my mother's side, who was intemperately against the bosses, was neither a socialist nor a communist. He was thought by his brothers and sisters to be unpleasant, and although he was the patriarch of that side of the family, he was regarded as too uncivil in his opinions.

My father had many friends among cigar makers of very diverse national origins, and they often came to visit us on Sunday afternoons. They never discussed politics. I remember only one political reference made by an old German, who was, I think, a very young soldier in the Prussian army during the Franco-Prussian War; it was a brief praise of Bismarck. For the most part, they spoke about their boyhood in "the old country" or about their fellow cigar makers, about the cigar-making business, about their employer, Mr. Herbert Shivers, and his prospective successor and heir, about their own kinsmen and their adventures, and other such topics. None of them read books.

My mother was better informed, since she read English very well, but she too took no interest in politics. She read the novels of Zola, Turgenev, Zangwill, and Tolstoy (at least *Kreutzer Sonata* and *Anna Karenina*), as well as short story writers. She was a great reader of Theodore Dreiser, H. G. Wells, Somerset Maugham, and Katherine Mansfield.

When I was ten years old, my parents purchased for me, on the installment plan, the eleventh edition of the *Encyclopaedia Britannica,* which I still possess and which I use frequently. There were no other books in our home except for those which I used to purchase for 5 or 10 cents from Leary's Bookstore—a great secondhand bookshop in Philadelphia.

Of course, I knew about the Soviet Union; it would have been impossible not to know about it if one read newspapers. My mother's eldest brother had returned to Russia early in the century, and there was much worry about his fate after the revolution. Neither of my parents had either interest in the Soviet Union or liking for it. It was thought to be a place where, despite the prominence of Jews in the revolutions, the Jews continued to have a very hard time. It was certainly not thought of in my family as the "workers' fatherland." In my boyhood, I shared those attitudes, which were a mixture of uninterestedness and distaste.

Of my immediate relatives of my own generation, who were numerous, only one had gone to university before I did, and not many followed. The few who followed mainly studied medicine, although one studied commerce and made a good name for himself as a teacher at the University of Pennsylvania. There was one very remote kinsman on my father's side who had gone to Germany before the First World War to study philosophy. He was a legendary figure; I never met him.

When I was an undergraduate, I read very widely. I became interested in sociology of the sort practiced by Max Weber. I was also greatly attracted by Sombart's writings, especially *Die Juden und das Wirschaftsleben, Der moderne Kapitalismus,* and especially *Der proletarische Sozialismus.* The latter was perhaps the first large German book which I read through from beginning to end. Tawney's *Religion and the Rise of Capitalism* and Troeltsch's *Soziallehren der christlichen Kirchen und Sekten,* about which I learned from Tawney and Weber, likewise attracted me. In this connection I also tried to understand the Marxist approach to the origins of modern capitalism and read the historical parts of Marx. I also discovered by accident Bukharin's *Historical Materialism.* I found him very cheeky and schematic, but I was impressed by the fact that he had written it while engaged in the political intrigues of the Bolshevik party in the early 1920s.

My one cousin who had gone to university—he was a son of the intemperate uncle—graduated the year before I did. He had studied architecture, but he also read books. He attached himself to me, *faute de mieux,* and we became uneasy friends. Like his father, he disapproved of the world. After I left Philadelphia, he ceased to read books, withdrew entirely into a private family life, and continued to have a disapproving view of the world. But before I left, he did interest himself in politics, primarily left-wing politics, about which he was sardonic, and secondarily ordinary politics, of which he disapproved completely. It was easy to disapprove of local politics in Philadelphia, since they had not become more virtuous over the years since Lincoln Steffens had investigated them. He had acquired a censorious view of bourgeois society from his father, and he had a certain cynical and contemptuous sympathy with communism; like his father he disapproved of "the Hilquits, the Thomases, and all the right-wing *shamases,*" but he was no admirer of communists either.

I had always been an explorer of the great city. Ever since I was ten years of age, I had gone alone every Sunday for long walks in the different districts and neighborhoods of Philadelphia. Such was the world in those days that my solicitous mother never seemed to worry in the slightest that I went off every Sunday by myself for about six hours. I became acquainted with practically every quarter of Philadelphia, looking at all the historically interesting buildings, peering into shop windows everywhere, going into churches and Quaker meeting houses, sitting in storefront missions, attending meetings of strange sects, seeing the external public life of the many ethnic groups of Philadelphia. I felt very much at home in Philadelphia, and even now, nearly sixty years after I left it, I still think of it with affection.

I was a patriot of a quiet sort from early on, and I have never ceased to be such. The Civil War was a very near presence to me, the Confederates having advanced as far as Gettysburg; I studied with pleasure and admiration the repulse of Pickett's charge. I adored Lincoln, admired greatly Grant and Sherman, and despised all those incompetent generals who nearly lost the war to the slavocracy. Veterans of the Civil War could still be seen in the streets in Philadelphia in my boyhood: I attended, on my own, Memorial Day commemorations in which volleys of rifle shots across the graves of Northern soldiers fallen in the Civil War gave me an acute feeling of kinship with those brave young men who had fought for the Union.

When my cousin attached himself to me, I continued my walks but also, on his initiative, I used to go to a communist "forum" on Sunday evenings where I heard most of the leading communists of the time, not only W. Z. Foster, Earl Browder, Benjamin Gitlow, Max Bedacht, Robert Minor, Robert Dunn, Scott Nearing but also the later dissidents—Jay Lovestone, Bertram Wolfe, James Cannon, Max Schachtman, and others of that ilk. They proclaimed the near-perfection of man's condition in the Soviet Union. I had a rather detached attitude about all that. If I had any politics in those days, they were the politics of H. L. Mencken.

At the beginning of these frequentations, I was not as distrustful toward the Soviet Union as I later became. It was perhaps the trial of the Industrial Party and later the Metro-Vickers trial which set me on my guard against the rulers of the Soviet Union and their tired and dusty American missionaries.

The deposition, exile, and denunciation of Trotsky, while not winning my sympathy for Trotsky, convinced me definitively that there must be something amiss in the Soviet Union. A minor incident which came to my attention in about 1931 sharpened this impression of communist baseness. On Sunday evenings, we had a sort of a *Stammtisch* at Horn and Hardart's on South Broad Street. It was there that I heard about the misfortunes of two young men—I think one of them was named Leon Goodman. I cannot recall the name of the other; he wore a "Lenin cap" of the type which was very popular in recent years until it yielded to the competition of the headgear of Mao Tsetung, and he obviously regarded himself as having a high calling as a revolutionary. These two young men were soft-mannered Jews who had been communists and then became Trotsky-ists. They had graduated from my high school, the great Philadelphia Central High School, a few years before me, so that must have singled me out for their attention. I did not know them at school. They must have also heard about my denunciations at the *Stammtisch* of the communists who were the authors of their misfortunes. One evening they came over to our table, perhaps—correctly—thinking that I would be a sympathetic auditor of their melancholy story. It was this: Attempting to win over to Trotskyism some homeless men, quartered in the disused Brill Locomotive Works at Broad and Spring Garden Streets, they were brutally knocked about by some communist partisans who were attempting to win the adherence of the same down-and-outers. The one who wore the Lenin cap was nearly blinded by a splinter of glass from his spectacles, which had been broken by their attackers. Their story, added to the "trials" and the morally scruffy impression of the communist leaders whom I had heard at the "forum," finished off the communists as far as I was concerned. After that I could not accept anything done by communists as virtuous or anything said by them as true.

At about the same time, the theory of social fascism was making the rounds; it was an obviously dishonest fabrication. I placed some of the blame for the accession of Hitler to power in Germany on the German Communist Party. The 1930s were one continuous exhi-bition of the hateful and arrogant ignorance of the communists, until the Seventh Congress, and of their patent hypocrisy thereafter. I followed their misdeeds closely throughout that decade and have done so ever since then. In the winter of 1934, I presented a paper on "Communism as a Social Movement" in Robert Park's seminar on "collective behavior" at the University of Chicago. For that paper, I read the *Daily Worker* from about 1927 onward; I also read carefully and benefited a lot from *Die Geschichte des Bolschewismus* by Arthur Rosenberg, the ancient historian who had separated himself from the communists after a long attachment. I also learned a lot from Waldemar Gurian's *Der Bolschewismus*. Both of these books and their authors are now forgotten; they should not be, since they were among the first to say what communism was. (I should include here Bertrand Russell's *Theory and Practice of Bolshevism*. That too helped to settle my mind on the matter.)

In 1932, my brother, who had graduated in engineering and who was always more idealistic than I was, took employment as an engineer in the Soviet Union; he spent about four years there. He returned to the United States in about 1936. While there, he had acquired a fluent mastery of Russian and an affection for his Russian colleagues and subordinates; what he told me about the Communist Party officials of the several parts of the Soviet Union where he worked and about the bureaucrats of the ministry with which he had to deal gave me additional ground for refusing to believe anything said by the American communists who always praised the Soviet Union as the one progressive force in the world.

I must add here that I was never a socialist either. I regretted the decision of the Bolsheviks to break the Second International. I certainly found offensive, for its trivial vilifications, Lenin's criticism of the "renegade Kautsky," whom I regarded as a probably quite boring but honorable person, and certainly no more of an "enemy" of the working classes than Lenin himself. I had more sympathy for Eduard Bernstein's criticism of Marxism, but I did not find his book on the presuppositions of Marxism very persuasive. His personal account of his years of exile in England was much more to my taste. Nevertheless, I had a feeling of sympathy with social democrats in Europe, and I continue to do so, even though I think that their ideas are wrong. They were clearly not such villains as the communists. Henry de Man's *Zur Psychology des Marxismus*, Robert Michels's *Political Parties*, above all Sombart's *Der proletarische Sozialismus* gave me a very skeptical perspective about socialist ideas. I also rather enjoyed Pareto's *Systèmes socialistes* for the sharpness of its criticism and its mocking attitude. Georges Sorel was, in general, more interesting to me than any other famous socialist and communist writer. I appreciated the primordial moralism of *Le Procès de Socrate* and his belief, equally unusual for a socialist, in redemption through the collectively transcendent experience of *la grève générale*. It was from studying Sorel that I learned the tradition of socialism was a historically accidental collocation of diverse elements which did not belong together with logical necessity. It was tradition rather than reason which held them together.

In the 1930s I met very few socialists. The handful of socialists at the University in Pennsylvania were very flimsy intellectually. There was only one of them who was of good character and who knew anything at all. His name was Sidney Sufrin; he was a practical socialist who was a partisan of economic planning. He had no interest in Marxism or in continental social democracy; he was very much inclined toward Fabian socialism. He was a very intelligent young man, rather moody; we did not often talk about politics, although I do recall one argument which we had about planning. This must have been in 1931, when the *Schwaermerei* for the accomplishments of the Soviet Union was just beginning; he did not share it, although I do remember his friend Maynard Krueger, who taught economics at the University of Pennsylvania, explaining away communist tyranny as a necessary condition of economic progress. (How often did I hear that same argument years later on behalf of the tyrannies of the new states of Africa after they gained their independence.)

Sidney Sufrin was very enthusiastic about the University of Chicago and especially about Frank Knight, the famous economist—Sidney had been a research assistant in economics there the preceding year. With his encouragement and help, I came to Chicago in the autumn of 1932 with the intention of studying sociology and economic history; I had read fairly widely in these two subjects while an undergraduate but never formally. I had studied Romance languages and literature when I was an undergraduate, and I intended to improve the study of nineteenth-century literature by applying to it the ideas of Weber and Dilthey; Georg Brandes was a hero of mine, a genuine "European" whose *Main Currents of European Literature in the Nineteenth Century* I wished to emulate and improve in a more sociological way. But since I had to support myself in Chicago, I obtained an appointment as a social worker in the Cook County Bureau of Public Welfare. I was responsible—after a fashion—for about 800 Negro families. I learned a great deal from my "clients" by this rather intense experience. I acquired a very warm feeling for them and regarded them as a brave and upright people who maintained their dignity under very adverse circumstances. In consequence of this experience, I could not but see straightaway the nonsense of the program of a "black republic," on which James Allen (*né* Solomon Auerbach) was a leading authority. I knew that the communists were seeking to exploit the Negroes for their own purposes, using some not very high-grade decoys like James Ford and Harry Haywood. They did not succeed. How could they have succeeded? The poor Negroes whom the communists were hoping to ensnare were surely uneducated, and many of them were probably not very intelligent, but they were shrewd enough to be utterly indifferent to the appeal to "Defend the Chinese Soviets." That was one of the demands displayed on the placards at a demonstration organized by the communist-dominated Unemployed Council in front of the building where my branch of the County Bureau of Public Welfare had its offices. (I also saw with abhorrence the brutality with which the police broke up the pathetically small demonstration.)

How could one have any respect for a movement so crudely unrealistic, untruthful, and manipulative? I will not go into the murderous dishonesty of the Moscow trials, which only the deliberately blind and the knowingly hypocritical could have said were justly initiated and fairly conducted. It was not only my reading about the monumental untruthfulness and cruelty, usually treated very indulgently in the *New York Times*, *The Nation* and *The New Republic*, which put me off this "one great hope of mankind." It was also my own immediate experiences and my own close observation of communists, with whom I had many contacts in the 1930s and very early 1940s.

At the University of Chicago in the 1930s, although Albert Walgreen, the owner of a chain of drugstores in Chicago, had instigated an investigation by a legislative committee of the state of Illinois into communist activities at the University of Chicago, communists and communist activities were negligible. It was not that the communists did not wish to make mischief; there were too few of them to do so.

One among them, whom I came to know very well, was by nature a mischief maker. He was Frank Meyer, a demonic figure with flashing black eyes, a mop of black hair before mops on the head became the fashion, shabby in dress, eloquent, voluble, excitable, a young man from a prosperous family in northern New Jersey by way of Oxford and the London School of Economics, from which he had been expelled. He was nominally a graduate student in anthropology, but his time was spent in agitation. He was very far from stupid—in fact he was rather bright—and he had his charms, but he certainly had no interest in learning anthropology. I came to know him quite well because he attended a course of Louis Wirth, to whom I was an assistant. In that course, he frequently interrupted Wirth's fluent if not very solid discourses with Marxist corrections, supplements, and reinterpretions. I knew more about Marx than he did and was not less forward, so that after a time he decided that I knew more than he did and that knowing so much about Marx and Lenin—in fact it was not very much but it was more than he knew—I must be sympathetic with communism. It was inconceivable to him that one could know the writings of Marx, Engels, and Lenin without being on their side. This latter error did not last very long; his more fundamental error lasted nearly ten years longer. Once he ceased to serve as educational director of the Communist Party in the state of Illinois, he became a zealous, regular, and much valued contributor to the *National Review*. In the last years of his life he became a prominent and deadly serious liberterian. Some years after he had ceased being a communist and long after I had last seen him—I last saw him at a street corner near the university on the evening when it became clear that the Soviet armed forces were about to invade Poland, and he was so despondent that I said to a common acquaintance that I thought that Frank Meyer was reaching the end of his communist tether—he wrote me that his current beliefs were undoubtedly as distasteful to me as his earlier ones had been. That amused me. It was also more or less true.

Despite Frank Meyer's sartorial effects, the Chicago Stalinists of those days were bourgeois gentlemen compared with the antinomians who thirty years later took over most of the heritage of Stalinist totalitarianism, touched it up here and there with a few criticisms, and placed a very heavy emphasis on its recessive antinomian element. Except for Frank Meyer, the communists at the University of Chicago, who were in any case very few in number, had no outstanding personality. The Trotskyists, or at least the small number of sympathizers with Trotsky, who were as anti-Stalinist as I was but for other reasons, included a handful of gifted young men who later made a name for themselves, such as Harold Kaplan, Saul Bellow, Herbert Passin, Isaac Rosenfeld, and Ithiel Pool. They enjoyed the friendship of Nathan Leites, then an instructor in political science, a passionate and extremely well informed anticommunist. Leites was certainly not a Trotskyist, but he liked the spirited and literate admirers of Trotsky, who were generally a rather attractive lot. For a time, their brightness was enhanced by the lively and eccentric presence of Lionel Abel. I was friendly with Leites, and the Trotskyists therefore regarded me as not too far from their position. As a matter of fact, I thought that they were rather foolish in their political and social views, but in their general culture and cleverness they were many cuts above the Stalinists.

Thus to the query which several of my students have put to me over the years, as to whether I was a communist or a sympathizer or a fellow traveler when those variant forms of totalitarian opinion were at the height of their influence, my answer is, of course, negative. I do not claim any credit for this. It did not take any exceptional intelligence, or imagination, or erudition, or strength of character to withstand the totalitarian temptation. One just had to be intelligent and self-respecting enough to withstand prevailing opinions. I had of course the advantages of knowing a little more of European history, of being a little more of a patriot, of knowing more of Marxism and of better ways of interpreting social phenomena than were given by Marxism, of having a little more of a sense of affinity with the American working class and with the lower classes generally, and of knowing a little more economics—thanks to Frank Knight—and much more about romanticism and about the tradition of antibourgeois bohemianism. I also had the advantage of having found an intellectual direction of my own before the great stampede of the American intellectuals began. Then too I had the advantage of being at the University of Chicago and not at Harvard, Columbia, Wisconsin, Berkeley, or the City College of New York. All those amounted to a considerable advantage when it came to seeing through the intellectually shoddy, arbitrary, and derivative character of the communist theories and policies. I also had the advantage of knowing about Marxism before it became the *dernier cri* of the intellectuals. Furthermore, I have always been repelled by running with the mob. In this respect, not being in New York helped; so did being pigheaded. It took nothing more than a sober eye to size up the brutality and the moral shadiness of communists, both in the Soviet Union and in Western countries.

Despite the rush of so many Gadarene academics and intellectuals toward the Soviet camp and its outposts in Western Europe and the United States in the 1930s, it was on a much smaller scale than the hectic stampede, in a similar but less specific direction, on university campuses in the United States during the 1960s and early 1970s. There was no pressure at all on me at the University of Chicago in the 1930s to "move to the left." Perhaps at Wisconsin or at the City College of New York or among the younger teachers at Harvard or Berkeley in that decade, I would have had to resist the pressure of environing opinion, but not at the University of Chicago. It was not that there no strong opinions at Chicago. On the contrary, there were many of them—there were neo-Thomists, there were anti-neo-Thomists, there were enthusiasts for the "great books," there were the equally dogmatic antagonists of the "great books," there were collectivistic liberals, there were individualistic liberals, there were the partisans of psychoanalytic interpretations of political activity, there were logical positivists, instrumentalists, there were even a few Christians. All of these views were strongly held. What was true among the teachers was also true among the students, especially the undergraduate students, who were, however, far outnumbered by the graduates.

Marxism had to take its chance among the other contenders,

and it was bound by its intellectual limitations not to come off well. Except for Frederick Schuman, who was in the political science department until about 1936 and who was a fairly conventional and not very sharp-witted fellow traveler for some years and later a devotee of Ron Hubbard's dianetic nonsense, there were no public fellow travelers or "running dogs" of the propagandistic efforts of the communists. There were a few professors who allowed their names to be used by the communists in order to gain more dupes. As I remember, Anton Carlson and Ernest Burgess were among the very few whose names appeared in communist declarations. Burgess was a good, gentle person who was naive enough to think that sociological research and "social planning" were made for each other. Carlson was an eminent physiologist, a "freethinker" of the old school; he looked and spoke like a Swedish carpenter from the North Side. He "believed in science"; the communists alleged they did so too, and that was enough for him. I think that there were "Marxist study groups" on the campus, but I was not invited to them, probably because it was thought that I would make too much trouble. No one known to me participated in them except Frank Meyer.

That is the story of why and how I did not yield to the totalitarian temptation between the early 1930s and the middle of the 1950s.

I myself had a much easier time than did the young persons of the 1960s and early 1970s. I was able to resist the totalitarian temptation, because I just did not find it tempting. When the temptation of antinomianism appeared thirty years later, I was not tempted by it either. For one thing, I was too old; that antinomianism was a "young people's thing." But far more important was my certainty that the ideals pursued were for the most part valueless, that the account which it gave of the world was wrong, and that the motives of those who saw and judged the world according to the antinomian world view were discreditable.

———— • ————

When the antinomian temptation came over the horizon in the 1960s, I did not expect it. But when I saw what it was, it seemed to be little more than a very intensely stirred-up continuation of recent tendencies and older traditions. I had always been opposed to the "cult of the self," skeptical about the romantic belief in the creative potentialities of all human beings; I despised *Gemeinschafts-schwaermerei*. That was armor enough.

The antinomian temptation is an elaboration of certain parts of the totalitarian temptation, with a certain shift in emphasis. It is an advancement of the emancipationist parts to greater saliency and a retraction of other features from the saliency which they occupied in their totalitarian variant. The ultimate utopian end—the first article of faith of the totalitarian temptation—is more prominent in antinomianism. At its innermost core resides, first, the fundamental and all-overriding value of the emancipation of the individual from the burden of obligations and, second, the unremitting insistence on his rights. This is the root of the matter. The highest ideal of antinomianism is a life of complete self-determination, free of the burden of tradition and conventions, free of the constraints imposed by institutional rules and laws and of the stipulations of authority operating within the setting of institutions. Neither God nor man is to be set over the individual self. (Charismatic authority is acceptable, but rational-legal or traditional authority is utterly repugnant.) All human beings, according to this view, are entitled to whatever any individual is entitled to. All human beings are entitled to be gratified as the promptings of the self require. The traditions of individualistic and constitutional liberalism—equality before the law, equality of opportunity, equality of electoral power, equality in the freedom of expression and in the representation of ideals and interests—are not only negated by this anarchistic liberalism; their postulates are denied. The traditions of individualistic and constitutional liberalism presuppose the effective working of institutions; antinomianism will have none of that. Of all institutions, antinomianism is most averse to private ownership of the means of production. Once private property in the means of production is eliminated, the conflict of interests which is the dominant feature of all previously known societies and especially of modern bourgeois society is bound to disappear.

With the elimination of the constraints of scarcity thrown up by private property in the means of production, the cessation of submission to tradition and conventions, the abolition of institutions in which authority operates, and the dissolution of the inhibitions and repressions inculcated by culture, human beings will enter the realm of freedom.

The program of the totalitarian temptation placed the realm of freedom in the future. Until then, class-conscious workers, whose class would be the beneficiaries of their exertions, must submit to the discipline of the Party until it seizes power and abolishes the bourgeois state. Once that has happened, then it will be necessary for the workers to continue to accept the dictatorial discipline imposed by the Party, which represents their interest.

The antinomians, by contrast, demand and wish to live in the realm of freedom before they have seized power. The culture of bohemianism was the forerunner of such an embryonic free society, living and practicing freedom, in the midst of the old oppressive, conflict-ridden, tradition-bound society.

The antinomian temptation shares with its totalitarian ancestor the anticipation of plenitude. It goes further and assumes that it already exists and that it is available through the activity of government. Governments can be made to act to provide plenitude if they are sufficiently pressed by the groups desiring more than they can acquire through the operations of the market.

In the totalitarian representation of the end and means of historical development there was a strain between the anarchistic utopian and oligarchic elements. The totalitarian tempters alleged that the utopian ideal of a harmonious freely expressive authorityless society could be reached only by the disciplined efforts of the working class led by the Communist Party. It was by this device of placing the two contradictory articles of faith in a temporal sequence that these two antithetical elements of emancipation and unquestioning submission to the will of the Party were made to coexist with a minimum of logical and political contradiction.

But even though the antinomian temptation places the emancipationist value far in the forefront of the several constituents of that ideal, it does not jettison the others. Since it is in favor of plenitude through governmental action and since it is in favor of the "social ownership of the instruments of production," it is committed to socialism—and therewith to authoritative institutions. Like the totalitarians, antinomians deride the institutions of traditional individualistic and constitutional liberalism; like the totalitarians, antinomians manipulate those institutions to conduct their war against traditional individualistic and constitutional liberalism and to live their emancipated lives in a state of plenitude.

The antinomians purport to distinguish themselves from the "old left" by criticism of the Soviet Union and their refusal to subordinate themselves to the Communist Parties of their respective countries. The disavowal is specious. The "New Left" collaborates with the "old left." It is not just on a tactical calculation that the collaboration rests, but rather on a fundamental agreement of values and ideas, with variations of emphasis.

The antinomians have opposed American society no less vehemently than did the old left. Indeed they might be more vehement, since they have added to their own hatred of the American economy and polity the anger of the feminists and the defensive nattering of the homosexuals as well as the fierce bitterness of the radical blacks with whom the New Left has made common cause.

Although the Soviet Union is criticized for its infringement on the freedom of artists and writers, its merit is unquestionable because it has firmly established the "social ownership of the instruments of production." A very important feature of this consensus of totalitarianism and antinomianism is the readiness of the antinomians, in discussions about the relation between the Soviet Union and the United States, invariably to give to the Soviet Union the benefit of the doubt. The aim is always to vindicate the Soviet Union and to put the United States in the dock.

The intellectual outlook of the antinomians is by no means as discontinuous from the totalitarian outlook of the fellow travelers and frontal deceivers of the early period as some of them think. Their declared abhorrence of "bureaucratic socialism"—a euphemism to dissociate the New Left from the Soviets—has not prevented their espousal of a standard Soviet communist interpretation of world events. The pervasive presence of the totalitarian outlook in the outlook of the antinomians had to occur, since the latter had its origin in the former. This consensus of a "vulgar" Marxist view of the world is what links the two; the numerous allegedly humanistic interpretations of Marxism drawn from the *Frühschriften* persist in acceptance of the basic postulates of "vulgar" Marxism regarding the nature of bourgeois society.

A simplified—"vulgar"—Marxist-Leninist-Stalinist image has come to dominate the antinomian view of the world. The social democratic variant of Marxism had lost its appeal to intellectuals, and the totalitarian outlook filled the vacuum in the minds of those who wished to abolish the existing order of society. Despite the judicious evasiveness of their terminology and their addition of some emancipationist wrinkles, the antinomians continue the primitive interpretation of bourgeois society that is to be found in the writings of C. Wright Mills, Paul Sweezy, Paul Baran, and Gunder Frank. They have lost faith in the industrial working class, they no longer believe in its revolutionary role; but they still demand a revolution which will introduce the "social ownership of the instruments of production." They still believe in an advance guard of revolution, variously found in students, the "Third World," the peasantry, and the generally disaffected. They have come to place more confidence in guerrilla actions and in terrorism than was ever the case in social democratic Marxism or in Leninist Marxism either.

The burden of 1917 has weighed as impressively on the minds of the antinomians as it did on the minds of the fellow travelers of thirty years earlier. Indeed it has weighed even a bit more heavily because it has been necessary to give an appearance of criticizing the Soviet Union while at the same time vindicating its principles.

Nevertheless one should not overlook the important differences. The greatest difference lies in the attitude toward emancipation. From this difference flow all others. In the antinomian outlook there is a resistance against discipline imposed from the outside, either in the form of a highly organized political party or in the form of a rigorous doctrinal orthodoxy. The antinomians reject the puritanism of the totalitarian temptation.

I had long seen through both the antinomian and the totalitarian elements in the nominally new temptation to which so many of my juniors and coevals were succumbing in the 1960s and 1970s. By the time the antinomian temptation appeared in its most seductive form, I knew personally some of the leading figures—although I had no close friends among them, as I had among the totalitarians. I had been reading the writings of the members of the Frankfurt Institut fuer Sozialforschung from their very beginning. I knew Horkheimer and his fellows from the 1930s, when Horkheimer and Adorno made a feeble and unsuccessful effort to draw me into their fold. Norman Brown had been a graduate student at the University of Chicago, and so had Paul Goodman. I had intermittent contacts with Habermas. I certainly was not even slightly tempted by their beliefs.

I myself had changed very little; my earlier beliefs had become more differentiated. What had been some tendencies toward a conservative liberalism became more pronounced. As an offspring of immigrant parents who would probably have been murdered in pogroms or been starved had they remained in Russia, I had good reason to be grateful to the United States. I knew of its imperfections, but given the imperfections of human beings in general, I did not expect perfection from it or from any other society. One could not contemplate the history of humanity and fail to see this unless one had yielded completely to the temptation to believe that ideal and total solutions to the problems could ever be found and realized. I felt very much at home with the ordinary, stalwart people of Chicago. I certainly was very aware of the horrors of life in the big cities of the United States in recent years, but that did not put me off American society. Indeed I saw the antinomian hand in some of these horrors.

As a university teacher, I had a good opportunity to see the seduction of the younger generation by the antinomian temptation. I regretted it greatly, not only because I disapproved of the actions in which they engaged under its influence but because of the losses these young persons were causing to themselves. From the standpoint of one who was advanced in middle age and who had spent much of his life happily among university students, it seemed to me that these young antinomians were wasting the best years of their lives in pursuing unworthy or unrealizable ideals and in performing actions which no one self-possessed would allow himself or herself to enter upon. (I exclude from this judgment the movement for the civil rights of Negroes, conducted with admirable bravery by Negro and white students.)

The war in Vietnam was a common point of departure and a common point of reference for antinomianism. It gave it the air of public legitimacy. Antinomianism was not, however, simply disapproval of American military action in Vietnam, nor was it simply a manifestation of a desire to avoid conscription.

The movement gained force from its association with the movement for civil rights for blacks and the "black power" movement. These added to the heterogeneity and profusion of demands. Central to the whole tumult was the hatred of institutions—government, academic, familial, military, and economic. This was above all hatred of authority.

As a patriot, I grieved over the hostility to the United States manifested in many wild actions, although I did certainly not deny the propriety of criticizing and even criticizing severely the policy of the government of the United States for its engagement in military activities in Southeast Asia. I myself thought that engagement justified, and I still regret that it had to be halted without success. I certainly agree that that policy was debatable, with respect both to its end and to its means, but the way in which the youthful antinomians conducted their frenzied battle against it was and is still utterly deplorable.

Still it is not against the youthful demonstrators, rock throwers, bomb layers, and grafitti daubers and sprayers that I would direct my criticisms. Nor will I waste words on such pied pipers as Dr. Spock, William Sloane Coffin, Frances Fitzgerald, Paul Goodman,

Susan Sontag, and the Berrigans. They played a villainous part and did much damage, to recover from which American society will take a long time. Still they had no special responsibility—aside from that of decent citizens and more or less educated men and women—for the universities against which so much of the "revolution" was directed.

The attacks against the universities seemed to me to be a compound of cowardice, arrogance, and ignorance. The cowardice was the easiest to discern. The antinomians knew that they were contending against an easy mark. In most universities and colleges, the administrators were fearful of ceasing to be "liberals" if they came out strongly in public against the refractory students.

My own direct contact with the disorders of the 1960s and early 1970s was much scantier than that of any of the contributors to *Political Passages*. They were participants or contemporaries or objects of the mad behavior of the antinomian and totalitarian students. I was an assiduous observer reading carefully many newspapers—American, European, and Asian—every day and writing a detailed chronicle each quarter in *Minerva*. (In 1968, I wrote 1,000 legal foolscap pages, subsequently printed there.) I had also studied the political attitudes and conduct of university students in Europe and Asia. But I was also close to the agitation in the universities of Cambridge and Chicago. About the former, I could cite some very striking instances of moral frivolity and faintness of heart among senior academics. On the whole, there was nothing in the universities of Great Britain in those years which could match the scale and intensity of what went on in the United States.

In almost all universities and colleges in the United States, students went on strike, boycotted classes, staged sit-ins in teaching and administrative buildings, abused teachers and administrators, damaged and defaced many buildings inside and outside. In a few cases they blew up buildings; in many cases they engaged in violence and noisy demonstrations. Publicity was what they sought and often obtained. There was no central control, no coordination, there was no strategy, no planning. Simple-minded conservatives thought that the simultaneity and similarity of the actions on so many campuses and in so many countries were evidence of a conspiracy. These actions were not a result of a conspiracy. Television and to a lesser extent the printed press were a school of disruption; they took the place of a conspiracy. The agitation was the product of a common culture.

In 1901, Ellen Key published a book which in English translation was entitled *The Century of the Child*. It was a fitting way to open the century. In the United States, the educational theories of John Dewey and popular sociologized versions of psychoanalysis, joined to a romantic conception of the purity and creativity of youth and the corruption of institutions, laid the intellectual foundations for the antinomianism of the students and the compliance of their teachers two-thirds of a century later. The productivity of the American economy, the strength of the trade unions, and humanitarian labor legislation rendered it unnecessary, impractical, and illegal for adolescents and young persons to hold remunerative employment. This made it easy for young persons to live in a mindless utopia. There was a consensus between adults and young persons in the United States, that youth was privileged estate and the youth in universities and colleges even more so.

American society after the Second World War became one in which "to be young was very heaven." At least, insofar as heaven is a realm of freedom, for the offspring of prosperous families youth was indeed a heavenly state. In such a state all things are possible.

Confidence in the compliance of the world with their desires was fostered in this situation. The desires of youth defined what was virtuous. Actions were made virtuous by being performed by young persons who were trying to "discover themselves." Universities and colleges were institutions in which young persons could discover their true, necessarily virtuous selves. This was the central article of faith of the consensus which comprehended many teachers and many students. The American universities were the incubators of this type of unreligious, unthinking antinomianism.

A very large part of the antinomian activity in the United States occurred on the campuses of universities. The disorders of antinomianism were to a very large extent the work of university students and teachers. Although the students appeared—thanks to the organs of publicity which they cultivated—to be the sole agents of the disruption, the truth is that their elders must share the discredit with them. Administrators were culpable by their cowardice; teachers were culpable for their instigation and encouragement of the troublemakers.

There was much resentment among the progressivistic university teachers against the federal government, but it had been held in check by their timorousness; there was much hatred of the dead Senator McCarthy and the living President Nixon, who was never forgiven for having brought Alger Hiss to book. The knowledge that students in many universities and colleges were with impunity offending authorities in the universities and the government gave teachers who held such views courage to cheer the students' offensive. In turn this support from their elders encouraged the antinomian students to be even more aggressive against the abdicating authorities when they saw them to be so weak. This encouragement came not only from teachers but also from university administrators, who out of ignorance and the desire to assure themselves of the benevolence of the aggressor praised the revolting students as models of high morality and civic responsibility.

The craven conduct of President James Perkins at Cornell University in embracing the black students armed with shotguns was surely one of the most infamous actions in the history of universities; it ranks with Martin Heidegger's rectoral address to the students of the University of Marburg in 1933. Perkins was not alone. He was furthermore only an administrator.

According to academics, administrators have not much interest in or solicitude about academic matters. They imply that they—the academics—do care about them. This was not, however, the case in the time of the antinomian uprising in the universities and colleges. Much aid and comfort was given to the antinomian students directly in conversations with colleagues and students and in declamations to large audiences in public, as well as within closed meetings of governing bodies and self-constituted committees.

In all of this deplorable countrywide scene of rampant disorder by self-indulgent excited antinomians, aided by the collusion and cowardice of their elders, the University of Chicago stood out in a singular way. It was of course not spared from the common troubles. In 1968, an incompetent young teacher of social sciences, Mrs. Marlene Dixon, thoroughly mediocre at best, was denied promotion to a rank conferring permanent tenure. She held an appointment in one of the weaker parts of the division of the social sciences, but she was also, by courtesy, an assistant professor in the department of sociology. Her continuation in the University of Chicago depended on her reappointment in that department as well as in the committee on human development, which had originally appointed her and which wished to reappoint her on permanent tenure. The department of sociology, in a series of decisions of a rare unanimity—both a special departmental committee which had been asked to assess her merits, and the department as a whole—voted against her continuation.

She herself, although backward in her studies, was not backward in building a body of supporters among students. In the condition of the general inflammability, her cause was taken up by the local representatives of the antinomian movement. A sit-in was undertaken—with her encouragement—and an effort was made to enlist wider student support for a strike and demonstrations. The students of the University of Chicago were at that time—they have always been—a fairly serious lot of young persons interested in their studies and enjoying quite good relations with their teachers. As a result, efforts to arouse the entire student body were unsuccessful, but the sit-in was put into operation and the usual "unnegotiable demands" were put forth.

It happened that at the time the president of the University of Chicago was Mr. Edward Levi, a man of exceptionally high intellectual standards and of no less exceptionally strong devotion to the university. The teaching staff of the university has had over three-quarters of a century a very strong corporate solidarity. Partly because of pride in membership in a university highly esteemed for its intellectual achievements, partly because of an intense earnestness about the common performance, by individual teachers, of the central tasks of a university, the University of Chicago, while having much heterogeneity in substantive views, has been marked by an unusually high degree of solidarity of its teaching staff and its students, each within its own circle and within the circle which encloses both students and teachers. When the sit-in began, there were a few teachers who supported the sitters-in, but these supporters were unsuccessful in calling forth any echo. Against them, there was an extraordinary outpouring of written expressions of concern to maintain the integrity of the university. Mr. Levi arranged for these letters, some addressed directly to him, others addressed to the entire body of teachers, to be reproduced and circulated. Whereas in other universities, the teachers who disapproved of the antinomians were isolated and those who supported them were very aggressively outspoken, the opposite occurred at the University of Chicago. The sit-in ended in about two weeks. No concessions were made to the disrupters.

While the latter were in occupation, certain members of the teaching staff and the dean of students passed through the areas of the administration building which were under occupation. They identified some of the intruders so that disciplinary action could be taken against them when calm was restored. It was rare in American universities for teachers to cooperate with the administration to enable sanctions to be taken against the malefactors. In the end, more than forty were expelled without the possibility of returning to the university, and about eighty were suspended for as long as two years. This was very unusual in American universities in those years. In most institutions there were divided counsels within the teaching staff, and those administrators who had not been intimidated and who refused to submit to the demands of the disrupters were refused the support of the teachers.

My own part in this was rather meager. I was teaching in Cambridge during the term when the sit-in took place. I was asked by the president to return, which I did almost at once. As soon as I returned, I was asked to prepare an assessment of the scholarly work of Mrs. Dixon. There was very little of it, and it was of rather poor quality. I studied it carefully and then summarized and assessed it with special reference to her knowledge of other work in her field of interest and the merits of her achievement in comparison with that work. In both respects, she came off poorly. I wrote my summary and evaluation with especial care to make the whole thing intelligible to persons not acquainted with sociological ideas, literature, and procedures. The report was circulated to all members of the university. The report was taken seriously. A considerable number of colleagues outside the social sciences told me that until they read my report, they had not made up their minds about the justice of the decision of the department of sociology or about the merits of the demands of her supporters among the students that she be given permanent tenure. The report persuaded them that the agitation was baseless.

Of course, nonsociologists, and particularly those who had not read Mrs. Dixon's writings, such as they were, were not really in a position, even after reading my report, to arrive at well-founded judgments of their own. The fact that many persons who read the report were persuaded by it was evidence of the trust and respect which are necessary for the good morale of an institution. I was generally known to be one who spoke straightforwardly, as one who, so one colleague said to another, "does not look over his shoulder," who knew the literature of sociology well, and who had an exigent intellectual standard. My colleagues throughout the university, including many who had never met me, were willing to accept this characterization of Mrs. Dixon's work. Their willingness to do so was evidence of the moral health of the University of Chicago under Mr. Levi's presidency. There was nothing like this at Berkeley, Cornell, Harvard, or Columbia, and that is one of the reasons why their troubles were much more prolonged and much more injurious.

Civility is the antithesis of both the totalitarian outlook and the antinomian outlook. I had the good fortune to have grown up academically at the University of Chicago, where, except for a few breaches, a fundamental civility has prevailed almost from the beginning of the university. It was really in my contemplation of the University of Chicago that I formed my ideas about "academic citizenship" and the "academic ethic." I did not simply imagine these things. I saw them in front of me, learned from them, and pondered them. I was not the only one at the University of Chicago who did so. These are some of the reasons why my own responses to the totalitarian and the antinomian temptations throughout my life have been so different from some of those described in this book.

———— • ————

I wish I could have called this essay "Good-bye to All That." But I cannot do so. It is true that the blatant aggressiveness, the confidence in their irresistibility, the resentful insolence against any authority to whom there is an obligation, and the dogmatic certainty reposed in Marxism are now less noisily expressed than they were in the high tide of antinomianism two decades ago. But the fundamental beliefs and disposition of the antinomians, wasteful of their own lives and destructive of others, have not evaporated. They are now less melodramatically expressed, but they still exist, and they are now entrenched in universities, as they are in American life. Whereas before they were the antics of students in a state of possession, they are now part of the ethos of adults in positions in which they exercise much influence, particularly in the educational system and in the media of mass communications.

Many of the antinomians have made their way as teachers within the universities which they denounced so scurrilously and whose teachers they spat on with such fearfully self-confident derision. There they continue the struggle; they express the same basic views without the exuberance and unthinking certainty of imminent triumph they had two decades before. They are no longer sure of the advent of a revolution; some of them even think that they have renounced the ecstatic politics of twenty years earlier, while in fact they still believe what they believed then. Their words have changed, their zeal has abated, but their society is still as repugnant to them as it used to be. They are like those ex-communists of whom a student of mine once said, "They have given up their friends, but they have kept all their old enemies." The latter is certainly true of a substantial minority of that generation of university teachers now nearing or in middle age in anthropology, sociology, political science, and English and American and continental European literatures; mathematics is not without some of these survivors. It is also true of a considerable part of the profession of academic historiography. It has even begun in its transformation to extend, in a very limited way, into Oriental studies. And the organized declaration of the intention to boycott research on the Strategic Defense Initiative is evidence that much of both the antinomianism of twenty years ago and the totalitarianism of forty and fifty years ago have survived in the present generation of teachers and graduate students of the natural sciences.

The antinomian movement is no longer so turbulent; it rumbles occasionally, as in the matter of "divestment," but it works quietly and unceasingly in offering the totalitarian and antinomian temptations to the oncoming generation. The prophets are more quiet. The *New York Review of Books* no longer expects "the revolution" to be just around the corner; it has not published a design for bombs for a long time. Noam Chomsky is not so frequently the bold knight in the lists. C. Wright Mills, who was a "hero of his time," scarely figures anymore. Susan Sontag has climbed down from being the passionate defender of North Vietnam and the Vietcong. *Esquire*, once the "haberdashers' *Partisan Review*," has given up the patronage of revolution and now caters to the tastes of "Yuppie" allrightnicks. Still the fundamental drift remains.

Nevertheless antinomianism can claim a great success; it has permeated American society to the point where homosexuality is regarded as being as normal as heterosexuality, where abortion is as normal as childbirth, where patriotism was regarded for a long time as protofascist, and where being in favor of "law and order" was unmentionable for an equally long time.

The totalitarian temptation was successful among intellectuals—mainly literary and artistic—and among some journalists and scenario writers. The antinomian temptation has been much more successful. It has reached into the academic world with a depth and scope which the totalitarian temptation was never able to attain. The quiet triumph of the antinomian temptation is a double triumph, moreover, because it has carried the debilitated totalitarian temptation with it in its wake. In fact, the antinomian temptation has won more victims for the totalitarian temptation than the totalitarian temptation in its own time was ever able to do. The totalitarian temptation never tempted as many persons into regarding communists as honest critics, as agents of humane ideals whom it is wrong to distrust, as the antinomian temptation has been successful in doing. The totalitarian temptation never tempted as many persons to join the denunciation of the American government or to disrupt the universities on the scale the antinomian temptation was able to achieve.

Why has the antinomian temptation been so much more successfully tempting than the totalitarian temptation? One tentative answer is that the antinomian temptation came on the scene when the belief that youth is the sacred time of life had become very strong. The reputed virtues of youth—purity of motive, freedom from self-seeking, devotion to ideals, straightforwardness of expression—were exploited by the antinomians. Their elders were already determined to believe that wisdom would come out of the mouths of babes. It was a time when the weight of responsibilities within society and in the dealings with other societies was becoming too heavy to bear. The seemingly endless conflicts of international politics, the frightful complexity of central government, the apparently limitless powers of science for good and evil, the difficulties of being rational and wise in a world without the comforts of religious beliefs and too intricate to master by unaided reason—these placed a premium on solutions with the merit of simplicity and purity. Large parts of American society found in the antinomian temptation a surrogate for the bucolic idyll which they were too sophisticated to take seriously. The antinomian ideal was against all the wrong things—authority, bureaucracy, technological risks, routines, far-reaching rationalization, wearisome traditions, postponement of pleasures into the remote future, sexual puritanism. It was in favor of all the right things—spontaneity, directness and frankness in speech, unencumbered expression of emotion, the ready gratification of desire, and the complete freedom to do as one wishes.

Yet the antinomian temptation kept enough of the negative side of the totalitarian temptation to furnish itself with a "theory" of modern society, of exploitation and imperialism, and the idea of a revolution which would break the rigid, inhumane bourgeois society. Most important, it retained one of the crucial elements of the totalitarian temptation, namely, the image and locus of the ideal center: the Soviet Union. For practical and fundamental reasons the Soviet Union cannot have the same place in the antinomian temptation that it had in the totalitarian one. It has done too much to discredit itself. The preachers of the antinomian temptation do not wish to be dragged down by the plain averment of a leaning toward the

Soviet Union. That would be too contrary to the emancipationist ideal. Yet that central part of the totalitarian temptation has not been renounced. No virtues are explicitly attributed to the Soviet Union; it has them attributed to it only implicitly when the United States has to be put in the wrong. Then the old devotion shines through. It has, after all, achieved one of the most valuable features of both the totalitarian and the antinomian temptations; it has achieved the "social ownership of the instruments of production." That after all is the precondition for emancipation.

Nevertheless, the mood which led to the rush toward the antinomian temptation, or which allowed it to attract many persons who affirmed it in a rather passive way, has by no means swept the field in the United States. Whatever may be the ravages of secularism and hedonism in American society—the ravages which have enabled the antinomian temptation so tempting—puritanism, patriotism, and piety still exist in very large parts of the population. There are also liberals—liberals of the type who believe in the freedom of contract, the rule of law, freedom of the press, freedom of association, free elections and representative institutions, and the practice of reasoned discourse in public affairs.

Most liberals in the United States are collectivistic liberals. They tend toward social democracy on the one side and toward antinomianism on the other. Nevertheless, many still adhere to the kind of liberalism which emerged when a great many traditional liberals began to divest their outlook of the primacy of private property and the freedom of contract and to interest themselves in the enhanced role of the state in promoting the common good through the provision of goods and services, particularly to the poorer strata of the population.

In the first third of the present century, American liberals, i.e., collectivistic liberals, thought of themselves as a beleaguered group in American society. They saw American society as a society of philistines, unreflective, avid in the pursuit and admiration of wealth, individualistic in their unconcern for their fellowmen, indifferent to the "finer things of life," harshly repressive toward individuals who were sensitive to "higher values" or who followed a mode of life or thought which departed from the prevailing pattern. The liberals, having already extended their views toward governmental intervention in the market, also reached out toward bohemianism, "free love" or sexual freedom. They also took to espousing the rights of "revolutionary" associations like the Communist Party and the Industrial Workers of the World. They not only defended the right to peaceful existence of these groups, they also were not unsympathetic with the substance of their views. They began to look upon the groups whose rights to existence they defended as fellow believers in the same social ideals. Thus it developed that in the 1930s and after the Second World War, American liberals—again emphasizing that they are collectivistic liberals—became the defenders of the Communist Party against accusations of subversion, espionage, and hypocrisy. (This was the beginning of the "anti-anticommunist" attitude.) From defending the right of revolutionary groups to believe as they did, liberals became defenders—and even the exponents—of their beliefs. Those who criticized and opposed communists and communism were regarded by collectivistic liberals as the enemies of liberalism. There were liberals in the United States who guarded themselves against this particular deformation of liberalism, but they were not in the majority.

Liberalism made similar mistakes when antinomianism appeared on the scene. The collectivistic liberals must accept much of the blame for the antinomian upsurge. Although in their heart of hearts they themselves were not antinomians, they did support and encourage the antinomians. For this they got little thanks.

Without distinguishing between collectivistic and constitutional liberalism, the antinomians hated liberalism as such because liberalism praises the exercise of reason, which was obviously repugnant to them. They hated it too because it respects the right of individual freedom rationally practiced; the antinomians wanted freedom for themselves and primarily for the immediate gratification of their desires, while both constitutional and collectivistic liberalism require some self-restraint, partly out of the respect for the rights of others to their freedom. The antinomians hated liberalism because liberalism postulates the stability and effective working of institutions; institutions are antipathetic to the antinomians. Liberalism requires governmental and institutional authority, and that is above all hateful to the antinomians, although they are partial to regimes in which authority is totalitarian and themselves expect to obtain all the benefits of an omniprovident authority within their own society.

It was very common for the antinomians to assert that liberalism had failed and had to be discarded on behalf of antinomianism. This, like nearly everything else said by the antinomians, was untrue. Liberalism had not failed except in the sense that the proponents of its collectivistic variant did not foresee the necessity of safeguards against its beneficiaries and its enemies. The collectivistic liberals viewed the former with unqualified benevolence, and they viewed the latter unthinkingly as like-minded allies.

Liberalism did not preside over the creation of universities in the Middle Ages and early modern times, but ever since the beginning of the nineteenth century, constitutional liberalism in all Western countries has contributed greatly to their growth and improvement. Collectivistic liberalism too has done much for them; it also owes a great deal to them, particularly in the academic social sciences. The presence of so many students in universities, and of so many teachers, was a triumph of liberalism, with its belief in enlightenment and in the value of inducting each generation into the cultural heritage; the greatly increased numbers owe much to the powers of collectivistic liberalism. The growth of scientific knowledge has been promoted by both kinds of liberalism. It may indeed be said that the growth and expansion of knowledge are central to liberalism; they are values of the same standing as individual liberty and the exercise of reason and civility, which subsume the free press and representative institutions as well as the rule of law.

At the same time the vehement and rancorous outburst of antinomianism was fostered by collectivistic liberals. Every one of the insane demands of the antinomians was an extension into an extreme form of some article of belief of collectivistic liberalism. The demands of feminists, homosexuals, and pedophiles and pornographers are all derivable from the postulates of the value of the freedom of the individual and the goodness of expressing one's true self. The aggressive, hate-filled denunciation of governmental authority is an extension of traditional or constitutional and collectivistic liberalism into an extreme form of the liberal demand for individual freedom and its effort to restrict the arbitrary exercise of authority. The demand for the legalization of drugs is an extension into an extreme form of the postulate of the value of individual freedom and of hedonic gratification, which had become a primary value of collectivistic liberalism. In fact, if liberalism is to be criticized, it is that it has encouraged and tolerated the antinomian tendency. It is characteristic of the self-centered ingratitude of the antinomians of the 1960s and 1970s that they took special pleasure in announcing the bankruptcy or death or wickedness of liberalism. All that they were they owed to liberalism, setting aside a strong admixture of their own bad characters.

Although I would exculpate liberalism as an intellectual and political tradition from the charges made against it by the antinomians, I do not exculpate the collectivistic liberals for their role in encouraging and helping the antinomians. The predominant collectivist tendency of liberalism in the United States has encouraged belief in the omni-competent, omniprovident state, and this has encouraged the demand-ingness of the antinomians while at the same time it has encouraged their hostility against the state. More serious is the deficiency of the collectivistic liberals in failing to draw the line between liberalism and antinomianism, just as from the 1930s onward, collectivistic liber-als were not and have not been courageous enough or perceptive enough to draw the necessary line between their kind of liberalism and communism. Senator Joseph McCarthy was a poor stick, but the collectivistic liberals who opposed him were wrong to think or to pretend to think that communist spies and traitors like Alger Hiss and the Rosenbergs were not spies and traitors. Of this particular tendency in collectivistic liberalism, the antinomians have been per-fect heirs.

One of the most disgraceful aspects of the antinomian episode in recent American history has been this inability and unwillingness of collectivistic liberals to see where liberalism ends and treason and subversion begin. It was the collectivistic liberals who either encour-aged or stood by approvingly when the students and their older confed-erates conducted their campaign on behalf of the Vietcong and the North Vietnamese communists. It has been the collectivistic and perhaps also the constitutional liberals who—fearful, unjustifiably fearful, of the "slippery slope"—have encouraged by their com-plaisance the free distribution of pornography.

Collectivistic liberals are like the members of the Democratic Party in a certain ward of Chicago, who were said by Mr. Dooley to be so loyal to their party that they would sooner die than be buried by a Republican undertaker. Liberals would sooner see their society ruined than learn something valuable to its preservation from conservatism. There is much that liberals must learn and assimilate from conservatism if they would conserve a regime of freedom. Tradi-tionality, nationality, normality, civility—these are among the values which collectivistic and constitutional liberals must acquire. It is be-cause they failed to make necessary distinctions and because they failed to see their affinities with conservatism that they have been so compliant in the face of the totalitarian and antinomian temptations.

1

A Virtucrat Remembers

Joseph Epstein

Well, I hope you think a little better of the world.
We mustn't make up our minds too early in life.

HENRY JAMES (*The Princess Casamassima*)

Famous American corners, permit me to name a few: Hollywood and Vine, State and Madison, Broadway and 42nd Street, Haight and Ashbury. Shortly before beginning this essay, I happened to be in San Francisco, staying with someone who lives in the Haight-Ashbury district, and over a three-day visit walked past the corner of Haight and Ashbury and along the street and in the neighborhood known as "the Haight" perhaps twenty times. I never did so without a rich stew of emotion boiling within me. If San Francisco was the spiritual capital of that period in recent history we think of with chronological inexactitude as "the sixties," then nearby Berkeley was its Finland Station and Haight-Ashbury its Red Square. To alter my trope rather abruptly, if the sixties were your idea of a good time, the Haight was Ciro's, the Chez Paris, the Copacabana; it was where, baby, the good times rolled.

Although some small changes have been made on the Haight—
a few new shops have gone in, a few head shops have gone out—
and although rising real estate prices presage other changes in the
near future, I found myself surprised how little the street seemed
to change, how very "sixties" it all still appeared, at least outwardly.
Block after block of shops sell handcrafted jewelry, homosexual and
feminist books (such as the Anarchist Collective Bookstore), used
clothing, berets, (putative) health food, aggressively uninteresting
paintings—in short, as Zorba the Greek might say, the full catastrophe.
The street's denizens are got up in sixties regalia: beards, long hair,
dreary denim, backpacks, bedrolls, bandanas. Walking past the corner
of Haight and Ashbury, I noted a man of perhaps my own middle
years, red-eyed and in an advanced stage of scragglitude, who plunked
his guitar and intoned, "Oh, ya drop dead in the street and they
give ya a ticket for littering." A block or so farther on, I heard,
behind me, one man say to another, "Whaddaya say we go up to
Montana, get hold of some shit, and take it down to Mexico?"

On the Haight I felt like I was Rip Van Winkle in reverse—as
if I fell asleep and awoke to find not that it was forty years later
but twenty years earlier. Except of course it wasn't, and there was
ample evidence to prove that it wasn't. The young, blond, long-
haired, be-sandled girls who seemed so much a part of the counterculture fantasy—a pipe of pot, a book of *Howl,* and thou—are now
older, gray, still long-haired and be-sandaled women, looking much
the worse for wear. The man who sang about dropping dead in the
street, the chances are, may do just that. While many of these aging
hippies sleep in Buena Vista Park, where they are not disturbed by
San Francisco's highly tolerant police, others drop off on stoops before
pastel-painted houses or in doorways. When they wake in the cool
San Francisco morning, they are not a charming sight; they are,
instead, a reminder of the good sense of Santayana's remark that
"the state of nature presupposes a tropical climate."

As I walked along the Haight, I, who am perhaps about as square
as one can get on this earth this late in the century, felt no hostility
directed at me. Yet I felt a good deal of my own hostility directed
toward them, these sad and aging hippies, who seemed to be standing
around awaiting a bus into the past. I felt about them a sense of
revulsion, and loathing, and above all depression—the latter, especially, when I would notice a young adolescent who looked to me
as if he might be a runaway come to the Haight to live the countercultural dream. Looking into the drug-besotted eyes of these people

who are now pushing middle age, I thought, my God, the squalor, the waste, the horror! And I also felt, what good luck that the counter-cultural dream progressed no further than it did! Passing a clutch of these people, men and women, on the very corner of Haight and Ashbury, I muttered to myself, "What you do with your own life is your own business, but I'm awfully glad that, in the battle of competing visions, yours lost."

But did it? The pathetic creatures lingering on the Haight are but the lost remnant of a now dead movement, people who bought the whole package of inchoate philosophy, quarter-baked politics, and sappy transcendentalism that made up the intellectual content of the movement. And yet in diluted form much of the spirit of the sixties lives on; and in some quarters it seems not merely living on but very nearly prevailing, even if not in the preserved-in-amber form one finds it in on the Haight. I find this spirit alive and all too well in the universities, for example. Those professors now in their forties, and hence coming into dominance as full professors, department chairmen, and deans, were all in their twenties in the late 1960s. Wherever they actually went to school, the true alma mater for most of them is the sixties, when they were graduate students. One sees the sixties influence not only in their dress and ubiquitous beards—theirs is surely the first generation of full professors to teach in jeans—but in their chumminess with students, their readiness to subvert tradition, their rush to align themselves with what they construe to be virtuous causes. The generation of the sixties was above all the generation of virtue. They set out to make America better. America, unfortunately or fortunately, was not as good as they and, in their view, still isn't.

The sixties, I have come to believe, are something of a political Rorschach test. Tell me what you think of that period and I shall tell you what your politics are. Tell me that you think the period both good and bad, with much to be said for and against it, and you are, whether you know it or not, a liberal. Tell me that you think the sixties a banner time in American life, a period of unparalleled idealism, a splendid opportunity sadly missed, and you are doubtless a radical, sentimental or otherwise. Tell me that you think the sixties a time of horrendous dislocation, a disaster nearly averted, a damn near thing, but a thing nonetheless for which we are still paying and shall continue to pay, and I shall tell you . . . well, I am not sure what you are precisely, but your views, friend, are close to mine and I am pleased to meet you.

— . —

Can there have been nothing good about the sixties, which, to become chronologically more exact about the period, I should date as beginning in 1965 with the Free Speech Movement at the University of California at Berkeley and closing with the resignation of Richard Nixon from the United States presidency after the revelations of Watergate in 1974? The role of student and left-wing protest in bringing about the withdrawal of U.S. troops from Vietnam, of which the protesters of the day were so exaltedly proud, must now receive credit as well for what happened after American withdrawal, which includes leaving Vietnam in a death grip of totalitarianism and permitting the massacre of millions in nearby Cambodia. Such progress as was made in the late fifties and early sixties in race relations—and it was serious progress at the state and institutional levels—was in many respects nullified by the surgent black consciousness movement, which claimed not only that Black is Beautiful but more than implied, corollarily, that white was mean, racist, and generally soulless, and in the process put an end to the dream of an integrated society, where things remain today. During the sixties, too, the black plaint of oppression was picked up by women, by homosexuals, and by every other group that found it useful; if you weren't a member of a group that could claim a heritage of oppression—and almost everybody could set out such a claim—you were in bad shape psychologically. A society that felt itself so widely oppressed needed to discover a regular supply of oppressors, and here the nation's journalists came to the rescue, tirelessly pumping out fresh conspiracies, hidden plots, secret deals.

The investigative journalist, Seymour Bob Halberstein (as I tend to think of him), became one of the heroes of the sixties. College-educated, usually middle or upper middle class, secure and happy in his work, the investigative journalist, when successful, won fame and sometimes vast fortune from a society that he portrayed as corrupt, decayed, sick. A man well paid and highly honored by his society for telling it how rotten it was, the investigative journalist lived a contradiction, and it is fitting that he be one of the heroic figures of a period in American life in which, for a long stretch, it appeared that the law of contradictions itself had been rescinded. It was the sixties, let us not forget, that brought us those splendid contradictions, not to say oxymorons, known as "open marriage," "free and easy abortion," and "repressive toleration."

The sixties also brought us the initials SDS, JDL, and LSD, not to speak of such nonacronymous but plenty acrimonious organizations as the Black Panthers, the Weathermen, and The Fair Play for Cuba Committee. It was a time of vast national yearning, when youth was revered and everyone, including the young, seemed to forget that the chief problem of youth is that it doesn't last. Men left their wives, wives smoked their adolescent children's marijuana, and everyone spoke—tsk, tsk—of the sad misunderstanding between the young and the adult known as the generation gap. Standards were lowered in education, Norman Mailer and Andy Warhol became leading figures in literature and art, and the misnomer "gay" entered the language as the official liberal word for homosexual. All kinds of essential responsibilities ceased to be people's "bag," and every kind of trivial irresponsibility became known as "doing one's thing." It wasn't quite a matter, in Yeats's famous formulation, of "Things fall apart; the centre cannot hold"; it was more a matter of people taking joy in the prospect of things falling apart and nobody claiming even to represent the center. Really to hate it you had only to have been there.

I was, and did, but not at first, and not unequivocally.

Let me begin with the year 1968, in some ways the height of the madness, the year of the riots at the Democratic National Convention in Chicago, the closest in some ways that America has come to having a year like 1848 in Europe. That year Hubert Humphrey was running against Richard Nixon, whose portrait then had primacy of place in my personal American political rogues' gallery. As a down-the-line, pull-the-lever man of the left, I was not too keen on Humphrey either. Humphrey had an honorable record as a liberal on domestic matters, true enough, but on foreign policy, as vice president under Lyndon Johnson, he had become an administration spokesman for continued prosecution of the Vietnam War, which, again as a man of the left, I detested. Lyndon Johnson didn't leave those who worked for him much, especially in the way of dignity, and certainly this was true of poor Hubert Humphrey. Yet for me Hubert Humphrey had one powerful thing going for him in 1968—he was not Richard Nixon.

Around this time I attended, purely as a sightseer, a large rally in Grant Park in Chicago, a block or so away from the Conrad Hilton Hotel, headquarters of the Democratic Party during the convention. I was there chiefly to see Genet, the French novelist, who, along with Norman Mailer and Terry Southern, was in Chicago to cover the convention for *Esquire* magazine. A compact little man with a bald head shaved on the sides, Genet was most unimpressive on the platform, muttering a few revolutionary banalities. Norman

Mailer, who also spoke that afternoon, adopting a Southern noncommissioned officer's accent for his platform appearance, had not even attained the level of unimpressiveness; he was merely ridiculous. The principal theme of most speakers was the crudity of Mayor Daley, the brutality of the Chicago cops, the racism of the United States. And then the police arrived, perhaps a hundred of them. They lined up in formation outside the crowd; they had gas masks and billy clubs. "Fuck the pigs," someone shouted, and then someone else threw a bottle into the police formation, and then another and yet another. That was the ball game. Gas masks were clamped on, tear gas canisters let loose, the police, cutting a swath with their clubs, marched through, dispersing the crowd, myself among it, choking with tear gas.

This little outing was my initial, firsthand hard evidence that an antiwar crowd was not necessarily an antiviolence crowd. Worse is better, said Lenin, and it was clear, at least to me, that most of the people who came to the protests connected with the 1968 Democratic Convention were interested in making things a whole lot worse—and as dramatically as possible. These same people knew they couldn't hope to bring off anything like the same spectacle at the Republican Convention. The Democratic was their party, disaffected though they might be from it at present. The Democrats, they felt (and acted on the feeling), owed them sympathy, had to put up with them, could not with a clear conscience put them down, whereas the Republicans owed them nothing. As the time of the election drew nearer, it occurred to me that a vote for Hubert Humphrey meant a vote for greater chaos. Left-wing though I was, I was not for chaos, I was not for tearing down the universities, I was not for the party of Allen Ginsberg and Abbie Hoffman and Paul Goodman and Joan Baez and the revolution-in-consciousness, polymorphously perverse, pot-minded, guitar-playing, commune-living culture of the radical left. Of this I was convinced. Yet to vote my convictions I would have to vote for Richard Nixon, which, at that time, I could not do. But to every liberal dilemma there is a liberal solution, usually involving political cowardice. My solution, as I recall, was not to vote and hope that Hubert Humphrey lost.

I refer to myself as a liberal in the above paragraph, but I then thought of myself as a radical. "Radical" at that time seemed to me an honorific term—radical, as radicals used to be fond of pointing out, as in going to the root causes of any problem. Let pass that there was something terribly self-congratulatory about thinking oneself a deep thinker, for after all that is what "going to the root" implies. Although I had worked as a director of an antipoverty program in Little Rock, Arkansas, I did not think of myself in any serious sense a radical activist. I carried no placards; I took part in no demonstrations; I had not the least touch of what an acquaintance of mine, feeling a twinge of jealousy of people who went to jail for political causes, once called "subpoena envy." No, in thinking myself a radical I chiefly thought of myself as a man of the left who thought things were radically wrong in the world and was not fearful of applying radical solutions to right them.

How did I come to hold the political views I then held? That is a question I have pondered, and ponder still. Our politics come from the air we breathe, from our background, our prejudices, our social class, our ethnic origins, our education. Except perhaps in rare instances—and mine is not one of them—we do not arrive at our politics through careful, or even careless, reasoning. "You cannot," wrote Swift, "reason a person out of something he has not been reasoned into." Few of us having been reasoned into our politics, few can be reasoned out of them. I know that I have never lost a political argument in my life, a statement that will seem rather less impressive when to it I add that I have never really won a political argument either. And I have engaged in lots of political arguments, especially since, having reached the age of fifty, which after a reasonably well-mannered life I have unofficially declared the age of tactlessness, I do not hesitate to make my own views known. But what I have found is that arguing a person out of his politics is akin to arguing him out of his religion. Swift was correct; it cannot be done.

This much about my youthful politics I can say with moderate certainty: I did not acquire them at home, at least not directly. Mine must have been one of the least overtly political households on record. In his best-selling book on the Jewish immigrants to America, *World of Our Fathers*, Irving Howe implies a strong connection between Jews and the labor movement and, beyond that, between Jews and socialist and utopian politics. This, though, was not the world of my father, nor of my father's father, both of whom were in business for themselves, the former very successfully, the latter rather dismally. I had an uncle, whom I never met, who died in the Spanish Civil War, but he appears to have been less a political character than an adventurer, one of those boys who ran away from home when he was fifteen to go to sea. Politics was never more than a passing subject at our table, never anything remotely like a consuming one.

As an adolescent, none of my friends was the least bit interested in politics, though I believe we all thought of ourselves, somehow or other, as Democrats, and this chiefly because Jews were not then Republicans, or at least we knew no Jewish Republicans.

Yet being Jewish, even if one wasn't at all an observant Jew, was a subtle influence upon one's political consciousness. Looking back, I at any rate feel it has been on mine. In an interesting essay entitled "Jews in the Russian Revolutionary Movement," the late Leonard Schapiro notes that some Jews threw themselves into revolutionary politics owing to oppression, but that more did so in the belief that, with the coming of the revolution, they would be fully the equal of anyone in Russian society. Boy and man, I have never felt the least oppression in America owing to my Jewishness, but, as a child, in the 1940s, it was difficult not to know that there was a good deal of anti-Semitism in the United States, some of it quite open and some of it quite close to home. A country club less than a mile from where I lived did not permit Jews; many a nearby neighborhood was, to use the term of the day, "restricted"; and there were restaurants, hotels, resorts where Jews did not attempt entrance.

As a small boy, I recall once returning from the school playground and chanting before my father "Eenie, meenie, minnie, moe/Catch a nigger by the toe," and his flying into a rage. My father was not a man easily enraged, but this was during World War II, when Jews in vast numbers were being killed in Europe, which my father, cooled down now, explained to me, rounding off his explanation by adding that "our people" had a special responsibility not to use a word like "nigger," which was a word of hate. Six or seven years old at the time, I remember taking his point, but also wondering what kind of world it was that would kill "our people." Out of the soil of such incidents does political consciousness take root and grow.

In my particular case, political consciousness grew very slowly indeed. Later, as a student at the University of Chicago, I met contemporaries, many of them from New York City, who had been reading *The Nation* and *The New Republic* since early in high school; some of their parents had become enmeshed in sectarian politics in the thirties, from which they never freed themselves, and about which, naturally enough, their children, from table talk alone, became fairly well informed. Politics was never part of the table talk in our home, unless there was a passing reference to some fresh piece of corruption at city hall, of which, in Chicago, there was never a paucity. Of politics in the larger sense—that is, of politics as an expression of views about how the world ought to be organized—there was no talk whatsoever. Had there been, I am not sure I should have been much interested in it. I seem to have been a fairly normal adolescent boy, which means that my head, filled with dreams of athletic glory and sex, had no room for a vision of the good life lived through politics.

Just as well, I have no doubt. If I had had political views at fifteen or sixteen—as so many people who grew up in the Depression did—I should have been an insufferable little prig. At twenty or so, when I began to have such views, behind them were the standard set of proper liberal humanitarian principles. They were very moral— and, worse, moralizing—and there was scarcely a politician about whom I could not have told you whether he was on the absolutely right or the absolutely wrong side. Need I add that I, invariably, was on the absolutely right side?

Although I was not a good student, I did go to a good school, the University of Chicago, whose implicit political orientation was liberal, even if none of the professors I encountered there pushed a liberal political line. But one had to be rather thick not to know that, in the 1956 election between Dwight David Eisenhower and Adlai Stevenson, for the thinking man there could be no real choice. (Ike and Adlai were supposed to have a meeting before the election, the comedian Mort Sahl joked at the time, but they had to call it off because they couldn't find an interpreter for Ike.) Along with providing me with some of the appropriate language with which to talk about politics, the University of Chicago put into my head the desire to be that odd excrescence of scholar and philosopher—without the learning of the former or the depth of the latter—known as "an intellectual." Here was a fateful decision, for my politics and for my life.

In those years—the late 1950s—the decision to be an intellectual implied the decision to be something of an outsider. In the presidential elections of 1952 and 1956, for example, Adlai Stevenson was frequently referred to as an "egghead," the dysphemism for an intellectual (which, apart from his using language with some nicety, Stevenson really wasn't), and to be considered an intellectual was clearly a mark against him. To the larger society, to be an intellectual meant that there was something insubstantial, untrustworthy, possibly even slightly dangerous about one. As a liberal has been defined as a person whose interests aren't at stake at the moment, so an intellectual has been defined as a person whose only stake is in his ideas. Intellectuals have often felt that this only proved their disinterestedness and hence redounded to their greater glory; nonintellectuals have construed it to mean only that intellectuals have nothing to lose—and, as any sensible businessman will tell you, you want to be a bit wary about entering into a deal with someone who has nothing to lose.

Part of the pleasure for me of being an intellectual was in the position of permanent nonconformity it seemed to provide. (I had not then heard Harold Rosenberg's devastating phrase, "a herd of independent minds," which has on more than one occasion been pressed into service to describe the collective behavior of intellectuals.) In *The Secret Agent*, Joseph Conrad remarks that "the way of even the most justifiable revolutions is prepared by personal impulses disguised into creeds." I know that by the time I was in my late adolescence, the impulse of, or at any rate toward, nonconformity was already powerful in me. Mine was, I like to think, a nonconformity not of manner but of spirit. When I was in high school, for example, I was invited to join an exalted senior boys' honor club, but turned it down—the first boy, I believe, in the history of the school to do so. It was my manner that got me invited; it was my spirit that would not permit me to join. At various times in my life, something in me has caused me to turn my back on conventional success, to swim out of the mainstream, to want to make do without the world's more obvious rewards. As a self-appointed intellectual, I was able to achieve all this in one swoop, for in determining to live my life for intellectual things, I guaranteed forfeiture of a clearly tracked career, a normal middle-class existence, and anything resembling serious wealth.

As a self-appointed intellectual, I was also taking on a fairly heavy ideological cargo. My notion of what an intellectual was came in part through my sketchy undergraduate study of history—here I learned that Voltaire, that splendid troublemaker, was an intellectual—but in even larger part through reading the intellectual journals of the day, which I began to do in a passionate way in my last year in college. Chief among these journals were *Partisan Review*, *Commentary*, *Dissent*, and *Encounter* (in London). All, be it known, were strongly anticommunist; but, let it also be known, none was probourgeois or even mildly in favor of capitalism. These journals were edited by that species of the genus intellectual known as New York intellectuals (including *Encounter*, whose dominant coeditor was Irving Kristol). The New York intellectuals of the day seemed to me, viewed at a distance of 800 miles, brilliant and radical, and the two qualities seemed to me interwoven, each dependent upon the other. They were too clever (any longer) to be taken in by communism, and also too clever to let up on criticizing their own country. As David Riesman once put it, "Were not intellectuals of more use to this country when they had less use for it?" As such, intellectuals functioned, permanently, as a not particularly loyal opposition—or, to put it more precisely, as loyal principally to the idea of being in opposition.

The idea of being in permanent opposition suited both my temperament and my youthful recalcitrance. As a boost to my morale, I retained only the white squares in the checkered history of intellectuals in politics: the distrust they had often shown for empty authority, their yearning for equality, their hunger for social justice, their belief in the possibility of greater freedom of a kind that would perhaps one day bring nearer the prospect of an earthly paradise. I now also began to read history rather more selectively, with an eye out for intellectual heroism. Men who could make moot the question of which was more powerful, the pen or the sword, by possessing both, particularly impressed me: T. E. Lawrence, André Malraux, Leon Trotsky. I soon became fairly well read in not the workers' but the intellectuals' revolution of 1917 in Russia, for the Russian Revolution was nothing if not a revolution choreographed, orchestrated, and staged by intellectuals. Although I now believe (not entirely without evidence) that the Russian Revolution was one of the great catastrophes of world history, I nonetheless know more about it than I do about the American Revolution, and probably even now know more Russian than American history; I can tell you a good deal more about the Decembrists, for example, than I can about the presidential administrations of Van Buren, Harrison, and Polk. Nor, my guess is, am I alone among intellectuals in this regard. The reason, I strongly suspect, is that intellectuals tend to become highly stimulated by revolution—by the actuality, the prospect, even the idea of it. In *Hope Against Hope*, Nadezhda Mandelstam noted; "My brother Evgeni Yakovlevich used to say that the decisive part in the subjugation of the intelligentsia was played not by terror and bribery (though God knows there was enough of both), but by the word 'Revolution,' which none of them could bear to give up."

By the time I graduated from college, at twenty-one, my politics were pretty well set for the next decade. I should describe these politics as highbrow liberalism. A student of literature, a devotee of Proust and Joyce and Kafka, I discovered a way to carry over my tastes in literature to politics by choosing British models: George

Bernard Shaw's socialism, John Maynard Keynes's economics, E.
M. Forster's "aristocracy of the sensitive, the considerate and the
plucky." A continental modernist in literature, an English Fabian
in politics, Brooks Brothers in dress, hey, daddy, they didn't make
'em much more sensitive, considerate, and plucky than I at twenty-
one.

Yet I don't wish to make too much fun of my younger self. For
one thing, he can't fight back; for another, there is a lot about the
kid that I really like. I think he was genuinely offended by the
world's injustice. I think he would have done what he could to diminish
it; and, in extenuation of the fact that he didn't do anything to do
so, it must be added that nobody else had many bright ideas on
the subject at the time. But this much must be said against him:
there was undeniably an element of snobbery in his youthful politics.
Leftism was not so endemic among the educated classes then as
now. The writers from whom he took many of his political notions—
Lewis Mumford, Paul Goodman, C. Wright Mills—were still a minority taste. He considered himself a radical, true enough, but above
and beyond that he thought of himself as a member of an even
smaller band, an unashamed idealist. This put him, he felt, in a
select company of the happy few—and the important thing always
about the happy few is that, in politics and in culture, the fewer
the better.

Why, though, didn't the snobbery inherent in my youthful politics
as easily turn me rightward? Why was I not an admirer of the intellectuals around *L'Action française* or the cultural theories of T. S. Eliot?
Why didn't I insert a first initial in front of my name (F. Joseph
Epstein), carry a walking stick, deplore progress and modernization,
and live in America as if I were in exile, as I have seen many a
right-wing youth do in the 1980s? Too strong a sense of the absurd,
I should say. Then there is the unblinkable fact that much of right-
wing intellectual life has been besmirched by anti-Semitism. (So,
as I would later learn, has been a good deal of left-wing intellectual
life.) But the attraction of left over right was also to be found in
snobbery of another kind—in this instance, moral snobbery.

The right is the side of the liver, as everyone knows, the left
that of the heart. To be on the left, then, was to be on the side of
the largehearted, the good, and (though the odious term had not
yet come into vogue) the "caring." Part of the appeal of being on
the left is that it puts one among the implicitly virtuous, and to
believe virtue is on one's side is no small thing in politics. (Just

now a belief in its own superior virtue—see Mario Cuomo's keynote speech at the 1984 Democratic Convention—may be all that the left in America has remaining to it, but it is a lot.) On the right, one can always accuse the fellow to the left of one of being unrealistic, which is nice. But on the left, one can always accuse the fellow to the right of one of being cold and callous, selfish and insensitive, which is better. I know that when on the left I always did, and I found it exhilarating.

My politics also fitted in nicely with my chosen vocation. I wanted to be a writer, not an easy thing to be, in America or any other country, for in writing, unlike many another line of work, there wasn't much room for mediocrity—at least not on the level of writing to which I aspired. If I failed, my politics would prop me up. Being an anticapitalist, after all, how could I hope to succeed under a system I contemned? (In later years, I would appreciate the rich irony with which capitalism seemed to reward its enemies; I am thinking here of such best-selling novelists as E. L. Doctorow, Kurt Vonnegut, and Robert Coover.) Being an anticapitalist and hence being able to blame capitalism—often known more simply as "the system"—for any failure I might encounter through my own lack of talent or absence of energy not only provided me with a fine fallback position, but permitted me to view anyone who labored at a workaday job in the system with a rather lofty contempt. Even if I didn't win, in other words, I couldn't lose.

Every idea has its psychological uses. The chief use of the political ideas I held when young was to make me feel quietly but confidently superior. Their other use was to furnish me with something I thought was a point of view but realize now was only a set of opinions. The problem with such opinions is that they can intercede between experience and feeling, coloring the one and blocking the other. I recall a particularly vivid instance of this when I was a soldier, an enlisted man, in basic training at Fort Leonard Wood, Missouri, in the late 1950s. Our company was returning from a 25-mile march undertaken with full 40-pound packs, steel helmets, and rifles. (I labored under the additional weight of the autumn number of *Partisan Review* in the pocket of my field jacket.) The day was clear, the weather crisp, we were within a mile of reaching our company area, our whippet-lean black sergeant, Mr. Andrew Atherton, was booming out cadence count, and, flush with pleasure at having survived a minor hardship and filled with camaraderie shared with the men in my platoon, I thought, God, this is fine!—when, wait a minute, I remembered that, as a socialist and a man of the left, I hated the military and all it stood for. And so I finished out the final mile of the march in a proper mood of cynical detachment.

Our opinions can exert a powerful tyranny over us, especially when we are simultaneously uncertain whence they derive yet nonetheless determined to live lives congruent with them. One of the advantages that the left has over any other political grouping in the struggle for the minds of the young is that it provides them with the most complete set of opinions. In my own youthful time, I held them all. One might imagine a free-association game called Left-Wing, in which one responds quickly to flash cards: BUSINESS— "A swindle." THE MILITARY—"Barbarian institution." CON-VENTIONAL PATRIOTISM—"For Mencken's Booboisie." RELI-GION—"Opiate of the people; also beside the point." RACISM— "Endemic in America." Then, too, the left provides a rich cast of conspirators and secret controllers of society: Wall Street, Madison Avenue, the CIA, the FBI, the military-industrial complex, and so on into the dark night. In the left-wing mind, people are regularly polluting, poisoning, pillaging, corrupting, carcinogenating. There are the utility boys, agribusiness, the pharmaceutical companies, the lobbyists, and surely I don't have to mention the weapons manufacturers. It's a wonder that a reader of *The Nation* can get any sleep at all.

Even in my hardiest, most confident left-wing days, I never suffered the full political paranoia available on the left, but I was not above doing what I now think of as "an opinion check" as a means of judging not only acquaintances but writers and public figures. As a young writer, I published essays on Henry Luce and Adlai Stevenson that were essentially opinion checks. In other words, I investigated their public utterances and writings and publications to discover what their opinion was on this or that issue or event, question, or problem. Where their opinions differed from my own, which were the standard received liberal wisdom of the day, I found them wanting.

I do not mean to mock the importance of opinions. I have lost friends over opinions, as I suspect many an intellectual has, for opinion is the chief stock in trade of the intellectual. As Santayana says, "the person of the friend is distinguished and selected from all others because of exceptionally acceptable ways of acting, thinking, and feeling about other things or persons." Yet in the realm of opinion conservatives have a natural advantage over liberals. Conservatives may think what they believe; liberals may only think good thoughts (except of course about those who disagree with them). Conservatives can often surprise one with the large discrepancy between their opinions and their actions. I think here of H. L. Mencken, behind nearly every one of whose harsh opinions one can find a kindly action that contradicts it. Liberals, being under the burden of espousing lofty opinions, can only disappoint—and usually do. With only a single exception, which I shall get to presently, I have never met a liberal who did anything serious to help any member of the working classes, apart from giving money to one or another cause (and the test of giving, I have always believed, is not how much one gives, but how much, after having given, one has left) or allowing one's cleaning woman to call one by one's first name. The truly largehearted people whom I have either known or heard about—a middle-aged woman in Chicago who has given her life to looking after stray animals, Mother Teresa of Calcutta—seem to be above politics.

The one exception in my lifetime that I can think of is the behavior of certain young white men and women during the glory years of the civil rights movement. These were the years from the first sit-ins in the late 1950s through the passage of the Civil Rights Act of 1964, shortly after which whites were told by young blacks in the movement, in effect, to bug off. But these young men and women put their heads on the block for a cause; and a good cause it was, perhaps the last altogether morally clear cause in the politics of this nation: the removal from the books of a number of Southern states of certain indisputably unjust laws. To challenge these laws required courage, physical as well as moral courage, from blacks and whites alike; and if I underscore here the efforts of whites, I do so only because, in the highest sense, their contribution to the civil rights movement of those days was the more immediately disinterested.

I was living in the South during a part of this time, and, though never called to the test of physical courage, was greatly impressed by those who came through the test—and, in the case of some civil rights workers, came through it again and again. When lives are risked (and sometimes lost) in a good cause, it enhances—ennobles, even—the lives and the cause. Living in the South at that time was strange in many respects, not least among them that one's life revolved around a single political issue: race. How one felt about segregation-integration defined one. One's opinion on this subject not merely loomed large but eclipsed the moon and the sun. It was all and it was everything. Karl Jaspers used to claim that each of us is our situation personified. For nearly everyone living in the South, race was *the* situation, and it took over nearly everyone's life. Living in the South in the early 1960s must have been a little like living in South Africa during the past few years.

It was during these years, when I worked as the director of the antipoverty program in Little Rock, Arkansas, that the salad of illusions I now think of as my liberalism began first to show signs of wilting. Such a job demonstrated that social arrangements were not as malleable as one might have thought. Large infusions of federal money, such as the antipoverty program then offered, tended to excite the greed and corruption in everyone. To cite but a single instance, when in Little Rock a legal aid program was set up under the antipoverty program, the secret political hope was that the poor, now supplied with lawyers, would sue the city and the school district and other institutions that ostensibly had made life all the harder for them. Instead the poor tended to sue one another. Blacks, as all but a liberal of my kind would have recognized at the outset, were fully the equal of whites in self-interest, greed, and petty-mindedness. My sentimental education was beginning to be under way at last.

There remained, however, the thrill of virtue, which liberalism, like many a religion, holds out to its adherents and which I was myself not yet ready to relinguish. Even after the coup de grace was delivered to the civil rights movement by the racist ranting of Stokely Carmichael, H. Rap Brown, the Black Panthers, and other of the madder brothers, I still did not want to renounce my belief in its righteousness. Or was it my own righteousness in which I did not wish to renounce my belief?

Shortly after the Free Speech Movement got under way at Berkeley in 1965, soon spreading to other universities around the country, violence began to be threatened more and more insistently. At first this violence was to be upon property and not upon people, but when the riots broke out in such cities as Newark, Los Angeles, (Watts), and Chicago, the line between property and people became more than a little blurry. Under the direction of Martin Luther King, Jr., the power and the glory of the civil rights movement derived in great part from its brilliant deployment of Gandhian nonviolent resistance, which lent the cause of civil rights in the South a splendid moral authority. I may have been a hypocrite, but I was not entirely a fool. I was not one of those people on the left who, to use their word, "empathized" with the rioters in black slums or with the students who took over buildings and destroyed university property, including in some instances professors' manuscripts. Thugs were thugs, violence violence, and when violence is approved, or even sympathetically understood, a social movement has taken a serious turn from which it cannot hope ever to re-turn.

As someone who wanted to continue to think himself a man of the left, much that was now going on in left-wing circles felt to me very wrong. It was clearly wrong, I felt, for professors beyond the draft age to encourage their students to burn their draft cards as a protest against the Vietnam War. It was wrong for a rather twerpy journalist named Andrew Kopkind, in the *New York Review of Books*, to instruct Martin Luther King, Jr., that "morality starts at the barrel of a gun." It was wrong for Lewis Mumford, in the pages of *The New Yorker*, to link Richard Nixon's name alongside those of Hitler and Stalin as among the moral monsters of the twentieth century— wrong for a writer who claimed a historical imagination to be so historically ignorant and wrong for a magazine as reputable as *The New Yorker* to let him get away with such ignorance. It was wrong, and comic into the bargain, that Mr. and Mrs. Leonard Bernstein would throw a fund-raising party for the Black Panthers, though fortunate that they were obtuse enough to invite Tom Wolfe to it. It was wrong, and not at all comic, that the radical left would at the first opportunity declare itself anti-Israel (wrong but scarcely surprising, given the guru Marx's opinion that the Jews were a kind of recurrent international disease produced from the intestines of bourgeois society). That such wretched excesses had long qualified as part of the tradition of the left any reader of Stendhal, Balzac, Henry James, and Conrad ought to have known. "Everything is eternal," as Santayana once remarked, "except our attention."

Yet one mustn't blame Christianity because of the quality of the Christians, or so at the time I continued to feel, substituting leftism and leftists for Christianity and Christians. In other words, there was nothing wrong with the left, I decided, it was only leftists I abhorred. Virtue, as the subtitle of the old melodramas often read, finds a way. True enough, this position of mine kept my sweet virtue intact, but this does not mean that, whatever my falsity on that front, I did not immensely despise what in the late sixties and early seventies was going on in the name of left-wing politics, and especially in what I think can properly be termed left-wing culture. Here of course I have in mind drugs, let-it-all-hang-out sex, and the general idealization of youth that infiltrated so much in the life of the country.

I might have felt differently about all this if I had been, say, five years younger—if, that is, in 1968 I had been twenty-six instead of thirty-one. If I had been twenty-six, unmarried, without responsibilities, I might well have loved every moment of the vaunted sixties culture: puffin' on the good stuff, rappin' the nights away, making plenty of love, and no war whatsoever. But not my age but my having two stepsons in their teens made this impossible. To have teenage children in one's charge during those years gave a whole new sour perspective on the Age of Aquarius. One saw kids frying their brains kitchen-testing drugs; one saw all discipline break down in high schools, especially middle- and upper-middle-class schools; one saw that ultimate act of racism well under way, not asking the same standards of performance from black kids as one asked from whites (and then eventually lowering those asked from whites), all in the name of good-heartedness, liberal version. So much garbage in the air, if a slight euphemism will be allowed, and everybody rushing to turn on fans.

Had I been five or so years younger and unmarried, I should also have had to face the question of what to do about the draft. Had I been drafted, would I have served in the Army? Opposed to the Vietnam War though I was, I am confident that I would not have had the courage to declare myself a conscientious objector if it meant a certain prison term, with the prospect such a term held out of such jailish delights as, say, homosexual rape, which has never been my idea of a swell time. Would I have fled the country, jumped to Sweden or, more conveniently, to Canada, where I have relatives? Doubtful. More likely, I suspect, as with so many of the confreres of my social class, I should have saved my rosy middle-class bottom by hying off to one graduate school or another, where, unmolested, allowing the poor boys and the black boys to fight this nasty little war in my place, I could protest in peace if not quiet.

I must say that I am extremely grateful never to have had to make that choice. Had I chosen to avoid the draft through hiding out in graduate school, behind alma mater's skirts, I should my life long have been in doubt about the authenticity of my protest: was it the war in Vietnam I hated or the above-mentioned rosy middle-class bottom I loved? It has always seemed to me that the authenticity of the antiwar protest movement of the sixties generally has been in doubt, owing to the undeniable fact that, though the war slogged on to its horrendous conclusion, once the United States draft law was abrogated, all protest abated (so to speak) radically. I do not claim a pattern here, but in recent months I have talked with two men, both in their early forties, one a professor of English at a Southern university, the other an editor in Chicago, who each separately told me he had misgivings about not serving in Vietnam. One felt that that war was the central experience of his generation, and he had missed it; the other felt a plain bad conscience about letting the working class do all the fighting, and he regretted it.

Visited with no such complicating emotions, I was able to hate the Vietnam War with a cool and evenhanded contempt. When such figures as General Westmoreland, Robert McNamara, and (for reasons now lost to me) particularly Dean Rusk appeared upon my television screen, I felt the want of a brick. What, I now ask myself, made me so angry? There was of course the lying, there was the ineptitude, there was the sense of sheer waste. But every war offers such spectacles. No, I think I was offended by what I construed to be the immorality of this war. In its foreign policy, my country was not as moral as I should have liked—not to put too fine a point on it, it was not as moral as I.

I was never procommunist; I was never for a moment so deluded as such heavy American thinkers as Susan Sontag, Noam Chomsky, and Mary McCarthy, who believed in the gentle, peace-loving people of North Vietnam. Yet nowhere is it written, or so I then apparently believed, that one could not be anticommunist and anti-American both. I was in those days, I now see, a plague-on-both-your-houses man; and as generally is the case with such men, I had even more complaints about the house I happened to be living in, the United States. And yet why? Why did I wish my country to lose a war that we all know, and ought to have known, to have been a war against a tyrannous communist country that immediately proved its true nature after its victory? If someone had asked me this question then, I think I might have mumbled something about our betraying our ideals in this war. (I now think that all we betrayed were the noncommunist countries of Southeast Asia.) I now think that my anti-Americanism was a part of my believing myself to be a man of the left, and hence antimilitary, and a part of my believing myself to be an intellectual (I still think of myself as an intellectual), and hence someone whose first duty is to criticize his own country. I was locked into clichés and false traditions of my own choosing.

If you think these clichés and false traditions are not powerful, you are mistaken. Take, for example, the three great American political trials of this century: Sacco-Vanzetti, Hiss-Chambers, the Rosenberg case. As anyone who has even dipped a big toe in the oceanic literature of those trials knows, one could easily drown in their vast and choppy waters. Yet, being a man of the left, self-declared, I took it as axiomatic that Sacco and Vanzetti were innocent, that Hiss was framed, that the Rosenbergs, though probably guilty, should nevertheless not have been executed. I took all this to be so because I assumed that every political trial was essentially a rerun of the Dreyfus trial, with the government being in the wrong, the defendant a victim, the proceedings in some way rigged on the side of injustice. Some may argue that this is healthy intellectual skepticism; I would argue that it is automatic left-wing thinking—that, with its taste for conspiracies and its distaste for authority, it goes with the liberal-left territory. (For the record, I have since come to believe that Sacco and Vanzetti were probably guilty, that Hiss clearly was, and that the Rosenbergs absolutely were, though they still didn't deserve to be executed.)

Another left-wing axiom, this one involving a paradox, is the belief in progress joined with the refusal to admit that much has ever been made—or, where some progress has indisputably been made, the denial of its importance. This is conjoined with the liberal-left belief in the slippery slope, which holds that one false political step is not merely likely to send a society rolling down a hill, but more likely start an avalanche. One sees the slippery-slope argument brought into play in the contemporary university fairly frequently. When one suggests, for example, that professors ought not to be permitted to teach courses that provide sheer political propaganda—at my own university, for example, a famous left-wing journalist this past year taught a course entitled "Reagan and the Crisis of the Modern Presidency"—one is warned of the slippery slope: start telling people what they cannot teach and pretty soon you will be telling them exactly what they can teach and pretty soon you will have a McCarthy-like atmosphere and . . . in short, you will have fallen down the slippery slope, with an avalanche of the Inquisition, fascism, McCarthyism, and Salem witch burning to follow.

For an interesting example of these axioms and assumptions at work, permit me to draw attention to an extremely well-written essay that appeared in the spring 1973 issue of *Dissent* under the title "The New Conservatives: Intellectuals in Retreat." Close readers will note that the very title is a dead giveaway. Retreat? From what? From the spirit of Onward Left-Wing Soldier, it turns out. The gravamen of the essay is that a number of intellectuals—among them Irving Kristol, Daniel Patrick Moynihan, Norman Podhoretz, and Nathan

Glazer—have left the political fray, chiefly through an uncritical acceptance of something that looks suspiciously like the status quo. A
careful polemicist, the author of this essay begins by giving these
intellectuals full credit for their devastating criticisms of radical excess,
and joins them in their condemnation of the antinomian strain of
that "congeries of personalities, organizations, and trends that went
by the name of 'the Movement' " during the late sixties and early
seventies. But haven't they, he now asks, gone too far in the other
direction? His is of course a rhetorical question. Damn right they
have gone too far in the other direction. They have come to accept
such Tory notions as that the chief responsibility for reform may
not fall upon the government; that personal reform may not be a
task that government regulation can bring about at all; that the arrangements of society are immensely complex and ought not to be tinkered
with until we have a reasonably sophisticated understanding of them;
and that—unforgivably—we must recognize that in many areas of
American life real progress has been made, and ought not to be
gainsaid. Granting the subtlety and high intelligence of these new
conservatives, our author nonetheless concludes that "the bitter sadness is that . . . [the new conservatism] may well end up a more
geniune obstacle to the alleviation of social pain than the obtuse
and retrograde conservatism of the privileged that preceded it."

Our author—"Hey," as the kids nowadays say, "you gotta love
him!" Maybe, though, you don't, if only because it is evident that
he sure loves himself. Note that sensitive phrasing—that "bitter sadness," that "social pain." Note, too, how neatly he has positioned
himself politically. There he stands, triumphantly in the middle,
the red hordes (sixties radicals and others) to his left, the Black
Hundreds (conservatives old and new) to his right, a good man ready
to continue to fight the good fight. One can almost hear him humming
to himself as he completed writing this essay, "Give me one man,
who's a stout-hearted man, and I'll give you. . . ." Perhaps I can
hear him better than you because it was I who wrote that essay.

The only use that that essay has for me today is to delineate
with some precision what my politics were in the spring of 1973.
As a document in the history of my opinions, it shows me to be a
still fairly young man (at thirty-six) who has quite had it with the
antidemocratic, procounterculture antics of the left of the day but
someone who is not yet ready to eschew the label of left or with it
the appearance of high public virtue necessary to the political type
I myself once termed "the virtucrat." Not dramatically but gradually

over the next four or so years this, too, would change. Far from wishing to retain a sentimental attachment to the left, I developed a strong antipathy to it—strong enough, at any rate, not to mind thinking of myself as antileft. How did this happen? Somehow I have the feeling that my explaining it by saying that I got smarter is not going to be adequate. Too bad, because I think that is what happened.

I am well aware of the cliché that has it that as one becomes older, better established, perhaps achieves a modicum of success in the world, one becomes more conservative. Irving Kristol once remarked that he has come "to believe that an adult's 'normal' political instincts should be" conservative, which is a kindly way of formulating it. A less kindly way is to remark, as people on the left do, that as some people grow old they get hardening of the arteries, especially those that lead to the heart. I am not sure that growing older has all that much to do with political change. What I think does is the strength of the emotional investment one has had in certain political ideas in one's youth. Some people—some astonishingly successful people—can never shake these ideas; and some others—I think here of the current-day university—live in an environment where holding on to the ideas of one's youth ensures the security that, in a contentious atmosphere, only careful conformity can provide.

In my particular case, nothing dramatic—no falling star, no shaft of sunlight on the forest floor, no weekend spent staring at the ocean—caused me to shed what I now think the political illusions of earlier years. Instead, as illusions most often do, mine decayed and fell away, rather like baby teeth. Like baby teeth, too, some of these illusions needed to be nudged, even yanked a bit before they came out. Here reading joined with observation helped enormously. Coming upon Edward Shils's *The Intellectuals and the Powers and Other Essays* gave me a more rounded view of intellectuals than any I had had before—of their social origin, their multivarious functions, their propensity for mischief making, and also their grandeur. One illusion that Professor Shils's book knocked permanently out of my head was that intellectuals ought to consider themselves in permanent critical opposition to the society in which they live. I was especially lucky in living in the same city as Edward Shils, whom I met and who befriended me. I discovered that there were no seams between his writing and his life: what he wrote, he lived. Belief and action are for him utterly congruent, and this requires a consistency and courage that one rarely finds in the world, and even more rarely among people who think themselves intellectuals. Intrinsically, the categories of left and right had little to do with the intellectual vocation; the attempt to grasp the truth in something approximating its complexity, through learning, insight, and common sense, had everything to do with it. Such were among the lessons taught by Edward Shils, in his books and through the example of his life.

Around the time I met Edward Shils I also began, at the age of thirty-seven, a career as a university teacher. The year was 1974, and though the revolution of the sixties was officially over, it didn't always seem so on university campuses. It was Edward Shils who once described the sixties to me in the metaphor of an enormous wave that rolled over the country, then slowly rolled back, but not without leaving a vast amount of debris on the beach. The university, I now at first hand came to see, was the beach. Debris was everywhere. It was found in university teachers (obviously not all of them) casually sleeping with their students; it was in a curriculum that was increasingly organized less to educate students than to please them; it was there in the new teacher evaluations that students were encouraged to make; it was there perhaps above all in the newly organized consciousness-raising academic units known as Afro-American Studies and Women's Studies.

And as the years went by, it would not get better. It would get worse, as the young graduate students and instructors of the sixties grew into the associate and full professors of the eighties. Marxism became a hot item, and scarcely any academic department in the humanities and social science (with the exception, interestingly, of economics) felt it could carry on without one or two Marxists. Open protest, it is true, was now for the most part passé, left to those small student groups who, over divestment in South Africa or U.S. involvement in Central America, could work off their sixties envy by marching with a banner or building a shack in front of the administration building. But open protest isn't any longer needed; no need to carry placards outside the gates when the barbarians are already inside, boring—in my view, in all senses of the word—from within.

When I say "the barbarians," I mean a modest number of hard-core characters who actively proselytize students and teach a fairly straightforward Marxist menu featuring distaste for America, in peace and war; unstinting admiration for the struggles of the people of the Third World; hatred of capitalism; and that old favorite the class struggle, served with a generous side order of alienation. Nothing new about any of this. What is new is the general tolerance for this dreary fare. The tolerance is so great because the general spirit prevailing in the preponderance of contemporary universities is that of liberalism. But it is liberalism which has lost its moorings, and which stands chiefly for tolerance for activities well to its own left and is finally convinced only of its own virtue. When a liberal myself, I used to wonder why people so despised liberals. I used to think it was owing to the liberal's avoidance of extremes, of his desire always to occupy the middle ground. No longer a liberal, I no longer think liberalism is, in its contemporary incarnation, informed by balance and fairness; I think it is instead motivated by fear and self-righteousness. Midge Decter once remarked that we should do away with the word "liberal," which has lost its old character anyway, and simply substitute for it the word "left." There is something to that; I would only add that to catch the spirit of the new liberalism, we require the adjective "weak" before the noun "left."

Something that it is not easy to convince people who live outside the university but that is evident to anyone who lives within it is that in the United States there are two political cultures: the culture of the country, which has twice now elected Ronald Reagan; and the culture of the university, in which, if an election were held today between Ronald Reagan and Louis Farakhan, the outcome would not be all that easy to predict (the largest number of votes, my guess is, would be abstentions). It is this political culture, for the most part composed of the weak left, that makes possible the almost continuous inroads of Marxism, feminism, and other isms too numerous to mention. As a rather chaotic teacher at my own university once put it at the close of a memorandum proposing an honors seminar in "gender and literature," our school and, in particular, our department had shown itself woefully behind the times in not having more such courses. When I suggested that being behind the times in this regard might not be such a bad thing, I received looks that could only be described as strange. When I went on to say that I was concerned about the built-in political content of such a course, it was as if I had loudly belched at a small dinner party for the French ambassador. How gauche! But then in the contemporary university just about everything that is not *gauche* is gauche.

Not in every university, I hasten to add, but chiefly in those that think of themselves as the better universities. Thus, the faculty at Stanford makes plain that it is not eager to have the Reagan Library; thus, when Harvard is beset by left-wing demonstrations against speakers, it boldly steps in and cancels the speeches; thus, school after school proudly announces it is divesting itself of its South African holdings, all duly reported in the section of the *Chronicle of Higher Education* called "The Divestment Watch." There is a very heavy traffic in the universities caused by everyone rushing to get on the right side.

In my anger at what I think of as the weakness of the contemporary universities and its baleful effects on the life of the country, am I merely like Ambrose Bierce's conservative, "who is enamoured of existing evils, as distinguished from the liberal who wishes to replace them with others"? In politics, is it enough to know what one doesn't like? Do not one's aversions and fears imply preferences and desires? On this score, after my early years of looking at the world from the left, I must say that today any revolutionary zeal I might once have felt is quite gone. Having come through what I have to conclude is something in the nature of a political deprogramming, I feel like Henry James's young hero Hyacinth Robinson, in *The Princess Casamassima*, of whom James writes, "What was supreme in his mind today was not the idea of how the society that surrounded him should be destroyed; it was much more the sense of the wonderful precious things it had produced, of the fabric of beauty and power it had raised."

Like Hyacinth, after dropping my leftism, I feel the world has become a more interesting place—and I mean the world as it is. I have no strong impulse to reform it, outside those pockets of alterable injustice and organized cruelty where change is necessary. I wish people were wiser and better—I wish *I* were wiser and better—but I know of no clear or certain way to bring this about. I no longer see life as requiring a crescendo of reform, in which every day and in every way my neighborhood, my city, my nation, the world gets better and better. I haven't the least hint how to bring this about, and I am not sure I would if I could. I only wish the world, my nation, my city, my neighborhood to be more habitable—less dangerous, less diseased, less dirty, less dreary. I do not want people to suffer, and I am willing to do all that I can to alleviate this suffering, but I am fairly certain that the old left-wing methods of bringing about this alleviation are less than worthless—they are often, as in the case of so many welfare programs, part of the problem. I do not expect the United States to behave itself with greater moral rectitude than any nation in the history of the world simply because it is the country in which I live and therefore must come up to my standards of rectitude. I expect it instead to act in a rough consensus of what its citizens judge to be its self-interest, protecting itself from its enemies, coming to the aid of its friends, ensuring its own continued prosperity and hence that of its people. In sum, I haven't a utopian notion in my head, and I do not expect to have another such notion this side of the grave.

Shedding my left-wing views has left me much happier without, so far as I can see, making anyone else in the world more miserable (except perhaps those who violently disagree with what I write). But then figures on the left—Marx, Bakunin, Bentham, Mill, Lenin, Trotsky, reformers or revolutionaries—are not a famously happy crew. Being on the left, they are not supposed to be happy, for surely the whole point of being on the left is that one is dissatisfied with the world as it is and ardently desires to change it. I do not mean to say that being leftist condemns one to being humorless. Not at all. But there is, not so very deep down, an element of serious and perhaps immitigable discontent with life, of discomfiture with the world as it is, that turns most people left to begin with and that must remain if they are to stay on the left.

As a writer, someone primarily interested in understanding and not changing the world, I found removing the furry blinders worn through my left-wing youth an immense aid. In my writing I no longer did opinion checks; I no longer sought out heroes and villains through the measure of whether a particular figure's views gibed with my own. Whereas once such men as Henry Ford and John D. Rockefeller would have been boobs and rotters to me, I now found them, not necessarily heroic, but extremely interesting. Cliché terms such as "the robber barons" no longer held any real meaning for me; nor could they for anyone who cared to investigate that fascinating and varied generation in the round and without the bandages of ideology that a committed left-wing writer such as, say, E. L. Docto-row prefers to wear. For myself, once the blinders of liberalism came off, the present became much more enticing than the future—the way the world *is* became a subject of greater fascination than the way it *ought* to be.

To say that one has shed one's leftist views, even to think oneself antileft, does not necessarily mean—I know it doesn't in my case— that one has automatically acquired the reverse of these views. In striving not to be deluded, for example, I don't think one has to drop one's compassion; in some respects, I have come to believe, it can grow even greater. Nor need all idealism begin, as left-wing idealism does, in dissatisfaction. Not all idealism, corollarily, need be invested in hope, where it is almost certain to be disappointed and turn sour; there is also the idealism of the actual, those instances of actual courage, altruism, and goodness. Released from bondage to the whole earth catalogue of left-wing views, one can take up more modulated and realistic ones.

I have, for example, recently seen H. L. Mencken and Justice Holmes described as approving capitalist economics without approving capitalist culture. On the practical level, I understand this to mean that one is permitted to approve the system of rewards for initiative and hard work that is at the heart of capitalism and still despise, say, the Waldenbook chain because it treats what it sells as no more than another commodity. Under socialism, I hear my younger self stepping in to say, there would be no Waldenbooks. True enough. Unfortunately, under socialism, thus far along, there hasn't been much culture either.

I no longer have to be *for* some hopelessly vague entity called the Third World, an entity that includes Bangladesh and Saudi Arabia. Instead I can attempt to distinguish among those Third World countries that are run by clowns, those run by butchers, and those genuinely struggling with horrendous problems. I no longer have to give a hustler such as Jesse Jackson special dispensation from criticism because he is a black man. (How fine it was to read, as I recently did in a biography of Martin Luther King, Jr., that King, too, greatly distrusted Jesse Jackson!) I can agree with George Orwell, who was of course staunchly antitotalitarian, that all revolutions are failures but that they aren't all the same failure—but I can add, because unlike Orwell I do not consider myself a socialist, that they sure are beginning to look like damn near the same failure.

My political deprogramming has given me a fine new sense of intellectual freedom. The impulse to criticism always came readily enough to me, but I see that formerly it only did so within the constraints of left-wing catechism. Now I feel fully free to criticize anything or anyone, from any side or angle. Better yet, I feel free *not* to criticize—not everywhere to find the connection between something I don't like and capitalism, to discover over and over again that my country is not finally good enough for me, or to blame something called "the system" for my own deficiencies of talent and character. Without such false, if not to say wholly imaginary, connections, discoveries, and accusations, the world seems a livelier, a brighter, an altogether more interesting place. At the age of fifty-seven, Henry James, unable to bear any longer the beard he had worn for several years, shaved it off, after which he wrote to his brother William that he felt "*forty* and clean and light." There are, I have come to realize, other ways to acquire that same feeling without having to shave off a beard.

2

Notes of a Journey

Julius Lester

Winter 1987
Amherst, Massachusetts

I stare through the window at the snow covering the earth and the Berkshires on the horizon. They are gentle reminders of that reality beyond time and space, of that shocking encounter with the Self I seek continually. That seeking has been the blessing and curse of my life, compelling me into solitude even as it propels me into intimacy with the world.

I am not sure, even after all these years, which is the blessing and which the curse. I am beginning to believe that the two are the same, that blessings are curses and curses are blessings and it does not matter if I do not know which is which.

It is not a disappointment that I did not find God keening with the coldness of a February full moon in the civil rights movement. When I was young I did not know how important it is to learn where God is not.

I think about the years I worked for the Student Non-Violent Coordinating Committee (SNCC) in Mississippi, Alabama, Georgia, and New York. Those years happened to another person. But he has my name. That is why Native Americans bestow a new name on you after a significant change in your life. How can the name given me by my parents be expected to express who I have become, especially when I become again and again?

Yet the person sitting here now is not wholly different from that young man who published a book in 1968 called *Look Out, Whitey! Black Power's Gon' Get Your Mama!*—that young man whom book reviewers still identify as a "former black militant." I know that I am unrecognizable to many I knew then, especially since my conversion to Judaism. But the constant of my forty-eight years has been the soul's reality, my soul's poignant and brave yearning to be a love song to God. I thought the civil rights movement could be that. It was not. It could not have been. But I had to risk my soul before I could know.

———— • ————

July 5, 1964
Clarksdale, Mississippi
10 A.M.

Hot already like Grandmomma's kitchen on a summer day when she was heating irons in a tub of coals and cooking on the wood-burning stove at the same time. It is what I would expect in the Mississippi delta.

I am here as part of what is being called the Mississippi Summer Project. Eight hundred to a thousand primarily white college students have come to organize an alternative political party, the Mississippi Freedom Democratic Party, as a way of protesting the exclusion of Negroes from political power in the state.

I am not white; I finished college four years ago, and I do not believe in political action. During the sit-in movement in Nashville in 1960, I did not sit in, nor did I go on Freedom Rides the following year. That is not my way. Yet I am here.

In the evenings I lead the singing of freedom songs at mass meetings for an hour or two; during the days I travel to another town and stand in another packed church or dance hall, my guitar over my shoulder, my voice like a clarion—"Ain't Gonna Let Nobody Turn Me 'Round"—calling the people to let their souls march to Freedom's heartbeat. It is not possible to be anywhere else. History has become a song as compelling and irresistible as the Siren's and I am unable to remain tied to the mast.

I was there at the beginning, February 1, 1960. I noticed the brief article on an inside page of the Nashville *Tennessean* about four students at North Carolina A & T sitting in at a lunch counter in Greensboro and refusing to move when they were asked. They were arrested. I knew something significant had happened. Nine days later some students from Fisk University and the other black colleges in Nashville held a sit-in. I was a senior at Fisk, but I was not one of those who made history by sitting on lunch-counter stools.

I am not one of them this summer either, them being the summer volunteers and the full-time civil rights organizers from SNCC and the Congress of Racial Equality (CORE). They are committed and dedicated to social change. Their bodies gleam with a fervor that would make them saints. My body recoils from belief that transforms mere mortals into crusaders. I am committed to something within me for which I have no name.

I remember arguing with friends at Fisk about whether the artist was supposed to be *engagé*, committed to social change. They said yes. I was unsure. Could Joyce have written *Ulysses* and *Finnegan's Wake* if he had been *engagé?* They accused me of being an "individualist," as if that were an obscenity. They did not understand what an achievement it was to have grown up in the South and become an individualist.

Autumn 1959. A close friend told me about a new group on campus which planned to meet with and hopefully persuade the owners of stores in downtown Nashville to eliminate the segregated lunch counters, bathrooms, and water fountains. "Would you be interested in joining us? We could really use you."

"I have better things to do," I responded angrily, coldly.

That was true. I wanted to complete enough paintings to have an exhibit in the spring; I was studying piano again and was to perform in a recital; I was working on choral arrangements of Negro spirituals for the university choir to sing, taking voice lessons and studying guitar in order to give a vocal recital of traditional Negro music, and I was working on a novel. She understood, she said.

She couldn't have. I had given her a plausible excuse, not an honest answer. Not wanting to hurt her feelings more, I had not said that because she was from Pittsburgh, Pennsylvania, she was as foreign to me as a white person. I could not imagine what it was like to live in a place where you could get on a bus and sit anywhere, walk in the front door of a movie theater instead of going down the alley and up the back stairs to the balcony, be downtown shopping and stroll into any restaurant and be served. What was it like to go into the world each day and not see signs reading COLORED ENTRANCE COLORED FOUNTAIN COLORED WINDOW NO COLORED ALLOWED WHITES ONLY COLORED SIT IN THE REAR? I had traveled with my parents to exotic places like

Philadelphia, New York, and Chicago, had sat in the fronts of buses and eaten in restaurants where white people did not even look at us. I could not relax into the bizarre atmosphere of social equality because in a week or two I would have to return to a place where dailiness was an undeclared war in which the objective was my soul. My friend did not know what it was to have your humanity mocked and doubted day after day after day.

The previous year I had lived for nine months in California and had learned to trust the world, to take for granted my existence in it. Thus, on the train ride home, I forgot and went into a cafe in the St. Louis, Missouri, railroad station and sat down at the counter. I was remembering that I had been born in St. Louis and had lived my first two years there, and thus I didn't notice how long it was taking the waitress to come over to me. Finally, she did and asked what I wanted. I told her. She asked if I wanted to take it out. I smiled and told her no. It was then she said, "I'm sorry but we can't serve you if you don't take it out." I left, angry because I had trusted the world once too often. I remained hungry because I could eat on the train only if I submitted to having a black screen placed around me so that the white diners would not get indigestion from seeing me.

Desegregating the lunch counters of Nashville, Tennessee, would not and could not heal the still bleeding wounds of my twenty years. My father had raised me to walk to town rather than ride the bus, not to see a movie if I couldn't walk in the front door, never to buy a hamburger or soda at the COLORED WINDOW of some cafe, or relieve myself in a COLORED BATHROOM, or quench my thirst at a COLORED FOUNTAIN. But whether I acceded to segregation or not, it defined my life. To protest as my friend wanted me to would be to continue living in relation to segregation as the primary force in my life. My friend could desegregate every lunch counter in Nashville. I didn't care. I was going to leave the South forever and ever when I graduated in June.

Forever has lasted four years, four years during which it has been increasingly difficult to justify a life of playing the starving writer while friends risk their lives on back roads in Mississippi and Georgia and are changing, if not the face of History, at least the clothes it wears. Last summer I lived in a small house at the end of a long dirt road in New Hampshire. I worked on a novel and wrote haiku while a quarter of a million people marched on Washington. The next month four girls were killed when a church was bombed in Birmingham. Since then writing has seemed like an act of selfishness.

July 7, 1964
Hattiesburg, Mississippi
Late evening

People look at me as if I am a hero. They call me a "freedom rider," their name for anyone involved in the civil rights movement, and thank me for coming to "help us get this burden off our shoulders."

I feel guilty because it is not the call of freedom I hear. I should. Don't I, too, shiver in the shadow of slavery? Yes, but something other than FREEDOM NOW calls.

During the sit-ins that spring of 1960, I had long conversations with Candie, a white exchange student from Pomona College in California. She had been arrested on a sit-in, and neither of us understood why she, a blond Californian immune from segregation, was willing to go to jail to end it while I was not.

I told her about Tillich's *Dynamics of Faith*, a book I'd read in a philosophy of religion course. I didn't understand it, but Tillich's definition of faith as ultimate concern had helped me name something in myself. "I love that phrase—ultimate concern," I told her. "If I know my ultimate concern, then I know the ground of being and I have this feeling that the sit-ins might change things on one level but unless things change on the level of ultimate concern, then the kind of change you're involved in won't add up to much."

Concurrent with the beginning of the civil rights movement was the Beat Generation. I had read Kerouac and Ginsberg and John Clellon Holmes, and my classmates called me a "Beatnik" because I wore jeans and walked around campus with a guitar. I was not sure I was, but the Beat Generation, like Tillich, cared about the values by which people lived their lives. Candie could not convince me that political change would lead to spiritual change.

In the novel I was working on, I described a religious experience I'd had the previous spring in California. The prose is so romantic that I am embarrassed by it, but I am not ashamed of this first statement of self-definition:

> I was sitting on a rock that was about six feet above the sea. The waves were crashing on the rock and running up to me before they slid and tumbled back down. As I sat there it struck me force-

fully as the waves slammed against the rock: This is God talking to me. I was partaking of eternity. "Before Abraham was, I am." The indomitable rock said this. It stood there, unconquerable. The ocean said it also. Everything around me breathed the essence of eternity. I knew then why I loved Bach and Michelangelo and Basho. They were telling me what the ocean and the rock were saying. . . . I didn't exist. I became a part of infinity.

Now I feel love everywhere. Love is the one universal. It is God. My entire becoming now is *consciously* directed toward manifesting this Love I feel. Art is a love letter to God. I must spend my life loving Him. It's completely irrelevant if He loves me. I must love in every way I know how. I can't spend my life loving just one individual but every person in whom I feel a soul. I must love.

That value has remained. It is a value of the civil rights movement, too. To the extent that it is, I trust love and nonviolence to make the kind of change I tried to articulate to Candie. But I don't know how many in the civil rights movement really believe in nonviolence as a spiritual discipline, as a way to live in the world. I think that many in SNCC see it as a tactic only.

July 8, 1964
Laurel, Mississippi
11 P.M.

The intensity of emotion with which people sang tonight was frightening. This is not the first time I've seen it, but tonight I was repelled. I know these songs release the frustrations of years and confer the courage to face what is to come. But standing at the front of the church and leading them in singing "Wade in the Water," one of the old songs, leading them into the new ones—"Ain't Gonna Let Nobody Turn Me 'Round," "Which Side Are You On?," "I'm on My Way to Freedom Land"—I did not know what to do with the pain and anger in those hundreds of voices.

The teenagers were more emotional than the adults. The emotions of the adults were tempered by knowledge and patience, by age and the psychic guerrilla warfare they have waged all their lives. The young are so tender and their emotions are so raw.

I was emotionally removed from the songs and the people. I believe that "we shall overcome someday." I know that I'm not going to "let nobody turn me 'round," but as I sang, I knew that my enemy was within—lack of integrity, the absence of imagination, callousness, cruelty. Even when Negroes are politically free, the absence of humanity will mock that political freedom. No Congressional legislation can overcome that which makes us slaves to the forces within.

That is part of what I was trying to tell Candie. Does it matter if a black and white person sit next to each other at a lunch counter if they do not know there is a realm beyond the narrows of time for which and to which they are responsible?

July 11, 1964
Biloxi, Mississippi

Reality has become heat attacking the body like burning needles, singing freedom songs, sleeping in a different town each night, being alone, and fear. I do not seek to escape the heat but concentrate on it. As long as I complain about it, I forget how afraid I am.

My mind takes a picture of the license plate on any car of whites moving too slowly. When I hear the loud slam of a screen door or the backfire of a truck, I wait for a scream. When none comes I know that a door is a door is a door. However, the next sound may be followed by a scream, and it may be mine.

I don't want to die. Others are willing to die for freedom, however. I'm not and I feel ashamed and unworthy. How I wish that the passion for freedom would illumine my face like a page from a medieval Bible. But freedom is not a feeling to be conjured by songs and fiery speeches. Freedom is an act of faith made with the future. It is a promise that cannot be fulfilled and yet must be made. Marking a ballot and putting it into a box is not a way to keep that promise because there can be no change unless the person marking the ballot knows he is the promise and the act of faith, that he is an offering to God and humanity.

What do we have to offer, we who are so young, so earnest, and so well-intentioned? Have we lived long enough to understand that freedom is a train on its tracks, as one of my professors defined it once? I still do not understand what he meant, but his statement has overtones of truth which FREEDOM NOW does not.

Our days are haunted by the disappearances of James Chaney, Andrew Goodman, and Michael Schwerner who vanished last month near Philadelphia, Mississippi. We know they are dead and wait only for their bodies to be found. We know they were murdered and it is impossible not to wonder each day, will one of us be next?

I did not know them, but I know Mickey Schwerner's brother, wife, and parents. I remember sitting in Steve Schwerner's apartment in Brooklyn one evening this past spring. We were listening to John Coltrane records and remembering having seen him at Birdland. We talked about the Mississippi Summer Project and the fact that his brother was going, that I was going. Casually and callously, we agreed that what needed to happen was that some white kid needed to get killed. That would make the nation do something about Mississippi. It happened, and I am so sorry. There is still enough of the primitive in me to wonder if it would have if Steve and I had not spoken thoughtlessly.

I think about the bodies of those three boys younger than me. I am twenty-five, but I am alive. They are not. Is FREEDOM NOW worthy of three young men's lives? No. There is no justification for their deaths. Some historical personage said that the tree of liberty was watered with blood. How obscene! Yet here I am, exposing my precious life to the hatred and rifle of any Mississippi redneck who would be applauded by his friends for pulling the trigger.

If I die this summer, I will hate myself for having come, will hate it that my blood watered the tree of liberty.

July 14, 1964
Vicksburg, Mississippi

I am no longer certain where I am in time and space. Last night I slept on a bed as hard as disappointed hope. The night before I slept on bedsprings. The night before that, a mattress on the floor, and the night before that, in the back of the car. I've drunk mega-gallons of soda pop, beer, water, coffee, and bourbon. I've sweated so profusely while leading singing in churches and dance halls that the matches in my shirt pocket were too damp to use afterwards. But one day soon, I will walk out of the Port Authority Bus Terminal in New York, see the traffic clogging Eighth Avenue, look up at the Empire State Building across town and smile a silly smile—NEW YORK! Without thinking, I will break into my New York stride and walk downtown to my apartment on 21st Street.

The memory of Mississippi will remain, but the pulsating despair will not. What is it like to live in some of the towns I've passed through—Mendenhall, Mississippi; D'Lo, Mississippi? Outside D'Lo I saw an old Negro couple hitching a ride. I stopped the car and they got in. They were going to town, to D'Lo for a bottle of pop. He was so drunk he could barely stand. She could do that much but not more. I let them out in front of the grocery store and she borrowed a dime. Will the Civil Rights Bill about to be signed by the President make a difference in D'Lo, Mississippi? Driving from Moss Point, I saw a young couple sitting beside a car. I stopped. They'd had a flat and didn't have a spare. The girl was pretty in her dirty, torn yellow party dress. Her hand was bleeding, and she was holding it with a piece of dirty paper sack.

"Where're you from?" I asked.

"Chicago," she smiled. Then she laughed. "Collins, Mis'sippi."

She bummed a cigarette and asked if I was a "freedom rider."

She and the man refused my offer of assistance and as I drove away, they sat back down. Maybe they're sitting there now, unperturbed, waiting for Godot.

The longer I am here, the less I understand. How am I supposed to understand the truck filled with white kids who screamed obscenities at me? What I am supposed to do about that pretty girl in the yellow dress sitting by the road? What can I do to relieve the injustices, the miseries? Say a kind word, sing a song, register a voter? But there'll always be D'Lo. And simultaneously there will be love and laughter, sex and children, dancing and playing, the beauties of mountains and rivers, Bach and Coltrane, Rembrandt and Joyce, and there will be me unable to reconcile the joy and the sorrow. Yes, they are one and each is necessary and should not be thought of as just or unjust, beautiful or ugly. I remember that much from studying the *Bhagavad Gita*. Nonetheless, it angers me that beauty has to walk with ugliness, that suffering is eternal and injustice even longer, and that we cannot make peace with each other until we make peace with ourselves.

I haven't enjoyed singing here because no one is ready to hear what I have to say—that death is awful, that you should see that my grave is kept clean, that there is no FREEDOM NOW because we will only be free when we love, really love, and we can't do that as long as we are suffocated by our own selfishness, as long as we want others to exist as reflections of our own images, that there is no freedom until we know another in his separateness and difference. Until I touch what is alien in another with what is alien in me, there can be no freedom, not now, not ever.

That is what I want to say, but my voice is not strong enough to be heard while history swells with the majesty of a wave to break on the land with all the fury of a *tsunami*.

———— • ————

Spring 1966
Itta Bena, Mississippi

I have returned. Mississippi is different now. Few civil rights workers remain in the state. The Civil Rights Act of 1964 and the Voting Rights Act of 1965 have made the civil rights movement unnecessary.

It doesn't seem that way. I know better than to walk into the white cafe downtown and expect to be served, and no Negroes in Itta Bena have tried to register to vote. But it is only a matter of time before someone tests the new laws and change will come. One kind of change, at least.

SNCC is in a mass of confusion. "Whitey," "black people," "black consciousness," and "power for black people" are the code words for a new sensibility. I'm not sure what I think of it. SNCC has created an African Bureau, a result of the two trips SNCC people made to Africa in the fall of 1964 and last year. A document has just been issued calling for a conference to discuss the movement's relationship to the African liberation movement. I seem to be the only one disturbed by it.

It is extremely polemical with perorations to "our glorious African past" and appeals for Negroes to identify with Africa and their African past in order to achieve "black consciousness." But with its emphasis on the Negro's connection to Africa, it denies the Negro's uniqueness as an Afro-American.

Yes, identity with Africa, but to the extent of learning African languages, adopting African styles of dress? Maybe I don't understand because I haven't been to Africa. Well, one thing's for sure: Northern white liberals are going to be amazed and consternated when they find out what SNCC is up to.

I am here on a grant from the Newport Folk Foundation to collect the old music, but it may be a while before I go back to New York. I am thinking of working full-time for SNCC. I'm still not willing to die for FREEDOM NOW, but because of the civil rights movement, there is now a Civil Rights Act. I travel the South with less fear and anger and no longer see signs telling me that I am an inferior being. I see a look of hope that was not on faces in 1964. Political change does make a difference in the dailiness of people's lives, and I was wrong not to see that. It was idealistic to think that people can care about Ultimate Concern when dailiness is lived in anxiety.

Could political action be another road to Ultimate Concern? Can one express love for God and humanity through political action? I have never experienced such love and selflessness as I do in SNCC people. Maybe I want to join SNCC because I love these people who live with a simplicity and commitment that is monk-like. Their idealism is not an intellectual abstraction, but is as palpable and warm as sunshine. They have submitted their egos to something greater, something bigger—the ideal of a society in which it will be normal for people to care about each other. Isn't that an expression of Ultimate Concern?

Summer 1966
Atlanta, Georgia

We are making history and we feel helpless. Each evening at six o'clock all of us working in the SNCC office gather in the basement to watch the news. The lead item is about our new chairman, Stokely Carmichael, and SNCC's new cry of Black Power.

We laugh. We know Stokely and don't take him that seriously. The walls of his office are covered with photographs of himself, and we tease him mercilessly about it. Each evening when we see the film clips of Stokely shouting "Black Power!" before thousands of black people in cities across the North, and then, a day or two after he leaves, blacks take to the streets in that city, fighting the police and setting buildings on fire, we do not understand. How can people take Stokely seriously?

Obviously, the Stokely we know is unimportant compared to what he embodies for blacks in the North. His anger is not one person's aberration, but the ethos of a generation. That is frightening.

There is a subtle and unacknowledged difference in SNCC between those of us from the South and those from the North. I am not sure if the Northern Negroes—blacks—are aware of it. We Southerners ask each other, "What are they so angry about? They didn't grow up with segregation. Why are they more angry than we? Why do they hate white people and we don't?"

America is burning this summer, and if one believes Huntley-Brinkley, SNCC is to blame. We are called "militants" and "revolutionaries." We are denounced on the floor of Congress and in newspaper editorials. But we did not create racial discrimination; we are not responsible for the racial inequities; racism is not the Frankenstein's monster of our souls. Why don't white people direct their anger at the institutions they created? Why don't white people denounce the racial attitudes of superiority embedded in their psyches? Are we revolutionaries merely because we are tired of being regarded as subhuman? Are we militants merely because we will no longer allow ourselves to be regarded and treated as less than what we are—American citizens? If we were Hungarians or Poles or Russians denouncing communism, we would be hailed as "freedom fighters" and the U.S. would give us millions in aid. But we are only niggers and we get shot.

———·———

The national office of SNCC is in a former warehouse building. On the top floor are offices. I work in the basement. The printing presses and darkroom are down here. I seldom go up to the first floor. As head of SNCC's photo department I spend my days and nights planning publications and working in the darkroom. I work until I can no longer stay awake and then I go to sleep on a mattress in one of the storerooms.

I like the silence and aloneness down here. Only when I am alone do I feel that I am truly myself. I can endure only so much talk about "whitey" and "honkies" and "black consciousness." The twelve-hour shifts in the darkroom give me uninterrupted solitude in which to try and understand myself.

I do not like what I am learning, namely, that I do not have the strength, the fortitude, and the courage to be wholly who I know myself to be. Until I do, I am helpless. I am caught between my collective self and my individual self trying to be born.

My collective self is very persuasive and argues, "Who you are as an individual does not matter. What matters in America is that you have a black skin. Because of that, white people think they know you to the very marrow of your soul, and nothing you do can change their minds, nothing, that is, except revolution. To think otherwise is to indulge in illusion and self-deception. These white folks are not going to change unless you put a gun to their heads and keep it there. You hear me? It doesn't matter if you're bright and creative and talented and all that. What matters is the masses of black people. What matters is that you use your intelligence and creativity to speak for them, to serve them. That is your moral duty!"

My individual self does not know how to answer. It stammers things like: "There is a reality more vast than the political one. It is a reality called God. It is a reality called the soul. And it is the soul's reality that creates the political one. One can change a political system but if the soul does not change too, inhumanity will continue. The best way to love humanity is to care for my soul."

I am not convinced by what I know is true.

July 1967
Havana, Cuba

I am with Stokely at a meeting of the Organization of Latin-American Solidarity. There are revolutionaries here from South America, Vietnam, and Africa, men and women engaged in armed struggle against their governments. I am ashamed to shake hands with them, to even pretend I am their equal.

Stokely has no such qualms. He considers himself an equal among equals and was very annoyed when the North Vietnamese delegation was not receptive at first to his coming to visit Hanoi when he leaves here. "They must not know who I am," he said angrily when we were back in our suite on the top floor of the Havana Libre Hotel.

Our visit coincides with violence in the streets of Detroit, and President Johnson has sent in federal troops. Stokely called a press conference and said that this was "the beginning of urban guerrilla warfare" in the U.S., which made headlines here. It also made headlines back in the States because I received an angry phone call from someone on the SNCC Central Committee telling me to tell Stokely to keep his "damned mouth shut." I wish I could. Stokely lowers rhetorical exaggeration to the level of a comic strip.

Being with him twenty-four hours a day, I see that his politics and rhetoric come as much from his ego as from a sense of caring about the lives of blacks. The first time I ever saw him was in May 1966, in Lowndes County, Alabama. He was surrounded by a group of reporters and I was disturbed that he did not appear to be unhappy with the attention. I asked someone who knew him well if he was enjoying himself as much as it appeared. She sighed and nodded. Two months later I was sitting with him in his office in Atlanta, and told him, laughing, that his picture was in the latest *Jet,* and it had described him as having the eyes of a "Near Eastern mystic poet." I was laughing so hard that it was a moment before I realized he wasn't. "Where's the magazine, man? Let me see it." I gave it to him and he read the story about himself several times before putting *my* magazine in *his* back pocket. It was not long before we were calling him Starmichael. Stokely feeds on attention like a puppy at its mother's teats.

Most distressing are the evenings we are alone in the suite. I need the quiet, but Stokely fills the air with words like someone throwing flares to brighten the night. He talks about the tailor-made sharkskin suits he bought in London and recounts sexual adventures like a white hunter telling tales about big game. He talks, drinks rum, and swallows pills.

"Are you sick?" I ask.

"Unh-unh. These are painkillers I got from my dentist."

"You got a toothache?"

"Naw, homes. I couldn't bring no smoke into Cuba and I can't sleep if I ain't high, and damn! This rum and these painkillers ain't doing shit!"

I sit here with the Mick Jagger of revolution and think about all the people who believe in him, and I am frightened—for him, for them, and for myself.

———·———

Stokely and I have returned from spending three days with Fidel Castro. I first saw Fidel at the July 26 rally in Santiago. Having read many times of what the American press calls his three-hour "harangues," I didn't know what to expect and was not prepared for what transpired. Fidel arrived late, which seems to be customary, and his appearance on the podium evoked loud cheering and applause from a crowd estimated at half a million. However, the ovation was quickly and abruptly stopped by the playing of the Cuban national anthem. His two-and-a-half-hour speech seemed to last no longer than a half hour. He did not address the crowd, but held an intimate conversation in which he shared his thinking about what it means to be a revolutionary. He has the extraordinary ability to make you feel that he is talking only to you. A love emanates from him unlike anything I've ever experienced. When he finished, the crowd started to cheer but once again the playing of the Cuban national anthem stopped it, and Fidel left. A leader who refuses to allow his words to be applauded or his person adulated is impressive. Stokely didn't seem to notice.

The next day Stokely and I were taken to a small town in the mountains where Fidel spoke. His subject this time was, believe it or not, the artificial insemination of cows. He spoke as a peasant to peasants about the problems of increasing cattle production. He spoke at length about a massive bull the government had purchased, how much semen the bull would produce and how many cows could be impregnated over how many years. He said that the CIA had tried to prevent the purchase of the bull and had also tried to kill it. He also pledged that once Cuba's cattle production needs were met, he would give, not sell, the bull's semen to any country that needed it. That is truly revolutionary!

The following morning we met him. Whether he is talking about baseball or the Cuban economy, there is a contagious passion about him. He is the embodiment of Che Guevara's dictum that "the revolutionary is guided by the highest principles of love." What an extraordinary human being!

October 1967
New York

> After being in Cuba for two weeks and seeing that it is possible to create a society based on something other than making money, I hate everything that frustrates, stifles, and destroys beauty and love. I hate it so much that I will kill to see that another kind of society comes into being. To kill can be an act of love and I look forward to the day when I will place a person in my rifle sight, squeeze the trigger, hear the explosion, and watch that person fall. And after the shooting has stopped, I will continue that act of love which began when I started to hate by helping to build a country that will be a servant of its people instead of vice versa.

Winter 1987
Amherst, Massachusetts

The paragraph above is a direct quote from an article I wrote in 1967. I read and reread the words with disbelief and shame. What happened to me that I could write so casually, so lovingly even, about killing another human being?

It is not difficult to explain.

Political movements offer the security of identity. This is so, regardless of ideology. They offer a vision of utopia and the means to achieve it. Nothing is required except to submit your ego and individuality.

One can become mesmerized by staring at a snake one knows to be lethal, and political movements are as fatally seductive. They relieve their participants of the need to take responsibility for themselves, answer all questions, and eradicate all doubts. They attack the very concept of the individual, which is why political movements of the left become as totalitarian as those of the right. The individual is denied value; the collective is crowned with every value.

The people! They are the standard which judges and by which all actions are evaluated. If what you do, think, and say does not serve the people, it is destructive. Power to the people!

In 1968, *Arts in Society,* a journal published at the University of Wisconsin, devoted an issue to "The Arts and the Black Revolution." I was interviewed for it and was asked: "Do you think the Negro artist has any degree of responsibility to commit his art to the fight for Negro equality? If so, in what way?"

I responded:

> If the black artist does not commit his art to the liberation movement (not the fight for Negro equality as you have it), he is not fulfilling his responsibility. The artist is a privileged person, having the ability to communicate the feelings and thoughts of a group of people. It is his responsibility to do this. At this point in history, the black artist has no other responsibility. For too long have black artists spoken to whites and left their own people to be lied to by whites. No more.

I had become a cliché of my time, mouthing platitudes in cliched prose. I had been swallowed by the savage appetite of the collective. Yet one aspect of my life which I withheld from the collective was my marriage and my children. I was stubborn in my insistence that these belonged to me and me alone.

Summer 1968
New York

My daughter is three and my son, one. On Sunday afternoons my wife, the children, and I walk to Greenwich Village. I ignore the stares better than I did when we married six years ago. Too, mixed couples are not as rare now.

It is more difficult to ignore the reactions of friends in SNCC. They seldom say anything directly, but I doubt they talk as much about black men and white women when I am not around. There is a silent but definite pressure on me to leave my wife. One of my closest friends ended his relationship with a white woman, and he is hurting. He truly loves her, but he cannot reconcile "talking black and sleeping white." The news has been reported to me gleefully by more than one black woman that a well-known black writer has left his wife because she's white. Recently a friend asked me if I had ever thought about doing what that black writer did. "Yes," I finally said, "but not for the same reason."

I did not marry her because she's white. Thus, I cannot leave her for that reason. Whom I choose to love is no one's business but mine. Having grown up in the South where interracial relationships were forbidden by law, I'll be damned if I am now going to let blacks tell me with whom I can and cannot have relationships.

Another friend from SNCC was at the apartment one afternoon recently, keeping me company while I stayed with the children. Suddenly he blurted out, "I don't think you should be married to a white woman."

He knew my wife; he played with our children; he had eaten at our table. I looked at him, the hurt visible on my face. Before I could respond, he continued, embarrassed, "Well, I guess you say that's my problem, huh?"

"You're right," I responded coldly.

We sat in tense silence for a few moments and then he got up. We managed to mutter a few phrases of politeness, but we both knew that our friendship had ended.

Is it a contradiction for me to be the author of *Look Out, Whitey! Black Power's Gon' Get Your Mama!* and be married to a white woman? Only if one makes the mistake of confusing whites with white individuals. More and more blacks are making that mistake. By doing so, they are in no way different from those whites who cannot see the personhood of an individual black.

What hurts the most, though, is that none of the people whom I considered friends care what it would mean to my children if I left my wife because she is white. My children are half white and to leave their mother because of her race would be to express hatred for them. My friends think there is something wrong with me because I am not ashamed of my children's light skin and curly hair. They glow with self-congratulatory generosity when they imply that my marriage to a white woman and our having children was an understandable mistake. However, now that my "consciousness has been raised," I know better, and should atone for my sin. I will die before my "consciousness" is "raised" to the place where I consider these children as sins to be repented.

————— • —————

Spring 1987
Amherst, Massachusetts

In the fall of 1967 I began writing a weekly column for *The Guardian*, the leading radical weekly newspaper. Through it I tried to find the point of convergence between my collective and individual selves and to articulate a vision that political involvement and action could be a vehicle for ultimate concern.

Many of those *Guardian* columns were collected and published in 1969 in *Revolutionary Notes*. A few weeks ago my agent called to say that the publisher was taking the book out of print. "Thank God!" I exclaimed. For eighteen years I had gone into bookstores and seen it on the shelves. For eighteen years college students thrust well-worn copies at me to be autographed. How well I understood Tolstoy's repudiation of his work.

Sometimes I try to read an essay in it and cannot. The voice of those essays is not authentically mine. It is the voice and thought of the collective self.

> The feeling that revolution is a necessity is the mere beginning and is really nothing to compliment oneself for feeling. Anyone who is not afraid to feel his humanity feels the necessity for the creation of a society in which man can truly be man and women can truly be women.
>
> (October 6, 1968)

> To break down the old and build the new is not a task accomplished in one generation or several, or by one individual more than another. It is accomplished only when each feels as responsible for the other as he does himself and acts in accordance with that responsibility.
>
> (February 1, 1969)

I was attempting to infuse the collective voice with something of the authentic me, but the attempt could only fail. Political movements cannot be vehicles for Ultimate Concern because they exist for themselves, and nothing threatened a political movement more than an individual who insisted that his individuality was his birthright.

In the spring of 1969 I became embroiled in a controversy that portended the end of my days in the movement. Students for a Democratic Society (SDS) issued a statement in which it called the Black Panther Party "the vanguard force" of the black liberation movement. "Their development of an essentially correct program for the black community and their ability to organize blacks around this program have brought them to this leadership."

I will not go into the details of the factional struggles between SDS, SNCC, and the Black Panther Party. Nothing is more boring and irrelevant than leftist factionalism. (It was boring even at the time.) My *Guardian* column of April 19 was the longest I'd ever written. One brief quote:

> What is at issue is SDS's ability to know what is correct or incorrect for the black community. And being an organization of whites, SDS is not in any position to define or analyze for blacks. If SDS is going to attempt to do so, then it must discuss why the Panther program is correct and why the programs of the Republic of New Africa, the Black Muslims, SNCC, the National Welfare Rights Organization, the Southern Christian Leadership Conference and other groups are incorrect. SDS does not do so.

My column was seen as a covert attack on the Black Panther Party, who were the darlings of the white radical movement. The military posturing and Marxist rhetoric of Huey Newton and Eldridge Cleaver appealed to an infantile romanticism among young white leftists, giving the Panthers an immunity from criticism. My April 19th column sent shock waves through The Movement, so much so that friends feared for my life. The Panthers were known for physically threatening those who disagreed with them.

The May 3rd *Guardian* published a response from the pen of Eldridge's wife, Kathleen, secretary of communications for the Black Panthers. I'd known her since 1966 when she was a young woman from Tuskegee, Alabama, who came to work in the Atlanta SNCC office. We had a friendly relationship and laughed and joked with each other a lot. I was unprepared for her personal attack on me.

> The entire apparatus of U.S. pig law enforcement is waging a full-scale campaign to destroy the Black Panther party and radical white

groups along with black people all over the country are moving to defend the Black Panther party. Now Julius Lester raises his whine in chorus with the opposition. He is definitely on the opposite side—opposite to the Black Panther party which stands firmly rooted on the side of serving the basic needs and desires of the people in the black community. It becomes relevant to question exactly on whose side this black employe of Time Magazine is on because it is clearly not the people's side.

Having had a book reviewed by *Time* did not make me an employee, but Kathleen was only warming up. She called me "a snake groveling in the grass," claimed that "Che Guevara and Panther Apprentice 'Bunchy' Carter both died at the hands of monsters who share thought patterns very similar to those articulated by Lester," maintained that "all Julius Lester does is waste newspaper space with his narrow-minded, pseudo-intelligent and devious argumentation backed up with *nothing* directed to serve the people's needs." She concluded by referring to the name of my *Guardian* column, "From the Other Side of the Tracks," and wrote: "So exactly what's over there on that side of the tracks I don't know, but I have a feeling it's a bunch of punks, sissies and cowards, so fuck them and fuck Julius Lester. All power to the people!"

Many friends told me they agreed with her. Others sat back and waited for me to attack Kathleen. I did not. I wasn't angry with her. How could I be? She is what was born when one merged collective and individual identities. She was what I could've become.

Though I was increasingly isolated in the movement and had drifted away from SNCC, I continued writing for *The Guardian*. When the end came, it was in a way I could not have anticipated. But I should not have been surprised. After all, one category of persons Plato did not want in his Republic was poets. Why had I thought the New Left and black radical movements would be different?

September 1969
Martha's Vineyard, Massachusetts

We have been here since June living in a house on the beach. Only in America would a revolutionary make enough money writing about revolution that he could spend the summer on a resort island where, of course, he writes about revolution. Oh, well. . . .

But my days as a revolutionary writer have come to an end. On the morning of September 3 I awoke to the news on the radio that Ho Chi Minh was dying. I listened to the radio throughout the day until finally, that evening, it was announced that he was dead. I wrote a poem and sent it to *The Guardian* to be published as my regular column.

The Third of September

Half awakened by the light of morning
choking in the greyness
of a third of September Wednesday,
I reached out for the
roundness
softness
fullness
allness of her
and she, awakened,
began to move,
softly,
silently,
gently,
and my hand found that place,
that hidden place,
that secret place,
that
won-
der-
ful place
and in the quiescent light of
a third of September Wednesday morning,
I felt my penis being taken into the
salty
thick
fluidity
of her swirling movement
easily
softly
gently
(as the children were waking.)

Afterwards,
my penis, moist and warm,

resting on my thigh like some
fish washed onto the beach by full moontide,
I turned on the radio
and we heard that
Ho Chi Minh lay dying.
(The fog covered the seagulls that
sit on the rocky beach when the tide is out.)

I retreated from her,
not talking that day as the radio told us
(every hour on the hour)
that Ho Chi Minh lay dying.
Finally, when night had covered the fog,
we heard that
Ho Chi Minh was dead
and I came back to her.
Ho Chi Minh was dead.
I wanted her again.
The softness
the roundness
the fullness
the allness.

Ho Chi Minh was dead.

When the next issue of *The Guardian* came, the staff had published
a poem of Ho Chi Minh's in the space where my column normally
appeared. I was angry and when I called the editor and said so, he
did not understand why. He claimed that my poem was not an appropriate response to appear the week of Ho's death and that publication
of my poem had merely been delayed for a week. That he had not
spoken with me before the decision or informed me afterwards did
not seem important to him. It was for me.

In my next column I announced that it would be my last and I
wrote about George Best, a college student who had died under
mysterious circumstances while working for SNCC in Mississippi in
August 1967. George and I had not been close friends in the sense
of sharing the intimacies of each other's lives. Our closeness was
that of the shared smile, respect, and a liking of each other based
on nothing more than that the other was. George had a habit of
driving up from school in Florida and arriving at the SNCC office
in the middle of the night. Since I lived in the basement, I was

always the one who answered the startling ring of the doorbell at 2 A.M. to let him in.

"Can't you ever show up during business hours?" I'd say, in mock anger.

"If I did that, you'd think something was wrong with me."

What I loved in George was the bright shining of his youth, that quality of innocence and idealism which made him as fragile and vulnerable as if newly born. I was in Cuba that August of 1967 when I read in *Granma*, the daily Cuban newspaper, that he had died. When I returned to Atlanta, I asked about his death. I was told it was an accident. He had driven off a bridge and drowned in the little creek. Others in SNCC were convinced that he had been forced off the bridge and then killed. There wasn't enough water in the creek to get a drink of water. Maybe I wanted to believe that George had been murdered. Maybe I needed to believe that George couldn't die in something as stupid as a car accident.

Then I learned that SNCC had not sent flowers to his funeral. There hadn't been any money for flowers, the treasurer told me. How could it be that we who were so intent on creating the brighter tomorrow did not send flowers to his funeral, that no one from SNCC had attended the funeral even?

> SNCC was George's life and it was while working for SNCC that he died. Was it too much to think that money could have been gotten from somewhere to send flowers, even one long-stemmed rose in all of its crimson fragility? But I wasn't sure. Maybe there was something I didn't understand. . . . Was I unmindful of human frailty? Would I have sent flowers had I been there? I couldn't answer.

And because I didn't know, I realized that something was happening to me, and that if I did not leave the organization soon, I too might find myself one day proclaiming undying love for black people and be incapable of loving one person. I was still innocent and idealistic enough to believe that the only purpose of revolution was to create a society in which all the institutions made it easier for individuals to love each other. A year later, in 1968, I left SNCC. Another year had passed, and now I was leaving *The Guardian* because it cared more about proper revolutionary etiquette than persons.

> During the two years this column has appeared in the Guardian, it has been published without question, whether it expressed the

views of the staff or not. When I turned in my column two weeks ago (the poem on the death of Ho Chi Minh which appeared belatedly in last week's Guardian), I knew that few, if any, of the staff or readers would consider it appropriate for the occasion. However, it never occurred to me that publication of the column would be delayed and without my being informed. The Guardian has the right not to print what I or anyone else writes, but when it exercises that right, it also has the responsibility to inform me or anyone else that that right has been exercised. If one cannot expect total honesty in his dealings with his "revolutionary comrades," then one cannot expect it anywhere. Being no longer able to expect that honesty from the Guardian, I can no longer write for the paper.

Through it all I haven't been able to rid myself of the feeling that the Guardian would be too busy meeting its deadline, too busy "making the revolution" to send flowers to my funeral. But I don't like flowers anyway.

Somehow, though, it matters.

(September 27, 1969)

I should've known the revolution wouldn't be erotic.

———— • ————

Winter 1971
New York

For almost two years I have been writing a monthly column for Dave Dellinger's magazine, *Liberation*. Dave offered me the space after I left *The Guardian*. It has been my last remaining link with the movement. My *Liberation* column has an honesty my writings for *The Guardian* lacked because I have written in a personal voice. But there is no space in the movement for the individual voice, I have learned yet again. I wrote an essay about the trial of the New Haven Seven, members of the Black Panther Party accused of murdering another member of the party. *Liberation* held it for three issues without publishing it. Reading it now I can see I wrote my farewell to the movement without knowing it.

Alex Rackley, a member of the BPP, was tortured and murdered. Warren Kimbro and Lonnie McLucas were charged with the actual murder. George Sams was an active accomplice, giving the orders. According to Sams, he was merely carrying out orders he had received from Bobby Seale, thus making Seale a coconspirator. Except for Seale's alleged complicity, the facts are indisputable. McLucas and Kimbro have each admitted participating in the torture and of firing one shot each into Rackley. Sams has admitted his role. From the legal point of view, it is an open and shut case. . . .

People in the movement did not agree. The underground press called George Sams "a psychotic and agent provocateur" and made him the scapegoat. The official movement "line" was that the Panthers were being persecuted and the defendants railroaded. The verdict of the Movement was that the Panthers were not guilty of murder, even when they admitted it.

This is sad. We self-righteously cite the verdict of the Nuremberg Trials when we want to condemn the military establishment and the politicians. We say to them that you are personally responsible for what you do, that you do not have to follow orders and there are no extenuating circumstances. Yet, we can turn right around and become Adolf Eichmanns, eloquent apologists for the Movement's My Lai. Our morality is used to condemn others, but it is not applied to ourselves. We react with outrage when four are murdered at Kent State, but when a professor is killed in the dynamiting of the Mathematics Building at the University of Wisconsin, we don't give it a second thought. When they kill, it is murder. When we kill, there are extenuating circumstances. It was an accident, we say. The blast went off too soon.

What kind of revolutionaries are we? Or, do we even deserve that name anymore? The murder of Alex Rackley was an important occurrence in the history of the Movement. It was the logical culmination of the politics we have been espousing, a politics of violence-for-the-sake-of-violence, a politics which too quickly and too neatly divides people into categories of "revolutionary" and "counter-revolutionary." The murder of Alex Rackley is the result of a politics which more and more begins to resemble the politics we are supposedly seeking to displace. . . . Because we have invested ourselves with Absolute Virtue, we cannot see when we are wrong. We perform incredible mind-calisthenics to remove all responsibility from the shoulders of McLucas. Yet, McLucas is responsible for what he did.

But the responsibility was not his alone because he belonged to an organization which required the individual to give his mind to the organization and any deviation from the official "line" meant expulsion, or worse.

The responsibility [for the murder of Alex Rackley] lies with the kind of politics [we] have been articulating. It is not the Government which is responsible in this instance; it is us. We have become the good Germans. We see the troops go by, the blood dripping from their hands, and we cheer, "Power to the People" and "Right On." Our involvement in the rhetoric and emotions of violence have so distorted our vision and warped our minds that we are now capable of perpetrating the same acts of inhumanity as the Government.

It should be impossible for a revolutionary to conceive of doing certain things. Torture is one of them. To torture another person means suspending all human feelings not to feel the pain of the other. McLucas testified to his own sickness and revulsion at the torture. Yet, his humanity was not strong enough to force him to risk his own life to stop it, or (and this is more likely) his humanity had been sifted through the sieve of dogma and doctrine and his head tried to justify what his heart was sickened by. But the revolutionary's politics, while guided by his head, are never disconnected from his heart. It is the feeling of love for humanity in his heart which his head seeks to make concretely manifest. That is the soil, the only soil, from which the revolution can grow.

There is no glory surrounding [the New Haven Seven]. They are deserving of all our compassion, pity and tears, because as we cry for them, we cry for ourselves and what we have allowed ourselves to become.

We must stop trying to excuse the murder of Rackley. There is no excuse. We must face that very painful fact and learn from it. If we don't, it will happen again and again.

We are never so much the victims of another as we are the victims of ourselves.

After three months of not seeing my column published, I requested a meeting with the editors. Dave argued that they were holding the essay because the district attorney could use my words against the Panthers at the trial. It was implied that I was giving "aid and comfort to the enemy."

"Don't you care how your words are used and by whom?" Dave asked.

There are moments when we know our souls are hanging in the balance and what we decide will resound in the hidden places for the rest of our lives. Sitting in the offices of *Liberation*, once again looking at friends, people like Barbara Deming, a revered and respected veteran of radical politics whom I respected, I knew this was such a moment for me. I did not hesitate, though I knew what it would mean.

"Yes, I care," I responded to Dave quietly, "but I think truth is more important."

For the first time, perhaps, my soul knew it had a home in me, that I would care for it, and allow myself to be guided by it.

It is to the credit of *Liberation* that they finally published the essay in Autumn 1970, but I stopped writing for them.

Never again will I write for anyone but myself.

Spring 1987
Amherst, Massachusetts

The university has been in the national news a lot recently, thanks to Abbie and Amy Carter. I knew Abbie Hoffman when he had short hair and was shy. We've always liked each other because we both have outrageous senses of humor. When he heard that I'd converted to Judaism, he called me and his first words were: "Julius! I've got a great idea! Let's have a public debate about Israel. I'll take the black point of view and you argue the Jewish side."

I laughed, long and loudly. That's the Abbie I love, the one for whom almost nothing is sacred. But he believes in social change and protest action in ways I never did. He wants to change the world and create utopia. (My wife would consider it revolutionary if she could get me to change my socks.) I see social change and protest as actions. But as carriers of numinosity to engage my soul? Never.

Last December, Abbie and Amy Carter were among seventy students the university had arrested for occupying a building to protest against the CIA's being allowed to recruit on campus.

At the trial Daniel Ellsberg and former CIA agents testified about CIA involvement in overthrowing governments. The argument is that the CIA violates international law, and therefore extreme measures were necessary to prevent it from recruiting on campus.

Unbelievably, the jury found this argument convincing and the defendants have been declared not guilty. I am outraged. I love Abbie dearly, but this time he is wrong. Not about the CIA but about denying those six or twelve students the opportunity to talk with the CIA recruiter.

As a member of a racial minority, I am acutely aware of the fact that the Bill of Rights was designed to protect minority belief or practice from government interference. I feel obligated to defend the right of those 6 students out of 24,000 who wanted to talk with a CIA recruiter because I do not want those who might not want black studies taught to feel that they have the right to disrupt my classes.

I did not see or talk with Abbie while he was here for the trial. I was afraid that our differing positions might end our friendship, and I would miss it. But I feel as if the worst of the sixties is returning, and it seems that Abbie has forgotten the difference between protest and coercion. To protest CIA recruiters on campus is legitimate. To coerce the university into not allowing them on campus is not. Maybe the Golden Rule should be, Do not coerce others because they can coerce you.

But what disturbed me about the movement in the sixties was how quickly it became antidemocratic. When students would shout down Secretary of Defense McNamara as he sought to defend the Vietnam War, I did not understand why they were so afraid of his words and viewpoint. Democracy is like a marketplace in which all ideas are represented, and may the best idea carry the day. Shouting down a speaker and taking over a building are easy. Much more difficult is to present your ideas in a cogent and convincing manner. Rather than prevent CIA recruiters from coming to campus, engage them in debate and let the student body judge for itself whose world view makes the most sense.

I am frightened by those who think they possess the truth by which I should live and will do anything to make sure I live by it. Nothing is more threatening to democracy than the self-righteousness of the ideologue. I hope that is not what Abbie has become. I hope he has not become an "aging radical," as I heard him described on the local news.

I am aging but I am not a radical. Neither am I conservative, though I must sound that way to some who knew me when. But neither am I a liberal, thank God. None of those categories is big enough to contain my need to protect the trembling vulnerability of the individual soul. For that reason I will take my chances with democracy, as imperfect, slow, and tattered as it is.

I need a fragile vessel in which to live and that is the agony and joy of democracy. It attempts to confer collective identity even as it gives one the space, encouragement, and support to oppose the collective.

That is a profound and humbling paradox.

3

How I Spent My Summer Vacation

Martha Bayles

"The Freedom Rides are over, you know." Steve was an anti-poverty worker in southwestern rural Georgia, and he had just handed me my suitcase. Climbing back in his dusty van, which said "U.S. Government Interagency Motor Pool" on the side, he chugged off without another word, leaving me standing in the middle of the red clay road. His comment didn't register at the time; I was too preoccupied with the combined strangeness and familiarity of the scene. On my left, a dense kudzu vine swallowed a row of old trees. On my right, a smaller red clay road humped over the railroad tracks and led past a group of wooden shacks to my destination: a tiny patched-up prefab, vaguely pink, which confronted a long low shed, vaguely green, across a meadow complete with picturesque hand pump and authentic live mule.

The scene was strange because I had never been in the South before. I was a Bostonian, a Yankee in both the Southern and the New England senses, and a Radcliffe student caught up in the ferocious muddles of the late sixties. A notice on a campus bulletin board had announced that a New York–based public service organiza-

Because of the private and complex nature of the events and relationships described here, I have changed the names of the people and places involved.

tion wanted college volunteers to travel to the deep South and spend the summer working with underprivileged black children. Fed up with Cambridge, estranged from my family, and intrigued by things black, I was ripe for such an errand into the wilderness.

The scene was also familiar, in the sense that no young American with a literary education could see, for example, her first Southern mule and not recall the passage from Faulkner which details exactly how long and hard a mule will toil for a human being in order to deliver a single satisfying kick. The novelist Alice Walker touches on this phenomenon when she describes how, for one of her characters who is a white Northern civil rights worker, Southern blacks were not people, they were Art. Expand this notion and you have the larger perception that for someone like me, the whole South was Art.

Especially in 1969. Steve was right: the Freedom Rides were over. I had arrived too late for the civil rights movement's sunlit agenda of moral, legal, and economic protests against state-sanctioned segregation. Martin Luther King was dead, black militancy was ascendant, and for politically active youth the action was no longer to be found along dusty Southern byways choked with kudzu. It's likely that Steve made his comment in response to a dose of predigested radical rhetoric, since I was fresh from the hothouse of Harvard campus politics—the student strike had occurred that April—and probably I could think of little else to say to impress a nice-looking white male peer whose acquaintance I had just made at the Albany bus station. I never got to know Steve well, so I never learned why he ended our 40-mile conversation in that chastening manner.

Why was I in Pine Top, Georgia? I suppressed the complexities of the question while hiking over the railroad tracks to the pink prefab, where I was greeted by a dozen black children whose accent I could barely understand, and by Doreen, a female antipoverty worker who had offered to accommodate two of us summer volunteers. Doreen was stocky, blue-collar Irish from Philadelphia, and even more corrosively sceptical toward summer volunteers than Steve. She did, however, favor the idea of a day camp for local seven-to-nine-year-olds, to be organized out of the aforementioned green shed, which I quickly learned was not a shed at all, but the Pine Top Community Recreation Center. As long as my covolunteer and I were willing to knock ourselves out providing a stimulating summer for twenty kids who might otherwise be idle, Doreen was willing to let us invade her tiny digs.

My relationship with Doreen started out cool, when on the first night she got a snootful of my meaningful life at college and I got a snootful of her father the policeman and her cousin the Army officer in Vietnam. Fortunately my covolunteer, a blonde Southern belle antipoverty worker named Jill, turned out to be sufficiently tactful to get along with both of us. But needless to say, we three did not begin the summer with a bull session exploring the complexities of why any of us was in Georgia. By itself, Doreen's and Jill's refusal to engage in consciousness raising was enough to give me culture shock—never mind all those black people out there whose accent I could barely understand. Three years of Cambridge in the late sixties had ill prepared me to be left alone with my own motives.

Now, looking back on that summer, I regard it as a blessing that my living companions were not cut from the same cloth as my radical friends. I didn't realize it at the time, but my journey to Georgia was a flight, not just from family, WASPdom, and elite education—all the things my radical friends agreed I should flee—but also from my radical friends themselves. In some areas, I was happy to accept their tutelage: politics and economics confused me, so I absorbed my boyfriend's strong views on the need for socialism in the United States; I was weak in political history, so my roommate was able to convince me of the moral righteousness of Ho Chi Minh's cause. The activists in my circle regarded me (correctly) as an aesthete, a dyed-in-the-tweed preppie from a background so reactionary and sheltered that my parents could actually remember having voted Republican in my lifetime. Naturally, my activist friends felt obliged to provide enlightenment.

When the subject was less abstract than a faraway war or a utopian economy, however, my aesthetic inclinations made me less happy with my friends' tutelage. I was simply too accustomed to trusting my own senses. Supposedly it was an era of liberation from personal ambition, as high achievers on deluxe college campuses nationwide joined together in collective struggle against the evils of competitive capitalism. Still, most of my acquaintance kept a watchful eye on the medical boards, on the law boards, or at least on what was going into their dean's office files. My ambitions were less focused, but they did move me to excel in poetry contests, and to try wowing my fine arts tutor with apprentice formalist/existentialist/crypto-Marxist criticism. Like all but my most extreme classmates, I never let my political radicalism interfere with my undergraduate egoism. Because the area I excelled in was neither politics nor economics, but sensibility, that same egoism prevented me from allowing radicalism to dictate how I would see, hear, taste, smell, and feel.

After a summer of having their ears bent by my SDS-style rhetoric, Doreen and Jill might not concur with this assessment. But in fact, I was relieved to be around people like them. As experienced anti-poverty workers, they both knew a lot about mundane matters such as planning budgets, scheduling daily activities, arranging field trips, and supervising children. As a transplant from the campus hothouse, I was ever so sophisticated about the vital issues of the day; but I was also useless. If I hadn't shown some rudimentary ability to entertain the kids, I'm sure Doreen in particular would have sent me packing. As it was, I spent the first few weeks following orders, and after that I did what I was told.

Not that Doreen and Jill—or Steve, had I gotten to know him— were the people who would make the deepest impression on me that summer. As peers, they were refreshingly different from my Cambridge cronies. But as peers, they were also unable to provide the one thing I was anxiously seeking in the wilds of Georgia: authority.

It sounds like the wrong word. "Question Authority," say the peeling bumper stickers on the rusting automobiles of graying sixties loyalists. Whatever else my generation was seeking back in 1969, authority was not it. The word had only negative connotations: adult repression, moral compromise, hypocrisy, and lies. The fact remains, however, that we were young, and youth cannot help but seek instruction and guidance. My two closest radical friends—one Jewish, one not—were red-diaper babies; leftist politics had entered their bloodstream with their mothers' milk, and would remain there even after the effects of the sixties wore off. We dismissed the significance of this inheritance at the time, but it's hard to dismiss it today—especially given the researches of Kenneth Keniston and others. These friends defied the authority of the liberal establishment, and specifically of the university in its more traditional postures. In small things, they even defied their (relatively) more cautious parents. But all the time they were trying to live up to their particular inheritance.

It was different for babies like me, whose snowy white diapers had been fastened with "I Like Ike" buttons. We had more in our backgrounds to defy, so it's not surprising that many of us remained fellow travelers at best—spending the night of the strike in Memorial Church instead of in "liberated" University Hall; and scattering in the chilly April dawn, when the visored, powder-blue Tactical Patrol

Force actually came marching toward us wielding 4-foot nightsticks. Who knows how we followers might have behaved if the Harvard authorities had disciplined us more consistently? If we deserved to have our heads cracked open, then perhaps we also deserved to be confronted with a few tough choices, such as between protesting and passing our courses. Classes, papers, and final exams should never have been suspended, regardless of the inconvenience to us or to the Harvard administration of properly finishing the semester. Our elders should never have succumbed so easily to our charms, then reacted so spasmodically to our threats. In rueful retrospect, I admire those few adults who tried to ignore the whole business and carry on as if life were still normal. But even their statement was too passive.

I followed the radical leaders because they seemed so sure of themselves. But as time went on and I got to know how their minds worked, I wearied of their crude but all-consuming ideology. There were too many intellectually interesting subjects that didn't lend themselves, even in jest, to radicalization. And there were too many things in the quotidian world that I longed to accept, not reject in the name of a brave new world currently under construction by my classmates. Put simply, the only authority I acknowledged to be valid—that of my radical peers—was eroding. I didn't understand what was happening, but I did feel a sickening dismay at no longer being able to locate wise, all-knowing people who could help me with my problems.

For I had problems. My older brother, who was about to turn thirty, was in the deteriorative final stages of chronic alcoholism. His wife, whom he had married while in the service, had recently taken their little daughter and gone home to her own family in the Midwest. My older sister, who was closer to my brother than I, was out on the West Coast, paralyzed by her own struggle with alcoholism. And my mother and father were trapped in the indescribable agony of trying to help a loved one who would not, or could not, be helped. Against this backdrop of family misery I was the successful one, presumably a source of pride to my parents and strength to my siblings. In fact, I treated all of them with appallingly brittle indifference.

Among the protesters of the sixties, I'm sure there were others like me who threw themselves into the fray hoping to alleviate individual pain. But because such psychological motivations were not typical, I will not dwell at length on my family's unhappiness during the spring and summer of 1969. Obviously, I was strongly motivated by it. Obviously, it should be weighed in the balance along with my budding disaffection from my peers, and with the fact that, like my peers, I was emotionally out of control due to Harvard's abdication of responsibility. Obviously, it meant that my battle was not the same as that of my aforementioned friends, as they disagreed with their leftist parents more about style than substance. Between me and my proper Bostonian family there wasn't so much disagreement as dissociation; we moved in painfully separate spheres. (How much more primal this dissociation must have been for other students from backgrounds even less tied than mine into the social and cultural roots of the New Left!) All these factors boil down to the proposition that I went to Georgia in search of an alternate source of encouragement, discipline, wisdom . . . in a word, authority.

Not that I expected to find it among the good folk of a New York–based public service organization. My Jewish boyfriend's parents knew the history of that particular outfit, and although they were too pessimistic about America's race problems to put faith in its tepid goal of "promoting racial harmony," they assured me that a summer spent under its auspices wouldn't hurt me. My boyfriend even tolerated my stated desire "to see what the South was really like"— although as I've explained, direct experience was not a high priority with radicals. For people so young, they worked hard at being jaded about things they had never seen.

Actually, the organization and I came to loggerheads when the Caplans, an elderly couple who oversaw its efforts in Georgia, decided to pay our day camp a visit. It was during the second week, when Jill and I were still adjusting to the daily routine of rising at dawn, driving 20 miles to collect our twenty charges, delivering them to the Pine Top Community Recreation Center for four hours of constructive fun followed by a hot lunch, and then driving them another 20 miles home. It sounds easy enough; but add in the 100-degree heat, the rough red clay roads, the "U.S. Government Interagency Motor Pool" station wagon that never stopped hemorrhaging oil, and most of all, the stupendous energy of twenty unfamiliar children whose idea of fun was rarely constructive, and it gets a little more demanding.

Our saving grace was not Doreen, who was making herself scarce those first weeks, but Mrs. Roundtree, Doreen's closest neighbor, a handsome middle-aged woman who was earning some spare change by preparing the day camp's hot lunches. One word from Mrs. Roundtree, and our exuberant campers would climb down off the roof, quit punching each other and tormenting the mule, hush their mouths, and line up at the hand pump to wash off the morning's dirt. No matter how frazzled Jill and I got, we took comfort in knowing that Mrs. Roundtree would be there during the lunch hour. She rarely showed herself until it was time to serve the Kool-Aid, hot dogs, collard greens, chicken wings, government surplus beets, and greasily delicious corn pone that always disappeared instantly, despite the simmering heat. But I was convinced that the kids were behaving better each day, not because of anything Jill and I were doing, but because it was gradually occurring to them that at high noon they were going to have to face a real grown-up.

Enter Mr. and Mrs. Caplan, a little before noon, in a new-looking, air-conditioned car. I had gone sufficiently native by that second week to find the sound of their New York accents harsh. I was already starting to mimic the melodious local dialect, and it seemed to me that this well-heeled white couple were being deliberately insulting by not doing the same. To their shiny car and gleaming camera equipment my reaction was, I fear, typical of well-heeled young people who choose to sojourn among the poor: downplaying my own advantages, I was offended by other people displaying theirs. When Jill volunteered to show the Caplans around the seemingly tornado-stricken Pine Top Community Recreation Center, I sidled off in the direction of Mrs. Roundtree's, perhaps hoping that she would take charge of this situation, too.

It was the first time I had made bold to knock on her screen door, and I was relieved when she responded in her usual bluff manner. "Hold your water, girl," she said. "Lunch ain't goin' to cook itself." But instead of bantering back, I grew tongue-tied. All I could think of was how, any minute now, the Caplans were going to patronize Mrs. Roundtree, she was going to withdraw into uncommunicative dignity, and I was going to lose her respect. Full of disproportionate anxiety, I went back and made a stab at organizing the kids, but as usual they preferred to wait for Mrs. Roundtree's voice to transform them into angels. When she came out and took command, and Jill and I stood at the pump, one working the handle and the other inspecting small hands and faces, Mrs. Caplan signaled to her husband to fetch his best camera. "Oh Abe, it's perfect!" she exclaimed as he set about focusing and setting, snapping and rewinding. So far, neither Caplan had said anything, pro or con, to Mrs. Roundtree, but that scarcely mattered to me. The moment I dreaded had arrived.

I don't recall my exact remarks, but my gist was that Jill and I resented being portrayed as white Ladies Bountiful brought in to teach personal hygiene to a bunch of ignorant pickaninnies. I informed the Caplans that it was not we who enforced cleanliness and good manners at lunch, but Mrs. Roundtree. And I deplored their neglect of Mrs. Roundtree. Why wasn't she a fit subject for their elaborate viewfinder and costly high-speed film? The Caplans' immediate reaction escapes my memory; I was in too high dudgeon to notice it. But they later wrote me a respectful letter explaining their need for compelling brochure illustrations to attract brilliant and dedicated young people like me to their organization's ongoing projects. Given how rudely I behaved, I marvel at such flattery.

I also marvel at the emotional symmetry of that little scene. There was I, a young woman in emotional and cultural free fall. And there were the Caplans, elderly do-gooders mistaking my plummeting for exhilarating flight. And there was Mrs. Roundtree, providing twenty black children with solid ground. I must have wished she would do the same for me, to have defended her so passionately. I must have felt forced by my own desperation to choose between the authority of radicalism, as exemplified by the Caplans, who were clearly not radicals but who reminded me of my boyfriend's parents; and that of blackness, as personified by the unwitting Mrs. Roundtree.

For as long as there have been whites and blacks in America, there have been white Americans smitten with blackness. Sometimes their motives are noble, sometimes base; certainly their behavior changes from era to era. Back in 1969, when the survivors of the first phase of affirmative action were about to graduate from elite universities, it was easy for young whites to pick up the message that black was not just beautiful, it was more beautiful. The most effete aesthetes acknowledged the power of Afro-American culture, especially music. And for all their arrogant defiance of authority, most radicals humbly deferred to the authority of black classmates when it came to defining the finer convolutions of oppression. Depending on one's major, one expressed solidarity with blacks either through the beauty rap or through the oppression rap. Much as the twain were intertwined in reality, they rarely met in our minds—probably because it was a conceptual strain to view blacks simultaneously as tragic victims and as cultural masters.

My fascination with blackness may have sprouted in Harvard's hothouse, but it bloomed in the sultry heat of Georgia. Fond as I was of Mrs. Roundtree, my affections soon found a more responsive object. To liven up our existence, and no doubt to regain a little privacy, Doreen hit upon the bright idea of sending Jill and me 20 miles away every weekend, to stay with two fellow antipoverty workers named Crystal and Jan in the tiny hamlet of Choochapulga. To be frank, we were glad to go. Brooklyn black and San Francisco white respectively, Crystal and Jan had a much more active social life than Doreen. Weekends in Choochapulga were a mellow but frequently hilarious round of barbecues, softball games, swimming parties, church socials, and drop-in beer bashes at the two young women's shack. It was at one of these latter, with the cold beer bubbling and the soul music thumping on the stereo (the shack had electricity but no plumbing), that I met Quennel.

Later on in Cambridge, when asked to describe this terrific guy I'd known in Georgia, I would say (accurately) that he looked like the young Jomo Kenyatta. Probably I was the only person Quennel had ever met who noticed the resemblance. His demographic profile was modest: a semiliterate high school graduate, age twenty-one, making $80 a week working in a nearby "stone crush," or quarry producing highway construction materials. Already a little deaf due to the constant din of the stone-crushing machinery, he took a certain satisfaction in explaining to me how tricky it was to drive a 12-ton loaded dump truck up and down the narrow paths scored into the steep sides of the quarry. He lived in the next town over, and knew Crystal and Jan through a buddy of his, who was sitting next to Jill. He talked about the recent death of his grandmother, his regret at having cut so many classes in high school, and his admiration for the Edwin Hawkins Singers while their gospel hit, "Oh Happy Day," resonated through the floorboards. After about an hour, his buddy absorbed too much beer and began making drunken passes at Jill, so Quennel declared it was time to head home. He thanked Crystal and Jan for the beer, told me that he had enjoyed our conversation very much, and was halfway out the door before I caught up with him, awkwardly blurting that I hoped we would meet again. He smiled shyly and said he hoped so, too.

It's probably clear by now that mine was not the sunlit agenda of the civil rights movement: black and white citizens marching arm in arm to register a public affirmation of brotherhood. Those days were over, as Steve had succinctly observed. Nothing politically significant had happened in the South for the last few years anyway, as my Harvard friends had windily observed. If I rejected the tepid goal of racial harmony, what did that leave? Only a moonlit agenda: the psychological-cultural residue of a political-legal struggle that had moved elsewhere. Obviously, interracial flirtation had been very much a part of the Southern civil rights movement. But only as subtext. For latecomer me, it became text. I spent the following weekend in Choochapulga feigning enthusiasm for the same social occasions I had earlier relished, because now they disappointed me by failing to produce Quennel. Perhaps if he had reappeared sooner, he wouldn't have gotten such a grip on my imagination. But by the time we did meet again—two weeks later, at the refreshment stand during a softball game—I cared more for his interest than for other people's good opinion.

"Other people" began with Doreen. A few days after the beer bash, the word came down from Choochapulga, via Doreen, that Quennel was married. Not only that, but his wife was up in arms, threatening physical violence if the poverty program sponsored any more orgies full of loose white women.

I can still see Doreen's expression when she hit me with this bombshell. She had already informed Jill and me, with the same beefily earnest look, that she made it a policy never to go out with the local men—a remark which we found endlessly amusing, especially her choice of the word "policy." I remember quipping that in Doreen's case, necessity was the mother of policy. Doreen's moralism, which my female cattiness took for sour grapes and my Boston snobbery chalked up to Irish-Catholic prudery, was an easy messenger to mock for the bad tidings that some half-crazed local girl considered Quennel her property. Perhaps if I had heard the news directly from Crystal, who was just as burly as Doreen but possessed the crucial authority of blackness, I would have reacted more soberly. But I doubt it. As a radical of the sixties, I coolly dismissed marriage as a bourgeois institution. And as a white bourgeois, I just as coolly dismissed the overwrought jealousy of some poor black girl I didn't even know.

Besides, I told myself, my intentions were innocent. All I wanted to do was talk with Quennel and bask in his wonderful smile. I felt no guilt at sharing a beer with him at the aforementioned refreshment stand, a platter of ribs at the softball play-offs barbecue, or a Coke at the lake where the poverty program held its swimming parties. Somewhere along the line, Crystal and Jan admitted to Jill that Quennel behaved like a gentleman, which comment Jill passed along to me and I regarded (naturally) as vindication. Jill became my staunch ally, confiding that she had once been in a similar situation, only to be amazed at the kind of filth people had in their minds. In our shock at the shockability of others, she and I found a new rapport.

"Oh Happy Day." That gospel rouser, heard on every radio and jukebox that summer, celebrated the day "when Jesus washed my sins away." For me it celebrated the day when Georgia washed my unhappiness away. I was not just infatuated with Quennel, I was enchanted with every detail of my new life. Like the Apollo astronauts cavorting on the moon, I rejoiced in the success of my long-distance mission. Didactic friends, demanding relatives, grim todays, apocalyptic tomorrows—I felt I had flown the whole coop. The astronauts looked back and contemplated the beautiful, cloud-skeined marble they had come from. I didn't bother to look back.

I could have floated through the whole summer in this rarified state of grace, but Quennel's instincts were a bit more down to earth. He was paying a heavy price for being seen with me in public, and eventually he must have decided to get his money's worth. Still treating me with the utmost deference, he made a series of minutely escalated allusions to romantic walks in the piny woods before actually coming up with a proposition: would I meet him after dark on a certain weeknight, on a side road off a side road slightly north of Choochapulga? Yes, I agreed after demanding multiple assurances that the rendezvous wouldn't get him into any trouble. (I must have been imagining a Choochapulga lynch party, made up of either white men or black women.)

He brought the peach brandy and I the blanket, and in many ways that first tryst was romantic. He led me uphill to a stand of tall, long-needled pine trees, where we spread the blanket on the soft, mossy ground, swigged the brandy, and gazed at the moon. He related how some folks he knew were so ignorant, they had sat through the entire lunar landing on TV without realizing that it was real, that it wasn't just a "story." "Ignorant," he repeated, shaking his head. I imagined he was talking about his wife, so I charitably suggested that people had good reason not to believe what they saw on TV; look at all the lies TV told about Vietnam. At that point I was a short step away from bringing up the issue of lunar missile bases, but Quennel preferred a giant leap: our first kiss.

Many moons later, when I was teaching English in the public schools of Boston, a black friend remarked that in her opinion, interracial sex was one of history's most overrated experiences. Color, she said, was right up there with death and taxes as a subject she did not want to have on her mind while making love. I won't speak for Quennel, except to say that he never seemed so remote from me as when we were physically close. But I will speak for myself. No matter how tenderly I reached for him that summer, I always embraced a tangle of barbed emotions instead. Guilt, anxiety, self-hatred, despair—how many of these strands were tied to the racial and class differences which so obsessed me at the time? How many were connected to the moral fact of our adultery, to say nothing of my own betrayal of a devoted boyfriend? And how many were bound up with my family? To this day, they cannot really be separated. But they can be ranked right up there with death and taxes.

Nevertheless, I kept playing "Oh Happy Day" and fantasizing about sticking around after the end of my volunteer stint. Once or twice I mentioned the idea to Jill, and she asked how I would manage. My flip reply was that luxurious shacks like Crystal's and Jan's rented for $10 a month; I could probably afford that. My daydreams of crisp fall air, frost on the kudzu, and a profounder relationship with Quennel were not disturbed, evidently, by the question of how somebody like me was going to make herself useful, never mind socially acceptable. But Jill knew better than to reason with romance. After all, it was only the first week in August; sooner or later something was bound to happen that would bring me to my senses.

Something did—sooner. Their softball tournament having ended, Crystal and Jan took up the recreational slack by organizing extra swimming parties at their "private" lake (so called because, for some reason, they always had it all to themselves). Despite my being a better swimmer than a softball player, I didn't favor the swimming parties. First, they attracted more children than adults, thereby providing less relief from the company I kept all week. Second, I was convinced that they discouraged Quennel. Risky as it was for him to talk to me in public, it was riskier when we were both wearing bathing suits. I told myself that our private meetings were better because they were more intimate. But the truth was, I missed seeing his face in the sunshine. I missed other people's half smiles whenever he laughed out loud at one of my corny jokes. I missed the illusion of belonging.

The next Saturday morning was especially sweltering as Crystal and I made the rounds picking up as many Choochapulga water babies, large and small, as could cram themselves into her van. It was also humiliating, because I started out foolishly assuming the same familiarity with these kids as I had with my campers in Pine Top. After a couple of feeble attempts on my part to "get over," one teenage girl asked Crystal coldly, "What is *she* doing here?" And Crystal replied with a shrug. "I dunno. Does it matter?"

The kids tittered, and I spent the rest of the trip staring down at my hot splotchy palms.

At the lake we met Jill and Jan with another load of strange kids, and later Steve showed up with a gaggle of equally strange teenagers and a white guy from Albany who turned out to be a Marine on leave from Vietnam. Since a smattering of local whites were involved in the poverty program's activities, I wasn't taken aback by the Marine's color so much as by the appalling fact that he was a Marine. Just the sight of that bullethead with its savage haircut was enough to awaken all my dormant New Left sensibilities. "What is *he* doing here?" I asked everyone, in a mild paroxysm. But no one would answer—except Steve, who said mildly that with all these kids, it had seemed a good idea to bring an extra adult.

By this time I was glum. Faint as they were to start with, my hopes of seeing Quennel that day were now dashed; and I still smarted from Crystal's quip. I got glummer as the afternoon broiled on and the Marine fired the same friendly salvo first at Jill, then at Jan, then at me. In response to the dismal prospect of debating the Vietnam War with such a person, I decided to indulge my taste for swimming out farther than anybody else, to the middle of the 5-acre lake, and playing porpoise in the deep, warm, silty water. After a long time I swam back and sat among the younger kids playing in the sand, hoping the randy leatherneck would take the hint and leave me alone. After teaching the kids how to make dribble castles, I looked around and noticed that I was the only white on the beach, as well as the only adult. Besides my dozen dribblers, there was one teenage boy paddling around in an inner tube, and three teenage girls sitting nearby intently cornrowing each other's hair. One of the girls was my nemesis from Crystal's van, so I hesitated before asking where Steve and the others had gone. The first time I asked, she didn't answer. The second time, she jerked her cornrowed head toward the field at the top of the hill where the cars were parked: "Up playin' ball." The hilltop blocked my view, so I just nodded. These girls didn't mean to be rude, I told myself, inspecting the pockmarks left on my legs by the gravelly sand. If I took a different tack, perhaps we could still become friends. That would show Crystal.

I must have been quite absorbed in the challenge of befriending those girls, because I gazed at the lake for several seconds before noticing that the boy's inner tube had drifted out past the shallows. As for the boy, he was now beside the tube, splashing and waving gaily at somebody on the beach. Probably at the girls, I mused. Maybe I should use that as my conversational opener.

Then I took a better look. The boy was splashing and waving all right, but not gaily. After a long, absolutely vacant minute I turned to the girls. "Who's that boy in the inner tube?"

"My brother," vouchsafed my nemesis. "Donnie."

"Can Donnie swim?"

"Uh-huh."

Another vacant minute went by, and I asked her again. "Are you sure? I mean, can he swim like me? Can he stay up in the deep water?"

"Not really . . . I mean . . . Donnie!"

Now I had her attention. She sat bolt upright and clapped both hands over her mouth, while I lapsed into a soothing trance, my mind slithering lazily over the various possibilities of what exactly was happening out there and what exactly I was supposed to do about it. The water looked inviting; but to me, water had always looked inviting. Water had never given me any trouble, although I dimly recalled that it occasionally gave trouble to other people. Perhaps this was one of those occasions . . .

And so on. Who knows what permutations looped through my brain as I rose to my feet and waded into the water, falling against it and thinking how cool it was? Perhaps the coolness restored my wits; I turned and ordered the girls to run up and fetch Steve. Then I began to swim, calmly and steadily, toward the empty inner tube. When I reached it, I scanned the surface: no splashing, no waving, just mockingly placid ripples. My mind rippled, too, methodically circling every possibility except the obvious one, that I would have to dive. I skipped that one because it terrified me. The boy was too big, he would drag me down. I didn't want to dive.

At length, however, I concluded—perhaps because I knew the others were coming and would see me—that I had no choice. I took a breath and ducked, rolling my eyes in the gloom. The water in that lake was the color of gravy, shading down into pitch. I kicked hard, but my body refused to sink a single inch. Almost immediately I ran out of breath and bobbed back up, gasping. I locked in a second lungful, but again I couldn't fight my body's terrible buoyancy. On the third try I dove a little deeper, groping downward in the murk and wincing at every imagined touch. Then I shot back up and gulped air, staring at the gilded, rippling surface as if I'd never seen anything so beautiful. "Don't go back down there," it gurgled at me in a soft, masculine voice. "Just come over here." I ignored the voice and dove once more, to approximately the same depth. But then something—probably a fish—brushed against my outstretched hand, and I recoiled so violently that the air exploded out of my mouth. Watching the bubbles rush upward, I felt my labored lungs shift into reverse, eager to suck their first deep breath of water. No, I told them as I forced my limbs to start moving. Not until we get there.

Would we have gotten there? The question is moot, thanks to the United States Marines. A steel tourniquet closed on my wrist, spun me around, and became a steel band across my chest. In a few seconds, my head was lolling back beneath a wide brightness—the sky. The air was finding its way into my mouth. And that same soft, masculine voice was murmuring: "Relax, babe. Take it easy. You did the best you could."

That's what everybody said: I did the best I could. Jill, Crystal, Jan, and Steve all reserved their moral outrage for the person at the local sheriff's office who had listened to Steve's frantic account of a possible drowning at the lake and then drawled, "White or colored?" Steve was furious with himself for having told the truth; evidently, white or colored made the difference between immediate response with an ambulance and delayed response with a truck and a set of grappling hooks.

Along with the children, I was hustled out of there long before the truck arrived. Steve and the Marine stayed behind, diving until it was time to start dragging instead. Later that week I was told that the grappling hooks had found Donnie on a snag near the bottom of a steep incline, where the water was over 20 feet deep. This news was intended to comfort me, since few unaided swimmers could have performed such a rescue at such a depth. But all I could think about was how horribly long it had taken me to swim out there and start diving. Had I suspected that Donnie was drifting deeper? Had I dawdled on purpose, waiting for him to drift so deep he could no longer grab me? Was my rescue attempt a sham, intended to cover up my earlier inattentiveness when I realized I was the only adult on the beach? Tangled with excruciating guilt, I felt excruciating resentment. The others mouthed comforting words at me, but it was they who had organized this swimming party for youngsters who couldn't swim. It was they who had gone off to play ball without making damn sure I knew I was in charge. I longed to blame them, and I was gratified to hear that they were blaming themselves. But the machinery of blame refused to grind them down without implicating me, too. The others had failed to provide foolproof water safety measures. But I had provided the fool.

Then the word came down from Choochapulga: no more weekend visits for the likes of Jill and me. Today I can see the reason for this edict: Donnie's mother was threatening a lawsuit, and the whole poverty program felt like it was on eggshells. The last thing Crystal and Jan needed was another screwup by another freeloading outsider. At the time, however, I saw only my own pain. Despite their comforting words, I knew that they blamed me. And I knew this was my punishment: to be cut off from Quennel. Since nobody had a telephone in those parts, Quennel and I had to arrange our meetings through his buddy who lived in Choochapulga. His buddy would tip me off which night Quennel could get away, and I would try to be there. It was a slender grapevine at best, and now it had been deliberately snapped by Crystal and Jan. I was so hurt and angry that I quit brooding about the drowning and took action.

The next afternoon I told Jill and Doreen I was borrowing the station wagon to run an errand and drove 30 miles to the stone crush where Quennel worked. The white guard at the gate asked me what I wanted, and I told him sweetly that I was a commercial artist who wanted to sketch the machinery and the pit. (I thought it a stroke of genius to have added the word "commercial.") He gave me a funny look but waved me in, and I spent the next few hours wandering around pretending to sketch that bizarre moonscape, but really studying the dust-covered figures perched high in the cabs of the colossal, Chartreuse-colored dump trucks. Eventually, after several attempts, I got a few of the drivers to speak to me as they changed shifts. Looking me over with suspicious black eyes set in grayish-white faces, they admitted the remote possibility that they might know a person named Quennel; and when I begged them to give him a message, they didn't refuse. What was the message? Grasping at this one straw, I said, "Tell him I'll be there every night at nine."

They guffawed. One of them wiped away a tear, cutting a brown swath through the stone dust. "OK, miss!" he roared. "We'll tell him! Every night at nine! Whoo-ee! And if that man ever gets tired, miss, just remember. There's plenty more sweets at the store!"

I stood there turning red, wanting to explain but realizing that no explanation was possible. Then I went back to Pine Top and killed the evening, not talking to Doreen or Jill but just waiting until it was time to get back in the station wagon and drive the 20 miles to Quennel's and my meeting place. Whether it was that night or a subsequent night I don't recall, but it was soon enough that I saw his short-sleeved yellow shirt glimmering in the darkness and rushed forward, eager to escape my world and everybody in it.

It didn't work out that way. Quennel wanted to know if I had really gone to the stone crush, and when I said yes, he shook his head, whether in amusement or annoyance I couldn't tell. Then he listened while I poured out all the details, physical and emotional, of the drowning; and he said, "You did the best you could." Then he listened while I launched into the larger reasons for my guilt: that I was a spoiled white girl in a racist society that sent black men to die in a racist war against a yellow people; and he said, "Don't talk like that. We're all God's children." Then he listened while I asked rhetorically where the hell he thought he'd be right now if he hadn't gotten a deferment; and he said, "I would have gone to fight for my country." Then finally he listened while I spun out my fantasy of staying in Georgia; and he said, "You said your folks had some troubles back home. Ain't they worried about you?"

With this question he smiled, as if taking secret pleasure in being the cause of my white parents' worry. But that was the only unconventional sentiment he expressed that night, and indeed one of the few he expressed that summer. I had gone along assuming that sooner or later I would pierce his old-fashioned Negro politeness and reveal his true attitudes—whatever I imagined those to be. But during this conversation, so full of echoes, I realized that Quennel was not about to fly away with me to a separate planet. He was going to make love to me again, but that was it. He was not going to save me from myself.

I went home. In September my brother died, alone in his house, from an overdose of alcohol. I joined the family for the funeral but didn't stick around. I felt compelled to hurry back to Harvard, where among other successes I had been admitted to Robert Lowell's poetry seminar. Later that fall I wrote a poem about the drowning, which, in addition to its own significance, had clearly acquired meaning as a metaphor for my brother's death and for my inability to pull my loved ones up from the bottom. One of my classmates who liked the poem remarked on what he called its "negrophilia," and suggested that I read Norman Mailer's essay "The White Negro." From that essay, and from most of my subsequent explorations into the literary-cultural symbolism of blackness, I learned a great deal about sex— especially black sexual prowess as mythologized by the imagination of white people. Far be it from me to dismiss this ubiquitous cultural "truth." Certainly it forms part of the story of how I spent my summer vacation. But somehow this white person's imagination keeps skipping over the moonlit dalliance and settling on the sunlit dailiness. Along with authority, the thing I craved most that summer was a thing neither valued nor provided by the late sixties: normality. Perhaps I craved it more because my home life was unhappy—who knows? But take another look at the images of my Georgia "happy day": children's day camp, Mrs. Roundtree's corn pone, softball tournaments, barbecues and picnics—even church. A community close-knit enough to keep an eye on the morals of its young men and women. Any resemblance to normal life in small-town America is purely intentional. It's just one of the many ironies of the sixties that my "radical" heart could accept these good things only in blackface.

4

The New Left: Reflections and Reconsiderations

Jeffrey Herf

It was really very, very brief. My first contact with the New Left was as a member of the SDS chapter at Grinnell College. I joined SDS because it stood for the things I stood for: civil rights, peace, and something different from the suburban life I had enjoyed but found too complacent. My interests in politics and ideas were nurtured by my parents and by the Jewish culture in which I grew up in Milwaukee. My father left Hitler's Germany in 1937. My mother's parents escaped the Russian pogroms before World War I. My mother taught in a predominantly black school. My father talked to me often about the Holocaust. My heroes were Jack Kennedy, Martin Luther King, and "the older kids" who went to the South to participate in the civil rights movement. Like many of the members in 1965, I joined SDS on the basis of liberal values I shared with my parents. It was really beyond my imagination that anyone who was young, Jewish, intellectually inclined, and at all compassionate could be anything but left-leaning.

I cannot underestimate the Jewishness of the following five years. The left in Madison, in particular, was not an escape from this Jewishness, but its expression. It was also a middle-class melting pot of Jews and gentiles. The Jewishness, the liberal values, the opposition to discrimination on the basis of race and sex, the intellectualism, and a few of the close friends made in the sixties all remained long after I had moved away from the New Left and it had ceased to be the wonderful community I recall from the early years.

The New Left was always more than the antiwar movement, but its rapid growth was due above all to the Vietnam War. As it grew, it moved away from the features that had drawn me to it in 1965. In October 1965 I went to an anti-Vietnam War demonstration in Washington partly sponsored by SDS. I recall Carl Oglesby's (then president of SDS) impassioned attack on the "button-down liberals" of the Kennedy and Johnson administrations, as well as his denunciation of liberal anticommunism. Attacking liberals—they tended to listen—was easy and for me expressed a sense of being let down by boyhood heroes. I still argued that the war was not in America's national interest—I cared about what I still spoke of as *our* national interest—that we were ignoring the possibility of a third force between the Saigon regime and the communists, and that the insurgency in the South was homegrown.

I recall repeating arguments about the propagandistic nature of the State Department white paper on aggression from the North and having a member of something called the May 2nd Movement from Columbia say to me that of course the State Department white paper was correct. The real problem, he said, was that North Vietnam and, especially, the Soviet Union were not doing enough to overthrow the Saigon regime. Of course, it was a good idea to attack the credibility of the State Department for propaganda reasons, but radicals, he continued, should be clear that it would be a good idea for the other side to win the war. I was a bit taken aback by this. Anti-anticommunism was not yet part of my vocabulary. There was an honesty to his position I respected. If you called for an American withdrawal from Vietnam, it was obvious that the communists, not some vague third force, would win. Many people in the antiwar movement either denied that fact or tried to convince themselves it wouldn't happen, but few, especially in 1965, thought it would be a good idea. When people say that part of the appeal of the New Left, as any radical political movement, was precisely its radicalism, they mean that people in such movements have a way of taking premises to logical or illogical conclusions in a way that tamer political thought does not do. For example, in 1965 we could not be certain that a Korea-style stalemate in Vietnam was not in the cards. Yet we were so certain that the South Vietnamese government had *no* support among the population that we believed that *only* an complete American withdrawal was the morally and politically right course. If there was a chance for some middling resolution, our radicalism became a self-fulfilling prophecy in helping to prevent its emergence.

I have very fond recollections of the period from 1965 to 1968. But the years from 1966 to 1969 in Madison were particularly intense. I read the New Left canon: C. Wright Mills, Herbert Marcuse, Noam Chomsky, Paul Baran and Paul Sweezy, Paul Goodman, Malcolm X, Frantz Fanon, Simone de Beauvoir, Sartre and Camus, Raymond Williams, E. P. Thompson, and William A. Williams. I read some fiction and poetry as well—Melville, Blake, Lawrence, Mailer, Nathanael West, Bellow, and American social criticism by Randolph Bourne and Dwight Macdonald. In 1966, one of the first underground papers in the country, *Connections*, was begun, and as its name suggested, it specialized in what at the time seemed like rather complex juxtapositions of impersonal Midwest dormitory architecture or scenes from mass culture with photos of the war. In Madison, the student union, the libraries, and our off-campus apartments offered wonderful places to gather and talk, and we talked about what we had read.

I was drawn to two of the refugee scholars in Madison, the historian George Mosse and the sociologist Hans Gerth. Together with a remarkable community of graduate students and undergraduates—Paul Breines, Andy Rabinbach, Charles Sourwine, Stuart and Elizabeth Ewen—I read Kant, Hegel, Marx, Nietzsche, Max Weber, Freud, and Karl Mannheim. I read Isaac Deutscher and E. H. Carr on the Russian Revolution, George Lichtheim and Leszek Kolakowski on Marxist humanism, and Georg Lukacs's *History and Class Consciousness* in the French edition. In 1966, I began to read Marcuse extensively, and then Theodor Adorno, Max Horkheimer, Walter Benjamin. I debated the Marxist and liberal interepretations of national socialism with Gerth and Mosse while reading Hannah Arendt's *Origins of Totalitarianism* and *Eichmann in Jerusalem* as well as Franz Neumann's *Behemoth: The Structure and Practice of National Socialism*. The impact of the European left was pervasive. We read and discussed the British Marxist historians and cultural critics and French situationists who prefigured the spirit of May '68, and Gramscian concepts of hegemony, but the key European beacon of radical theorizing for me was the German and largely German-Jewish traditions of Marxism and critical theory. For me, the New Left in Madison entailed a revival of old traditions of the radicalism of the 1920s in Europe. "Culture" and "consciousness" were our central slogans, with which we sought to take on the pragmatic, atheoretical American left and its neglect of history. Madison became famous for the scope of its demonstrations in the late sixties. But for me its uniqueness lay in the degree to which the left was also an intellectual community, and the close friendships inside and outside the left that grew in those years. Marcuse's *One-Dimensional Man* was the most important of all the books I read in the mid-sixties, and I did read it very carefully. I now regard its contentions concerning American society and politics as wrong. But at the time, I found it to be very compelling, perhaps partly because of my father's disdain for American mass culture and partly because of growing up in a Midwest suburb. It was not the empirical validity of specific theses in Marcuse's argument alone that made it so compelling to me. Attacks on the military-industrial complex, complaints about the lack of difference between the political parties, and regrets that the American working class was more anticommunist and more satisfied with American society than the intellectuals were commonplaces of the literature of cultural criticism and politics in the 1950s. Moreover, as someone who grew up with a very intense awareness of the technological efficiency of the Holocaust, criticism of the dark side of technological development was hardly a revelation to me.

What was most compelling to me about the Marcusian vision was the promise of "grasping the totality," of connecting the apparently disconnected. It gave me a sense of great power and clarity, a framework, or what Clifford Geertz later called an ideology as a cultural system. Why, for example, was positivism crowding out interpretive approaches in the social sciences? Because capitalism demanded the "penetration of technical reason into all spheres of life." Why did the United States construct a triad of nuclear forces? Not because there were real, external threats to the security of the United States, but because anticommunism and a focus on the External Enemy were functionally useful in dampening potentially explosive class antagonisms. Why were there so many different kinds of cars and deodorants? Because the capitalist system rested on a firm foundation of waste and production of junk. Why had there been no socialism or revolution in the United States? Because the working classes had succumbed to a one-dimensional consciousness fostered by the system. The role of intellectuals in politics was clearly to "pierce false consciousness" with the aid of theory. Not only did Marcuse's analysis have an answer to everything; it also attributed to intellectuals a central role in political and social change.

Critical theory and the cultural left in general appealed to me because they seemed to account for so much: why there had been no revolution in the West, and why the revolutions that had taken place had not turned out as expected. It seemed like the most intelligent form of alienation from American society, one which did not lead to an enthusiastic endorsement of the Soviet Union. (Cuba and Vietnam were another matter.) In this sense, it was a precursor of the more pervasive mood that Jeane Kirkpatrick was to call "the doctrine of moral equivalence." At the time this refusal to make clear distinctions between free societies—such as ours—and tyrannies of the left struck me as a sign of independence from a "cold war mentality." Only later did I come to the conclusion that this "critical" stance contained a strong element of what it elsewhere found so objectionable, namely an inclination to reduce different phenomena to one common denominator, a refusal to make distinctions, and an inability to appreciate differences.

The Vietnam War speeded everything up. The two great outbursts of leftist cultural revolution in the West in this century, that of the 1920s and that of the 1960s, were both linked to revulsion with war. The interminable slaughter of the trenches radicalized European politics, led to the Russian Revolution, and was an essential backdrop for the radicalism of Lukacs, Ernst Bloch, and the Frankfurt School theorists. Like World War I, the American participation in the Vietnam War lasted longer than political leaders anticipated, and it appeared to us to be a war of senseless brutality. It is often said that the war radicalized our generation. That is a half-truth. The war accelerated a process of radicalization already under way. The war radicalized me, but I was ripe for the picking. My lenses of interpretation, my ideological and cultural system, fostered a view of the war as immoral and as the product of our political system. I accepted the view that this was a war against the people of Vietnam, waged with unprecedented brutality and no less unprecedented disregard for the lives of noncombatants. The evil means were inseparable from the political goal, for, we argued, it was only possible to defeat a peasant revolution through the most brutal means of intimidation of the population in general. Just as the slaughter of the trenches in World War I encouraged hostility to capitalism, so the Vietnam War fed our suspicion and dislike for "technological unreason" and "late capitalist society."

Alongside these moral objections, I had a "political" objection to the war: it was not a mistake, but a microcosm of the American imperialist system. Ending the war required an end to American imperialism and capitalism. Both moralists and political sophisticates in the left dismissed press reports of North Vietnamese and Vietcong brutalities and either rejected the notion that a communist victory would be a disaster or, more commonly, failed to reflect much on what it would mean. At times we presented the Vietnamese communists as successors to the American revolutionaries; at others we spoke more darkly about the need to break eggs to make omelettes. There were many instances of bad faith. Often, especially in our speeches and leaflets, we tried to discredit press reports—most of which turned out to have been true—about aggression from the North or Vietcong terror, but on the other hand, and usually when talking only amongst ourselves, we made arguments justifying "revolutionary violence" if there were no other way to end the "violence of the status quo." If, as we said, the war was a revolutionary war against an imperialist aggressor, then wasn't it likely that the Vietcong did engage in terror? Wasn't revolutionary violence necessary to overcome the structured violence of the status quo? Rather than deny that the Vietcong received outside assistance, in private moments we regretted that the Chinese Cultural Revolution detracted from Chinese support for the North Vietnamese, and were more than a bit perplexed that it was the "boring" and "bureaucratic" and at times "counterrevolutionary" Soviet Union that was the major supplier of arms to the North Vietnamese war effort.

At the time, there were other voices—albeit an increasingly silent minority on a campus such as Madison—which sought to make a moral and political case for American intervention in Vietnam. But because I had a theoretical framework concerning the totality of American society, I "knew" in advance that efforts to present facts not in accord with my own views should be dismissed as ideological fabrications. I read newspapers and magazines that confirmed my point of view, spent my time with friends who largely shared my beliefs, and gradually found it simply difficult to believe that any thinking person could think differently. It was very gratifying to believe that I was unequivocally, morally right and those who disagreed with me were absolutely morally depraved. I did not really confront and engage arguments and facts supporting the government's position. Rather I approached each new piece of evidence that conflicted with my view of the war as yet another example of ideological mystification to be demolished. I was the smasher of myths, a "critical intellectual"—though in retrospect it is clear that this "critical" stance left no room for the possibility that my own views could be mistaken.

If you were a New Leftist in this period, you probably thought that South Vietnam would be much better off if the National Liberation Front won the war. Our morality was thus based on an unflinching double standard. American atrocities should be denounced, while communist atrocities were the regrettable unintended consequences of revolution. The American war was one "against the people," while the Vietcong owed their support to having addressed popular grievances. The American effort to win the war was immoral, while the Vietnamese communists' effort to do so was a matter of national self-determination. At the time, my own views were a mixture of New Left radicalism and the more widespread opposition to the war based on liberal, internationalist principles. The moralist in me would denounce the conduct of the war, as if following a different American "policy" was in order. As a New Leftist, I found this moralism dishonest, a ruse, and a tool with which to attack the imperialist system. But the New Left was most successful when it could link its "political" agenda to the "moral" revulsion widespread in the universities.

The solidarity of the New Left grew with opposition to the war. I participated in opposition to the draft, demonstrations against recruiters for the CIA and Dow Chemical Company, countless marches and rallies to denounce the latest American escalation of the war or support civil rights activities. All of these demonstrations added to the strong sense of in-group solidarity. Though the radical left at the University of Wisconsin was probably never more than 500 students out of 30,000, we were able to set the political tenor of the campus with our solidarity, activism, level of organization, and commitment. It must have been a very lonely and difficult period in which to be a young conservative or anticommunist liberal.

In the 1970s, some analysts of the New Left described a golden age before 1968 when a still relatively small group of radical intellectuals entertained visions of "postscarcity communism." This golden age was destroyed, according to these accounts, by the introduction into the New Left of Marxist-Leninist sects—first the Maoist Progressive Labor Party and then youth groups from the Communist Party, "Revolutionary Youth Movement II," and finally, of course, "Revolutionary Youth Movement I," or Weatherman. What these accounts fail to explain is why such obviously lunatic groups were able to gain so many adherents at some of the best universities in the United States. The golden age contained the seeds of later troubles. The basic problem was that by 1968, a critical mass of leftist students wanted to make a revolution in the United States but had neither the foggiest idea of what it would accomplish or who would make it. Clearly students and black people were already "in motion," but the working class was either inert or hostile. The faction fight that led to the self-destruction of Students for a Democratic Society from 1968 to 1970 was focused on where radicalized students should look for allies. PL chose the American working class. Most of the rest of us looked instead to "white youth in the mother country," that is, our fellow students, and to "national liberation struggles in the Third World," that is, to communist movements trying to over-throw governments of which the North Vietnamese and Vietcong were the paradigmatic example.

The Marxist-Leninist sects exacerbated tendencies evident in the New Left from the beginning. They did not create qualitatively new phenomena. They made basic assumptions more explicit, but the assumptions were not qualitatively new. They enforced conformity with an unprecedented rigor, but the large size of the New Left generation obscured to us our own previously existing conformism. The decisive advantage of the Marxist-Leninist groups over the more diffuse New Left they sought to dominate was that they had "posi-tions" on "questions," no matter that they were invariably expressed in Orwellian language and absurd on the face of it. I remember, for example, being asked to decide if American blacks should have their own nation-state in the American South or if instead blacks would be the vanguard of a revolution in the whole country. I rejected the alternatives, but what was important was that these groups were remarkably successful in determining the terms of debate and its language. As a result, they encouraged the rest of SDS to elaborate an ideological response no less coherent and no less complete. In this way, small Marxist-Leninist groups hastened the process by which diffuse radicalism gave way to highly disciplined sects.

At the famous SDS national convention in Chicago in 1969, we gathered to destroy the organization which had provided the frame-work for the diffuse radicalism of the 1960s. We were now in a period of organized vanguards each of which had decided that either SDS would pursue its particular outlook or SDS would cease to exist. Either you belonged to some group, parroted a "clear line," and knew who was "objectively" revolutionary and reactionary or "the revolution would pass you by." This was the message of all of the contending factions: Join one of us or be relegated to the dustbin of history. The time is now. The train is leaving the station. If you don't get on, you will be left behind, shut out, irrelevant. In this situation, those in SDS such as myself who did not belong to any of the contending factions, and who thus were more likely to see merit in more than one argument, were powerless to influence the course of events. No one who was at the convention could ever have any doubt about the power of organized vanguards to exert disproportionate influence over comparatively disorganized majorities.

To its credit, the Madison SDS contingent, perhaps due to the "backwardness" of life in the provinces, looked on with both fear and disbelief at the spectacle played out before us by the groups from Chicago, Columbia, Harvard, and Michigan. The relatively diffuse radicalism we had known in Madison was now outclassed by the sectarians from the elite universities. Although I had been in many demonstrations, I still looked on in disbelief as the Harvard and Columbia SDS chapters screamed at one another in unison chants such as "Ho-Ho-Ho Chi Minh, people's war is going to win," or "Mao-Mao-Mao Tsetung, dare to struggle, dare to win." Here were people my own age, who had gone to fine universities, who appeared to be out of their minds. Here were the real vanguards of anti-intellectualism and fanaticism. Yet by their very fanaticism and collective delirium, these groups of educated chanting robots radicalized me. They upped the ante of what was regarded as radical and militant. Positions that were "absolutely crazy" soon became "quite reasonable" as one group made sure not to be outflanked by any other on the scale of revolutionary militancy. With the ante going up by the minute, I realized I was afraid not of the "fascist state" but of being left out in the cold, of being thought cowardly, of losing my friends, and of not being in on the action when the revolution took place. The "Weathermen," later the "Weather underground," represented the greatest challenge to most of the New Leftists there, for however "crazy" we said they were, Weatherman captured the alienation and indeed hatred of American society and politics that had become pervasive in SDS. This anti-Americanism was expressed in quintessentially American terms and thus was less off-putting than the more stolid Marxist-Leninists. Above all, however anti-American it was, Weatherman promised success. At home we might be weak, but the New Left was a link in the chain of international revolution including millions of people, especially "the Vietnamese people." The "movement" was a thing of the past; the "revolution" was already taking place all over the world. The only question now was whether white Americans would be part of the problem or part of the solution.

Were we not alone? Was the war not immoral? Wasn't the Third World the new collective subject of history, the new class with radical chains in place of the well-fed and ideologically blinded working class? I was both appalled and attracted. By spring 1969, I was not averse to apocalyptic interpretations of American politics and an "either-or" style of political thinking. Either one stood on the side of the oppressed peoples of the earth or one was an "objective" ally of American imperialism. Either America would be engulfed in the flames of a race war or we would see to it that the race war would be transformed into a—more constructive and presumably slightly less violent—class war. At last, here were people who were going to put their money where their mouths were and unite theory and practice.

The Weather statement was fundamentally New Leftist in a cultural sense as well. It promised to demonstrate that "the personal is political." Politics was not one sphere of life separated off from others. Politics and life were to become one. No aspect of personal life was to be kept from political scrutiny, just as no aspect of political life was to be saved from assessment by existential criteria. The best political position became one which manifested the greatest commitment and authenticity measured by willingness to sacrifice career and comfort. Those who were most willing to sacrifice for the cause (often those who were wealthiest had the most to sacrifice) had the potential for the greatest power over others. What was a sensible and cogent political argument worth compared to the reality of someone dropping out of school, living on next to nothing, and then being willing to risk his or her life for the revolution?

Because of the potency of this totalitarian conception of community, Weatherman and the mystique surrounding it made us feel guilty, small, and self-regarding by comparison. One of its most potent aspects was its intense moralism, which presupposed that the truth had been revealed and that any who failed to follow were immoral. The outward expressions of unbounded confidence, the ease with which complexity collapsed into a coherent program, a camaraderie between people who shared basic ideas and common dangers—all combined to place the rest of us on the defensive. Weatherman said to us, Come join and be in the vanguard of the revolution, if, that is, you have the courage to do so; end your pointless, alienated life of on again, off-again political activity for a 'total' commitment. To continue your career while the revolution was beginning was simple cowardice and greed. Start a new career as a full-time revolutionary and be successful and win with us rather than lose with the cowardly movement. I resisted the call, but I was not unmoved and felt considerable guilt over not joining up. Were my intellectual arguments against the Weather statement a rationalization for simple lack of courage? It was a question thousands of people who did not join the Weather underground asked themselves in 1969.

In 1969, we adopted a caricature of working-class–black-underclass profanity as everyday speech in political affairs. Huey Newton and Ho Chi Minh were "far fuckin' out." An obviously mistaken opposing political viewpoint was "jive-assed" and, of course, almost anyone to the right of SDS was a "motherfucker" or a "jive-assed motherfucker" of some kind or another. We thought the use of this coarse and dehumanizing discourse as a regular part of everyday political discussion served to distinguish us from the namby-pamby, effete, nonstruggle wimps who were staying in graduate school. But, for me and many others, it was a daily ritual of self-repudiation, of rejection of years of carefully nurtured linguistic and intellectual refinement and sensibility.

The dehumanization of our political language fostered the appeals of violence, at first as an abstract, distant activity. Much has been written about the link between repression of the New Left and its radicalization, and there certainly were people who had been hurt and arrested in demonstrations. But the factor of repression has, in my view, been overemphasized. In spite of having caused havoc at major universities, few SDS members or leaders were spending much time in jail. On the contrary, the future leaders of the Weather underground were flushed with success and self-confidence. The process was one Tocqueville would recognize. Radicalization grew at the point at which civil rights for blacks had improved, the United States was very slowly beginning to leave Vietnam, and the intellectual and political climate on the campuses ranged from violent radical left to left liberalism. The much praised idealism and moralism of the New Left were the source of the push toward violence. If American society was so hopelessly repressive, how could palliatives suffice?

The results of the 1969 convention are well known. PL was expelled, and SDS became "better smaller but better." After a meeting in Cleveland in August of that summer, Weatherman became explicit about its intention to form an armed underground, for which several "days of rage" in Chicago in October 1969 were to be a preparatory step. After the Cleveland meeting, a friend—who in the early seventies became a vice president of a Hollywood movie company—kept urging me to accept the Weatherman position and then to join after the Cleveland meeting. The revolution was beginning, he said. The movement was over. Private life, family, children, and career would have to wait. At times he said the conditions for revolution were ripe, at others that fascism was around the corner and we had to prepare ourselves for the coming clash.

I lived on Manhattan's Upper West Side in the summer of 1969. At the end of the summer, I returned from a trip home to find that my friend the Hollywood executive-to-be had invited the New York "Weather collective," composed mostly of Columbia SDS members, to stay in our apartment. Thirty people were lying on the floor, "smashing monogamy" in between chants of "Pick, pick, pick up the gun, the revolution has begun." One fellow was torn: how could he join Weatherman and continue in psychoanalysis? A woman was yelling at her older brother on the phone: "What do you mean, you can't give me $10,000? I know Daddy put five times that much in your trust fund." A Marcusian intellectual who'd written a pamphlet entitled "Consumption: Domestic Imperialism" insisted that Weatherman followed from the analysis in *One-Dimensional Man*. Several people had returned from a summer trip to Havana, where they had "talked with the Vietnamese," who had urged them to "open up a front in the United States." I left to go to grad school. My friend denounced me as a "wimp," and I felt miserable, convinced that they really were going to accomplish something and that I had chickened out at the decisive moment.

The invasion of Cambodia and the shootings at Kent State and Jackson State once again brought our apocalyptic visions to a fever pitch. My last political meeting in a New Left organization was in May 1970, when I gathered with the members of a Black Panther "support group" called the December 4th Movement or D4M, to consider possible courses of action. The meeting began with a sober assessment of the political situation by a former SDS leader from Columbia. According to him, the United States was on the edge of going fascist. Perhaps six months were left for legal publication of left-wing magazines and newspapers. Now, he said, it was time to "prepare work in the country and in the city, to move stuff from one to another." He was not trying to be histrionic or impress a crowd. He really believed what he was saying. He ended by looking vaguely in my direction and saying, "Those of us who are less well known [i.e., me] will be able to go underground first, while those of us who are more well known [meaning him] will be forced to remain above ground for the time being."

I had finally had enough. I said to the group that this was where

I got off. America was not the Weimar Republic, 1970 was not 1933. Neither revolution nor fascism was around the corner. They could do what they wanted but without me. My friend, the future Hollywood executive, denounced me again, as a wimp who couldn't overcome a "nonstruggle attitude." As far as I know, neither of the two male honchos of D4M ever made good on the rhetoric, but Sylvia Baraldini, one of my good friends from student days in Madison, certainly did. I last saw her in 1970. For the next ten years, rumors floated around about a furtive Sylvia who belonged to strange groups. In 1983, I picked up the *New York Times* to see that she had driven a getaway car during the Brinks robbery in Nyack, New York, a robbery in which a policemen and a security guard were killed. She is now in prison.

From 1969 to 1971, I drove a taxi part-time in New York, managed to finish a master's degree in history at the State University of New York at Buffalo, did some organizing to support the Black Panther 21 in New York, was arrested at a demonstration and then paid a $25 fine for disorderly conduct. It was a bad time. The glory years of the New Left were over, yet the Vietnam War continued. Many people were experimenting with LSD and mescaline, not to mention marijuana. Later that spring, I moved to Boston to be close to some Madison friends and to put my life together again.

It became commonplace in the 1970s to bemoan the lack of theory and anti-intellectualism of the late sixties. I drew a different lesson. No one who was at all remotely familiar with the maelstrom of 1968–1970 could say there was a lack of theory in the movement. The atmosphere was laden with abstractions, from abstractions about the contradictions of imperialism and the nature of a mythic working class, to abstractions of mythic heroes and heroines—the Panthers, the Vietnamese people, and so forth. Certainly the "theory" was wrong, crude, and destructive, but political ideologies usually are. The ideas of 1968–1970 were coherent, closed systems which promised their adherents that they would be on the right side of history, that the dialectic would move in the direction they desired, and that the contradictions of imperialism would "explode" in patterns compatible with their morality. In a period of great confusion—and the late sixties were if nothing else confusing—such simplicity, clarity, and discipline were very appealing for many people, including many highly intellectually inclined members of SDS. For all of our hostility to intellectuals, it is a half-truth to say that the SDS crack-up was primarily a revolt against the intellectuals. Without intellectuals, however dogmatic and anti-intellectual they may have been, the competing fanaticisms would never have come into being in the first place.

I did not believe, then or since, that Weatherman represented a total repudiation of the New Left legacy. However clear Marcuse's personal objections to political violence were, I believed that if the working class was not going to emerge as the revolutionary vanguard, then it logically followed that the young and minority groups were the primary candidates. In this sense, I interpreted Weatherman and the mood that surrounded it as one perfectly logical extrapolation of the assumptions present in *One-Dimensional Man*. Some of my New Left intellectual friends sought to have it both ways by placing great importance on the role of theory but then insisting that every form of practice was a divergence from their understanding of theory. But I believed that the practice, though never as elegant or pleasing as the theory, could not be separated from it. I thought it bad faith to plead for a unity of theory and practice and then disclaim any responsibility for the results.

There is no question that the New Left was a far more congenial place for people who loved to read and talk about ideas before 1968 than it was afterwards. But illiberalism was such a prominent part of the ideas we loved to discuss that we did not put up a very good fight when totalitarian ideologues took over the movement. We wanted community and equality rather than liberty and political freedom. We took the latter for granted or else we saw it as a sham. It was not in spite but because of our utopianism that we were drawn to political ideas hostile to a free society.

From beginning to end we in the New Left saw ourselves as a intellectual, political, and moral elite, as the conscience of American society. I think its end was an example of the arrogance of power, rather than, as has often been stressed, the desperate rage of the powerless. The New Left was now going to "fight back." The NLF would win. The Panthers were "the vanguard of the revolution." "White youth in the belly of the monster" would join with "national liberation struggles" to "smash U.S. imperialism." SDS would "open up a front in the mother country." For liberals and many in the radical left, the New Left's message of gloom about fascism and repression, about the details of police violence or the conduct of the war in Vietnam, were decisive. But it was the smell of success, moral absolutism, and the lure of power mixed with the language of despair and frustration that I recall most from those years. No wonder the factionalism was so bitter: the prize was leadership of The Revolution.

In retrospect, it is not surprising that as we repudiated intellect, scholarship, a world full of moral ambiguity for one of "imperialists" and "revolutionaries," our political judgment also failed. After 1975, when this self-appointed moral and political elite saw that its judgments about Vietnam turned out to be wrong, it responded as most people do when faced with a difficult past: repression and silence. The course of events in Indochina after 1975 was not what the conventional wisdom of the New Left had led us to expect. Our predictions, to the extent we made any, about what the Vietnamese communists would do with their victory were completely wrong, while the warnings of American conservatives were on the mark. We chose not to believe those voices. We were wrong and they were right. Those who actively opposed the war *and* were aware of how horrible a communist victory could be for the people of Indochina were a minority. And even they tended to keep their fears of a communist Vietnam to themselves while focusing on the folly of continuing American involvement in and support for the South Vietnamese government. Generally, we simply did not think very much about consequences, but to the extent we did, we all thought a North Vietnamese victory was preferable to continuation of the war.

I am convinced that if North Vietnamese domination had led to anything remotely approaching the "humane collectivism" the New Left foresaw, there would be a host of American leftists rushing to take credit for the great event. Instead history after 1975 confirmed the worst fears of Americans who supported the war: a genocide did take place in Cambodia under the leadership of communist leaders who had studied Marxism-Leninism in Paris; an Asian gulag was established in Vietnam; a war with China soon followed; the Soviet Union acquired a vital strategic asset in Cam Ranh Bay; the boat people made poignantly clear what we had refused to believe for a decade, namely that thousands of Vietnamese citizens really did not want to live under a communist dictatorship; and with the extinction of political liberty in Vietnam came economic collapse. We continuously minimized and even ridiculed the idea that a terrible tyranny could follow from our good intentions and a communist victory. When the debacle occurred, our supposedly so critical generation shut up. That is perhaps good taste, but hardly the moral high ground we always said we owned. We did not stage demonstrations in front of the Cambodian embassy in Washington or at the United Nations while the Holocaust in Cambodia took place. Instead, American leftists figured out a way to blame the United States for the genocidal madness of the Khmer Rouge, whose leaders had studied in Paris with some of the same Marxist luminaries whose works found favor in seminar rooms in Western European and American universities.

The end of the war in Vietnam, which we in the New Left had initially greeted as a victory for the forces of liberation, became a spectacular refutation of our political judgment. I am not going to add my opinion on whether it was wise for the United States to enter the war in the first place or to pass judgment on how it was fought. Historical scholarship has demonstrated to my satisfaction that the image we had of the war as a war against the people of Vietnam was not true. But what is clear to me is that for all of the imperfections of the South Vietnamese government, for all its corruption and authoritarianism, it was preferable to what has followed. Our greatest political misjudgment concerning that war was to believe that the communists really represented the will of the Vietnamese population and that their victory would bring a better society to South Vietnam. Debates over the wisdom and morality of the war in this country too often take place without consideration of the basic fact that the triumph of communism in Indochina has brought with it levels of political oppression, murder, economic collapse, and yet more war which we insisted would not take place.

Because the war dragged on so long, we in the New Left tended to underestimate our own political significance. Then when the "victory" turned into such a disaster, the impulse to minimize our political significance was all the greater. Our political vocabulary was one that focused on the overwhelming power of a nearly omnipotent System faced with a failed opposition. While we overestimated our political and moral insight, we underestimated our political impact. I did not understand at the time that the New Left actually was an important political actor. It was reading Henry Kissinger's memoirs of the Paris negotiations with the North Vietnamese that made clear how important the American antiwar movement was in North Vietnamese strategic calculations. While the main battle of the war was in Vietnam, our efforts to raise the cost of staying in Vietnam to the American government were more important than many of us realized at the time.

It is more difficult for me to retrace my steps away from the left. Perhaps by its very nature as a process of reconsideration and reassessment, deradicalization is a more private, quieter, less dramatic and long-term process than is radicalization. There is no one dramatic event or set of events, no clear "before and after," no "Kronstadt"[1] comparable to the Hitler-Stalin pact, the Russian invasion of Hungary in 1956, or Khrushchev's secret speech that led to a massive exit from the left. Nor can I report any sudden revelation or overnight conversion. Perhaps the very unorganizational character of the American left, especially after the 1960s, its existence as a mood expressed in a set of journals, networks of friendships, and tacit assumptions rather than as an organized party, also made the need for dramatic decisions to "stay or leave" less necessary than for the leftist generation of the 1930s.

By the early 1970s, I had come to the conclusion that the New Left's hostility to liberal values contributed to its end in factionalism and violence. Previously I viewed capitalism and its mass culture as a threat to individual autonomy. After the crack-up of SDS, the leftist vision of political community took on more sinister connotations in my view. The loyalists to the New Left in the 1970s bemoaned what they viewed as a failure to unite theory and practice in the late sixties. What struck me about those years was an unfortunate unity of theory and practice.

From 1974 to 1980, I worked on a doctorate in sociology at Brandeis University. I studied and learned much from Kurt Wolff and Egon Bittner, both sociologists who are steeped in European traditions of sociological theory and historical sociology, but my Brandeis years left much to be desired. The department suffered from the influence of the counterculture on the faculty. Its disillusionment with professional sociology, combined with the abysmal academic job market of the seventies and eighties, made graduate student life very difficult in any case. Being a white male working in nonquantitative traditions of social science certainly did not help in an era of affirmative action and growing quantification of the social sciences.

I immensely enjoyed working on my doctorate, which I published in revised form as *Reactionary Modernism: Technology, Culture and Politics in Weimar and the Third Reich*. The thesis and then book posed the problem of how the German right and then the Nazis reconciled political irrationalism with a fascination for modern technology. How could the Nazis reject reason and embrace the machine at the level of ideology, and how did such a reconciliation affect Nazi politics? The thesis and book were a labor of love as well as a coming to terms with the Frankfurt School's critical theory. The analysis of Nazi ideology drew extensively on insights first developed by the critical theorists, yet finally I concluded that more conventional, liberal interpretations of modern German history were more adequate than were Marxist or neo-Marxist efforts to locate the German catastrophe in the perversities of the Enlightenment or capitalism. Historians and social scientists of the left too often failed to grasp the distinctive character of anti-Semitism, the distinctive contributions of German history, the uniqueness of the Holocaust, or the autonomous power of cultural and ideological traditions. Instead they tended to write general analyses of capitalism which slighted the importance of ideology in politics, particularly in the history of Nazism.

The seventies were very much an aftermath, a period in which the political framework I had constructed in the sixties unraveled. I mulled over the 1960s in and with other contributors to *Telos* and *New German Critique*, hoping with them to sustain a "nonauthoritarian" and democratic left. I read Solzhenitsyn and pondered the link between the romanticism of the young Georg Lukacs and his subsequent attraction to communism. In the summer of 1975, I visited with some of Lukacs's students, the "Budapest School" of philosophers and sociologists in Budapest. I was moved by their commitment to humanist and democratic socialism but even more struck by the reality of political harassment due to political views. The East European dissidents played an important role for me in rethinking the importance of the liberal political tradition, and I am grateful to them for looking at our taken-for-granted traditions with fresh eyes.

There are a number of intellectuals who came from the New Left and now have sought to integrate liberal political theory into their enduring antipathy to capitalism. I recall a panel discussion on Solidarity held at the Center for European Studies at Harvard several years ago in which the theme of civil society was central. I asked the audience why it was that political democracies with electoral competition between political parties that were willing to peacefully alternate between government and opposition, and with individual political liberties and freedom of speech and the press, did not exist anywhere where capitalism had been abolished. Was there after all— dreaded thought—a causal link between capitalism and freedom? In view of the many dictatorships that have coexisted with capitalism, clearly capitalism is compatible with dictatorship. But democracy and individual liberty have existed nowhere in which there are not also private markets and private investment decisions not controlled by states. Max Horkheimer, one of the Frankfurt School's central figures, coined the aphorism "He who does not want to talk about capitalism should remain silent about fascism." Yet the opposite is certainly more true: he or she who does not want to talk about capitalism has left out a major part of the argument concerning why free societies exist. Once I reached that conclusion, I could not call myself a leftist in any meaningful sense anymore.

I first visited West Germany in 1975 and have returned regularly. Like other American Jewish scholars of my generation, I was both drawn to a West German culture on the basis of shared interests in social theory, philosophy, and history and kept at an emotional distance because of the memories of Nazism. The relations between Jews and the West German left, at the level of political controversy and scholarship, became tense in the seventies. Some West German terrorists made common cause with Palestinian terrorists. Much of the Marxist analysis of "fascism and capitalism" had little or nothing to say about the particular problem of anti-Semitism or Nazi ideology. We Jewish scholars found ourselves stressing the particular dimensions of the Nazi regime, while Marxist and left-leaning counterparts tended to assimilate it more to a general view of modern capitalism.

Those postwar West German scholars, especially among historians, who did devote special scholarly attention to the origins of the Holocaust were liberals or moderate conservatives, not scholars inspired by Marxism or critical theory. So my scholarly concerns moved in different directions from my political affinities for the left. Yet many West German conservatives voted in the West German parliament to bring to an end prosecution of those accused of committing war crimes and crimes against humanity.

In the late seventies, the myth of Third Worldism came to an end for me. The United Nations resolution equating Zionism and racism and the callousness of the OPEC cartel toward the suffering it caused in the seventies in other poor countries did much to undermine any lingering view of the Third World as a repository of virtuous suffering. Without minimizing the links between anti-Zionism and anti-Semitism in the American left, my problem with the left was that it could not accept the need for a strong *American* military establishment if Israel was to survive. The Yom Kippur War of 1973, during which the Western European governments refused to allow the United States to resupply Israel from Europe for fear of Arab retaliation, made it abundantly clear that it was the United States and only the United States that was the ultimate guarantor of the survival of Israel. But reconciliation to the military power of the imperialist monster was simply beyond the pale for the left after Vietnam.

In 1981, I came to teach in the Committee on Degrees in Social Studies at Harvard, an interdisciplinary program in history and social science. There I reread the classics of nineteenth-century social and political theory—Adam Smith, Tocqueville, J. S. Mill, Marx, Max Weber, Durkheim, and Freud. By then, I had become utterly disenchanted with leftist utopias and was rereading the classical social and political theorists with a renewed sense of the value of the liberal political tradition. Individual liberty rather than equalitarian leveling, free speech and pluralism rather than "repressive tolerance," in Marcuse's terminology, a sense of the dark side of human nature, the importance of trying to separate scholarship and ideology, the moral arguments for economic growth—all of these liberal conceptions fell on my very receptive ears. It all felt like a great relief, a wonderful rediscovery, all the more so as I could share it with fine students and intelligent colleagues.

I came to Harvard ready to learn as well as to teach. My years at Harvard from 1981 to 1985 are the only time that compares in importance to my Madison years. In both cases there was a fortuitous combination of openness to ideas on my part with a climate in which I could develop them. I was not inclined any longer to utopianism in politics and thus warmed to Stanley Hoffmann's skeptical realism in international politics, and then turned again to the work of Hoffman's teacher, Raymond Aron, whose political commentary and scholarship in the fields of international relations and sociological theory have been an inspiration for my own more recent work in these areas. My disenchantment with ideological politics and with the antitechnological mood of the sixties made me more open to learn from, get to know, and befriend Daniel Bell. I had learned much from him through his writing for years concerning the nature of the coming of postindustrial society, the role of technology in society, and theoretical and epistemological problems in the social sciences. Now I appreciated his sense of civility in discussion, his sense of fairness in confronting the argument and not attacking the individual, and his appreciation of how important a thick skin is if one intends to challenge the conventional wisdom of one's colleagues. I discovered that Samuel Huntington and a remarkable group of graduate students were engaged in a revival of strategic thinking which entailed a critique of ahistorical, technocratic approaches to strategy, a critique that struck a chord with my own past criticisms of such approaches in other fields of social science. I taught a section of a course given by David Landes on the historical origins of inequality between nations which helped me enormously in rethinking the issues of capitalism and inequality on a world scale. Landes has challenged us to examine capitalism's moral contribution to reducing human suffering in a way that avoids the complacency of some procapitalist argumentation. I shared in the very stimulating life of the Center for European Studies, though my criticism of the peace movements and growing distance from the left placed me at odds with many fellow Europeanists.

Marty Peretz and Ronald Radosh were the only friends I knew who had been left-leaning in the sixties and had subsequently moved away. In the early eighties I came across a new phenomena: younger intellectuals, some five and ten years younger, who were serious scholars and writers but who were not on the left. They had no radical youth against which to rebel and held their views with a certain ease and lack of anguish that was refreshing. Some of these younger friends concluded that the left had become too powerful a veto group in sociology and political science and thus instead decided to go to law school. Much to my regret, the evolution of my political views away from the left in the eighties was at the price of some old friendships.

Things came to a head with my involvement in the controversy over the deployment of American missiles in Europe. The controversy over the Euromissiles was the most important challenge of the left since the sixties and one of the most important political battles of postwar European politics in general. I followed developments in Europe, especially in West Germany, closely. Initially I was sympathetic to some arguments of the peace movements, but at Harvard I heard intelligent arguments made on behalf of the NATO decision. In contrast to my Madison years, I no longer possessed a theory of ideology with which to dismiss the arguments and evidence of those with whom I disagreed as the work of Pentagon propandists or "exterminists." Having seen my political judgment falsified by the outcome of the war in Indochina, I was determined not to make the same mistakes again. I was not going to dismiss the arguments made by the Western governments as propaganda and was going to give the arguments of the Western governments a fair hearing. I was not going to dismiss an argument simply because it was made by a conservative politician or came from the Pentagon, nor would I accept an argument because it came from the left in Western Europe. I was not going to assume that the Western governments were most likely lying while protest groups had a monopoly on peace and morality or that there were no important differences between the United States and the Soviet Union.

I found the very term "peace movement" reminiscent of the

moralism and Manichean character of my own views in the "antiwar movement." If the New Left had been so wrong about the outcome of the war in Indochina, why should the left of the early 1980s be any more right about the Soviet buildup and its political implications? Just as the "antiwar movement" had failed to address the issue of the war waged by North Vietnamese communism against the South Vietnamese but focused instead on opposing the American war in Vietnam, so I thought it presumptuous of "peace movements" to claim the mantle of peace. They meant to suggest that they were more in favor of peace and more opposed to war than those who disagreed with them, just as we had believed that the debate in the sixties was between those who favored an obviously immoral war and those who supported it.

In the New Left, we understood that the antiwar movement "objectively" helped the Vietnamese communists, whatever our subjective views may have been. In the Euromissile controversy, it seemed clear to me that the peace movements in the West and the political parties that adopted their positions if not all of their rhetoric "objectively" helped the Soviet position in arms control negotiations with the United States. The great fear of nuclear war, in itself a rational fear, became a powerful tool of Soviet coercive diplomacy directed against the Western democracies, where alone peace movements and political dissent existed. I thought it obvious that an American exit from Western Europe or a collapse of NATO would inevitably lead to greater Soviet influence in Western Europe. The radical left in West Germany, the Low Countries, Scandinavian, and Great Britain wanted the United States out of Western Europe, while the moderate left wanted us to stay but without preserving a balance of nuclear forces. I was convinced that it was utterly naive and irresponsible to believe that a Western Europe without an American presence was likely to sustain a balance of power and will against the Soviet Union. I also believed that without such a balance, the Soviet Union could pursue a course of coercive diplomacy that would erode Western Europe's political freedom. Having been wrong about the consequences of the success of communist strategy in Indochina, I felt a particular responsibility to raise questions about Soviet goals and their consequences for Western Europe.

I plunged into reading essays and books which in the sixties I would have dismissed out of hand as propaganda for the war machine. Without losing interest in political and social theories, I sought to confirm or disconfirm them in regard to facts. In the sixties, my

attitude toward uncomfortable facts was expressed in slightly exaggerated form by Lukacs's view that if facts did not conform to theory,
"so much the worse for the facts." I was determined to make the
ethics of scholarship apply as well to my partisanship. I became increasingly interested in facts. I surprised even myself with my interest
in charts showing the military balance of power in Europe in numbers
of tanks, planes, missiles, soldiers, artillery, and ships. Without a
theoretical framework to tell me in advance that the NATO assess-
ments of the balance of forces in Europe were simply propaganda,
I was able to look closely at the facts of the Soviet military buildup,
examine the standard criticisms of American policies, and try to interpret the political implications of the changing military balance.

The result was an essay published in *Telos* in summer 1982 and
a shorter version in *Partisan Review* in spring 1983. *Telos*, under the
guidance of its editor, Paul Piccone, was a unique journal of the
left. As far as I know, there was no other journal which began in
the sixties (outside France) which fostered a libertarian critique of
communism and Marxism—not just Marxism-Leninism—with equal
consistency. In the late seventies, *Telos* also published essays on
the Soviet military buildup and the naiveté of Western liberals and
leftists in denying it. In my essay of summer 1982 I sharply criticized
the peace movements in Western Europe for failing to take seriously
the reality of the Soviet threat and for uncritically repeating Soviet
propaganda about the purposes of the NATO decision to deploy
missiles and negotiate with the Soviet Union.

I went further, however, and made a case for the NATO deployments. Just as we in the New Left knew that an American exit
from Vietnam would mean a communist victory, so I was convinced
that a failure to sustain a balance of military power in Europe would
lead eventually to an American exit from Europe. I argued that while
no one could predict with precision exactly what the consequences
of an American exit from Western Europe as a result of having lost
a major political battle with the Soviet Union would be, neither
were these consequences incalculable. That is, the most likely consequences would be an erosion of freedom, and peace as well. The
governments of Western Europe were obviously worth defending.
These were not the right-wing dictatorships in the Third World it
was so easy to dislike. With the memories of the exit from Vietnam
still vivid, how could we fail to respond to pleas from the Western
European governments to see that a balance of forces was preserved?
Did we not have some responsibility to the West Europeans to be

a loyal ally? Why should the Western governments revoke a decision of democratically elected leaders because a leftist intelligentsia had come into positions of influence in the parties of the left and in parts of the media in northwestern Europe?

I also argued that the NATO decision was *not* the insane culmination of instrumental rationality, an American plan to limit nuclear war to Europe, part of a strategy to facilitate a first strike at the Soviet Union, or a manifestation of American control over a reluctant Europe. On the contrary, I wrote that there were sound political reasons to be given on behalf of this decision. It would help to deter any war from beginning by reducing the likelihood that the Soviet Union could escape retaliation in the event it attacked Western Europe. The facts were that this decision was a response to West German chancellor Helmut Schmidt's warnings in London in 1977 to America not to neglect the preservation of a balance of power in Europe upset by Soviet deployments of the SS-20 missile in the hopes of attaining an arms control agreement with the Soviet Union at the level of strategic nuclear arms. Finally, I argued that the Western negotiating position, especially after adoption of the "zero option," was perfectly reasonable and the best way of really reducing the level of nuclear arms in and for Europe.

In 1987, Mikhail Gorbachev accepted the zero option first proposed by President Reagan in 1982. Had the peace movements had their way in 1983, Gorbachev would never have had to contemplate dismantling his SS-20 intermediate-range missiles deployed at such great cost. The defeat of the peace movements, the firmness of Western governments, and the common sense of the electorates especially in West Germany and Great Britain led to at least a short-term failure of the Soviet strategy of using Western dissent as a lever against the Western governments. A better deal for Europe was now conceivable because the Western governments and publics did not accept the arguments made by the intellectual and political left in West Germany, Great Britain, and the Low Countries or the freeze movement in the United States. I noticed the irony of my arguments. Whereas in the sixties it was the true consciousness of the intellectuals, my true consciousness, that sought to pierce the false one-dimensional consciousness of the deluded masses, in the eighties I had come to view the dissent of the intellectuals as politically misguided and the electorates as repositories of common sense.

The New Left did not create feminism, but it added immeasurably to its impact on all of our lives. Feminism is probably the most important continuing legacy of the New Left for our personal lives. Feminists within the left were among the first to break with the authoritarian political style it had come to adopt by the late sixties. But the appearance of "Weather sisters," women who aspired to be no less effective as revolutionaries than the SDS men, soon disabused me of the idea that women had some special inclination to nonviolence. I support feminism as a realization of liberal ideals of equality for all individuals. My wife is an active scholar of women's studies and American history. I am very involved with raising our daughter and think, on balance, equality between men and women has enriched the life of men immeasurably. But I have difficulty with the idea of affirmative action, which seems to me to be one of the more illiberal ideas of the past decade.

The enduring value of the 1970s for me, and I think for many veterans of the 1960s, was a return to scholarship and intellectual work. I learned that anti-intellectualism in politics is almost always the prelude to utopian and then totalitarian excesses, and that the Marxist and neo-Marxist ideas we thought to be so daring in 1968 were more often rehashes of what was daring in the late nineteenth century or in the 1920s in Central Europe. If it was an antiauthoritarian left we wanted, it already existed. Its name was social democracy, and its most recent battle against totalitarianism was the cold war. The authoritarianism it had in mind, especially after 1917, was called communism. Anticommunist American liberals and European social democrats of the 1950s, the New Left's main targets, were an anti-authoritarian left.

My odyssey from the New Left to an eclectic mixture of conservative and liberal views today marks a journey away from a search for certainty and a yearning to grasp politics and history in an all-encompassing system. The New Left promised a great deal, answered many questions, and gave meaning to apparently disconnected phenomena. But the great hopes I placed in "theory" could not survive the factual outcome of the Vietnam War. In the eighties, my turn away from political utopianism put me at odds with the left's passion for nuclear disarmament. In the eighties, the theories that had once seemed so profound and insightful were serving as pretexts for refusing to face uncomfortable facts about the growing military power of the Soviet Union. Utopia in my twenties was understandable. By my late thirties, I simply knew too much to still seek to unite these theories with practice or to believe that because facts did not fit my paradigms, they could be ignored.

Today, my political values are liberal in the classical sense. I believe that a free society must be a differentiated society in which the different spheres of economics, politics, and culture should not be subjected to one overarching principle. Attempts to do so always end in tyranny. Literature, art, scholarship have an autonomy that should be respected. Personal life is far too complex to be adequately grasped in the categories of public, political life. Political judgment requires thinking through the links between intentions and consequences. Political judgment also calls for the capacity to make distinctions, a quality of mind that has suffered greatly since the sixties. The most important of such distinctions is between societies that nurture political freedom and individual liberty and those that do not. But, as the budget deficits of the 1980s make clear, conservatives alone cannot sustain a firm Western foreign policy. A vital center that encompasses impulses for compassion and equality should be part of any meaningful notion of a bipartisan foreign policy.

I am sure that my involvement in the New Left deepened a conviction that ideas and ideologies are major driving forces in political life and led me to want to devote my career as a scholar to understanding these issues. Among scholars in the social sciences and history of my generation, a focus on intentions and ideas was somewhat out of fashion. But it is returning, and as it does, I think those of us who have paid attention to the beneficial and harmful impact of ideas on political life will exert a constructive, if mediated, impact on the political life and climate of American society.

Note

[1] "Kronstadt" refers to a revolt of Russian sailors in the early years of the Bolshevik regime which was suppressed by the new government. Afterwards many supporters of the Russian Revolution saw the suppression of the revolt as the starting point for their disillusionment with the Bolsheviks. Since then the name Kronstadt has been a shorthand way of signifying the moment of disillusionment among those drawn to communism and the radical left.

5

Liberal in the Middle

John H. Bunzel

The time was ten o'clock on Monday morning in the first week
of February, the opening day of the 1969 spring semester at San
Francisco State College. The stage curtain in the auditorium was
drawn, but the policeman's feet were clearly visible to the jeering
students out front. When I entered backstage, I looked with dismay
at the uniformed members of San Francisco's Tactical Squad. The
police had been on the campus for weeks, but I had not asked that
they be sent to my class. The sergeant in charge told me he and
his men were there to provide any protection I might need. "We
have word you may be in for some trouble. We'll be back here if
you need us."

The television cameramen and newspaper reporters were standing
in the hallway. I had refused to admit them into the auditorium
while the class was in session, promising instead to meet them afterwards. For over a week there had been many rumors about what
might happen at the first meeting of the class. On Friday five or six
black students had spotted me walking across the campus to the
library and followed within taunting distance. "Hey pig, hey pig
Bunzel," they shouted. "We'll get your ass on Monday. Be there,
pig—you hear? Be there."

My upper-division course in community power and politics had
been moved to Knuth Hall from a much smaller room because of a
sudden surge in enrollment. Normally about 40 students took the

course, but this time over 100 had signed up. The turnout was not a tribute to my pedagogical skills. I had simply been designated a major target by student radicals. Among those "enrolled" in Political Science 151 were the leaders of the most militant groups on campus— the Black Students Union, the Third World Liberation Front, and Students for a Democratic Society.

I glanced at my watch. We were already late getting started. From my pocket I pulled out a note I had found in my mailbox that morning from a close friend and colleague. "Luck," it said.

The doors in the back of the auditorium were finally closed. There was no turning back now from this, the most improbable experience of my academic career. When I stepped onto the stage, the auditorium erupted with catcalls. I could barely make myself heard.

BUNZEL   I would like to talk today about the general outline of this course . . .
STUDENT   Mr. Bunzel—pig, dog, racist, sir . . .

About twenty-five students joined in the disruption. They milled in the aisles. They shook their fists and shouted epithets. One student waved a copy of Chairman Mao's Red Book.

BUNZEL   I'd like to give you some idea of what this course is about. It's a course in community power and the politics of leadership.
STUDENT   You seize power by armed force.

Cheers and applause.

BUNZEL   I want to ask for order.
STUDENT   Revolutionary war is inevitable.
BUNZEL   Those of you who'd like to discuss the problems on your mind, I'd be willing to meet with you any time today . . .
STUDENT   Right now, pig.
BUNZEL   Ladies and gentlemen . . .
STUDENT   Get the pigs out of this classroom.
BUNZEL   At the appropriate time I will take questions.
STUDENT   Teach, Mr. Bunzel. We're here to learn.

Laughter.

BUNZEL   There'll be no discussion until I'm allowed to make an observation.

Booing and yelling.

BUNZEL   I intend to talk to those students who . . .

STUDENT   Mr. Bunzel, don't you know anything? We're not here to be intimidated, Mr. Bunzel, sir—racist, pig, dog. Understand that? I'm not going to be forced to come into this class and be taught racism.

BUNZEL   Just a minute . . .

STUDENT   Don't intimidate me, Mr. Bunzel.

BUNZEL   It's perfectly clear to me this class cannot conduct its business today, and perfectly clear I'm unable . . .

Cascade of catcalls.

BUNZEL   This class will meet here on Wednesday. Appropriate measures will be taken to permit me to teach.

General pandemonium.

———— • ————

Thus began the climax of an extraordinary academic year. For six months I had received anonymous threatening telephone calls at home and at the office. I even became accustomed to being called "pig." Now a large number of black militants had come into my class determined to disrupt it. To them I represented the enemy— it had been that way since the beginning of the fall semester in September and would continue when the class met again on Wednesday. What I had not anticipated was that the events of this week would spill out of the classroom and receive the attention of the national press. My parents called from Florida, and my brother, a journalist, came down from Seattle to see for himself.[1] The *Los Angeles Times* editorialized on the "larger meaning and importance" of the attacks on me by the student radicals. The *New York Times* ran a front-page story on the difficulties of a "New York–born political scientist." Soon I was getting letters from all over the country, from friends who sent warm personal messages by way of extending a supporting hand as well as from people I did not know who wrote to express their own concern and best wishes. A Congressional Subcommittee on Education asked me to testify in Washington. The reason for all this attention was the symbolism of my plight. My brother put it very simply: "The object of continuous radical abuse was a middle-aged liberal whose activist record encompassed more than 20 years: from his tumultuous undergraduate years at Princeton to his selection in 1968 as a Robert Kennedy delegate from California to the Democratic National Convention."

It was not by chance that my classroom was singled out for attack, as were my office and home in previous weeks. A leader of the Third World Liberation Front at San Francisco State told a reporter for the *Washington Post* the militants were determined to "stop the functioning of Bunzel's class and educate people on what the class was about. Any class Bunzel will be teaching will have his attitudes and perceptions of our society and that is hurting the people. We're saying he's in direct opposition to our struggle at this point. And as such he's an enemy." One of the members of the Black Students Union said: "Bunzel's much more a dangerous thing than a man like George Wallace. With Wallace, every one knows where he stands. But when Bunzel says something people say, yeah, he's a liberal so that must be right."

There was an uneasy truce at the beginning of the 1969 spring semester. The militants were finally negotiating their "nonnegotiable demands" with then acting president S. I. Hayakawa, and a settlement was supposedly being hammered out. Nevertheless, policemen were still posted in each building on the campus. Not having much to do, they spent their time reading the student SDS-oriented newspaper, which called them "pigs." They also read the mounds of mimeographed strike literature cranked out by every group and faction on campus. I remember being struck by the sight of blue-uniformed officers, their clubs and revolvers at their side, quietly leafing through the revolutionary quotations in Chairman Mao's little Red Book. When they were through with these daily diversions, they turned to the more familiar and less complicated pleasures of *Playboy* and *Sports Illustrated*. When they were not reading, they were listening to students explain the promises of Marx's dialectic or why, as members of the working class, they were the best hope for America's future, or, from those who looked upon them with less warmth and enthusiasm, how they were "occupying troops" and "racists" hired to crush the people. The police would shake their heads, no doubt envious of the students whose classes and instruction lasted only fifty minutes.

The San Francisco State campus is located on 94 acres in the southwestern part of the city. Its more than 20,000 students are mainly middle and lower middle class, many of whom are married and hold down full- or part-time jobs. They arrive by bus and streetcar each morning and return home the same way. The wide-open quality of the place—its very liberalism—is widely known and accepted by everyone. It had not always been torn apart by student rioting or disruption. The campus had had its lighter moments too. Early in the fall semester of 1967, a "nude-in" was staged and directed by the part-time poet and self-proclaimed founder and president of the Sexual Freedom League, who bore the unlikely name of Jefferson Poland. A kind of fey, gentle soul with a single fixation from sunrise to sunset, he was dedicated (or so he told the press) to liberating the college from its sexual repressions. Naturally, everybody wanted to help. The student newspaper and local press were advised of Poland's plan well in advance of his scheduled performance in order to ensure a massive turnout.

The day he had chosen dawned cold and foggy, but Poland, always the trouper, was determined that the show must go on. Shortly after lunchtime he arrived at a prearranged spot in front of the cafeteria accompanied by a young lady. Both were wrapped in heavy overcoats. Responding to the cheers of the multitude, Poland removed his clothes and ran around on the cafeteria lawn. Short and slightly built, he appeared pale in the gray afternoon light. "He doesn't even look very healthy," one girl remarked as she bit into a cookie. "I think he looks positively rabid," said another. Poland's companion, perhaps because of an attack of middle-class modesty, seemed reluctant to follow suit. Suddenly several security guards appeared to escort the now shivering Poland off campus. That moved his girlfriend to take action. She rose to her feet and took off her coat. To the delight of the crowd she had nothing on underneath, and for a brief moment stood in the buff. However, the suggested orgy never materialized as they were both led away by the campus police. Within a few hours a few of San Francisco's outraged citizens phoned the college, the mayor's office, and, inexplicably, the Post Office to demand a stop to the "pornographic" behavior. The problem for those who stand guard over the public's virtue is that people cannot be arrested for indecent exposure until their clothes have come off, but by that time their worst fears—the naked truth—have come to pass.

In the fall of 1968 San Francisco State blew up. Virtual guerrilla warfare broke out on the campus. On November 6 the leadership of the Black Students Union and the other minority groups that made up the Third World Liberation Front began putting into operation their plan to immobilize the college and shut it down. Using hit-and-run tactics and terrorism, groups of black and brown students, later joined by whites, succeeded in disrupting the campus with a violence unprecedented in the history of American higher education.[2]

During the first week of the fall semester I was called to the office of the vice president for academic affairs. "I don't want to alarm you," he said, "but the word up here is that the Black Students Union is out to get you. I'm only telling you what I've heard," he added, "and I thought you ought to know." As it turned out, he was right. My troubles started with an article I had written on black studies at San Francisco State[3] in which I was critical not of the idea of black studies, but of the particular perspective of Nathan Hare, a sociologist with a Ph.D. from the University of Chicago, who had been hired during the summer by President John Summerskill to draw up a proposal for a department of black studies. Hare had been very clear about the kind of program he wanted in various forums on and off the campus. He said that in his model of a black studies department he wanted teachers who would work solely within a "black revolutionary nationalist framework. I don't want any assimilationists," he said. My article raised questions about this approach—among other things, I was concerned about whether it would allow for enough diversity in points of view. I had written:

It is true that for many students in this country, the history of man has too often been treated as though it "started in Athens and ended in California," with the Afro-American story simply left out. The question now is whether a Department of Black Studies would substitute propaganda for omissions, or, as some have said, new myths for old lies.

In a public speech Hare had said, "I think this is a time for hate." I did not agree. Further, I did not believe that such a sentiment had any place in the college curriculum. But I soon discovered that in the kind of polarized, combustible environment that prevailed on the campus, one either supported Hare's program in its entirety or was tagged a "racist" and an "enemy of the people."

One morning in October around 8:30 a crude, homemade bomb was found outside my office door by one of my colleagues who happened to pass by and heard it ticking. The building was immediately evacuated, and an ordinance team from the nearby Army post was called to dismantle it. Fortunately, no one was hurt. There was no way of knowing who put the bomb there, and the police never found out.

Campus authorities advised the police department where I lived, some 20 miles away, to keep our house under surveillance, which it did for most of the academic year. From then on, particularly in light of what took place in the months to come, my wife lived in almost daily fear. About two weeks after the bomb incident I returned from work one Friday afternoon to discover that our house had been broken into and burglarized. No one was ever caught. Whether the robbery was related to my difficulties at the college was never determined. In any event, we had chain locks installed on all the outside doors, and the police asked us to keep a light burning at night in the kitchen and carport. A number of friends suggested we get a big dog for protection. The problem was we liked cats.

Two days after the black-led student strike began, five people wearing masks tried to break into my office. It was locked—only because the dean had received some advance warning that my office might be "hit" and had urged me and the department secretary to go home for the rest of the day. They settled for the office next door, where a young woman hired as a research assistant was working alone. She watched helplessly as books, papers, and typewriters were hurled to the floor. "I ordered them to get out," she said afterwards, "but they just smiled and kept right on looting."

Early in January 1969, the campus chapter of the American Federation of Teachers, led and dominated by sympathizers of the student radicals, joined in "the struggle" by piggybacking on the strike of the Black Students Union and Third World Liberation Front. Although I had been a strong union supporter most of my life, I opposed the teachers' strike. For one thing, I had always felt that a strike, if it was to be effective, should at the very least have solid backing—and that is precisely what the striking teachers did *not* have. In the preceding year the AFT union had been specifically repudiated as the faculty's bargaining agent in a mailed ballot. A few weeks after the strike was called, almost two-thirds of the faculty voted against it in a mail ballot referendum. Besides, I was strongly opposed to a union of professors treating a college in the same way an industrial union might treat a reactionary employer. The use of confrontation, the weapon of the strike wielded by a faculty minority against the majority of its colleagues, the withholding of grades at the end of the semester as if students were an economic commodity—these tactics had no place on a campus and could do serious damage to an academic community if they became a permanent way of life.

The faculty strike was many things to many people, generating a wide range of attitudes and behavior, making me realize that my split with the radicals of the left had become a chasm. After a particularly active day of confrontation on the campus, Acting President Hayakawa told the press, "This has been the most exciting day since my tenth birthday, when I rode a roller coaster for the first time." The statement was probably true in that, as one of the striking teachers himself pointed out, "the strike reflected what everyone experienced, a new energy that changed our connections to each other and to our institution."[4] Swept up in a group experience with its own force and vitality, many of those who had left the classroom for the picket line experienced a new excitement, a feeling of "really living" as action replaced talk and striking became the badge of authenticity. Going on strike sometimes represented a revulsion from what was seen as the shabbiness, the hypocrisy, and the mediocrity of the college community, including its alleged racism and complicity in the war and the draft. For some it was also a revolt against the tediousness of day-to-day existence, an antidote to being bored. Another faculty striker spoke candidly and perceptively on this point:

> I didn't realize it until some time later, but I had been bored for a long time—bored with teaching the same dull classes year after year, with students who aren't that bright or interesting, with my own life in general. Now suddenly I was on strike, walking the picket lines, doing something for a change that was shaking up the place. I think a lot of us almost felt young again, but for all of us there was a real communal spirit. We had broken out of a mold and were in this thing together for better or for worse.

Thus for many of those on strike the absorption in confrontation became the most important experience they had known in years. There was a kind of mass therapy at work, and for some it took its most expressive turn in the romantic expectation that "the system" (which meant not only San Francisco State and the Board of Trustees, but the whole political structure of California) would be turned around in response to the pressure of their direct action and made to reorder itself into a new network of relationships reflecting their demands and priorities. Further, the AFT strike provided for many of its participants a real sense of theater. It took on symbolic meaning and significance and became a dramatic and liberating experience. The theatrical components of the strike became "real," and reality was dismissed as irrelevant.

Another component of the strike was that it provided a vehicle for some faculty members to lay claim to and confirm their own self-esteem. They became political activists not only to show that they were truly sensitive to the needs of young people, but to affirm their support for the one group they really wanted to be identified with—the student radicals. One member of the AFT who resigned during the strike put it this way: "I began to see some of the dynamics of this thing last fall when the students tried to shut the College down. Some of my faculty friends in the AFT simply had to show their support. What the AFT strike did was to give them another chance to show the students they were with them all the way. For a lot of them," he said, "that association with the students was a way of legitimating their own behavior." The other side of the coin was that the radical students wanting to take charge of the college were always looking for whatever support among the faculty they could pick up. They found some of their staunchest compatriots in the ranks of the AFT local.

It may be that an instinctive or reactive craving for "action" has always been inherent in academic life and, for some students and faculty, the fundamental mode of self-expression. Thus it is not surprising that the AFT strike leaders, propelled by what Professor Richard Hofstadter has called "the full-bloom bravado of their actionist creed," were able to make quick and easy connection with those faculty members who felt that the "body on the line" tactic was the only way to meet the emergency. The strikers' urgency ("Unless our strike demands are met, San Francisco State may not survive") did not allow consideration of anything as abstract or remote as what a striking faculty member in the humanities deplored as "ivory tower research instead of standing up for humane goals and values." An underlying theme of their strike rhetoric was that empirical research is the safe refuge of the social scientist who prefers—the language is that of a striking graduate student in English—"research inaction to moral action and winds up a reactionary supporting Reagan and Hayakawa." As David Riesman pointed out, the white radical activists tended to regard research "almost as black activists do: as Whitey's hangup: 'We know already we should act. We don't need to go find out. Society is rotten, and research a delaying tactic.' "[5] By throwing themselves into action intended to shut down the college, the faculty members on strike dissociated themselves from those of their colleagues who did not wish to turn their scholarship (or classrooms) into instruments of political action. Furthermore, the nonstriking faculty members felt themselves to be as moral as those on the picket line.

The members of the faculty who went on strike with the AFT local claimed they were fighting for academic freedom, improved working conditions, social and racial justice, and so forth. They repeatedly announced that these goals were the principles they believed in. The irony of their position was that they fought for their principles by attacking the principle of majority rule. As already noted, the AFT had failed to win the support of the faculty majority through the mechanism of the mailed ballot. The conclusion drawn by the AFT leaders was that it was more necessary than ever to resort to direct and decisive strike action—among other reasons (in a then current idiom) "to open fresh areas of consciousness" in those who needed to be "freed" from the limitations and errors of their thinking. As members of a culture of confrontation, the AFT strike leaders talked incessantly about the climate of repression at the college and its stifling academic conformism. To the black student militants leading their own strike, the repression on campus reflected the repression in the rest of society, which, as far as they were concerned, was openly blatant by virtue of the fact that America was capitalist, racist, and imperialist. But the notion of repression was given a different and more subtle meaning by many AFT faculty members. In their view repression at San Francisco State was indirect and hidden. It essentially worked in the mind. Most of the faculty, so the argument went, do not know they are repressed, and those who do know, e.g., those on strike, should try to free them. It was plainly an elitist concept because it implied, as Professor Zbigniew Brzezinski had observed in another connection, that by some miraculous redemption only they had become free of this bondage. Now it was their mission (and the strike was their method) to make "free men" out of their reluctant colleagues and liberate them from their unconscious state of enslavement.

Prolonged involvement in the crisis took a strange toll on everyone who was close to it. One example was the subtle but perceptible change in the meaning of words. Old and traditional meanings gave way to varying forms of self-serving rhetoric that mirrored an individual's personal biases and was used to justify his "side." The ancient Greek historian Thucydides understood what one English major has called "this slide into linguistic ambiguity." After five years of conflict between Athens and Sparta, he observed:

> Words began to change their ordinary meaning, and to take on that which was not given them. Reckless audacity came to be considered the courage of a loyal ally; prudent hesitation, specious cowardice; moderation was held to be a cloak for unmanliness; ability to see all sides of a question, inaptness to act on any.

This is what happened after months of strike action and steadily escalating tension. In the militant world view of things held by many striking faculty members, anyone's call for patience and moderation, or winding down the confrontation by working through established academic channels, was regarded as "gutless" or "liberal bullshit." The sight of striking faculty members walking the picket line shouting in unison "Power to the people" drove home two points: (1) that student and faculty radicals were using this slogan not for democratic majoritarian purposes, but for its symbolic value in enlisting partisans who would join in the "struggle for freedom," which in this case meant closing the college until their demands were met; and (2) that such contempt for language and the cogent use of words encouraged the appeal to raw emotions and the destruction of orderly processes of thought.

Trotsky once remarked that the success or failure of a revolution depends on the way the beleaguered elite responds. If it is split, the hordes will pour through the gates. In the university the elite is the faculty, and one of the reasons the university is so susceptible to the tactics of disruption is that the faculty is almost always hopelessly divided, especially when a campus is undergoing a crisis of serious proportions.

It quickly became obvious that under emergency conditions the San Francisco State faculty was unable to govern itself. The spectacle of mass faculty meetings, at which dozens of hastily drawn motions were introduced and ringing pronouncements and denunciations were made as everyone engaged in a frantic search for the general will, had to be experienced to be believed. But something else happened that was even more disturbing. The organized political minority on the faculty saw the mass forums as an opportunity to be seized. Capitalizing on the decline of leadership and faculty confusion, the activist leaders and supporters of the strike manifested a readiness to impose their standards and will on the unorganized majority by the processes of countless resolutions, endless debate, and continuous confrontation. A large audience of faculty, uncertain of what to do or how to proceed, was frequently responsive to the appeal of moral certitude and the call to action. The occasional suggestion (if it was heard) that the secret ballot—"that enemy of enforced consensus"— might perhaps be an appropriate way to determine faculty opinion was swept aside by fierce rhetoric in which polemical skill at the microphone replaced thoughtful examination of the issues and quiet listening gave way to diatribe.

As the strike wore on, most members of the faculty concluded that AFT local 1352 was not so much a union as a political faction. They rejected the strike because they believed it was the wrong strike at the wrong time led by the wrong people. They had raised a critical question from the very beginning: by what right did a small minority of union activists feel it could try to impose its strike and ideology on everyone else? These were the self-appointed moralists who, with little support from their colleagues, regarded every rejection of their demands as further confirmation of their right to call a halt to all teaching and to suspend the academic program. The real danger lay in their wish and determination to politicize the college or, failing that, to shut it down. As one member of the faculty put it in resigning from the union, "The tactics of the AFT, its style, its bullying, its covert alliance with mindless and irresponsible elements on the campus, its betrayal of common sense and decency, its fickleness, its doctrinaire reductivist sloganizing, its playing at revolution—these and much more clearly reveal an apocalyptic and immoral autointoxication that I find repulsive."

A single incident betrayed the arrogance of the union leadership. The president of the union, in a letter to all members of the faculty, arbitrarily divided them into "friend versus enemy." He announced the union's attitude belligerently: "You will not have the luxury of nice distinctions or Byzantine excuses," he told us, overlooking the fact that a community of teachers and scholars has a specific responsibility to make distinctions—nice, Byzantine, or otherwise. "He who observes our picket line is a friend—any one who plans to cross will be subject to moral force." Among others on the faculty, I was subject to more than moral force which, although unknown in origin, revealed the conditions that had become all too familiar. One night around twelve o'clock I was awakened by a phone call from a faculty member who was one of the leaders of the union strike. "As a liberal we had expected you out there on the picket line with your brothers.

You'll have to pay the consequences," he warned. "Don't threaten me," I said. "I'm not threatening," he replied. "I'm just informing you." My wife, whom I had asked to listen to the conversation on the kitchen extension, could not believe what she had heard.

Several days later I got up one morning to find our two cars vandalized. During the night, persons unknown had slashed all eight tires. They had also painted on the back of my car the words "facist scab." They had misspelled "fascist" but they got "scab" right.

Then, in February, came the classroom disturbances.

After the first meeting of the class I asked for an appointment with the police captain who was in charge of police operations on the campus. I told him I would like the Tactical Squad removed from the auditorium. "I'm quite sure I can handle the situation without their presence," I said. "It's your class. We'll do it your way," he replied. I pointed out that some two dozen heavy boots sticking out from beneath the stage curtain looked a little silly and did not really help. "I'm going to have the curtain pulled on Wednesday so that everyone can see the police are gone." I was not naive. I did not anticipate a peaceful meeting simply because the police were gone, but I wanted it unmistakably clear that I was there, alone, for only one purpose—to get the course under way for those who wanted to take it. The police captain agreed to go along. "But our men will be in the building in case there's any trouble," he said.

The disrupters returned for the second session. I began with a general statement about what the course would be about and some of my own ideas as to procedures and purposes.

BUNZEL   My premise is that before we can accept or reject any point of view, we need to consider all the arguments being advanced.

Shouts of derision. Students on their feet. Demands for recognition.

STUDENT   When we raise our hands, you should respond to that hand being up in the air as soon as it goes up.

BUNZEL   I will be glad to answer all questions at the end of the class after I have had a chance to outline . . .

STUDENT   Answer them now.

BUNZEL   Before we can begin to make some sense out of the tremendous complexities of community power, we will need . . .

STUDENT   Hey, Bunzel, you know community power comes out
           of the barrel of a gun. Hey, don't you know that?

More shouting and whistling from all sides of the auditorium.

BUNZEL   We will look at a variety of studies and approaches that
           have been developed over a period of many years.
STUDENT   Some of the things you say we don't understand. I'm
           asking you to come down to our level.
BUNZEL   I can't hear your question.
STUDENT   Man, you haven't been hearing all your life.
BUNZEL   I will recognize one question at a time.
STUDENT   What you're saying doesn't mean anything anyway.

Great cheers. Then a half dozen questions were shouted simultaneously.

STUDENT   I don't see anything on the reading list from a communist
           perspective. I don't see anything written by Stokely Car-
           michael. How about Huey Newton?
BUNZEL   There are hundreds of books and articles that have been
           omitted.
STUDENT   Answer the question, pig.
BUNZEL   Those of you who have read some of the books . . .
STUDENT   The books on the reading list are racist.
BUNZEL   There are no racist books on the list. Not Robert Dahl,
           or C. Wright Mills, or Robert Lynd. By what standards
           are these writers . . .
STUDENT   If you put it on the list, nine times out of ten it's a
           racist book.

Wild applause.

STUDENT   All an A will mean in your class is excellent in racism,
           B will symbolize good in racism . . .
BUNZEL   I want to make a final observation for today.
STUDENT   All observations you make this semester will probably
           be final.

Deafening cheers.

BUNZEL   I want to inform you that this class will not be allowed
           to continue under these conditions. I would also ask
           whether those of you who are not of a mind to permit
           me to teach this course wish to be here on Friday. I

intend to teach this course as it has always been taught—openly, freely, with opportunity for discussion. No one should have to shout to be heard.

Hoots of derision.

STUDENT   If we have to bring guns in here, you won't teach it. We'll teach you about community power.

Roars of approval.

BUNZEL   This class is dismissed. We will meet here on Friday.

On Friday I tried again, but the shouting and heckling continued. I knew what was going to happen today if I was not permitted to begin the course. I had carefully worked out plans with the college administration and the police. They would wait for a signal from me before making their move. Again the disrupters were on their feet before I had a chance to say anything. They hurled the usual epithets at me from all sides. One student, more charitable than the others, called me an "educated pig." Another called me "stupid" when I referred to Plato. "Plato's a ding-a-ling," he shouted. Several students were screaming quotations from Chairman Mao's Red Book. And so it went. I stood silently for a few moments. Then I read the following statement that I had carefully prepared in consultation with the college's attorney:

> I am obliged to inform you that your conduct is making it impossible for me and the other students in this course to conduct this class in a manner appropriate to the basic purposes of the academic community and to the particular procedures which have been openly, carefully and clearly set forth at this and previous meetings. I ask you to cease in your interruptions and disturbance of the business of this class. If you do not find this course suitable to your own interests, then I respectfully ask you to leave so that those who wish to remain may be allowed to pursue their own education.
>
> If you are not willing to accept this reasonable request and if you persist in your present disruptive behavior, you are hereby warned that you will be subject to immediate disciplinary action. I ask again that you stop your tactics of interruptions so that I may conduct this class in a manner that will allow me to be heard in the proper academic setting.

I read it again. More catcalls and defiant shouts. I stepped away from the lectern. A college official rose on cue and, pointing to students all over the auditorium, announced their immediate suspension, citing provisions of the California Education Code. "This student, this student, that student, you, you, you. . . ." At this point two campus security guards came down one aisle. Only two of the disrupters were apprehended. The rest ran up the other aisle and escaped through the rear door. It turned out later that no one was positively certain of the names of those who had fled the hall. Students complained about an identity crisis, but these security guards had an identification crisis.

I had invited Ernest Besig, the executive director of the American Civil Liberties Union of Northern California, to attend this particular class session. His credentials as a civil libertarian were impeccable. Furthermore, he knew of my own deep and long-standing commitment to First Amendment freedoms. I wanted him to be there so that he could see for himself what took place. At the end of the stormy meeting he came up to me, shook his head sadly, and said: "I have only one complaint. You were much too patient. I would have thrown them out in five minutes." Besig later told a reporter for the *New York Times*: "That was a rough place out there. Much of the disturbance came from girls. There were all kinds of questions, everybody talking at once, and someone was trying to sell papers while Dr. Bunzel was trying to lecture. Obviously," he went on, "it was a planned effort to disrupt the class. Bunzel was called stupid. I couldn't make out precisely what he was stupid about." He voiced surprise that only two students had been suspended for their disruptive tactics. He said eight or ten others could have been suspended "for interfering with the academic freedom of Dr. Bunzel and the serious students." He then announced that the American Civil Liberties Union would not intervene in behalf of those who had been charged with disruptive behavior.

Mr. Besig understood that the inviolability of the classroom is a principle that cannot be compromised because it involves, as he told the press, nothing less than the integrity of the academic process. What was particularly distressing and shameful was that this view was not shared by all of my faculty colleagues. After the disturbances were over and the class was moved back to its regular classroom, a resolution was introduced in the Academic Senate by history professor Theodore Treutlein reaffirming the right of the student to learn and the teacher to teach. It further asserted that any denial of such rights was unacceptable to the college community and that the Academic Senate would support the obligation of the administration and faculty to protect these rights. Nineteen members voted to support the resolution, but twelve either voted against it or abstained. As Professor Treutlein would say many times in the years that followed, the refusal of twelve members of the faculty to defend a colleague's academic freedom was one of the low points of his career and a sad day for the Senate. It was difficult to have much respect for those faculty members belonging to the American Federation of Teachers who, as members of the Senate, had put their political beliefs and preferences ahead of their commitment to one of the central values of academic life that transcends in importance any other divisions that might exist. If a faculty cannot agree that the classroom is inviolate, then it has moved one step closer to turning the academic community into a cockpit of ideologues and fanatics.

———— • ————

"But why you?"

I was asked that question more than any other throughout the turbulent year. Why had I been singled out for harassment and intimidation? One answer came from a former student of mine who at one time belonged to the left-wing Students for a Democratic Society (SDS). We were having coffee together in my office one afternoon, talking quietly about the crisis at San Francisco State. We had talked like this many times before. Although we did not agree on many political matters, we were good friends and had always spoken easily and candidly to each other. She had dropped out of SDS and began to tell me why. She had sat in on too many all-night sessions recently in which there was more and more talk about the need for violence. This bothered her. She had also been very upset, she said, about the attacks on me by black and white student militants. She paused for a moment and then smiled. "Would you like to know why you have been made a target?"

"I would," I said.

"I don't know who put the bomb here or vandalized your car at home or things like that," she said, "but I know why it's you. It's because you are a liberal. You're a perfect symbol of everything the student radicals hate. You believe in reason, you're open to different ideas, you're tolerant. When you talk in public, your arguments are organized and persuasive. Furthermore, you're white, you're over forty, and you have a Ph.D. You are a department chairman. You write books and articles and appear on television. You don't stay silent. You speak your mind. But worst of all," she said, "you're a liberal. You're part of the liberal establishment. You were on the Kennedy delegation before he was shot, you're opposed to the Vietnam War, you believe in racial justice. The radicals see you as their real enemy because you believe in change and free speech and equality and all the liberal values which undermine their tactics and goals. You're the kind of liberal who blocks their revolution"—in the same way, we agreed, that tolerance and discussion and democracy always reduce the potential for revolution. This was the "repressive tolerance" people like Herbert Marcuse were enthusiastic about at the time.

She was right. I was an academic liberal with the traditional credentials to prove it. I regarded conservatism in America as lacking intellectual respectability. I had taken on in print and public debates right-wing extremists who emerged in the heyday of Joe McCarthy and later in the John Birch Society and in George Wallace's movement. As a civil libertarian, I regularly defended the individual's political rights against the heavy hand of authority. Championing an economic liberalism that elevated equality over liberty, I supported an activist welfare state that promoted the economic rights of the poor and the powerless. What my friend didn't know and couldn't know—I was only dimly aware of it myself amid all of the agitation of mind and feelings I was experiencing that year—was that my liberal orthodoxy was being bent in ways that would make it impossible for me to straighten back into all of the old configurations.

When my brother was on campus during the strike, he wanted to talk to Nathan Hare. He sent him a note that revealed his identity— "the worst at the start: I'm Jack Bunzel's brother"—and asked for an appointment. Hare agreed. At one time in his career a professional boxer (which may explain why he once challenged me to a fight), Hare is a short, brawny man who speaks in a staccato fashion. "Liberals like Jack have had it," he told my brother. "He's from a different time and place. He *talks*, we *do*. The reason you find blacks setting bombs and lighting firebombs—and I don't admit they do—is to make themselves heard. They want academic freedom too. They have every right to disrupt classrooms."

I told my brother that was pure nonsense. I had told Hare the same thing many times. He was certainly entitled to whatever views about me he wanted, but I vigorously opposed his notion that he and his supporters somehow had a right to take over the campus by force and violence. A college has no elaborate mechanisms of self-protection, which is why it is always vulnerable to those who would use power, pressure, and muscle. I had thought that every member of the academic community, and especially those who prided themselves on their liberalism, would oppose the use of violence as a tactic to hijack the campus. I was wrong. There were many liberals who could posture with the good causes but skillfully avoided the deep waters of tough decisions required to deal with difficult and conflict-ridden problems that were having a serious impact on the college.

An important part of my own education throughout the year was what I learned about many white liberals on the faculty. For example, I discovered that they would do almost anything to avoid being called a racist. If a white student radical made a suggestion that went beyond all standards of what is right or decent, they did not hesitate to call it by its right name—wrongheaded or outrageous. But if it came from a black militant, they would say, "That's an idea worth thinking about." If the white members of SDS went on a rampage and tried to tear the college apart, many liberals would call for their immediate suspension. But when members of the Black Students Union used intimidation and violence to try to get their way, they said, "These students have something important to tell us." Blind to their own feelings of guilt and self-doubt, they could not see that they were treating black students in a patronizing manner. Their real preference, of course, was to avoid having to deal with the problem at all.[6]

The problem had larger overtones. The issue was academic freedom. When freedom to teach and to learn become imperiled, when libraries are ransacked, when professors are threatened, when ungovernable passions are deliberately inflamed, it is not important to inquire too much whether such extraordinary attacks come from blacks or whites or from the far left or the far right. What is important is that they become central facts of our existence, as they were for six months at San Francisco State. Those who condoned or approved them because of their particular source revealed a failure of sensibility, of philosophical clarity, of rationality and understanding of what academic freedom really is. Liberals and militants of the left have always jealously guarded against any incursions from the far right. It has both depressed and angered me that they do not always show an equal determination or readiness to react to the more novel threats in this area when they come from within their own ranks. They should be among the first to point out that this moral duplicity and double standard has the suggestion of fanaticism at its worst.

I take it as an article of faith that when freedom of thought and speech is attacked or suppressed, those of every political persuasion must take their stand in opposition. It used to be that the severest threats to academic freedom came from outside—in a word, from the primitives of the far right—with the result that the faculty was almost instantly united. But at San Francisco State in the late sixties, when the assaults came from inside and from the new brand of left-wing political moralists, the faculty was just as instantly divided. If the threat had been white and right instead of black and left, the faculty would have been close to unanimous. The attack on academic freedom from the left, of course, is by no means always tied to black militancy and extremism. But the question remains: when principles that are fundamental to the academic community are cynically exploited by the extremists of the left, why do so many liberal and moderate members of the faculty refuse to stand up to those who would impose their will by threats or coercion?

During the week that the student militants attempted to take over my class, I was astonished at some of the thoughts and comments expressed to me by many of my liberal colleagues on how I should handle the situation. The burden of their counsel was that under no circumstances should I call the campus police. "If you do that," one of them said, "you will be setting up a little fascist state in your own classroom." Another colleague said, "Instead of calling the police, why don't you show movies until the black students cool off?" I told him this course did not have movies. "Look," he said, "it's you the blacks are after. If you show movies instead of lecturing, the heat will be off." I tried to explain to him that the issue was my right to teach in the way I wanted and believed was most appropriate to the subject matter of the course. "If you do that, you'll only continue the confrontation," he replied, and walked away. Others suggested I use guest speakers or, if that did not seem practical, give the students a "research assignment" that would keep them in the library all semester—"anything to keep you out of the classroom." As one faculty member put it, "It's your presence up there on the platform that's provoking the militants." I said, "If I'm so provocative, maybe I should cancel the course altogether." "No, you don't have to go that far," he replied, taking me seriously. "But maybe there's somebody else in your department who could teach it this semester. Is that a possibility?" I told him it was not even remotely possible and that he was missing the point. Another professor took a different line. Instead of calling the police, he said I should "try to hold out against the disrupters by outlasting them. Even if it should take weeks," he added, "at least they'll be too busy in your class to break up anyone else's." He was serious. So were many others. They believed strongly in academic freedom, as they were all quick to point out. They just wanted to avoid any personal confrontation over it. They preferred their academic freedom in the abstract, pure and untested.

Many members of the faculty, especially those with a strong commitment to the liberal values of free development and protection of the individual, were profoundly cross-pressured during the months of violence and disruption. It troubled me that in spite of the evidence all around them, they continued to talk and behave as if there were no enemies on the left. With great self-righteousness they regularly denounced the right-wing elements off campus that were capitalizing on the explosive situation for their own political purposes, which was true enough. But they either refused or were unable to see that the left-wing forces *on campus* were subverting the very liberal principles they professed to support and on which the academic community depends for its life's breath. They had some overlapping sympathies with their colleagues on the left—civil liberties, social justice, the egalitarian ethic, and the like—but often disapproved of their unilateral methods and, in particular, the AFT faculty strike. The result of this split in their views was that they became, consciously or unconsciously, victims of a form of psychological and moral intimidation practiced by the radicals. In contrast, for example, to those for whom the need for strike action was unambiguous and whose moral vision was unobstructed, they were made to appear weak and vacillating. The immediate and practical consequence was to silence the middle, or, to put it another way, to engender the feeling that there was something shameful about speaking out or being in opposition. This had nothing to do with physical coercion. It was a subtle but effective control over people who might normally have spoken out but who, in an increasingly politicized and polarized arena, imposed their own self-restraints and remained silent or otherwise preoccupied.

Thus I watched many liberal faculty members resolve whatever personal conflict they may have felt by withdrawing altogether, on the grounds that "the problems were too massive" and the situation too volatile. Furthermore, the student and faculty militants on the left had outflanked them by establishing a powerful claim—vouchsafed by action—on certain words and ideas. It was the kind of cross-pressure that elicited in many faculty members the desire to remain "uninvolved."

On March 26, 1969, I testified before a House Subcommittee on Education probing student disorders. The committee's counsel had phoned two weeks before to ask if I would be willing to talk about my own activities and involvement since September and, drawing on my experiences, to discuss the crisis at San Francisco State. He explained to me that Edith Green, who chaired the committee, was particularly anxious to have me tell my story because, as he put it, "there are many liberals on the committee who share your political position and values who would like to hear firsthand what happened to you, and why."

Room 2261 of the Rayburn House Office Building provided a sharp contrast to my besieged classroom at the beginning of the semester. The audience in the high-ceilinged chamber was silent and attentive. Congressman Philip Burton of San Francisco added his own personal welcome, pointing out to the members of the committee that we were personal friends and had served together on the 1968 Democratic Convention delegation from California. Presiding was Democratic Congresswoman Green of Oregon, gray-haired, bespectacled, and businesslike, firm in her control of the hearing and fair and courteous throughout.

Facing the committee from the witness table, I gave my account of not only some of the incidents in which I had been personally involved but the larger problems that had emerged as a consequence of the new and heightened political pressures and passions that had intruded themselves into every facet of campus life. Congressman Louis Stokes, a black Democrat from Ohio and brother of the mayor of Cleveland, wondered if my radical tormentors might have been showing their disdain for liberals "who always jump to the defense of the Constitution and the principles of the American Civil Liberties Union but are really doing nothing about the inequities and the wrongs that exist in this society. Isn't this, in effect, why they are really disgusted with those who profess liberalism?"

"I think many of them feel that very strongly," I replied. "Part of it, of course, is that their vision or time span is different from that of someone who is, say, over forty. But when I am asked if liberals have ever done anything, I always have two answers: 'Yes, we have. But we still have much to do.' "

"Yes, but it is the slow process, this process of saying, 'Wait, be patient.' It is pretty difficult after 350 years to say to one sector of the society: 'You must continue to wait and be patient. We are going to take care of you one day.' "

"I assume you are talking about the young blacks in America

who now feel it is one minute to midnight and that time has run out.''

"The young blacks," he said, "and those who have now expressed sympathy with this cause, the whites who are also saying this."

"I would distinguish the people who want to move with urgency and make the system work from those in SDS who are ready to use whatever methods they can to destroy the system," I replied. "I am with you on the former, but I oppose the latter."

For two hours the committee members took turns asking questions. At the end of my testimony Congressman Stokes looked down from the elevated committee table and observed, "I just want to say to Dr. Bunzel that after hearing his recounting of his experiences, I certainly hope your alienation from the black community at San Francisco State is not permanent, because I think from having heard some of your principles enunciated here today that they have lost a very valuable ally."

"I can't tell you," I said, "how much your comments mean to me."

———— • ————

I spent 1969–1970 as a visiting scholar in the serene environment of the Center for Advanced Study in the Behavioral Sciences, a so-called "think tank" overlooking the Stanford campus. Each year the center provides some fifty men and women a chance to rediscover the pleasures of reading, writing, and reflection in an incomparable setting—what Professor Daniel Bell has fondly described as "the leisure of the theory class." One of its greatest virtues was that apart from deciding whether to play volleyball every noon or join the luncheon wine-tasting group (or both), there were no other decisions to make for twelve months.

For me, the year at the center served as a "decompression chamber." It gave me time to reflect on my own involvement in the events at San Francisco State and how the disorders of the late sixties had affected my "liberal mode of sensibility." In 1968, I campaigned for Hubert Humphrey for president (he was a friend and a man I had admired since the 1940s when he was first elected to the U.S. Senate) against Richard Nixon, but four years later I did not vote for either George McGovern or Richard Nixon. The Democratic Party had moved to the left under McGovern and the "new liberals," with the result that millions of Democrats defected and helped elect

President Nixon to a second term. Although no longer a "certified camp follower," I did not leave the Democratic Party. I voted for Jimmy Carter in 1976, and never voted for Ronald Reagan either for governor of California or for president. But my increasing alienation from many of the policies of those who dominated the national Democratic Party led me to join other disaffected Hubert Humphrey–Henry Jackson Democrats who supported the Coalition for a Democratic Majority, of which I think it can be said, regrettably but fairly, that never have so few been led by so many.

Unlike the journey of many intellectuals, writers, and others who at some point in their lives have renounced their political past, mine involved neither guilt nor self-deprecation, which is one reason I did not go through a process of recantation. There was no radical swing from left to right, no conversion to a new political church. Nevertheless, there was significant change. Toward the end of the year of upheaval and violence at San Francisco State I knew that the center of my political and moral gravity had shifted, resulting in my estrangement from a liberal-left outlook and temperament that I now realized had too often been characterized by habitual and uncritical thinking. In the years to come it was not always clear whether I had moved away from political positions I had long held or the rapidly changing culture and society simply made many of my views that were grounded in fundamental liberal values—for example, opposition to racial discrimination and quotas, or to the rampant "do your own thing" virus and "anything goes" dogma, or to the totalitarian mind-set of those who "bury their brains" in Havana or Hanoi—appear outmoded and irrelevant. But one thing was certain. The unreconstructed liberalism I had worn on my sleeve for more than two decades as a badge of my own authenticity no longer had the instant and reflexive ring of conviction.

However, I was concerned with more than the various strands of American liberalism (it has never had a single coherent theory). In the sixties as well as in the 1970s, I found myself increasingly repelled by the behavior of many left liberals in and out of the academic world. I have in mind instances not only of their hypocrisy (many of the wealthiest liberals, for example, were the most ardent advocates of busing for purposes of racial integration, yet wouldn't think of sending their children to public schools) but of their "selective intolerance" in action, for which I cultivated a healthy disrespect. I think of the faculty members and students who led campus teach-ins during the Vietnam War, sometimes praising the courage of Ho Chi Minh and the Vietcong but always denouncing the United States for its imperialism and racism. There was little attempt to illuminate, let alone to debate, the range of issues that surrounded the war because the war, as viewed from the moral enclaves of the "America stinks" crowd, was not open to dispute.[7] Or the time right after Martin Luther King was assassinated when six or eight liberal-left notables were returning by plane from Vanderbilt University where they had participated in a panel debate. As they approached Washington and Baltimore, someone turned on a radio. There was an anticipatory buzz of pleasure in the group at the news of the cities on fire. They rushed toward the front windows to get a better view of the burning cities, shouting their glee at the revolutionary ardor that had set the fires and glorying in the wounds inflicted on these troubled communities. Yet this was a time of crisis, and I can still recall the pain and sadness I felt as I watched these cities in flames on the evening news. I had seen violent behavior given legitimacy at San Francisco State by those who regarded it as a "cleansing force" and a weapon of liberation. In Baltimore, Watts, and other urban centers, it was also being cheered by those on the political left who justified violence as a form of social and moral regeneration. Once again I knew the gap that separated us.

In developing my own conceptual base and method of examining political and social questions during the past twenty years, it is hard for me to classify as either liberal or conservative the way I have tried to think about different issues. I am much more hardheaded today about the realities of politics at home and abroad (using William James's distinction between the "tough-minded" and "tender-minded"), which has led to a new skepticism and independence in my efforts to pull together various approaches into a paradigm of my own. I continue to support the basic underpinnings of the welfare state, a mixed economy, and a strong national defense, as well as the movements for women's rights, homosexual rights, and legal abortion. As a supporter of Martin Luther King's vision of an America free of every form of racial division and hatred, I found little to cheer about in the exclusionary movement of black nationalism, black extremism, and black separatism that in the late sixties and seventies stood opposed to what was called the "pathetic pursuit of white values." In testimony before a subcommittee of the Democratic Party prior to its 1976 presidential nominating convention, I urged it to reject the arbitrary imposition of preset mathematical proportions for certain groups in the delegate selection process, on the ground that Democrats do not believe that only a black can represent a black, a woman a woman, a Pole a Pole, or a college professor a college professor.

I have also come to believe that much of the permissive society that arose in the years of affluence has made a mockery of certain liberal values. I agree with Harvard historian Oscar Handlin that the fight against censorship has often been reduced to absurdity. The liberating doctrine in the cases of *Ulysses* and *Lady Chatterley's Lover* had rested upon the "redeeming social value" of great literature. But that qualification has disappeared. There is no pretense of redeeming social value in the steadily escalating scope of pornography. Out of a growing concern about the forces of disintegration in our society, I am now more inclined than ever before to consider the interests and demands of the community before invoking the language of unfettered individualism.

I have found other features of the traditional liberal perspective inadequate. For many years I had no demonstrable theory about the relationship between organized labor and society. It was part of my code—the liberal's code—never to criticize labor, which I think was understandable when the American trade union movement was still too weak to challenge the economic power of big business. Now, however, I find that the political rhetoric of many liberals is too often ill-equipped to deal with some of the exigencies of our highly bureaucratized society—for example, the problems of oligarchy in large-scale organizations such as trade unions. While I remain firmly committed to the efforts of working men and women to achieve social and economic equity, I do not believe that all of the current grievances against labor can be rejected simply as the familiar rantings of "union-busting reactionaries" or that liberals should automatically assent to whatever the unions say or want.

In the 1970s, when I was president of San Jose State University, I did not go along with many on the liberal left on some controversial educational issues. On the question of bilingual education, I was critical of bilingual programs that allowed students to linger on the margins of American life. I disagreed especially with those who said that the psychic costs of "Americanization," which includes the critical idea that a single common language is a strong force in binding this diverse continental nation together, were too high. (I had heard the same charge made by leaders of the black power movement in the 1960s, who said that American culture was an alien culture so injurious to the self-esteem of blacks that only institutions run by

blacks could repair the psychological damage of American racism.)
Although I have never favored a constitutional amendment making
English our official language, I have long felt that those who enter
our schools unable to read, write, speak, or understand English need
special help so that they can learn the language of jobs and success
in this country. Further, I have never thought that the bilingual
movement should be in the business of promoting group consciousness
and cultural separatism that can lead to a passive or even active
hostility toward American society. For generations this country has
represented values and opportunities that people who came here
were eager to embrace and that went far beyond ethnic affiliations.
It was not too long ago that liberals trumpeted the same theme and
were among the first to express their pride in the important role of
the schools in helping newcomers to our shores to participate in the
American dream by transmitting many of those values. Today, many
on the political left dismiss such talk of "Americanization" as a conservative (meaning spurious) idea, while many Hispanic and other minority leaders regard it as a threat to their political power.

I also developed a special contempt for liberal academics who
do not hold blacks to the same standards as whites—sometimes because the standards of definition are considered "white standards"
and therefore racist. "You would give a black kid an A for work
which would merit C from another student," the eminent Catholic
teacher and writer Andrew M. Greeley observed, "partly because
you felt guilty and partly because you were afraid he'd call you a
racist if you didn't." I had run into the liberal's guilt at San Francisco
State and knew that it could take many forms. Sociologist Sanford
Dornbusch of Stanford University has pointed out that black students
who do poorly are the most likely to report they are being praised
by their teachers, thereby getting "unrealistic images of their effort
and achievement." Put simply, they are not aware of how badly
educated they are. "Teachers now are expressing warmth toward
minority students without accompanying their friendliness with chal-
lenging academic standards. This," says Dornbusch, "is just as debili-
tating to students as the old overt hostility." One may argue whether
or not it is discrimination to favor blacks (or anyone else) by praising
them when they have not earned it. In my view it is worse. It is
condescending. Dornbusch calls it "institutional racism." I think liberals should be among the first to see their behavior for what it is.

One of the reasons the late 1960s were a watershed period in
my life is that they led to a reordering of certain basic values—to

take an important example, the rearrangement of some of my ideas about equality in America. Ever since my undergraduate days I had looked upon freedom and equality as "two virtues" standing together rather than in conflict with each other. Equality seemed to exist in my thinking almost in isolation, untempered by any sense of its connections with other values. I had embraced, in effect, a slogan or a utopian ideal rather than a political principle that could be made part of our lives and coordinated with other cherished beliefs. I favored strong governmental action to eliminate all of society's inequalities, as if this were "the only legitimate beginning of political life." The real problem for me now, however, is the noticeable and important differences between freedom and equality. I was recently struck by the observation of an Israeli socialist who said that those nations that have put freedom ahead of equality have ended up doing better by equality than those with the reverse priority.

The change for me is that over the years I have discovered I care as much for freedom as I do for equality. I am no longer satisfied with a social calculus that is blind to the fact that equality is not an absolute and should be inseparable from evaluating each person according to his or her individual merits and qualities, as well as inseparable from fair play, evenhandedness, and the like. This does not mean that I value equality less. It simply means that I do not view equality as the only goal of a democratic society. And I have come to appreciate the observation of England's Professor John P. Plamenatz that equality of opportunity in a free society differs from equality of opportunity in a society that is merely equalitarian.

———— • ————

In December 1980, while driving back from the city late on a Sunday afternoon, I stopped at San Francisco State. It was cold and getting dark. No one was around. As I walked across the campus, I could not help but remember the pervasive grimness of the place when it erupted twelve years earlier and became less a college than a battlefield. The striking teachers and student militants kept saying that what they had been doing all year was "saving" higher education in California. Yet the political reality was they had helped to galvanize a large majority of Californians into a kind of mass public motivated to act not with sympathy but out of anger. As I listened to the militants shouting day after day "Power to the people!" I realized they had become so intoxicated by their call to "revolutionary" ac-

tion—to strike, to occupy buildings, and to disrupt the college—
that they didn't know, or didn't care, who the people were who
really had the power.

The protracted struggle of 1968–1969 left scars on practically everyone. A number of friendships I had made during the 1950s and
1960s—and virtually all of my friends at the time were solidly liberal
or left—were broken, some never to be repaired. My intellectual
and political journey has its roots in the serious damage I saw inflicted
on an academic community I cared for, and some of those who helped
create an atmosphere of political division and enmity were colleagues
I had known well. I saw firsthand that the tactics of harassment,
intimidation, and lawbreaking were not the exclusive preserve of
the political wildlife on the right. The left had its own share of
hooligans who were willing to plant bombs and rough up those who
got in their way.

Today, my circle of friends includes socialists (there aren't too
many around any more), left liberals (the academic world is one of
their natural habitats), conservatives (neo- and not so neo-), libertari-
ans, and others who, like myself, are often given labels that are
seldom enlightening. I still remain hungry for intellectual stimulation,
only now I like to search about for ideas and arguments that come
from people who have wide and divergent interests and whose political
views may be sharply different from my own. In my odyssey I have
passed through many transition points and, along the way, have confirmed my commitment to such things as the importance of middle-
class values, the "beneficence of capitalism," and the special qualities
of our democracy. At the same time, I also recognize more clearly
than I ever did before the potentials within human beings for radical
evil and creative good.

By the end of the 1960s, the political center was in a state of
disorder and confusion, battered by crises it seemed unable to manage.
It had lost its moral compass. If I had to designate myself today, it
would be as a hardheaded realist who would like to see the rebuilding
of a "vital center" that would reestablish a new sense of community
and national purpose and provide "a 'moral core' for our public life."

Notes

[1] I am indebted to my brother, Peter D. Bunzel, for giving me years ago his own written
account and notes of his stay on the campus. I have made full use of them in different parts
of this essay where their value cannot be measured—as, for example, in his description (he
was there) of what took place in my class.

[2] On the afternoon of November 5, 1968, the Black Students Union made public their list of
ten "nonnegotiable" demands, including one which ordered the college to establish at once

a black studies department with twenty full-time faculty and staff. They refused the invitation of then president Robert R. Smith to discuss them, insisting on a yes or no answer. Two days later the Third World Liberation Front, a federation of groups whose members are of various nonwhite ethnic backgrounds, added five similar ones. On November 6, the Black Students Union launched a strike against the college.

In the weeks and months that followed a pattern was set. Students were "educated" on the aims of the strike. Teams of strikers, some all black and some all white, would rush into classrooms, announce the class's dismissal, and leave, often with a warning that there might be consequences if the class continued. The strike was used as an instrument of agitation not only to mobilize the already committed, but to radicalize the rest of the student body. The strike leaders understood that before they could seize power, their stated goal, they would have to employ their "guerrilla tactics" with such effectiveness that the college administration would be forced into repressive counteraction that would build support for the strike. Their "war plan" failed, but the strike lasted 133 days.

For an analysis of the ideology and tactics of the student strike, see my " 'War of the Flea' at San Francisco State," *New York Times Magazine*, November 9, 1969. For a more detailed account of the Year of the Strike from the perspective of President Smith's administration, see Robert R. Smith et al., *By Any Means Necessary*, (San Francisco: Jossey-Bass, 1970).

[3] The article in question, "Black Studies at San Francisco State," appeared in the fall issue (1968) of *The Public Interest*.

[4] Leo Litwak, "We Needed a Revolution," *Look*, May 27, 1969, p. 66.

[5] "The Young Are Captives of Each Other: A Conversation with David Riesman," *Psychology Today*, October 1969, p. 32. Professor Riesman writes, "Social Science today is as much feared as a hidden persuader or manipulator of men as a generation ago it was admired as a liberator."

It should be remembered that of the full-time faculty members who made up the hard-core group on strike, approximately 60 percent came from academic fields not connected with the behavioral and social sciences. That figure jumps to 70 percent if the psychology department is added. It is perhaps worth adding that most of the fifteen psychologists who went on strike were not experimentalists but clinicians and therapists who identified strongly not only with the political goals of the student strike but with the "humanity" and "honesty" of the student strikers.

[6] It should also be noted that these same white liberal faculty members, unhinged by guilt, helped to weaken the morale of nonradical black students who did not support the tactics of the militants and were made to feel that they were not "genuine" because of their (the term was used disparagingly) "middle-class values."

[7] The same intolerance by the left had been in evidence during the Cuban missile crisis in 1962. At a student rally at Brandeis, Herbert Marcuse proclaimed to wild applause, "Castro si, Kennedy no!" When challenged to debate by a faculty colleague, the scholar-author Max Lerner, his answer was that there could be no dialogue with a fascist.

6

Looking Backward: Memories of the Sixties Left

Peter Collier

It is true that history did not provide our generation of leftists with a great issue, as Stalin and Soviet communism was for the thirties, which would force a decision either to continue knowingly the commitment to totalitarianism or to denounce past belief and thus risk being stigmatized for apostasy. There was no great Rubicon to cross like the purge trials or the Stalin-Hitler pact. But there have been events over the past two decades—the fate of Vietnam after the U.S. withdrawal, revelations about the Cuban gulag, the invasion of Afghanistan—which should have prompted a rethinking about who exactly we New Leftists were in the sixties, what we did, and the heritage we left. The fact that there has been so little soul-searching reinforces what was obvious at the time—that the New Left, to put it charitably, was not a thinking movement. It was rather a movement that centered on vaunt and braggadocio. It always had an allergic reaction to ideas, and this is what has made it incapable, retrospectively, of grand disillusions. The thirties may have been a low, dishonest decade, but at least the main actors were adults—embracing adult evil and, for some at least, making adult atonement. The sixties were an era of adolescents—lost boys and girls who for the most part never grew up politically and have thus ignored the promptings of history to take stock of the consequences of their acts. This is why it is so difficult to imagine any of the movement heavies writing credibly, let alone eloquently, about such issues as belief and betrayal, about the political dark night of the soul none of them ever confronted.

New Left radicalism hectored the contemporary media into treating it more respectfully than it deserved; social historians since then have been even more generous. The nostalgia artists who write pop history and create the icons of pop culture almost invariably portray the sixties generation as passionate and caring, a collection of dewy-eyed idealists driven to extreme remedies by a world of cruel power. These radicals were right more often than they were wrong, we are told, but whether they were right or wrong is almost irrelevant because they were above all *authentic*.

It is obvious why there should be such affection for the sixties—those good old days when we were all so bad. In truth, however, they were anything but an innocent time. Most of the radicals I knew were, at least by the middle of their journey, confirmed cynics. Their god could never fail because they were atheists to begin with. They never really believed *in* anything. Certainly by the end of the decade their commitment was negative: they were *against* patriotic commitment; they hated the *idea* of America. What we called politics in the sixties was exactly what Lewis Feuer and many of our other political elders tried to say it was before we shouted them down—an Oedipal revolt on a grand scale; a no-fault acting out. We liked to think of ourselves as characters out of Malraux. As I think back on it now, it seems to me that we were always political Katzenjammer kids whose mischief turned homocidal somewhere along the road.

The sixties were a time which existed in the eye of history as few other times have, yet for all this they were oddly ahistorical years. There were great events—a cataclysmic war, assassination and fratricidal strife, the disaffection of an entire generation—yet the time itself has none of the perverse grandeur Arthur Koestler and others managed to salvage from the thirties. This is why the decade plays less authentically in the chambers of memory as tragedy than as melodrama and farce. If there is a tragic resonance in the era it comes from the fact that we have never really come to terms with the way we were then and thus continue to repeat those same destructive patterns in the way we are now.

—·—

Many of the people I came to know in the movement were red-diaper babies who had been political all their lives. They seemed still to be people with a political green card, immigrants who had never allowed themselves to be fully assimilated into America. Their status as aliens made me envious of them; by comparison I felt that I had spent most of my life in America's air-conditioned nightmare, and that my politics were not the outgrowth of an honorable adversarial tradition, but rather homemade and ad hoc. When these red-diaper friends of mine were growing up, I fantasized, they talked about Hegel and Marx at the dinner table. By contrast, my own parents, to the extent they discussed politics at all, focused on such things as FDR's capitulation to Stalin at Yalta and the ominous growth of big government. One of my strongest memories is of a drive our family was taking one afternoon on Sunset Boulevard when I was ten or so. My father saw a newsboy, slammed on the brakes, jumped out of the car, and came back with a paper whose heavy black headlines said that the U.S. was sending troops to Korea. "The bastards have done it to us again," my father said, quickly scanning the story. It was *them* (Washington, big government, etc.) against *us*.

I suppose my political "consciousness," as we radicals grandly used to call it, began in Berkeley in 1959. The city has since become a self-parody: the People's Republic of Berkeley, example of socialism in one city. It is a place where hacks from the Communist Party have been allowed to infiltrate city government (a development immune from discussion lest someone commit an inadvertent "McCarthyism"). It is a place where the school system, once one of the best in the nation, has been crippled by radical schemes and schemers; where elected officials have concentrated on an anti-American "foreign policy" while allowing problems of crime, housing, and economic stagnation to go unchecked; where a merchant, in an elliptical comment on the miasmic bureaucracy that has sprung up over the years of radical rule, posted a sign in his shop that drew universal assent: "Everything that is not expressly forbidden is mandatory." The last time I was there, a sewer had broken and spewed human excrement onto Telegraph Avenue. People were stoically walking through the mess, pretending not to see or smell it. The scene was right out of Kundera and offered itself as a metaphor for Berkeley civic life.

It was different in the late fifties. Berkeley was clean and bright; relatively small, yet conveying a sense of spaciousness; a refuge for creative eccentricity and an arena for personal exploration. California had not yet discovered its identity as a place of cultural early warnings where trends that would sweep the country could be seen a year or so before they arrived elsewhere. Berkeley was a liberated zone of cosmopolitanism within the provincial squareness of the state. Everybody seemed to be writing a novel; everyone was an "existentialist." The city was implicated in the Beatnik happening across the Bay, and indeed, an awed undergraduate might occasionally see Ginsberg and Kerouac themselves strolling down Telegraph Avenue.

But for me Berkeley's primary appeal was that it was not Southern California. I had grown up there thinking of it as the distilled essence of the fifties, a time and place of ponderous boredom, "conformity," and Ike. (Later on, while watching my own kids trying to grow up, I realized that the fifties had been bum-rapped; they were probably the last good time to be a teenager, the last time when culture played its traditional role by providing real rules an individual might define himself by breaking.) When I was a teenager, I could only think of getting away from "L.A.," getting into the *real* world.

I spent the summer of 1958 attending the University of Mexico in Mexico City. At one point a Mexican friend said, "Let's go to help Castro." Several of us tried lackadaisically to arrange for a private yacht like the *Granma* which would take us to Cuba. The deal, which had almost nothing to do with politics, fell through. Instead of going to Havana, I went to Berkeley.

Ann Arbor usually gets the credit for being the birthplace of the New Left because of the Port Huron Statement. But before Tom Hayden and the other founding SDSers made their manifesto, Berkeley was already feeling the first faint tremors of the eruption to come. There were vigils to protest against the execution of "red-light bandit" Caryl Chessman, and sit-ins against racial discrimination on San Francisco's Auto Row. There were demonstrations against HUAC in which the police washed students and other protesters down the steps of the Federal Building with fire hoses, taking obscene pleasure in aiming the spray of water at women and moving it up and down their skirts between their legs. The film *Operation Abolition* played for years afterwards. It might have been taken seriously in the hinterlands, but at Berkeley it was a joke, a little like *Reefer Madness* is now. Joe McCarthy was dead and we had insulted his corpse just as Khrushchev had Stalin's. Nobody knew what to call it yet, but we talked about a new politics that would avoid the ideological ossification of the Soviets as well as America's long status quo.

The first couple of years of JFK's presidency were our equivalent of the phony war. Everything was ready; we were geared up, although we weren't quite sure for what. Some of the people I knew at Berkeley went into the Peace Corps; others began to talk about going south to do civil rights work. There was an inarticulate sense of imminence: we knew that our chrysalis was about to open.

——.——

I was working on a graduate degree in English literature when JFK was assassinated. I realized at the time that something had snapped. It was more than a feeling of loss, or even the stunned comprehension that the era of the lone crazed gunman was at hand. It was more a realization that "the system" was perhaps incapable of protecting itself.

The Free Speech Movement offered many of us our first opportunity to test this proposition. As the protest ripened, this movement proposed that the university was actually an allegory for society at large—a place where power worked secretly to crush personal freedom just as the chancellor crushed our student rights. As we slowly paralyzed the campus by our protest, we felt that we were coming of age in a glorious rush. We would seize our destiny while we were in our prime. We had to because you couldn't trust anyone over thirty.

As the conflict with the university administration reached a head, we had the heady feeling that history was not something one reads about, but something one could actually make. People were *watching* us; we were *on television*. There was also a sense that under all its talk about the importance of rules, the system was riddled with self-doubt. I had always loathed Wordsworth, but as the Alameda sheriffs began to gather shortly before dawn for what would be the first mass arrests of students in decades, I kept thinking about his lines on the French Revolution: to be alive was bliss, and to be young was very heaven.

I found it impossible to pick up my studies where I had dropped them when the FSM began. I could no longer conceive of life as a methodical march through a career and other predictable stages. Now there were CORE marches against employment discrimination in the restaurant row of Oakland's Jack London Square, pickets at William Knowland's dread *Oakland Tribune*. In the spring of 1965, Berkeley had its Vietnam Day, one of the first major teach-ins against the war in the country. Previously Saigon had been a fantasy name like Katmandu or Sri Lanka. Listening to Isaac Deutscher, I. F. Stone, and other speakers, I integrated it into my developing political geography. It was a place, as one speaker said, occupied by American soldiers just as the Alameda County sheriffs had recently occupied our campus.

That summer I went to Birmingham to do voter registration work for SNCC and to teach at Miles College, whose president, Elijah Pitts, reminded me powerfully of the cagey college president in Ralph Ellison's *Invisible Man*. Miles students had been heavily involved in the demonstrations which had caused Bull Connor to unleash his police dogs the previous summer, and the Klan had responded with drive-by shootings. When I got there, President Pitts had hired a group of middle-aged black men in overalls to walk the perimeter of the campus with shotguns. I got to know one of them. His name was Raymond. He once gave me half of his lunch, a sandwich of rich, pungent meat he later told me was possum.

The experience was an intense one which I remember less as a whole than as a series of images frozen in montage. The swooping figure of a commemorative black Christ in stained glass at the Baptist church where three little blacks girls were blown up in a bombing. Whites angrily standing on the periphery wherever we went—people who all seemed to have lank blond hair and recessed chins, a menacing look of inbred sameness. A new bombing in Birmingham with an elderly white-haired black man standing in front of his charred house looking like a photographic negative. Young whites carrying baseball bats like homicidal semipros following us when we tried to register voters.

The Klan chased us every once in a while in rickety pickups. It seemed like some sort of ritual, war games carried out within pre-scribed roles, but once they took a shot at us and the back window of the car we were in collapsed on our shoulders in shards of glass. That was as close as I came to martyrdom.

All the blacks I met that summer idolized Martin Luther King except for a short, coffee-colored SNCC worker named John Jefferson. A director of the voter registration project, he ridiculed King as "Gee-zuz" and "de Lawd." He surprised me by saying during one of our discussions: "Its not important who's got the Bible. Its important who's got the power, who's got the guns." It was the first time I had heard of this kind of talk, and Jefferson was the first black I met in the South who regarded white civil rights workers with some-thing less than gratitude.

The summary moment of that Birmingham summer (although I didn't fully understand the lesson until later on) came from a girl named Hazel who was a student in one of the English classes I taught at Miles. She was very dark, almost blue-black, tall and thin with coltish legs and a perpetually startled quality like a deer surprised at water. She never said much in class but turned in essays I felt were remarkable, better by far than most papers I had gotten as a graduate teaching assistant in the English department at Berkeley.

In my fantasies, Hazel became part of a parable of wasted potential—the one who, if she could be saved, would help redeem an evil situation. I told her she should be thinking of going to a college in the North where she could develop her gifts. I said I wanted to talk to her parents so that we could figure out a way for this to happen. Hazel begged me not to, but I insisted. I borrowed a car and drove to their house, following a red dirt road to a terminus of automobile carcasses and old bathroom fixtures with rust leaking down onto the porcelain. Hazel's mother came to the door of a tar-paper shack and invited me in. She was a large woman sweating freely and using a fan to chase away the flies that attacked our faces in the afternoon heat. I talked; she smiled and fanned herself below a painting of JFK on velour, nodding in automatic agreement with whatever I said. I told her I was going to get her daughter away from all this, that I was going to get her into a school in the North where she could *be someone*. Hazel's mother smiled and nodded and fanned the flies away from her face.

A week or so later one of the other teachers at Miles whom I'd shown some of Hazel's work brought me an anthology of literature from the Harlem Renaissance. He opened the book to a certain page, set it down, and left my room. I picked it up and began to read. It was the same thing Hazel had written in one of her essays, almost word for word. As I read further in the anthology, I saw the sources for most of her other writing as well. I was devastated and told John Jefferson about the plagiary. He laughed until tears came into his eyes. "You been punching the tar baby all along," he said. "Now you're all caught up in that sticky stuff and don't know what to do. You white folks sure are something."

— . —

By the time I got back to Berkeley I had the feeling that people like John Jefferson would make Martin Luther King and white civil rights workers obsolete. But it didn't matter. I had already made a personal transition from civil rights to Vietnam. The question was not what to do. Like others I passed through the early stages of the foreign policy debate painlessly: it was necessary to support the NLF and work against the U.S. The only question was how to do it. How to become an activist, or, as we called it then, an "organizer"? Who to organize? How to get paid for it? These questions were answered when I became one of the coordinators of Robert Scheer's bid for Congress.

A radical journalist who had become a minor Bay Area personality, Scheer had been an early critic of the war. He was articulate and outspoken, and, after interminable wrangling about whether or not to work within the electoral system, we decided to run him against incumbent Berkeley Congressman Jeffrey Cohelan, one of LBJ's favorite liberals. We came close to winning the Democratic primary in a campaign that drew national attention. After the election, Scheer got me a job at *Ramparts*, where he was an editor.

The magazine was just then undergoing its transformation from a small quarterly published by liberal Catholics to a big-circulation monthly funneling radical politics into the mainstream. This metamorphosis came about as a result of two factors. One was the New Left, represented by several of us, notably Scheer, who had the ability to make the radical gestalt yield a journalistic point of view. The other factor was the salesmanship of Warren Hinckle, who was the same age as the rest of us but only faintly interested in the New Left. (He became political later on in the seventies, starting to celebrate just as the party was over.)

Hinckle liked to think of himself as an old-fashioned newspaperman, a muckraking troublemaker in the tradition of Ambrose Bierce and Citizen Kane, his heroes when he edited the college paper at the University of San Francisco. Coming from an out-of-pocket Irish-Catholic family, he was almost comically anxious to acquire panache and cultivated a style that involved a crude dandyism (patent leather dancing pumps and three-piece suits instead of the proletarian look the rest of us had adopted) and a patch covering a missing or mutilated eye whose fate remained a mystery. My son Andrew, then three years old, couldn't keep from staring at the eyepatch when I brought him to the office, and once asked of Warren, "Is he a pirate?" This was closer to the truth than he could have known, as the investors Hinckle convinced to pour a king's ransom into *Ramparts* over the next few years could have affirmed.

Ramparts seized the country's attention in 1967 with the first big exposé on the CIA—in this case the agency's infiltration of the National Student Association. Others followed. Soon the magazine was making news as well as reporting it. Featuring investigative reporting and splashy four-color art direction at a time when other magazines of the left were filled with interminable commentary and unrelieved blocks of type, *Ramparts* became a sort of synecdoche for the New Left itself—a triumph of aggressive self-dramatization, not particularly intelligent or at all introspective but very much on the scene, kicking the shins of the establishment and demanding to be taken seriously.

It was also a clearinghouse for people who eventually became part of the left-wing media establishment. People like Britt Hume of ABC and Daniel Zwerdling of National Public Radio were at one time or another affiliated with *Ramparts*, although in minor roles. Jann Wenner was a sort of glorified copyboy who tried to write rock criticism for the *Sunday Ramparts*, a newspaper we began during the San Francisco newspaper strike of 1967 and whose design he ultimately appropriated when he began *Rolling Stone.*

A then unknown Hunter Thompson came through San Francisco to meet us because of a flattering piece I had written about his first book on the Hell's Angels. At the time of his visit, Warren had a monkey named Henry Luce he kept in the office. Hunter left his rucksack near Henry Luce's cage while we went to lunch. Somehow the monkey got out and opened the bag. When we got back we found the floor strewn with the pharmacopoeia of red and white pills Hunter carried with him. Henry Luce had to have his stomach pumped.

Ramparts got Eldridge Cleaver out of jail after publishing the first essays of what became *Soul On Ice.* The first day Eldridge came into the office after being paroled, I could tell he was going to become an important figure in the movement. He walked with a cantilevered prison-yard strut; his hooded green eyes conveyed a sense of danger mitigated by an odd introspection and self-irony.

Talking to Eldridge was like playing tennis against a wall: the ball always came back just as hard as you hit it. He seemed amused that his background as a rapist was an aphrodisiac for certain women of the left, and he talked about "pussy" with the laconic humor of a stand-up comedian. (I remember coming into the office one Saturday afternoon and hearing noises in the only room with a sofa. Soon Eldridge came out grinning, followed by a blond girl whose picture I had seen on the *San Francisco Chronicle* society page and who was now rearranging herself in the manner of a hen fluffing her feathers after encountering a rooster.) Eldridge gave us a certain authenticity we had lacked with radical blacks, brokering a coalition between *Ramparts* and the Black Panther Party, which became, for a time at least, something like a wholly owned subsidiary of the magazine.

Eldridge was a kind of free-lance nihilist. I heard that he had approached James Baldwin at a party and given him a deep kiss, a noteworthy event primarily because he had earlier tried to establish himself as a black writer by attacking Baldwin (just as Baldwin himself had done by attacking Richard Wright). I think Eldridge liked to mock our solemn left-wing pieties. Once he caused a sudden silence in one of our editorial meetings which had digressed into an encomium on Trotsky by interrupting with "Trotsky was a bourgeois intellectual like you all. Stalin, now he was a brother off the block. More people were killed trying to see that brother's corpse than ever followed any Trotsky." We were horrified but dared not contradict him.

People occasionally ask about the strange twists in Eldridge's subsequent career—how, after his return from exile in Algiers and Paris (where he is said to have shared a mistress with Giscard d'Estaing), he got involved with the Moonies and other odd organizations. My only answer is that he is now what he always was—a hustler.

——·——

In truth, *Ramparts* did not produce much good journalism. The pressure to shoehorn the facts into our view of reality was too great. We did not just assign stories; we told writers to *do in* certain American personalities, to *destroy* certain American "myths," and to *attack* certain American organizations and institutions. Aside from its disregard for the truth, such an editorial policy, if it could be called that, obviously did not give most writers enough intellectual legroom to discover their subject and themselves. But it did demand a tough adversarial stance, a perception that there were moral issues in even seemingly "value-free" phenomena, and a commitment to comfort the oppressed, as Mencken had said, and to oppress the comfortable. And so for someone like myself whose views on life had been formed according to Jamesian laws of moral ambiguity, the atmosphere at *Ramparts* was tonic.

Our journalistic politics, like the politics of the New Left as a whole, invariably involved liberal-bashing. The Republicans and conservatives were not our enemies; they were irrelevant. It was the liberals we were after—the ones most identified with what Henry Luce (the man, not the monkey) had prematurely called the American Century. The liberals were the ones who were present at the creation; the ones who had, in the revisionist clichés which became the foundation for our journalism and for New Left thought, begun the cold war; the ones who had taken the anticommunism of the Truman Doctrine (not the buffoonery of McCarthy) as an excuse to extend American power into every crevice of the globe and to get us into

Vietnam. Irving Kristol later said that a neoconservative was a liberal who had been mugged; we identified ourselves as the muggers very early on.

As the "literary" one on the magazine, I got to take on some easy targets. One was Eric Hoffer, the "longshoreman philosopher" who had become a sort of poet laureate for the Johnson administration. Another was John Steinbeck, whom I attacked for forgetting his old sympathies with the Okies and other victims of power in his rush to embrace the President and his war. (After the piece appeared, I got a couple of fan letters from Steinbeck's son, then in Vietnam, applauding my attack against his father. During one of *Ramparts'* times of financial hardship, I sold them for $15 apiece to a rare book dealer). I also got to "attack" some cultural organizations, writing the first investigative report on Synanon (an organization that was then a favorite of the liberal media) because of what seemed to me its totalitarian tendencies.

Ramparts was "political" as opposed to "cultural," distrusting the shotgun marriage Jerry Rubin had tried to broker between these two opposites during the Summer of Love as a deviation that would pollute radicalism. For this reason we missed the significance of the Haight-Ashbury scene, for instance. And we not only missed but actually *dismissed* the significance of women's liberation, publishing an early article on that phenomenon in which we attacked Betty Friedan and convinced the leftist women we proposed as her betters to model for the cover of the magazine in elegant maxi skirts.

We didn't check facts very energetically, and paranoia and ideology always overcame professional skepticism. It is hard not to wince when leafing through *Ramparts* back issues (which, I am told, now sell for a considerable sum), yet it is also true that the magazine deserves at least an agate-type footnote in the histories of journalism to come. It midwifed the rebirth of investigative journalism, and it accurately—if often somewhat unintentionally—chronicled the temper of the times.

—— • ——

The year 1968 was a turning point. Tet, Johnson's withdrawal, the assassinations of Martin Luther King and Bobby Kennedy, the riots in Chicago: a writer will probably realize someday that this year is a metaphor that contains the whole story of the great unraveling of the sixties.

By 1968 the New Left had degenerated into sham and charade, a movement whose only truly necessary implements were the soapbox, the megaphone, and the suppository. The slogans were afflicted by moral scurvy. ("Bring the troops home" had become "Bring the war home".) A chic hatred of America had long since replaced any intention to make America better. Even the most quotidian forms of discourse were affected. I remember once getting a Christmas card whose cover showed a silhouette of a Vietnamese peasant woman with a rifle under the words "Peace on Earth"; inside the card were the words "By Any Means Necessary."

The war corroded our minds and brutalized our emotions, lowering our resistance to the intellectual toxins in the air. We had a weekly ritual of sitting in front of the television set and cheering as Walter Cronkite announced the ever-rising American body count on CBS. I carried a comb Tom Hayden brought back from Hanoi, where he had gone to pledge our solidarity with the Vietnamese war effort. It is made out of the fuselage of a downed F-105 and shaped like that plane, and is stamped with the words "The American Pirates 1700th plane shot down in North Vietnam."

We hated the war but loved it too. Vietnam made us special. It justified every excess, every violent thought and deed. Heaving a rock at some corporation's window, we banished guilt by the thought, "This is for the Vietnamese." Trying to set fire to a university library, we said to ourselves, "This is for the Vietnamese." The war gave us license; it also gave us an addictive sense of moral superiority. We daily committed small crimes of indecency that were justified by the much larger and more obscene crime in Southeast Asia. Vietnam was in our marrow. It was *our* war, the time of our lives. I remember one day in 1968 having a chilling thought after hearing that negotiations were possible: What if it ends? What will we do then? But I quickly put the thought aside. It was impossible that the war should end; it was the fountain of youth we had discovered.

Chicago became the *Kristallnacht* of the New Left. Jerry Rubin was there talking about putting LSD in the water supply. Hayden had the shrewd intention of provoking the cops, knowing that Mayor Richard Daley had already threatened to shoot looters. If one intention was to inspire a police riot while "the whole world was watching," the other was to deliver a deathblow to the centrists of the Democratic Party, the "cold war liberals" we hated so. We went to Chicago, in short, to have some fun, trash the liberals, and elect Nixon. This would "maximize the contradictions" and drive the country more swiftly and effectively toward "fascism," where it was ineluctably headed in any case.

The New Left did destroy the Democratic Party at Chicago, the party of Hubert Humphrey and Scoop Jackson which had been compassionate on domestic policy and obdurately anticommunist in its international world view. Like political body snatchers, the left then inhabited the party's corpse through McGovernism, reviving it as a party of special interests, of compromise and appeasement. Among the many ironies is the fact that Tom Hayden, who more than anyone else had masterminded the debacle at Chicago, was able to serve a brief and unrepentant apprenticeship and then to reemerge a decade later as a Democratic Party regular.

—·—

We were convinced that reform was not enough; there had to be revolution. We weren't sure what this meant exactly. But we were sure that it had to be. We awaited the apocalypse like huddled millenarians, scanning the skies for a sign. The 1969 People's Park riots in Berkeley, a combination of crackpot utopians and hard-core politicos, was one such portent. It involved the trashing of Berkeley: plate glass windows heaving and falling like icebergs; city cops looking frightened as they found themselves isolated within our circle. The "blue meanies" of the Alameda Sheriff's Department arrived once again. At one point during the riots I threw a piece of slag through the tear gas and hit one of them in the shoulder. Another pointed his gun at me. I held up my press card and screamed "Journalist!"

There was a sudden fad for Franz Fanon's notion of "revolutionary violence." We were the Americong, and it didn't seem implausible at the time to talk about "taking" Berkeley and making it a model for the "liberated zones" we wanted to create in strategic locales across the country. During the chaos on the streets, Tom Hayden was holed up in a garret somewhere drafting what he called the Berkeley Liberation Program (one part of which would call for protection of the community's "right" to use harmful drugs). He was also talking about the need to strike back against the sheriffs, an "occupying army" that must be defeated. White radicals and countercultural-ists couldn't do it, he said; they weren't ready. The only ones who could bring off "armed resistance" were the Panthers, whom Hayden had called "our NLF." Cleaver, Huey Newton, and Bobby Seale were all either in jail or on the run at the time of People's Park, so he went to David Hilliard, the Panthers' interim leader, to talk about the possibility of trying to shoot down an Alameda sheriff's helicopter. Rumor had it that Hilliard looked at Hayden in disgust and responded: "Just like you, Tom. Get a nigger to pull the trigger."

It was a time of breathless waiting, a time whose spirit was captured by The Doors' song about breaking through to the other side. My friend David Horowitz and I had taken over *Ramparts*, removing Robert Scheer and some others in one of those rites of radical purification that affected most left organizations during the latter part of the decade. But running the magazine didn't seem like a sufficient political act. Everyone else seemed to be stockpiling weapons and breaking into affinity groups. They were *getting ready*.

It was a time when many of those like myself who had been involved in the civil rights movement and had never quite been able to commit themselves to violence (other than rhetorically) were in danger of being upstaged by a younger group who'd come of age in the sixties rather than the fifties and seemed to have few qualms about anything. "The heavier the better" was the new slogan. A symbol of this second wave of the New Left was Bernadine Dohrn, who came through Berkeley with a tiny miniskirt and a sweet, heavy-chinned face—a radical pinup with a moue. "It's time to stop talking," she said. "We've got to *do it!*" She was about to go to Cuba as part of the SDS faction calling itself Weatherman which came home after meeting with the Cubans and Vietnamese with a commitment to begin acts of terrorism here in the mother country.

Although we had begun a few years earlier as a movement opposed to dogma, we now began to talk of ourselves as "Marxist-Leninists." People claimed to be reading *Kapital;* there were soporific discussions about parallels between 1970 and 1917. The main attraction in Berkeley was the Red Family, a collective whose principal personalities were Scheer and Hayden. Controlled by sexual politics (there were said to be brain-dwarfing struggle sessions over such topics as whether or not it was "bourgeois privatism" to go into the bathroom alone and shut the door), the Red Family waited for the revolution like the rest of us. One day not long after Kent State, David Horowitz and I were sitting on the porch of the collective with Hayden. "Well, fascism is here," Hayden said without any apparent regret. "There will be civil war soon." On Hayden's advice, I bought a gun so I could be armed when the revolution arrived. I hid the loaded clip in one place and the gun itself in another so that my children could never find them. I always forgot where the hiding places were and went for months unable to put the whole gun together.

We were driven to more and more radical gestures because the left had caught on and become chic. I realized this early in 1970. I got a call from a man in Hollywood who said he represented Jane

Fonda. He said that she had broken with former husband Roger Vadim, and just completed a session of transcendental meditation with the Mahareshi in India. She had read a piece I had written in *Ramparts* about the Indian occupation of Alcatraz. Because of it she had decided she wanted to come home and "get involved." Would I take her to Alcatraz and introduce her to the left? Naturally I said yes.

Later she herself called and said that she wanted to meet some Indians. Then she arrived one foggy morning in San Francisco, fresh-looking and self-confident, still in her shag-cut *Klute* phase. She said she'd been in exile for too long, that she wanted to be back in America because this was where it was "happening." I joked that perhaps she had waited too long; the sixties were over. A look of horror crossed over her face and she said, "Oh, I hope not." I took her to Alcatraz. She was an incredibly quick study, understanding immediately what the power arrangements were on the island, and picking up the radical lingo. She saw, for instance, that there was a factional fight between the Sioux and the other tribes for control of Alcatraz and that the Sioux were more "radical." By the time I left, she was over in their corner of the old prison exercise yard, smoking dope with them.

Later on, as Jane went off on a tour of the reservations I had helped arrange for her, she wrote me a note in a backhanded scrawl expressing her hope that she could be of use in the struggle. It ended with the slogan "power to the people!" Instead of a dot under the exclamation point, there was a little circle. (My wife and I were looking at it later on and she said, "I'm surprised it doesn't have one of those little smiley faces on it.") The next thing I knew she was on the Dick Cavett Show with Mark Lane arguing a Marxist line about Southeast Asia. We were there because our imperialism required the natural resources of the area, especially the "tung and tinsten."

I watched Jane's rapid progress through the movement over the next couple of years (culminating in her propaganda appearances in Hanoi) with appreciation and also amusement. I always remembered two things: that little circle under the exclamation point, and the classic spoonerism "tung and tinsten."

—— . ——

In 1972 David Horowitz and I met a young man from the National Security Agency who was disillusioned by the war. Once he had begun talking to us about the NSA—at that time a virtually unknown component of the U.S. intelligence apparatus—we realized that we had a gold mine. We debriefed him in a Berkeley hotel, and I wrote a story which showed the extent and effectiveness of the NSA's electronic surveillance of the Soviets. The story revealed material that one intelligence expert said was "incredibly sensitive." After it wound up on the front page of the *New York Times*, we began to worry about our possible exposure and consulted Harvard Law professor Charles Nessen, then assisting the Ellsberg defense team, and he told us that we were guilty of violating the Espionage Act, but would probably be OK because the government would have to give up more secrets to prosecute us. Like other radicals, our treason of the heart had incubated into a treason of fact for which there were no consequences. A few years later, we were talking to Billy Ayres, husband of Bernadine Dohrn and one of the founders of Weatherman, while doing a story on that organization, and he put the lesson all radicals learned in the sixties with eloquent malice: "Guilty as hell, free as a bird. America is a wonderful country."

Yet the movement itself was nearing the end of a prolonged dry labor by the early seventies. It was clear that the revolution, monstrous offspring of our fantasies we had awaited so long, was going to be stillborn. People who had gathered for the apocalypse were dropping off into environmentalism and consumerism, and (to the detriment of communities like Berkeley) into local politics. Some of my own comrades were going back to graduate school in the universities they had failed to burn down so that they could get advanced degrees and spread the ideas that had been discredited in the streets under an academic cover.

Among the odd developments of the mid-seventies, we noticed a new tolerance for members of the Communist Party. For nearly a decade they had hung around our meetings trying to find an organization, any organization, they could infiltrate. They were always boring from within in both meanings of the term, and we hated them, although for the wrong reasons: not because they supinely supported the Soviet Union, but because they were so *moderate*, always trying to find a way to vote Democratic while we were looking for things to blow up. Now the Communist Party was being revaluated, if not rehabilitated, as an organization that had been in it for the long haul. Party members were suddenly transformed into good old warriors who might have been a bit obtuse ideologically but who had nonetheless fought the good fight. Disregarding the nature of their commitments and what these commitments had wrought, people on the left in Berkeley began to wonder aloud whether or not the communists might be a better model for the future than the New Left, whose flamboyant theatricality and impatience, everyone now realized, had made it a burned-out case.

About this time, David Horowitz and I became interested in the Panthers for some of the same reasons that others were taking a kindly look at the CP. Huey Newton had disavowed the violence of the past, changing the focus of the group from shoot-outs with the police to community organizing. He said that revolution was not an overnight thing, but rather a patient process involving methodical political action and evolutionary change. "Put away the gun," he said. "Concentrate on survival, put together a real community program." After being in the New Left theater of the absurd for so long, such a message seemed refreshing. There was something about Newton himself, however, that I found deeply disturbing. When I went with David to see him at his Lakeshore apartment, it was like attending a performance which played well enough at the time but left the viewer with a shiver of doubt afterward.

There were always a cheering section of whites at his apartment (led by Hollywood producer Bert Schneider) along with black lackeys from the party. Huey always found some excuse, even on cold days, to take off his shirt and prance around his living room vamping everyone by flexing huge pectoral muscles. He would slap hands with his black bodyguards and grab whites around the shoulders in sudden embraces of solidarity. He would occasionally interrupt his nonstop monologues to peer out of a telescope he kept trained on the holding cell in the Alameda County courthouse where he'd first done time for killing an Oakland policeman back in 1967. He always carried a water tumbler with him, but it was filled with vodka instead of water. He had a great physique sculpted by pumping iron in prison workout yards, but there was a liverish and unstable look in his eyes that made him look sick and dangerous.

Our interest in the Panthers (David's always greater than mine) continued even when Huey fled to Cuba after being charged with the murder of an Oakland prostitute. After that, David convinced the *Ramparts* bookkeeper, Betty Van Patter, to get the party's books in order. Apparently she stumbled onto information showing that they were dealing in drugs and protection rackets. Wanting them to live up to her radical vision, she confronted them with what she had learned. The next thing we heard, she was found floating in the bay, her head caved in by a blow from a heavy object.

There had been rumors on the left for a long time that the Panthers had used the Santa Cruz Mountains as a sort of killing grounds, getting rid of members there they had decided, after councils of paranoia, were "police agents." We not only ignored these rumors; we said that it was *good* for a vanguard organization to purge its ranks of informers. But now one of our friends was the victim, and the fact that those who knew about it refused to say anything took on a different coloration. I went to a Berkeley police lieutenant and told him that they had to do something. He said he knew who was responsible for Betty's death and smiled bitterly: "Yeah, well how can we? You guys have been cutting our balls off for the last ten years. You destroy the police and then you expect them to solve the murders of your friends."

The Black Panther Party, which had begun as a street gang, had never really changed. They had just allowed us white radicals to project our violent fantasies about "avant gardes" onto them. They had remained a gang. The gang, it occurred to me, was an appropriate metaphor for the left as a whole.

———— · ————

As experiences such as this one made me draw back from the radical brink, I took refuge in my family. Because I had a "nuclear" family (my comrades used the term to distinguish it from their own "intentional" families, but it also carried the implication that old-fashioned arrangements such as my own were politically radioactive), I had often felt like an imposter, someone whose movement life was undone by his private life. I had seen others try to heal this dichotomy by forcing their intimate relationships to conform to their politics. They rearranged their marriages to eliminate "bourgeois sexual privatism"; they made their relationships obey the radical laws of the emerging feminism and raised their children to become the new men and new women of a future socialist utopia. Like others, I paid lip service to all this but kept it out of my own life, knowing instinctively that it would first trivialize and then destroy everything that was important to me. This conviction did not come in a rush, but in small *aperçus*. I remember one of them quite clearly. Two of my movement comrades decided to get married. After a ceremony filled with gibberish about liberation and the Third World, there was a reception with a large wedding cake decorated with the words "Smash Monogamy!" Needless to say, this marriage didn't last long, leaving in its rubble a pair of pathetic children whom I still occasionally see walking around Berkeley looking like the survivors of an airplane crash.

At about this time my daughter Caitlin was born. Soon after, my father was diagnosed as having terminal cancer. Being sandwiched in between birth and death not only took politics further out of focus for me but also told me something about life, about the fact that it was a game played for keeps, that I didn't want to hear. My father and I had fought over politics for years. I would occasionally tell him some of the things I was doing; he would flinch as if I had slapped him. He couldn't master all the facts about Vietnam ("I don't know Bo Dai from Bo Diddley," he once grumbled during one of my harangues about the French colonial experience). Instead of trying to argue with me about the war, he had tried to talk about what this country had meant to him—how he had come to California during the Depression so poor that he and his mother and father had survived by eating "road meat," domestic and wild animals killed by passing cars; how he had worked two jobs during the war and gotten a citation signed by FDR for an improvement he'd designed on a certain power lathe. I had ridiculed him for seeing himself as a stick figure in the national melodrama, and after a while he stopped talking about anything significant. We went through years of long silences.

But once I found out he was sick, all our past troubles seemed irrelevant. He was dying and history was dying with him. Not the Hegelian claptrap radicals had in mind when they talked of History, but lived life, the human record of an individual trying to make his way through real obstacles. He had created a world that would vanish when he died.

My father's last summer we decided to go to South Dakota, where he had been born. I watched him poke around in the crumbled foundations of the sod house where he'd lived his first years. We went to the Black Hills where he'd hiked as a boy and to the Pine Ridge Sioux reservation where he had watched warriors do the sun dance in a time before authorities prohibited it. We didn't talk much while we were there, but as we were returning home and his sickness was growing in him, he began to reminisce and talk about his life in a way he'd never done before. During a long stretch of Nevada highway, he said: "You know, I'm glad I was born a South Dakotan and an American. I'm glad I saw the beginning of the twentieth century. I'm glad I lived through the Depression and the war. I think these things made me a stronger man. I'm glad I came to California because I met your mother there. I'm glad we had you for a son."

It was the longest speech I'd ever heard him make. It was not maudlin or smarmy. It was a moment of simple acceptance and affirmation by someone whose life had often been disfigured by unremitting hard work and responsibility and to whom words had never come easily. What he said and how he said it were so different from the bitterness and anger I had lived with for fifteen years that I was taken aback. My comrades had been given a more comfortable fate than my father and his generation but they hated their lives despite all the talk of "love." They had projected that hatred onto everything around them.

As I sat beside my father in the hospital a few months later watching as the last breaths were snatched out of his body, I had a feeling that part of my life was ending too. It was like those artist's conceptions of stages of moon rockets separating: I could see my past decoupling from my future and falling away into deep space.

—— · ——

My father's death came at about the same time as the U.S. defeat in Vietnam. This was what we had worked for all those years, but it was an outcome that didn't give any pleasure. Many of my movement friends seemed to feel cut adrift. I felt something like what Orwell must have felt after the Spanish Civil War when he wrote, "This war, in which I played so ineffectual a part, has left me with memories that are mostly evil."

As the communists took over in Vietnam, Joan Baez and a few others tried to protest against their reeducation camps and revolutionary tribunals, the boat people and the new imperialism. But what was left of the left attacked the attempt to apply the standards of political morality we had claimed to believe in to the Hanoi regime. Tom and Jane, who were on their way to becoming the Mork and Mindy of California politics, were opposed to Joan. So, back east, was the coalition of old-line communists, neo–fellow travelers, and unreconstructed sixties radicals that was forming into the present "Solidarity" Left. No matter that our old allies in the National Liberation Front were among the first to be crushed; no matter that South Vietnam was conquered by the North; no matter that the Khmer Rouge, which we had supported with such great enthusiasm, had embarked on a policy of genocide. There were no enemies on the left.

To come to terms with what was happening in Southeast Asia—the fact that more people were killed in the first two years of the communist peace than had been killed in all of the anticommunist war—would have been a cleansing experience for the movement.

But the left wasn't capable of this reckoning. Like some sort of revolutionary cargo cult it was ready to move to the next cause—in South Africa, Central America, or wherever—ignoring the body count that began to pile up in the long totalitarian night we had left behind.

It was one thing to think such things, of course, and quite another to say them aloud. That would have meant stepping purposefully away from what I had been most of my adult life and leaving the community of the left with its powerful vision of humanity as a mass of victims requiring a few select caretakers. It was not only left ideas I found hard to disentangle myself from, but the community of the left as well, with its seductive conviction that it is on the side not only of morality but of history itself. What Kundera calls the "totalitarian poetry" of the left had a strong grip. I could see saying goodbye to most of that, but not all. I entered a period of dormancy and hibernation, hoping that events would take a turn that would reconfirm my old faith and help me be born again.

Writing was my middle passage. During the time that I had first been feeling traumatized by my left-wing commitments, David Horowitz and I had begun a book on the Rockefeller family. The project was actually an outgrowth of our successful efforts to fund-raise the guilt-ridden fourth Rockefeller generation, our contemporaries, as a way of keeping *Ramparts* alive so that it could publish attacks on Nelson, David, and the other Rockefeller family elders. We had started the book with the vulgar Marxist notion that the Rockefellers were a sort of executive committee of the ruling class, a Rosetta stone by which we could understand American imperialism and power. The truth turned out to be quite different. They were a family not even able to control their own children, who were running away from the Rockefeller name, money, and influence, let alone control the world.

After the Rockefeller book, I began writing fiction—short stories for little magazines and then a novel, *Downriver*, which explored, under a sort of artistic grant of immunity, the issues I couldn't yet bring myself to confront in my workaday life—the way people got caught up in movements and in history, the effects of political belief on the affective life, the tension between political commitment and love.

After being awarded a National Endowment of the Arts fellowship in 1980, I was asked by the USIA to lecture in Europe. The Soviets were already in Africa along with their Cuban lackeys and had just invaded Afghanistan; the Iranians were holding U.S. citizens hostage.

The Europeans I spoke to assumed I would join the parade of U.S. writers who, like some traveling freak show, attacked America for their amusement. Earlier I would have done it gladly. But now I found the double standard Europeans used in judging the U.S. and the U.S.S.R. revolting, especially since our defeat in Vietnam had so changed what we used to call the "objective conditions" and created a vacuum into which the Soviets had moved with such brutality. Not really relishing the role, I nonetheless found myself defending America in my talks. It wasn't what was expected or desired.

When I got back home, David Horowitz and I began another family dynasty book, this time on the Kennedys. We had gone through a lot together at *Ramparts* before it went under in 1973, and afterwards. We still had a political collaboration, but it was different from what it had been when we were radicals cruising along the party line with only minor deviations. We took turns playing devil's advocate, each of us creating arguments he knew would move the other forward in apostasy. We found ourselves in roughly the same mood—bruised by our past beliefs. There was the continuing wound of the murder of our friend Betty, a murder that had gone unsolved and unpunished. There was also the selective morality of the left, which might wax indignant about the Carter administration's rather moderate stand against communist guerrillas in Central America, but was yet unable to become aroused by the Soviet genocide in Afghanistan. (The *muhajadeen* were not "progressive" enough, one of our ex-comrades told us during an argument; they countenanced clitorectomies, after all, and believed in capital punishment.) We tried to bury ourselves in the Kennedy book, telling each other in long talks that we hadn't left the left but it had left us. But it was hard to accept the feeling of being in internal exile, and we began to explore our New Left experiences indirectly through a series of magazine articles. It was not just a coming out, we later realized, but a coming home as well.

Our first project was a piece on Fay Stender, the radical feminist lawyer who had been George Jackson's lover and attorney and who had been paralyzed years after his death when she was shot by one of his former prison followers. We had of course supported Jackson when we were at *Ramparts,* proposing him as an innocent victim of a conspiracy of the criminal justice system. But as we began to reconstruct Fay Stender's life and death (she had recently committed suicide), we discovered that Jackson had killed several people in prison, and that far from being a sensitive prisoner-poet, he had been a

deranged con. The slogan inspired by the passion of George Jackson—
"All prisoners are political prisoners"—seemed absurd to us in light
of what we had found. We saw now what authorities close to the
Jackson case had known all along: there are individuals who, for
whatever reason, are so flawed that they ought to be locked as deeply
as possible into the prison system.

We concluded this article by pointing out that the left had honored
Fay Stender as a fallen heroine but ignored her quintessential truth:
that she had been taken advantage of and debased by her left convictions. We were immediately attacked by such individuals as Jessica
Mitford, Queen Mother of the Bay Area's left, and by former *Washington Post* editor Ben Bagdikian, who refused to accept a service award
from a local media association because we were members. Previously,
attacks against our standing as radicals would have been devastating.
But these gave us a sense of confirmation. It was not *what* we had
said that was wrong, but the fact that we had said it at all. We
experienced the perverse pleasure of the fallen angel and of his slogan,
non serviam.

The next story we wrote was about what had happened to the
Weather underground. Among other things we discovered in our
chronicle of the rise and fall of this organization was the fact that
the bomb that had blown up three of the soldiers of the Weather
Army in the Manhattan townhouse had been intended for a dance
hall full of Army enlisted men and their dates at Fort Dix. When
our old friends attacked us for publishing the piece, we told them
that we felt that if someone had to die, it was better that it was the
Weatherpeople than the soldiers.

We next became involved in a story about the juvenile justice
in California, showing how liberal pieties had created a system in
which it was quite literally possible to get away with murder. Next
came an article about how the gay establishment—anxious to protect
the homosexual life-style—had pressured the elected leaders of San
Francisco to forestall public health measures that would have stopped
the spread of AIDS in San Francisco and saved countless lives.

Writing these stories had drawn us into a deeper reevaluation of
our past and a greater candor about where it had led. In the spring
of 1985 we published "Lefties for Reagan" for the Washington *Post
Magazine*. It was a piece about the atrocities the left had committed
in the sixties and defended in the seventies. We said that we had
voted for Ronald Reagan (whom we had attacked as a "fascist" when
he was governor of California) because he acknowledged the fragility

of American democracy and the degree to which it was on the defensive in the world. We were probably not the first former New Leftists to cast a ballot for the President, but we may have been the first to admit it. There was a lot of press attention and a lot of criticism from our old friends, who attacked us as "turncoats" and "sellouts." After one such encounter, I told David that I felt like an American for the first time in twenty-five years. As someone born into the emotional and political ghetto of the Communist Party with an alienation far greater than mine had ever been, he shook his head in agreement: "I feel like an American for the first time in my life."

——.——

The sixties seem very far away now. Yet I know they are still very much with us. Often it seems that we are now living out the consequences of original sins committed then. When someone brings up today's drug epidemic, I always think back to that promise in the Berkeley Liberation Program to protect the people's right to use harmful drugs. It is clear to me that the sixties' insistence on sexual liberation and protecting the "integrity of countercultural lifestyles" has played a major role in creating an atmosphere conducive to the spread of AIDS. And the New Left vision of the world—a vision that replaced the Munich metaphor which cautioned against appeasement with a Vietnam metaphor which holds that what may seem like Third World totalitarianism is really harmless nationalism in disguise—paralyzes our attempt to assert the primacy of democracy in this hemisphere and to protect our national interests.

Nor is it simply a matter of ideas. Some of our old comrades are active again. But not in the way of the New Left—in the streets candidly admitting their intentions to tear the mother down. Today's Solidarity Left operates more like the Stalinists we used to hate—through front groups and deceitfully layered organizations that appear to be "liberal" and for "peace" but are actually (in the case of the Committee in Support of Central America, for instance) following a party line developed in Havana and advancing the cause of Marxist-Leninists in this hemisphere.

The sixties thus continue to be with us today, in our memories and also in our politics. They were a curious time, serious but also foolish, destructive but also ineffectual. When thinking about the good old days, I always remember a story, perhaps apocryphal, about Bruce Franklin, a Stanford English professor who had gained notoriety in the Bay Area as a red-hot Maoist. It was 1969, when the apocalypse seemed finally to be at hand. One of Franklin's colleagues, a junior professor at Stanford, had escaped to the Bolinas Lagoon and spent the summer in the guilty pleasure of sunshine and ocean. When the fall term began, he ran into Franklin, who immediately asked him what he had been doing. It was a question freighted with a portentous subtext: what have you been doing *for the revolution?* The junior professor, looking sheepish, said, "Well, Bruce, I have to tell you that I did a lot of swimming." Franklin glowered for a moment and then, in the manner of many abstruse revolutionaries of the day, managed to find something redeeming in this apparent waste of time: "Well, that's OK. We're going to need frogmen."

The revolution never got far enough to require wet suits and underwater demolitions, thank God. But people from the sixties left are still out there—the dark shapes under our political waters. After my years as a New Leftist, I could never join another movement or subscribe to another oxthdoxy. But I feel that I still have a small role to play—keeping an eye on these deep swimmers, and, when I see one of them come to the surface, pointing out who he is, what he is doing, and what the consequences are likely to be. It may not be much to show for a fifteen-year indenture to the New Left, but it is the only way I know to put that perverse experience to use.

7

Letter to a Political Friend: On Being Totalitarian in America

David Horowitz

All that exists deserves to perish.

MEPHISTOPHELES (*Faust*)

The struggle of man against power is the struggle
of memory against forgetting.

MILAN KUNDERA (*The Book of Laughter and
Forgetting*)

Communism is the philosophy of losers.

DANIEL (*The Book of Daniel*)

Los Angeles, April 1987

Dear M.,

I'm sorry it has taken me so long to answer your letter. When I returned to California after my father's funeral, I spent a long time thinking about what happened during that weekend in New York. I thought about my phone call to you on Friday after I came back from the cemetery; how I had invited you to the memorial service we had planned for Sunday at my mother's house; how you had said you would come and how comforting that felt; how our conversation had turned to politics and changed into an argument, and our voices had become angry; how I had begun to feel invisible, and how the loneliness this caused in me became so intense I said we should stop; how, when we could not stop, I hung up.

I thought about my feelings when you did not call back that day or the next; and when you did not come to my father's memorial on Sunday as you had said you would. I thought about the plane ride back to California, when I began to realize how deep the wound in our friendship had become.

Our friendship had begun nearly half a century before at the Sunnyside Progressive Nursery School—so long in memory that I have no image of a life without it. In the community of the Left, it is perfectly normal to erase the intimacies of a lifetime over political differences. On the long ride home, it occurred to me that I might never hear from you again.

And then, a week after my return, your letter arrived in the mail. You were sorry, you said, about the way our phone call ended. *Because of our common heritage* [you said] *the personal and the political cannot really be separated.* Your words reminded me of the "Khrushchev divorces" of 1956—the twenty-year marriages in our parents' generation which ended in disputes between the partners over the "correct" political position to take toward his secret report on the crimes of Stalin. As though a political idea defined their reality.

But then, as though a political idea defined our reality too, your letter suddenly forgot about what had happened between us as friends and resumed the argument. And reopened the wound:

April 1986

Dear David,

I was sorry that your call ended the way it did. It was not my idea to get into a political argument, but apparently you had a need to provoke it. I would have preferred to talk more about personal matters. But because of our common heritage the personal and the political cannot really be *separated. And that is why I can't help thinking that the views you now hold are psychological rather than intellectual in origin.*

I want to add some things to clarify my position. I still consider myself part of the left, but my views have changed significantly over the years. I haven't been a Stalinist since I visited the Soviet Union in 1957, when I was nineteen. After that, like you, I became part of the New Left. I no longer consider the Soviet Union a model for the socialist future. But after all the garbage has been left behind I do hold certain basic tenets from my old left background. The first is that there are classes and the rich are not on the same side as the rest of us. They exploit. The second is that I am still a socialist. I still believe in theory socialism is better than capitalism. If it has not worked so far, it is because it has not really been tried.

What concerns me about you is that you have lost the compassion and humanism which motivated our parents to make their original choice. There can be no other explanation for your support of the vile policies of Ronald Reagan. Except that you are operating from an emotional position which surpasses rational thinking. Also, by assuming that because you are no longer "left" you must be "right," you appear to be lacking a capacity to tolerate ambiguity; and the real world is indeed ambiguous. Why do you feel the need to jump on establishment bandwagons? I assume they are paying you well for your efforts.

Your old (one of the oldest) friend,

M.

The wound in our friendship is really a mirror of the wound that a political faith has inflicted on our lives, the wounds that political lives like ours have inflicted on the time itself.

Let me begin with a concession. It is probably correct of you to blame me for our argument. *Apparently you had a need to provoke it.* I probably did. I had just buried a father whose politics was the most important passion in his life. Political ideas provided the only truths he considered worth knowing and the only patrimony he thought worth giving. When I was seventeen and had political ideas of my own for the first time, politics made us strangers. The year was 1956. My father and I were one of the Khrushchev divorces.

We never actually stopped speaking to each other, and mostly managed to be friends. But the distance was there just the same. After I had my own children and understood him better, I learned to avoid the areas where our conflicts flourished. I was even able to make a "separate peace," accepting him as the father he was rather than fighting to make him the one I wanted him to be. But he never was able to make the same peace with me. In all those thirty years that were left to us after my manhood began, there was not a day I was not aware of the line that politics had drawn between us, that I did not feel how *alien* my ideas made me to him.

Mourning emotions make a perverse chemistry. If I provoked you to attack me on my father's burial day, perhaps I had a need to do battle with the ideas which in ways and at times seemed more important to him than his son, to resume the combat that was his strongest emotional connection to other human beings and to me. Perhaps I thought I could resurrect his ghost in you, one of my oldest and dearest friends, who despite "all the garbage" you have left behind remain true enough to the faith of our fathers to act as his stand-in.

I don't mean to excuse my provocation, but only to remind you of what you forgot in your political passion that evening and in the silence that followed. Me. David. An old friend in need. I had been obliterated by a political idea. I felt like those ideological enemies of the past whom Stalin had made into "unpersons" by erasing the memory of who they had been. Which is what happened to my father at his own memorial that Sunday you did not come.

—— · ——

For nearly fifty years our parents' little colony of "progressives" had lived in the same ten-block neighborhood of Sunnyside in Queens. And for fifty years their political faith had set them apart from everyone else. They inhabited Sunnyside like a race of aliens—in the community but never of it, culturally and psychologically distinct. They lived in a state of permanent hostility not only to the Sunnyside community, but to every other community that touched them, including America itself.

The only community to which they belonged was one that existed in their minds: the international community of their progressive Idea. In all the real communities around them, they lived as internal exiles waiting for the time when the conditions of their exile would come to an end and they would be able to go home. "Home," to them, was not a place somewhere other than Sunnyside and America; "home" was a time in the future when Sunnyside and America would be different. The circumstance that made them exiles was the very existence of the communities they lived in. No sea passage could put an end to their exile, only a wave of destruction that would sweep away the institutions and traditions of the communities around them, leaving the international community of the progressive Idea to stand in their place.

To my father and his comrades the fantasy of this future was more important than the flesh and blood reality around them. All the activities of the Sunnyside progressives—the political meetings they attended five and six nights a week, the organizations they formed, the causes they promoted—were solely to serve their revolutionary Idea. The result was that after five decades of social effort, there was not a single institutional trace of their presence in the little ten-block neighborhood where they had lived. The result was that when my father's life came to its close in the community where he had spent his last fifty years, it was as a stranger he was buried.

My father lived the sinister irony that lies at the heart of our common heritage: the very humanity that is the object of its "compassion" is a humanity that it holds in contempt. This irony defined my father's attitude toward the people around him, beginning with those who were closest—the heirs of his Jewish heritage, whose community center in the neighborhood he would never be part of and whose synagogue he would never enter. Every Friday night his own mother still lit the *Shabat* candles, but as a progressive he had left such "superstitions" behind. To my father, the traditions his fellow Jews still cherished as the ark of their survival were but a final episode in the woeful history of human bondage, age-old chains of ignorance and oppression from which they would soon be set free. With the members of the real communities around him my father was unable to enjoy the fraternity of equals based on mutual respect.

The only community my father respected was the community of other people who shared his progressive Idea. To my father and his Sunnyside comrades this meant the orthodoxies that comprised the Stalinist faith. But when he was just past fifty, a Kremlin earthquake shattered the myth that held together the only community to which my father belonged. The year was 1956. The disintegration of my father's world was the biggest Khrushchev divorce of all.

In fact, like all "progessives," my father had no real community; he had only an Idea. My father lived as a stranger in a strange land. And when it came time for him to die, it was as a stranger he was buried.

By the time I reached Sunnyside from California, my mother had already decided that his burial arrangements would be made by the Shea Funeral Home on Skillman Avenue. The Shea Funeral Home was where the Catholics of the neighborhood had come to in the end for as long as I could remember. And for just as long I remember how my father hated its very name. To my father, the little storefront was a symbolic fortress of the enemy forces in his life—the Christian persecutors of his ghetto past, the anticommunist crusaders of his ghettoized present. My father took his hate to the grave. But for his widow, the battles were already forgotten, the political passions dead with the past. What was alive was her new solitude and grief. Her terror in the knowledge that everything had changed. To my mother, the Shea Funeral Home was an ark of survival, as familiar and comforting as the neighborhood itself.

My father's burial was attended only by his immediate family. We were accompanied to the cemetery by a rabbi I had somewhat disloyally hired to speak at the graveside after confirming with my mother that she would find his presence comforting too. Having been primed with a few details of my father's life, the rabbi observed that death had come to him the week before Passover, whose rituals commemorated an exodus to freedom not unlike the one that had brought him as an infant from Russia eighty-one years before. Not unlike the dream of a promised future that had shaped his political life.

The place of burial was Beth Moses, a Jewish cemetery on Long Island 50 miles away from Sunnyside, the last of my father's exile homes. It seemed appropriate to me that my father who had struggled so hard in life to escape from his past should find peace in the end in a cemetery called the "House of Moses." And that this final compromise should have been made for him by the international community of his political faith. The grave where my father was buried among strangers was in a section of the cemetery reserved for Jews who had once belonged to the International Workers Order, a long-defunct Communist front which had sold the plots as fringe benefits to its members.

On Sunday, the last surviving of my father's comrades assembled in my mother's living room for the memorial. No ceremony had been planned, just a gathering of friends. Those present had known my father—some of them for more than fifty years—with the special intimacy of comrades who shared the scars of a common battleground, lifetime cohabitants in a community of exiles.

I could remember meetings when the same room had reverberated with their political arguments in the past. But now that the time had come to speak in my father's memory, they were strangely inarticulate, mute. As though they were daunted by the prospect of their task: not to contend with my father's opinions as before, but to remember him as a man.

My father was a man of modest achievements. His only real marks were the ones he made in the lives of the individuals he touched. The ones who were there now. The memories of the people who had gathered in my mother's living room were practically the only traces of my father still left on this earth. But when they finally began to speak, what they said was this: "Your father was a man who tried his best to make the world a better place. . . . Your father was a man who was a teacher to others. . . . Your father was a man who was socially conscious. . . . progressive. . . . who made a contribution."

And that was all they said. People who had known my father since before I was born, who had been his comrades and intimate friends, could not really remember the man they had shared their lives with at all. All that was memorable to them in the life my father had lived—all that was real—were the elements that conformed to their progressive Idea. My father's life was invisible to the only people who had ever been close enough to see who he was. Reality to them was a political Idea.

The obliteration of my father's life at his own memorial is the real meaning of what you call "our common heritage": reality is a political Idea.

——.——

Our common heritage. Such a precious evasion. Our common heritage was totalitarianism, was it not? Our parents and their comrades were members of the Communist Party, were they not? Your need for this Orwellian deceit is revealing. It can hardly be for the benefit of an old comrade like me. In fact its camouflage is for you. "Our common heritage" betrays your need to be insulated from your own reality—the reality of your totalitarian faith.

I'm sure this idea upsets you. In your own mind, the only elements that survive of our heritage are the innocent ones: *I haven't been a Stalinist since I visited the Soviet Union in 1957, when I was nineteen. . . . I no longer consider the Soviet Union a model for the socialist future.* But what leftists who are able to enjoy the privileges of *bourgeois* democracy in the West think of themselves as Stalinists anymore, or the Soviet Union as a socialist model? Such vulgar convictions are reserved for the revolutionary heroes of the Third World who actually wield the power—the Vietnamese and Cuban and Nicaraguan comrades—to whom you and other left-wing sophisticates pledge your loyalties and faith.

Not an intention, but a totalitarian faith is what creates the common bond between revolutionary cynics like Stalin and Fidel and the Sandinista commandantes and progressive believers like you.

Totalitarianism is the possession of reality by a political Idea—the Idea of the socialist kingdom of heaven on earth, the redemption of humanity by political force. To radical believers this Idea is so beautiful it is like God Himself. It provides the meaning of a radical life. It is the solution that makes everything possible; it is the end that justifies the regrettable means. Belief in the kingdom of socialist heaven is the faith that transforms vice into virtue, lies into truth, evil into good. For in the revolutionary religion the Way, the Truth, and the Life of salvation lie not with God above, but with men below—ruthless, brutal, venal men—on whom the faith confers the power of gods. There is no mystery in the transformation of the socialist paradise into communist hell: liberation theology is a Satanic creed.

Totalitarianism is the crushing of ordinary, intractable, human reality by a political Idea.

Totalitarianism is what my father's funeral and your letter are about.

—— . ——

Your letter indicts me because my ideas have changed. But the biggest change in me is not in any new political convictions I may have. It is in a new way of looking at things. The biggest change is seeing that reality is more important than any idea. It is in gaining respect for the ordinary experience of others and of myself. It is the change that allows me to learn from what I know. To connect, for example, the little episodes of our progressive heritage with the epic inhumanities that its revolutions inspire. It is because you have not changed that these connections remain invisible to you.

What concerns me about you is that you have lost the compassion and humanism which motivated our parents to make their original choice.

Their original choice. Another Orwellian trope. You find its use necessary here, do you not, because in these words you reveal your loyalty to our common heritage. In these words you concede that this loyalty is what divides us now. The Orwellian trope is necessary because you cannot face the reality it hides.

Their "original choice" was Communism, was it not? Our parents were idolators in the church of a mass murderer named Joseph Stalin. They were not moralists, but Marxist-Leninists. For them the Revolution was morality (and beauty and truth as well). For them, compassion outside the Revolution was mere *bourgeois* sentimentality. How could you forget? Was it compassion that inspired their complicity in Stalin's slaughter of innocent millions? Or made them antifascists until the Soviets concluded their alliance with Hitler, and then neutralists unconcerned about the Nazi armies conquering Europe or rounding up their fellow Jews until the moment came when Hitler broke his word to Stalin and began an attack on their sacred Russia, at which time they became antifascists again?

Compassion is not what inspired our parents' political choices. Nor is compassion what inspired the Left to which you and I both belonged—the *New Left* which forgot the people it liberated in Indochina once their murderers and oppressors were red, which never gave a thought to the Cubans it helped to bury alive in Castro's jails, which is still indifferent to the genocides of Marxist conquest—the fate of the Cambodias and Tibets and Afghanistans that no longer exist.

Compassion is not what motivates the Left, which is oblivious to the human suffering its generations have caused. What motivates the Left is the totalitarian Idea. The Idea that is more important than reality itself. What motivates the Left is the Idea of the future in which everything is changed, everything *transcended*. The future in which the present is already *annihilated*. In which its reality no longer exists.

What motivates the Left is an Idea whose true consciousness is this: *Everything human is alien*. Because everything that is flesh and blood humanity is only the disposable past. Because *all that exists deserves to perish*. This is the consciousness that makes mass murderers of well-intentioned humanists and earnest progressives, the Hegelian liberators of the socialist cause.

In the minds of the liberators, it is not really *people* that are buried when they bury their victims. Because it is not really people who stand in their way. Only agents of past oppressions; only enemies of the progressive Idea. Here is an official rationale, from the time of Lenin, for the disposal of 30 million human souls:

We are not carrying out war against individuals. We are exterminating the bourgeoisie as a class. We are not looking for evidence or witnesses to reveal deeds or words against the Soviet power. The first question we ask is—to what class does he belong, what are his origins, upbringing, education or profession? These questions define the fate of the accused. This is the essence of the Red Terror. [M. Y. Latsis, a Cheka official]

The Red Terror is terror in the name of an Idea.

The Red Terror is the terror that "idealistic" Communists (like our parents) and "anti-Stalinist" Leftists (like ourselves) have helped to spread around the world. You and I and our parents were totalitarians in democratic America. The democratic *fact* of America prevented us from committing the atrocities willed by our faith. But impotence was our only innocence. In struggles all over the world outside America we pledged our faith and gave our support to the perpetrators of the totalitarian deed. Our solidarity with them, like the crimes they committed, was justified in the name of the revolutionary Idea. Our capability was different. Our passion was the same.

And yours is still. You might not condone some of the crimes committed by the Kremlin or Castro or the Nicaraguan *commandantes*. But you would not condemn the criminals responsible. Or withhold from them your comradely support. Nor, despite all your enlightenment since the time of Stalin, are your thoughts really very different from theirs.

Does it occur to you that you condemn me in exactly the same terms that dissidents are condemned by the present-day guardians of the Soviet state? *There can be no other explanation for your support of the vile policies of Ronald Reagan. Except that you are operating from an emotional position which surpasses rational thinking.* In other words, the only explanation for my anticommunist convictions is that I am "antisocial" (lacking compassion) or insane.

Devoted as you are to the cause of "the people," does it occur to you that the contempt you express for me because of my ideas is also contempt for the majority of Americans (including the sainted working class) who have supported the same "vile policies" of Ronald Reagan, a man they elected by a political landslide? Perhaps you have lived so long in internal exile in this country that you are not even aware of the degree of your alienation from the people who live in it.

What kind of revolution do you think you and your radical comrades would bring to the lives of people for whom you have so little real sympathy and such obvious contempt? The answer is evident: exactly the same kind of revolution that radicals of our "common heritage" have brought to the lives of ordinary people in every chilling episode in the past. For when the people refuse to believe as they should, it becomes necessary to make them believe by force. It is the unbelieving people who require the "Watch Committees" to keep tabs on their neighborhoods, the gulags to dispose of their intractable elements, the censors to keep them in ignorance, and the police to keep them afraid. It is the reality of ordinary humanity that necessitates the totalitarian measures; it is "the people" that requires its own suppression for the revolution that is made in its name. To revolutionaries, the Idea of "the people" is more important than the people themselves.

The compassionate ideas of our common heritage are really masks of hostility and contempt. We revolutionaries are the enemies of the very people we claim to defend. Our promise of liberation is only the warrant for a new oppression.

These are the realizations that have changed my politics. They were not clever thoughts that one day popped into mind, but, as you know (and choose to forget), conclusions I was able to reach only at the end of a long night of pain.

Until that moment I had shared your conviction that we all were radicals for compassionate reasons, to serve benevolent ends. However perverted those ends might have become in the past, however grotesque the tragedies that occurred, I believed in the revolutionary project itself. I believed in it as the cause of humanity's hope. And I was confident that we could learn from history and would be able to avoid its destructive paths. I believed we could create a *new* Left that would be guided by the principles of the revolutionary ideal, that would reject the claims of dictators like Stalin who had perverted its goals in the past.

After 1956 I joined others who shared this dream in the first attempts to create a "new Left" in America and for nearly twenty years was part of the efforts to make it a reality. But eventually I realized that our efforts had failed. I gave up my political activities and embarked on a quest to understand why. When it was over, I saw that what we had dreamed in 1956 was not really possible. I saw that the problem of the Left did not lie in sociopathic leaders like Stalin or Castro, who had perverted the revolutionary Ideal. It was the revolutionary Ideal that perverted the Left.

Because you knew me from the very beginning, you were aware of the road I had traveled, the connection between what I had lived through and what I had come to believe. No matter how different the traveler appeared at the end of the journey, you were a witness to his true identity. To the reality he had lived. But it is clear now that this reality—*my* reality—is something you no longer want to know. You prefer to erase me instead.

By assuming that because you are no longer "left" you must be "right," you appear to be lacking a capacity to tolerate ambiguity. . . . In these words you have forgotten who I am. In these words, you erase my memory, just as my father's old comrades erased his.

Let me remind you of the person you accuse now of being unable to cope with real life complexity, of responding to the loss of one ideological certainty by reflexively embracing its opposite.

The formative experience of my political manhood was the shattering of the Old Left's illusions by the Khrushchev Report and the events of 1956. You and I were seventeen at the time, now suddenly suspended between a political past that was no longer possible and a future that was uncertain. Our parents' political faith had been exposed as a monstrous lie. It was impossible for us to be "left" in the way that they had been. But I did not assume therefore that I had to be "right." I swore I would never be part of another nightmare like theirs. But I didn't want to give up their beautiful Idea. So I joined the others in our generation who were setting out to rescue the Idea from the taint of the past and create a Left that was new.

In the years that followed, I could always be seen in the ranks of the New Left, standing alongside my radical comrades. But in all those years, there was a part of me that was always alone. I was alone because I never stopped thinking about the ambiguous legacy that we all had inherited. I was alone because it was a legacy that my New Left comrades had already decided to forget.

It was as though the radicals who came to politics in the sixties generation wanted to think of themselves as having been born without parents. As though they wanted to erase the bad memory of what had happened to their dream when it had become reality in the Soviet past. To them the Soviet Union was "not a model" for the revolutionary future, but it was also not a warning of a revolutionary fate. It was—in the phrase of the time—"irrelevant." Radical theory was not a means to incorporate the lessons of the past in present politics, but something to improvise as the occasion required. As though what happened before was unconnected to what was to come. For radicals, there was no need to look at the past. All that mattered was to embrace the "future."

All during the sixties, I wrestled with the troubling legacies that my comrades ignored. While others invoked Marx as a political weapon, I studied the four volumes of *Capital* to see "how much of the theory remained viable after the Stalin debacle" (as I explained in the preface to *The Fate of Midas*). For New Left radicals who were impatient to "bring the System down," Marxism provided the convenient ax. Even if Marx was wrong, he was right. If Marxism promoted the desired result, what did it matter if the theory was false? To me it mattered. All the nightmares of the past cried out that it did.

In the mid-sixties I moved to London and came under the influence of Isaac Deutscher, an older Marxist who had written panoramic histories of the Russian Revolution and the lives of its protagonists Stalin and Trotsky. For me, Deutscher was the perfect mentor, steeped in the dark realities of the revolutionary past but believing still in the revolutionary Idea.

Inspired by my new teacher, I expanded my study of revolutionary history and intensified my search for a solution to the problems of our political inheritance. Before his untimely death in 1967, Deutscher encouraged me to expand one of the essays I had written into a full-length literary effort. When *Empire and Revolution* was completed in 1968, it represented my "solution" to the radical legacy. I had confronted the revolutionary Idea with its failure, and I had established a new basis for confidence in its truth. In Europe my book joined those of a handful of others that shared its concerns, but in America *Empire and Revolution* stood all by itself. I don't think you will find another book like it written by an American New Leftist during that entire radical decade. In living with the ambiguities of the radical legacy, in my generation I was virtually unique.

When it was published in America, *Empire and Revolution* made no impression. The willful ignorance of New Left activists had by then become an unshakable faith that long since had ceased to be innocent. Alliances had been struck with totalitarian forces in the Communist bloc; Stalinist rhetoric and Leninist vanguards had become the prevailing radical fashions. Even a New Left founder like Tom Hayden, previously immune to Marxist dogmas, had announced plans to form a new "Communist Party." As though the human catastrophes that had been caused by such instruments had never occurred.

In the face of these developments, I had begun to have doubts as to whether a New Left was possible at all. Whether the very nature of the Left condemned it to endless repetitions of its past. But I deferred my doubts to what I saw at the time as a more pressing issue—the issue of America's anticommunist war in Vietnam. Opposing the war was a moral obligation that in my mind took precedence over all other political tasks. The prospect of revolution which was the focus of my doubts was a reality remote by comparison. Even though I was uncomfortably allied with "Marxist-Leninists" I found politically dangerous and personally repellent, I didn't break ranks. As long as the Vietnam War continued, I accepted the ambiguity of my political position and remained committed to the radical cause.

But then the war came to an end and my doubts could no longer be deferred. The revolutionaries we had supported in Indochina were revealed in victory as conquerors and oppressors: millions were summarily slaughtered; new wars of aggression were launched; the small freedoms that had existed before were quickly extinguished; the poverty of the peoples increased. In Asia, a new empire expanded as a result of our efforts and, over the peoples of Laos and Cambodia and South Vietnam, the familiar darkness of a totalitarian night.

The result of our deeds was devastating to all that we on the Left had said and believed. For some of us, this revelation was the beginning of a painful reassessment. But for others there were no second thoughts. For them, the reality in Vietnam finally didn't matter. All that mattered was the revolutionary Idea. It was more important than the reality itself. When they resumed their positions on the field of battle, they recalled "Vietnam" as a radical victory. The "Vietnam" they invoked in their new political slogans was a symbol of their revolutionary Idea: "Vietnam has won, El Salvador will win." The next generation of the Left had begun. The condition of its birth was only to forget. To forget what really had happened in Vietnam. To erase the memory of its own past.

—— . ——

Perhaps the course of these events would have completed my journey in any case. But fate did not prove so kind. Before history had run its course in Vietnam, the refuge I had reserved for myself all these years in the Left had already been cruelly destroyed. The murder of an innocent woman by people whom the New Left had celebrated as revolutionary heroes and whom I had considered my political comrades finally showed me how blind I had been made by my radical faith.

The murder was committed by the leaders of the Black Panther Party. Originating as a street gang in the early Sixties, the Panthers had risen in the Left by promoting themselves as a Leninist vanguard and by promising to lead the movement from radical rhetoric to revolutionary violence. When the Panthers proclaimed, "It's time to pick up the gun," the white student Left acclaimed the Party as the vanguard of the political struggle.

This mindless adulation of the Black Panther Party crystallized the reasons I had remained an outsider in the radical ranks. Throughout the sixties, I had kept my distance not only from the Panthers but from all the Leninists and their self-appointed vanguards. But, at the same time, I shared the reasoning that made gangs like the Panthers part of the Left. According to this logic, the Panthers had become "politically aware" as a result of the "struggle" and had left their criminal past behind. By the same reasoning, their crimes were not something shameful, but "prepolitical" rebellions against their oppression as blacks. I accepted this logic for the same reason everyone else did, because it was the most basic tenet of our radical faith: reality was defined by politics, and could be changed by political ideas.

Like everyone else on the Left I could see that despite their new orientation, the Panthers still acted like a gang of thugs. But that was the way the other Leninist vanguards acted too. It was the ghost of Stalin that disturbed me about the Panthers, not the implications of their criminal past.

When the sixties were over and the war that had fueled its radical passions had begun to draw to an end, the political apocalypse suddenly receded. Almost overnight the "revolution" disintegrated. Its energies were exhausted, its organizations in varying stages of dissolution, its agendas quietly shelved. The Panthers survived to embrace the change with a new slogan proclaiming "It's time to put away the gun," and, as their actions showed, to put away the Leninist posturing too. It was a time for practical community efforts, a time for reality. For me, it seemed a time to end my long alienation in the Left. In 1973 I began a project with the Panthers to create a Community Learning Center in the heart of the East Oakland ghetto.

I had been persuaded by the Panthers that they did not intend to use the center as a Panther enclave, but to turn it over to the ghetto community as a model of what could be done. And I had persuaded myself that my intentions in working with the Panthers to accomplish this end were truly modest: to help the people in the community it would serve. But looking back afterwards, I could see that my intentions were not modest at all. Every aspect of what I did was informed by the revolutionary Idea. That was the bond that connected me to the Panthers in the first place. That was what made what we were going to do resonate with the socialist future. That was what made me so ready to trust intentions I should not have trusted and to forget the violent realities of the Panthers' past. That was what inspired me to ignore the surface betrayals of character that provided warnings to others but were dismissed by me as the legacies of an oppression that radical politics would overcome.

So I raised the necessary funds and bought a church facility in East Oakland to house a school for 150 children. I organized technical support systems and teacher training programs and a variety of community services for the center, and I found a bookkeeper named Betty Van Patter to keep its accounts.

In the winter of 1974, the Panthers murdered Betty Van Patter and ended my career in the Left. I suspected, and was later told by the Panthers, that they had committed the crime; and there were others in the Left who suspected them too. But none of us came forward to tell what we thought. We all knew that even if we took the risks of voicing our suspicions, our radical comrades would be the first to denounce us as "racists" and "agents" and worse. Because the Panthers were a "revolutionary vanguard," they had to be defended. To protect the revolutionary Idea. Betty's murder was an ambiguity that I could not resolve.

Betty's murder was only one of nearly twenty that the Panthers committed while they were an integral part of the New Left. The Panthers were (as they had always been) a criminal gang extorting the ghetto. But as a vanguard of the Left they were a far more dangerous gang than before. Whenever the police accused the Panthers of criminal activity, the Left responded with cries of "racism" and "fascist repression," defending their innocence in the same way as the Left in our parents' generation had defended the innocence of Stalin. For the Left, the facts were not what mattered. What mattered was the revolutionary Idea.

It was a familiar pattern: the cynical exploiters of the revolutionary cause, the faithful defenders of the revolutionary name, the "political" silences that erased the truth, the blindness of believers like me. The legacy that I had tried so hard to leave by joining the New Left had become the very center of my life.

— . —

The summer after Betty was murdered you and I shared a tragedy of our own. Our friend Ellen R., who had grown up with us in that overrich Sunnyside political soil, was brutally raped and strangled in her Englewood, New Jersey, home. Ellen had been more faithful than either of us to the heritage we shared (you even thought she was a member of the Communist Party when she was killed). All her life Ellen had been a missionary to the people she considered to be most oppressed—the blacks who inhabited America's ghettos.

She even named her third child Martin after Martin Luther King. As a high school teacher, Ellen was devoted beyond the call of professional duty to black youngsters whom others considered intractable problems, but whom she "knew" she could help. To Ellen, these youngsters were not problems at all, but victims of a racist society she was determined to change. She took them on as a "cause" and was willing to incur risks that others would not, making not only her talents and intellect available but her paycheck and her home as well. On that fateful summer night, it was one of the troubled youths whom Ellen had tried to redeem who returned to her house and murdered her in her bed.

That summer you and I were able to share a grief over the friend we had lost, but we were never able to share an understanding of why she was dead. In your eyes, Ellen died a victim of circumstance; in mine she died a martyr of faith. A political faith that had made her blind.

Because of this faith, Ellen's middle-class existence was constantly beset by unsuspected enemies and unseen perils. As a young instructor at Queens College, she helped black militants take over a SEEK program she was employed in that they had targeted as racist. By personally betraying her professional colleagues, she was able to provide the radicals with the keys to their triumph. But after they completed their takeover, the militants turned on Ellen too, denouncing her first as a racist and then firing her with the rest.

Ellen married a man whom she did not regard as an equal, whom she considered it her mission to uplift. But when her husband found out she was hiding guns in their house for the Black Panther Party, he threatened to report his wife to the police. Her husband's reaction confirmed Ellen's judgment of him as "bourgeois" and selfish and politically backward. But his real concern was the safety of his children, which was the reason he didn't want the Panthers' guns in his house. Their marriage could not survive conflicts like this, and by the time Ellen had reached her thirty-sixth year her husband was no longer around to look out for his family. That was why a psychotic youth was able to return that summer to the house he knew and strangle his redeemer as she lay in her bed.

Even though her three children were asleep in the house, Ellen had left her front door unlocked. If the door had not been unlocked, Ellen might still be alive. The door was not unlocked because the neighborhood was safe. It was unlocked because of an Idea. An Idea that to Ellen was more important than reality itself. The same

Idea was expressed in the place she had chosen to live, which was one of the first integrated neighborhoods in America. To Ellen, Englewood was a social frontier that showed whites could live together with blacks. To Ellen, a locked door was a symbol of racist fear, of a world divided. The night Ellen was killed, she had left her door unlocked to affirm her faith in an Idea. The Idea of the future that progressives like her were going to create—the future when black and white would be one.

It was not that Ellen never locked her door, but that locking it always seemed like a defeat. Some nights more than others it was important for Ellen—like other progressives whose ideas made them the people's vanguard—to stand up and be counted and to resist such defeats. In the months past, incidents of violence had been reported in the neighborhood and rumors had made its inhabitants afraid. As a good soldier of faith, Ellen would not allow herself to give in to this fear, the fear that was a threat to her Idea. On the night she was killed, Ellen's door was unlocked because it was unsafe.

Ellen had no more understanding of the black people who lived in her neighborhood than she did of the black militants whom she had helped to fire her or the troubled teenager who finally killed her. Ellen had made all of their causes her own, befriended them and given them her trust, until finally she gave them her life. But she never once really understood who they were. How could she possibly have understood? It was not because of who they were that Ellen had reached out to the black people she had tried to help. It was because of an Idea she had of them as people who were "oppressed."

The night Ellen was killed the black people in her neighborhood locked their doors. While Ellen set an example for everyone of a progressive without fear, her black neighbors worried among themselves about the recent incidents and talked about them even more ominously than the whites. Ellen's black neighbors knew their fear was not symbolic and what threatened them was not an idea. They had reason to worry that a dangerous criminal was stalking their neighborhood, because all his previous victims were black.

—— . ——

In Ellen's fate I saw a mirror of mine. Our progressive mission had been destructive to others and, finally, destructive to us. It had imbued us with the greatest racism of all—a racism that was universal, never allowing us to see people as they really were, but only as our prejudices required. With Ellen's death I had come to the last step

in my political journey, which was to give up the progressive Idea—
the fantasy of a future that made us so blind.

Why was this Idea so hard to give up? Since 1917, perhaps 100
million people had been killed by socialist revolutionaries in power;
the socialisms they created had all resulted in new forms of despotism
and social oppression and an imperialism even more ruthless than
those of the past. But the weight of this evidence had failed to
convince us. We were able to hold on to our faith by rejecting experience as a valid test. The ugly socialism of record, we explained to
ourselves, was not "really" socialism. It was not our Idea. (*If it has
not worked so far, it is because it has not really been tried. . . . In theory
socialism is better than capitalism . . . I still believe. . . .*) If there was
any validity to the Idea at all, to give up on it seemed an unthinkable
betrayal, like turning one's back on humanity itself.

The last question I came to ask was whether there was any reality
to the socialist Idea. In 1973, a conference was held at Oxford University with the same question as its main agenda. The organizer of
the conference was a Marxist philosopher who was one of the founders
of the European New Left and had traveled a road that ran parallel
to mine.

When East Europe's Communists rebelled against their Soviet
oppressors in 1956 in the aftershocks of the Khrushchev Report,
Leszek Kolakowski was one of their leaders. The rebellions were
crushed by the Soviet armies, but Kolakowski remained a New Leftist
until 1968, when Soviet tanks again crossed into East Europe to
quell the dissident Communists in Prague. In 1968 Kolakowski made
a last-stand defense of his New Left faith. When it was over, he
was expelled from his Party and driven into exile in the West. When
Kolakowski organized the Oxford conference, nearly twenty years
had passed since he had joined the struggle to create a New Left
in the Communist world. For two decades he had led the efforts to
create a new "humanistic Marxism" and to liberate socialism from
its totalitarian fate. But by the time he organized the Oxford conference, Kolakowski could no longer ignore what his experience had
shown. He was ready to admit defeat and give up the attempt to
resolve the ambiguities we all had inherited.

The paper Kolakowski read at the conference examined the idea
of a classless, unified human community—the goal to which we had
dedicated our lives. The catastrophic experience of Marxist socialism,
he showed, had not been an accident. It was implicit in the socialist
Idea. The forces required to impose the radical equality that socialism

promised would inevitably lead to a new inequality and a new privileged ruling elite. The socialist unity of mankind we all had dreamed of could only be realized in a totalitarian state.

Kolakowski's arguments had been made before by the critics of socialism in every generation since Marx himself. And, in every generation since, the societies that Marxists had created had only served to prove them right. And now they had been proved right in mine. In the light of all I had come to experience and know, Kolakowski's arguments were utterly and tragically correct. But I was still not ready to embrace their conclusions, whose consequences seemed as unthinkable as before. I decided to suspend judgment and take Kolakowski's arguments to my comrades in the Left. I wanted to know how they would respond and whether they had the answers that I did not.

For several years I pursued my quest, initiating discussions in radical circles and even organizing a seminar addressed to the question "Is Socialism a Viable Idea?" The reactions I encountered proved personally frustrating, but in the end they were finally instructive. Most radicals, I discovered, did not see the issue as one that was important at all: among people whose lives were absorbed in efforts to replace an "unjust" society with one that was better, no one was interested in whether their efforts might actually make things worse. The few who recognized the gravity of the issue reacted to my questions with suspicion and mistrust. To ask whether the socialist Idea was more than a fantasy was like asking believers about the existence of God.

My search finally ended when I was visited by a British New Leftist who had been one of my earliest mentors. In the days when we were all setting out on our journey, Ralph Miliband had guided me in my first encounters with the troubling legacies of the radical past. After Isaac Deutscher's death in 1967, Miliband was the Marxist whose intellect and integrity I respected most. I had not seen him for more than a decade, but I still read the socialist journal he edited. It was the only socialist publication that had printed Kolakowski's recent ideas.

After we had caught up on the years that had passed, I told him about the crisis I had reached in my political journey. I recalled the impact of Kolakowski's arguments and the resistance I had met when I confronted other leftists with the issues he raised. I told Miliband it seemed irresponsible for radicals like us to call ourselves "democratic socialists" while Kolakowski's arguments remained unanswered and—

even worse—when most of the Left didn't care if his arguments could be answered at all. I didn't see how I could justify a commitment to a political movement with a history like the Left's, which was dedicated to destroying society without a viable plan for what would come next. I was still ready, I said, to oppose injustices wherever I perceived them, but I could not be part of a movement that would not examine its goals.

When I was finished, I waited for an answer. Not an answer to Kolakowski (which I knew by then did not exist), but the answer I had been looking for all along. The one that would say:

> David, you are not as alone as you think. The experiences of these years since we all began have indeed shown that the crisis of the socialist Idea is the crisis of the Left itself. If this crisis can't be resolved, if socialism is not a viable future, then our radicalism is really nothing more than a nihilistic passion and the Left a totalitarian force. But there is another possibility. The possibility that answers can be found, that a viable conception of socialism will result, a new agenda for the radical forces and a renewal of the radical hope. Ours may be a small contingent in the radical ranks, but the consequences of failure are too great to give up without trying.

If my old teacher had answered me like this, perhaps my quest would have gone on a little longer. But when I was finished, Ralph Miliband said:

> David, if those are your priorities, you are no longer a man of the Left.

What my old teacher had returned to tell me was that the Left was really a community of faith.

For me it was over. The Idea was dead. Bankrupt intellectually and refuted by history, the socialist future existed only as a destructive illusion—the living God of the totalitarian creed.

My conversation with Ralph Miliband occurred sometime in the summer of 1979. I did not then leap to the right side of the political spectrum, but waited another five years before casting a vote for Ronald Reagan and the policies that you consider so "vile." During that time and for twenty-three years previous, I had lived in the teeth of political ambiguity—never free from doubts about the Left but never feeling I had to resolve my doubts by embracing the views of the opposite side. Your image of me not only denies the meanings of my life, but actually reverses them.

And finally misunderstands them. If I had to label the perspective my experience has given me, I would call it "conservative." And would mean by that, respect for the accumulated wisdom of human traditions; regard for the ordinary realities of human lives; distrust of optimism based on human reason; caution in the face of tragedies past. Conservatism is not the mirror image of radicalism, any more than scepticism is the mirror of faith. I have not exchanged one ideology for another; I have freed myself from the chains of an Idea.

——·——

Why was my freedom so hard to win? Why is the Idea so difficult to give up? When I asked myself these questions afterwards, I realized that to do so had seemed to me like giving up something I could not do without—like hope itself. It would be like life without meaning. The reason the Idea is so hard to give up is that a radical faith is like any other faith: it is not a matter of politics but of self.

The moment I gave up my radical beliefs was the moment I had to look at myself for the very first time. At *me*. As I really was— not suspended above my fellow human beings as an avatar of their future salvation, but standing beside them as an equal, as one of *them*. Not one whom History had chosen for its vanguard, but a speck of ordinary human dust. I had to look at the life ahead of me no longer guided and buoyed by a redeeming purpose, no longer justified by a missionary faith. Just a drop in the flow to the common oblivion. Mortal, insignificant, inconceivably small. Marx was a rabbi after all. The revolutionary Idea is a religious consolation for earthly defeat.

For the Jews of our Sunnyside heritage, it is the consolation for internal exile; it is the comfort and support for marginal life. A passage home. Belief in the Idea is the deception of self that makes people like my father and you and me feel real.

Self-deception is what links you to the common heritage which is so difficult for those who inhabit it to name. Communism was the center of my father's world, but the word never passed the lips of the comrades who rose to speak at his memorial. A political faith dominated both their lives and his, but in the end the faith could not be named. To name it would make their lives too uncomfortably real. In their silence was their truth: What my father and his comrades were finally seeking in their political faith was not a new reality for the world, but an old illusion for themselves. What they found was comfort for their lives of pain.

For my father it was the pain of a chosen son. My father was the only male child of poor immigrants who could not speak English and who were as fearful of the strange world they had come to as the one they had fled. His own father had failed as a provider, and when my father was still only a child he realized the family had already placed its fate in his hands. From that time until his death, he felt like a man treading in water that was over his head with the shore forever out of sight.

At the age of nineteen my father found a means to support his parents and a life raft for himself in a job teaching English to other immigrant youngsters at Seward Park High School on the Lower East Side. But until he was thirty he continued to live in his parents' apartment and his own life remained dangerously adrift. Clarity entered my father's life through the Communist Party and the socialist Idea. The moment he joined the Party he felt himself touch the shore of a landmass that circled the globe and extended into the future itself. As a soldier in the Party's vanguard and a prophet of its truth, my father gained wisdom and power beyond his faculty, and finally achieved what his own father had not, his self-esteem as a man.

But in the memorials of his comrades there was no mention at all of the Party that had given my father so great a gift. It was like a secret they all were keeping from themselves. And my father would have wanted them to keep their secret. Because he had a secret too.

My father had left the Communist Party more than thirty years before.

It was only toward the end of his life that my father felt able to tell me his secret, and then in a voice full of emotion and pain, as if it had all not happened so many years past. The events had taken place in 1953, when I was fourteen and my father was approaching fifty (which is my age now). The anti-Communist crusade of the early cold war was reaching its height, and my father was about to lose the first life raft that had kept him afloat. For twenty-nine years he had remained a teacher of English at the same high school on the Lower East Side, but now a new law had been passed that barred Communists from his lifetime vocation.

In the ordinary business of his life outside politics, my father had remained timid like his father before him, clinging all that time to his very first job. But in the drama of history which he now entered, my father was the tall man his faith had made him. He was ready to stand up to his inquisitors and bear the blows they were about to give him. To defend his Party and its cause, my father was even ready to give up his raft of survival and to swim for the first time in uncharted seas. It should have been my father's moment of glory, but instead it became his hour of shame.

For "political reasons" the Party had decided that my father would not be allowed to make his stand as a man on trial for his political beliefs. Instead, he would have to defend himself as the victim of an "anti-Semitic" campaign. All my father's pride as a man lay in the cause that he had joined, in the fact that he had reached the shores of progressive light and had left his Jewish ghetto behind. Even in the best of circumstances, the lie that the Party now required would have been excruciating for a man of my father's temper. But when the court of history called him to account, there was no place for my father to hide. Not only were the judges who condemned him Jewish, but a Jew had written the antiCommunist law.

The Party had lived so long by deception that it could not be swayed by realities like these. And through all its deceptions, my father had kept his faith in the Party. Because without his faith he was a man who was lost. When his moment came, my father followed the Party line as he always had done. In his moment of glory my father colluded in his own public humiliation and was fired as a Communist from his only profession, protesting his rights as a Jew.

When my father was betrayed by the Party he loved, he was forced to look at the truth. The Party was everything to him, but to the Party he was nothing at all. His faith in the Party had not given him power; it had only made him a pawn in their game. The secret my father could only reveal to me late in his life was the terrible truth he had seen.

The truth made it impossible for my father ever to go back, but he did not have the strength to go forward. He could not leave (any more than you can leave) the faith that was the center of his life. It was a dilemma my father resolved (as you do) with a strategic retreat. He quietly left the Party that had betrayed him, but he kept his political faith. He was never again active in a political way, but every day of the thirty years he had left, he loyally read the Communist press and defended the Party line.

All those years my father kept his secret as though he were protecting a political cause. But, as anyone else could see, all those years my father was keeping his secret in order to protect himself.

My father's deceit is a metaphor for all the lies of the political faithful. Its immediate intent was to conceal the reality of his political cause—its casual inhumanity and devious method, its relentless betrayal even of its own. But the real purpose of my father's deception was to avoid the reality that made his faith in the Party necessary in the first place, that makes the Idea so hard for all of us to give up. The reality my father could not confront was his own.

— . —

It is the same with you. When you deny my reality for a political Idea, what you really don't want to confront is your own. *I assume they are paying you well for your efforts.* Can you really think I sold the birthright of a faith that for thirty-five years gave meaning to my life for a mess of pottage at the end? How can you, who know the price that I had to pay for what I have learned, point such a finger of judgment at me? Only if you feel so deprived in your own life that your words really mean this: "I am not being paid well for mine."

Behind this complaint lies the vulgar radical "truth" about the world—which is really the vulgar truth about the radical heart: the "truth" that divides the world into them and us; the envious heart at war.

The rich are not on the same side as the rest of us. They exploit. The radical truth (which is your truth still) is the *class war* of the social apocalypse, the war that divides humanity into the "haves" who exploit and the "have-nots" who suffer, into those who are paid well for their efforts and those who are denied, into the just and the unjust, into their side and ours. The radical truth is the permanent war that observes no truce and respects no law, whose aim is to destroy the world we know.

This is the "compassionate" cause that makes radicals superior to ordinary humanity and transforms the rest of us into "class enemies" and unpersons and objects of contempt.

Take a careful look at what you still believe, because it is a mirror of the dark center of the radical heart: not compassion, but resentment, the envious whine of *have not* and *want;* not the longing for justice, but the desire for revenge; not a quest for peace, but a call to arms. It is war that feeds the true radical passions, which are not altruism and love, but nihilism and hate.

— . —

The farcical surfaces of the political divorces over the Khrushchev Report masked a deeper reality of human pain. Consider what terrors of loneliness inhabit the hearts of people whose humanity must express itself as a political construction. Consider what passions accumulate in such unsatisfied souls.

This is the poisoned well of the radical heart: the displacement of real emotions into political fantasies; the rejection of present communities for a future illusion; the denial of flesh and blood human beings for an Idea of humanity that is more important than humanity itself. This is the problem of "our common heritage," as you so delicately name it, and it is our problem as well.

Your old friend and ex-comrade,

David

8

On Hanging Up the Old Red Flag

Ronald Radosh

Like many others in the New Left, my political roots were in the radicalism of an earlier era. My parents were part of the Jewish immigrant generation who made up the militant cadre of the garment unions, whose activity in the thirties fueled the efforts of the newly born CIO. My father had run for president of the Hat, Cap and Millinery Workers in the 1920s under the aegis of the communist-controlled Trade Union Unity League. He came within an inch of winning. My mother came from Jewish anarchist circles. Her first cousin, whom I knew as a child, was Jacob Abrams. He and his cohorts were arrested for giving out leaflets opposing the U.S. Siberian expedition of 1919, and were sentenced to twenty-five years in prison for this offense. Their appeal became the basis of Judge Oliver Wendell Holmes's famous dissent in the Abrams case, in which the Justice laid out the parameters of the rights of free expression—the so-called "clear and present danger" doctrine.

As a youngster, I attended the left-wing Camp Woodland, where a noncompetitive environment was combined with pleas for world peace, justice, and the need to coexist with our socialist friends. Instead of "Olympics," we had World Youth Week competition—patterned after the Communist World Youth Festivals. High school assured that the trajectory I was following would be continued. I was sent to Elisabeth Irwin High School, a private institution affiliated with the more famous Little Red School House, which was familiarly known as "the little red school house for little reds." Among its illustrious alumni were Cathy Boudin of the Weather Underground; Angela Davis, the black communist leader; Michael and Robert Meeropol, the children of Ethel and Julius Rosenberg; Victor Navasky, editor of *The Nation;* and Mary Travers of the folk-pop group Peter, Paul and Mary that now sings the praises of Daniel Ortega. Of course we had our black sheep, like Elliott Abrams, who later became the hard-line assistant secretary of state for Latin-American affairs and patron of the Nicaraguan *contras.*

The school's principal and staff had been subpoenaed by the House Committee on Un-American Activities, and fear abounded that pressure might cause the institution to fold. Our political instruction was informed but continuous. At a time when communists were under a cloud of suspicion, my class's choice of graduating speaker was W. E. B. Du Bois, an outspoken communist fellow traveler. Some uncooperative parents let it be known they would pull out their children if Du Bois appeared. A compromise was arranged. Du Bois came to a special mandatory all-school assembly, and we had another graduation speaker, Arthur Miller, who told us that the main lesson to be learned from life was never to accept half a loaf. We thought he was speaking about Du Bois. We soon learned better, when the news came out that he had left his wife for Marilyn Monroe.

My high school history teacher was a Marxist, and that soon became my ambition too. After graduation I chose the University of Wisconsin, as the institution where I could pursue my goal best. It had a reputation for having a good history department, but, more important, was the only college in the country that allowed an organized Communist youth group on campus. I was already a member of the Labor Youth League, as the young Communists were then called. At Wisconsin, I became its secretary-treasurer.

Except for a few of us who declared ourselves openly, most of the cadre were secret members, who engaged in what we call "mass work." Our strategy was to infiltrate other groups, with the easily achieved goal of taking them over. At one time, we calculated that young Communists controlled virtually every major campus political organization, from the liberal Students for a Democratic America (the youth arm of ADA) to the campus film society.

I graduated in 1959, moving on to the University of Iowa for a year—where I actively organized a civil rights campaign in support of the Southern black students who had begun the Woolworth boycott. I also helped form the Iowa Socialist Club, whose members included future Democratic congressman Ed Mezvinsky and Sol Stern, who became one of the editors of *Ramparts* in the sixties. In 1960, I left to do further graduate work at the University of Wisconsin, where I could also continue my political activities.

By that time, however, world events and my intellectual understanding had drawn me from the official Party line. The LYL group had dissolved, and its remaining members had formed a "New Left" Socialist Club. When a visiting Communist leader who was passing through spotted one of Isaac Deutscher's works on my bookshelf, he was shocked. If I wished to be a good Communist, he said, I should not read such anti-Soviet garbage. Then he pulled out a copy of *World Marxist Review,* which the Soviets controlled, as an example of what I should spend my time on. I realized at that moment that he and I were living in different worlds, and I quietly left the Party's ranks.

I had not, however, left the ranks of the left. I was working for my Ph.D. under the dean of "cold war revisionists," William Appleman Williams. It was largely from the work of the radicals who had grouped around Williams that the intellectual underpinnings of the New Left emerged, through our new magazine, *Studies on the Left.* The journal in particular inspired the founders of Students for a Democratic Society, which became the main organization of sixties politics. Indeed, many of the radical theories that led them into precipitous action, particularly the concept that "liberals are the enemy," came from the scholarly-political analysis our journal developed.

If any one idea was identified with *Studies on the Left,* it was the theory of "corporate liberalism," which portrayed liberals as the "enemy" in the struggles that followed. It was "corporate liberalism," its editors wrote in an editorial that had far-reaching political implications, that had "essential responsibility . . . for the Cold War."

If we needed proof of our theory that liberal America was the real enemy, Vietnam came along to provide it. Others may have expressed surprise that the "best and the brightest" of the American elite had led us into the quagmire of Vietnam; it only confirmed what we had been saying all along.

By 1965, Vietnam had become the focus of everyone's political attention. I had completed my graduate studies and moved to New

York, where I threw myself into activity with the antiwar movement. In April, the first large antiwar demonstration in Washington was scheduled to take place. The SDS organizers of the demonstration had shocked their financial backers in the League for Industrial Democracy by announcing that no opponents of the war would be excluded from participating, including the Communists. The march was quickly endorsed by the organized Communist youth, who had now changed their name to the Du Bois Clubs, and by the Maoist communists of the Progressive Labor Party, whose members longed for a return to the days of Stalin.

Prior to the march, an event took place which crystallized the new development for me. Irving Howe, a veteran of the old anticommunist left, had agreed to debate New Leftist Tom Hayden at a small meeting hall in Manhattan. Hayden was one of the founders of SDS and an editor of *Studies on the Left*. Howe chastised Hayden and the New Left for failing to recognize the true character of communism, and for ignoring lessons of the past. As the debate grew hotter and hotter, Hayden suddenly bolted from the stage in anger and, with Jack Newfield, Nat Hentoff, and me directly behind, stormed out of the hall. Howe's social democratic followers were left staring in disbelief at the show of New Left arrogance.

The League for Industrial Democracy cut off its financial support, and SDS was forced to move out on its own. Much of the future of SDS was foreshadowed in that early walkout. How ironic that the organization would eventually collapse over the same issue of communism, as its last convention in 1969 dissolved in rival factions waving Mao's Red Book in each other's faces.

Howe and Michael Harrington also opposed those New Leftists who saw a victory for Hanoi as a result that would advance the "progressive" cause; they tried to oppose the war without endorsing communism or the Vietcong guerrillas. When SDS put together its 1965 march, Howe and Harrington could not in good conscience endorse it. They could not lend their support to what Howe called "harsh criticism of Saigon and either silence about or approval of Hanoi." Nor could they endorse confrontational civil disobedience that only worked to polarize the nation and minimize the political chances of fashioning a Democratic coalition opposed to the administration's foreign policy. New Left activists pretended to be engaging in civil disobedience, as Howe put it; in reality, they were engaging in prerevolutionary acts of civil disorder.

Meanwhile, Hayden and Yale historian Staughton Lynd were proclaiming in the pages of *Studies on the Left* that "we refuse to be anti-Communist," and that "anti-Communism" was no more than a term Americans used "to justify a foreign policy that often is no more sophisticated than rape." I agreed, along with most of the New Left. We saw the Vietnam War as a liberation struggle against the American aggressor. Hence we responded with hostility to the suggestion that Communists might be enemies of freedom, or that a Communist victory might be worse for the Vietnamese themselves. The candid arguments of Harrington and Howe only led us to define them as part of the liberal establishment enemy. *Studies on the Left* provided our answer: the war in Vietnam had to be seen as part of a struggle against American imperialism. In this struggle, the Communists were our progressive allies, and anticommunists our reactionary enemies. We saw any kind of anticommunism as a mask for counter-revolution, and we sided with the anti-imperialist revolutionaries of the Third World.

The other great moral struggle of the sixties was civil rights. At the University of Iowa in 1959–1960, I had worked hard to organize a picket line for the Woolworth boycott in support of the civil rights activists in the South. It was the first joint black and white picket in Iowa City's history. As a result of my activities, I was threatened with arrest by counsel from the department store, and with dismissal from the university by a red-baiting dean, who dug up my Communist affiliations at the University of Wisconsin. The tactic didn't work, and the picketing received favorable attention in the campus paper. I was still not satisfied. What I wanted was some way to use the civil rights struggle to develop "socialist consciousness," which was the realization that the "enemy" was not just the segregationists who supported "Jim Crow," but the "corporate system" itself.

Some of the leaders of the civil rights movement had ties to the Old Left anticommunists, like Norman Thomas's Socialist Party, and I was quick to see the signs of conspiracy. In an article in *Studies on the Left*, written a year later, I attacked James Farmer and CORE for using the civil rights movement to suck cadre into the orbit of anticommunist socialism. Describing American blacks as "a potentially revolutionary proletarian group within American society," I criticized reformers who favored making American democracy work for black people. Like the rest of the New Left, I cheered on those black nationalists who attacked "white liberals," and called for solidarity with "the anti-colonial and revolutionary movements of the [Third] world." One could not support U.S. policy in Vietnam, I argued, and advance civil rights at home. It never occurred to me or other New Leftists that whether the war was just or not, one could indeed do just that.

I advised white radicals to support the new "black power" movement led by Stokely Carmichael and the black radicals. When Bayard Rustin, the old-line civil rights leader, defended his strategy of "coalition politics," I rushed into print to condemn him. Rustin's strategy, I said, was a recipe for coalition with the Democratic power structure. I urged black radicals to unite with the white poor, and to seek power through mass action and a revolutionary strategy. And the only black leader I praised, naturally, was Malcolm X—then in his most fiery antiwhite Black Muslim stage.

During the summer of 1963, I met Staughton Lynd, who was teaching at an "alternative" institution in New York called the Free University. Lynd, who had gained fame for his work with SNCC, was teaching a course on black freedom. I went out for dinner with him after his class and showed him my analysis, which had not yet appeared in print. Lynd listened carefully, especially to my attack on Rustin, whom I accused of not being a theoretician "of the Negro movement," but a spokesman for "the moderate white liberals who fear radical change and . . . the Administration that continues to play politics at home and wage war abroad." Soon after this conversation, Lynd joined in the attack by accusing Rustin of advocating "coalition with the Marines," as if a coalition with white liberals meant that one was supporting the counterinsurgency war in Vietnam. Under pressure from New Left radicals, Martin Luther King himself eventually came to oppose the war and in a famous speech claimed that America had become the "greatest purveyor of violence in the world." But his own stance did not lead him to break with Rustin, the one prominent adviser he took with him to Oslo when King accepted the Nobel Prize.

Decades later, I finally met Rustin—who died in 1987—at a friend's party. "Bayard," I said, "I'm the one who attacked your strategy article and called you a sellout." I wanted to apologize, I said, for my arrogance then. "Think nothing of it," he replied. "When I was young, I attacked A. Philip Randolph for selling out when he called off his scheduled March on Washington protesting the Roosevelt administration's inaction on civil rights. I called him a toady of fascism." (Rustin, of course, had gone on to become Randolph's protégé.)

When Norman Thomas died in 1967, I wrote what may have been the only negative assessment of his life. In Dave Dellinger's magazine *Liberation*, I scorned Thomas for regarding American imperialism "as an ally in the new fight against world Communism." Thomas had been an active supporter of the moderate SANE Nuclear Policy Committee and had spoken out against atomic testing in the 1950s. I argued that his opposition was so tame that it actually served the interests of the American establishment. I also discussed his opposition to Lyndon Johnson's introduction of bombing in Vietnam as only a "tactical" difference and actually accused him of favoring a continued American presence in Vietnam. Thomas believed that the Vietnamese National Liberation Front deserved some representation in a new government. When Thomas wrote, however, that he did not "regard Vietcong terrorism as virtuous," I said he had provided a new way for leftists to attack the heroic Vietnamese people, instead of concentrating their energy on attacking only the United States, the real enemy of the world's people. My final judgment of Thomas was that he had "accepted the Cold War, its ideology and ethics and had decided to enlist in fighting its battles" on the anticommunist side.

Of course, my attack on Thomas was intended as an attack on all the cold war liberals and anticommunist leftists in groups like Negotiations Now, a movement, ironically, in which the American communists had entered en masse. New Leftists like me had put their efforts into a movement whose slogan was "End the war," which called for "immediate withdrawal" from Vietnam. Our "Independent Committees to End the War," as we called them, were an attempt to create a revolutionary socialist mass movement.

Our effort quickly collapsed. Instead of paying attention to Vietnam, our time was spent in internal dispute with the Trotskyists of the Socialist Workers Party, who through shrewd Leninist manipulation had taken over the national movement to end the war. The Trotskyists, who already had a socialist party, sought to build a single-issue movement. Their hope was that as they recruited people to the mass marches, the result would be a growing membership in the SWP, which would become the "vanguard" party of the left.

Hence the Trotskyists sought minimal agreement and concentrated on getting the biggest establishment names to participate in their rallies, while leaving politics to the SWP. We, on the other hand, sought ideological agreement on a socialist strategy around uniting the "new working class." It meant many stormy meetings. One, in particular, began at 8 P.M. and was still going on at 3 A.M. Clearly, the Trotskyists would always win, since their cadre had strict orders to stick it out to the bitter end and they were all there when a final vote was called.

Our analysis in the struggle with the Trotskyists was laid out in one of the most influential theoretical statements of the New Left. One of its authors was David Gilbert—who subsequently became one of the Weather Underground, and who was sentenced to life imprisonment for his role in the Brink's robbery and murders committed by the remnants of his organization at the end of the seventies.

A decade before, Gilbert was a leading spokesman against the Maoists of the Progressive Labor Party, who were attempting to take over SDS just as the Trotskyists had taken over the movement against the war. The Maoists insisted that the blue-collar working class was still the revolutionary vanguard. Gilbert and other New Lefists argued that students too were also "workers" and were inherently revolutionary. I remember Gilbert's theoretical lectures at our local "Independent Committee to End the War in Vietnam" meetings, in which he informed us that our work to end the war revealed our true destiny as revolutionaries.

Soon after, Gilbert and his then girlfriend, Laura Foner, were put in charge of political work at the campus at which I taught—Queensborough Community College. The QCC students carried out a massive sit-in and protest, one that tied up the school in 1968 and led the president of the college to call in city police to have a few hundred of them arrested.

The QCC disturbances were not triggered by the war, but rather by a local campus issue, the college's not granting tenure to a member of the English department named Don Silverman. It happened that Silverman was also a self-proclaimed communist of the PL variety, although no one knew that until after he was fired. Silverman seized the moment to go public, maintaining that he was fired *because* he was a communist. The facts were otherwise, but building upon the guilt of the liberals over McCarthy era witch-hunts, Silverman prevailed upon cartoonist David Levine to draw a picture of our college president on a broomstick carrying off the persecuted professor. The caption proclaimed the birth of a new McCarthyism. Personalities from the literary community like Joseph Heller, and President John F. Kennedy's chief counsel, Theodore Sorensen, spoke at the sit-in. Students were cajoled to come to Silverman's defense by the SDS leaders, who explained that the college was their factory and that their strike was really a strike against the "system." I joined them in their daily vigils but, unlike the more militant professors who showed true commitment, did not jeopardize my job by canceling all my classes and joining the sit-in or assigning A's to all those on strike. The semester ended with the school in disarray, students spending their summer in city jails, and the college eventually restored to its good senses, through no fault of ours.

The election of Richard Nixon had the effect of revitalizing an almost dormant antiwar movement. By the end of the 1960s, campus protest against Vietnam had become the pattern rather than the exception. The country was polarized, and instead of dialogue, one saw provocation followed by repression. Students occupied Harvard University buildings, protesting the college's refusal to take a stand against the war. At Berkeley, Governor Ronald Reagan brought in police to confront 5,000 students who seized a vacant lot owned by the university, and who were demanding it be turned into a "people's park." The tragedy reached its finale at Ohio's Kent State University after Nixon announced the invasion of Cambodia in May of 1970. Students had protested the invasion by rioting and firebombing the campus ROTC building. The governor called out the National Guard and declared martial law. Student radicals, he said, were worse than "brown shirts and the Communist elements." On May 4, his Guardsmen suddenly aimed rifles at scores of demonstraters holding a peaceful campus rally. They opened fire, shot four students dead, and left eleven others seriously wounded.

This event produced a momentum of protest around the nation's colleges. Thousands took to the streets, and universities throughout the nation closed their doors in protest, often with the approval of antiwar administrations. After Kent State, students had spread out through the country, urging their peers to express solidarity with the victims and to oppose Nixon's "secret war." I was then active in a group called the New University Conference, which was the young academic version of SDS. Cambodia caught us off guard. We had been meeting regularly for two years, and now students were acting spontaneously on their own. We saw this as proof of Rosa Luxemburg's theory of spontaneous revolutionary movement by the working class, and our vanguard rushed to catch up with our masses. I moved to take charge of events on my own CUNY (City University of New York) campus.

Leaflets were handed out for a mass rally, calling for a student strike that would unite our students with those at Kent State, Harvard, and other campuses throughout the nation that were shutting down. This time we had support in high places. Many college presidents were proclaiming their approval of the student insurrection, and on their own were closing down their campuses and creating so-called "freedom schools." These, supposedly, would replace the forced education going on in captive colleges. At the rally, we were fortunate to get students who claimed to be part of the rebellion itself—comrades from Kent State. To this day, I have no knowledge of whether they were really Kent State students. What was important was that they sported Kent State jackets and sweaters, had red armbands, and raised clenched fists. They also all seemed to be Trotskyists. The school officials were trying to prevent another disturbance such as the sit-in, and to see to it that their college was kept open. The dean of admissions strode to the podium and expressed sympathy with the students, but pleaded with them to not let their feelings of the moment interfere with the business of education.

It was good advice, and I sought immediately to offset it. As I approached the microphone, the dean attempted to prevent me from speaking, saying something to the effect that "we don't need to hear from rabble-rousers." I pushed him back hard, and he almost fell to the ground. I then gave the most demagogic speech of my career. Quoting lyrics from a recently released Jefferson Airplane album, I said the enemy was the System. By closing down the school, we would strike a blow against the System. In perfect *Waiting for Lefty* style, I raised my hand in a clenched fist and yelled, "Strike, strike, strike, strike!" The students responded in unison. Some approached the stage, held me on their shoulders, and marched out of the building. One of them approached the flagpole and pulled down the American flag. The strike began a few weeks before semester's end, and the college administration was forced to cancel final exams. At a faculty meeting, one professor complained about this side effect of the strike. She argued that her commitment to her students and their education came first. She intended to keep her classes going, and would not cave in to left-wing tyrants who claimed to have all virtue on their side. I jumped up in my best New Left fashion to protest: "There are many ways to kill," I said. "Some do it with the National Guard's bullets, others with grades." I had joined the ranks of those whom Irving Howe had dubbed "guerrillas with tenure."

My activism was not without cost. The administration of my CUNY campus held my action against me for many years. Despite a sustained record of scholarly achievement, my requests for promotion were regularly denied. I certainly felt that my behavior on campus should not have any bearing on the rank I wished to attain within the university system. Thus, I took action to gain my due.

My first step was to bring the professional associations into action on my behalf. I filed a protest with the appropriate academic freedom committee of the American Historical Association. This committee in turn appointed a committee of distinguished professors from Columbia University to investigate my case. They unanimously concluded that at any other institution, my work would have guaranteed my promotion. The decision of this committee may have embarrassed the administration, but it did not convince it to act on my behalf. My next step was to turn to the AFL-CIO affiliate that was our bargaining agent—the very union apparatus I had previously condemned as having but one role, to integrate the labor force into the mechanism of the corporate state. The union representative arguing on my behalf was a firm supporter of the war, a member of my department whom I had debated at a campus teach-in. The union chapter of the Professional Staff Congress—the faculty union at CUNY—instituted formal proceedings to secure my promotion, even threatening to move the case to federal court should my promotion be blocked. Eventually, the Chapter's intervention proved successful, and I was promoted.

At the same time, I continued with my efforts to build a new socialist movement. The catalyst for this was James Weinstein, who had been the main editor and financial backer of *Studies on the Left*. Author of a study of the early American socialists, Weinstein believed that the time was ripe for creation of a new socialist party. He had more luck with creating journals. Eventually he moved to San Francisco, where he started both a bookstore and a new magazine, *Socialist Revolution* (now called *Socialist Review*). Later, he moved to Chicago and founded the independent socialist paper *In These Times*.

Weinstein had called together a working group to fashion a new socialist party. The group seemed to be almost completely composed of fellow radical historians. It included Christopher Lasch, Warren Sussman, Eugene D. Genovese, myself, and other representative culprits. We met every Saturday for a year. I remember only one discussion of note. Genovese, who would later start his own short-lived journal, *Marxist Perspectives*, was concerned that any movement he was part of respect rank and hierarchy. "I'll be in the same movement with student comrades," he put it, "but they better realize that they are talking to Professor Genovese, and that if we publish a journal, those of us with rank are listed separately." The classless society, he wanted it known, would maintain the status ranking of the bourgeois university.

We also organized the Socialist Scholars Conference. The first conference was held at Columbia University, where the keynote speaker, Conor Cruise O'Brien, was mugged by neighborhood black residents, who obviously failed to differentiate O'Brien from the regular racist "honkie." The second was held at the old Commodore Hotel, a site that emulated the location of professional academic meetings. The third and fanciest was held at the New York Hilton. When the group subsequently shifted back to the less glamorous milieu of campus settings, the attendance and excitement dimmed. I recall one of the last sessions being held at a particularly depressing public high school in New York—a big comedown from the Hilton.

At the Hilton meeting a packed session heard Herbert Marcuse expound on "Radicals and Hippies: Youth Responses to Industrial Society." The presentation was regarded as phony by one of the scheduled commentators, a young man who called himself a Yippie and who did not like the academic socialists. Thus Abbie Hoffman, decked out in a cowboy suit with two toy guns, which he shot caps from, rushed on stage, lit up a joint, and demanded that Marcuse stop talking and start smoking. The learned Hegelian professor did not appreciate Hoffman's antics, and the session ended in pandemonium.

The convocation at the Commodore featured a panel on "Socialist Man," with Isaac Deutscher, the biographer of Stalin and Trotsky. Deutscher was regarded as a bridge to the Old Left. His candid evaluation of Soviet socialism was cherished by those of us who thought we were breaking with Stalinism and old traditions but who still wanted to share Deutscher's hope that Marxism showed the path to the future. We greeted Deutscher at the airport, only to discover that he was smoking South African tobacco. Our first words to him were, "Mr. Deutscher, we're shocked. How can you do this?" He blushed and discarded the offending tobacco immediately. It was not an auspicious start.

One of the other speakers on the panel with Deutscher—on the topic of new paths toward socialism—was a Trotskyist named Shane Mage. One of the founders of the sectarian Spartacist League, Mage had been expelled from its ranks for Menshevism. One would have to search far and wide to find someone expelled for Menshevism in the mid-1960s, but Mage had been. But unbeknownst to us, by the time he was invited to speak for the SSC, Mage had gone through another transformation. He had met Timothy Leary, the prophet of LSD, who had just begun to preach the gospel of "Turn on, tune in, and drop out." In true Marxist fashion, Mage announced to the assembled socialist scholars that Timothy Leary was the Lenin of the sixties, and that the Leary gospel, which he repeated with gusto, pointed the way to personal and political liberation under the conditions of late capitalism. Those who were truly Marxist revolutionaries, Mage told us, would drop acid with him, give up the old Marxist schemes, turn on, and drop out. Deutscher went white and, grasping his hands in front of his face, shrieked out loud in his distinct Polish accent, "Drooggs." Mage's disquisition on Acid Leninism, perhaps unique in the history of the Socialist Scholars Conference, did not find its way into the official book of papers of the conferences published by Oxford University Press.

Perhaps our academic and political activity reached its high point at the annual conference of the American Historical Association in 1969. At that meeting, we attempted to pass a resolution calling for a U.S. withdrawal from Vietnam. Eugene D. Genovese, then a professor at Rutgers University, was a central figure in what transpired. He had become the target of a red-baiting campaign by the Republican gubernatorial candidate, who was running for office on the slogan "Rid Rutgers of Reds." The right wing had never forgiven Genovese for a speech he had made at a teach-in in 1965. Condemning America's war in Vietnam as "a war of aggression," Genovese added: "Unlike most of my distinguished colleagues . . . I do not fear or regret the impending victory of the Vietcong. I welcome it." Richard Nixon and others called on the university to fire Genovese, declaring "the line must be drawn." But the Democratic governor of New Jersey did not agree, and Genovese stayed.

Since Genovese was a self-professed Marxist and revolutionary, we expected him to be a strong supporter of the resolution we now put before the members of the American Historical Association. To our dismay, we found on the other side Genovese himself. Staughton Lynd and Arthur Waskow, representing what they called the Radical Caucus of Historians, had introduced our resolution at the AHA business meeting. A session that usually attracted 100 or so stalwarts was packed with 2,000 historians who met for two nights into the wee hours of the morning to settle the issue. The radical motion failed. A substitute resolution, favored by antiwar moderates, which simply deplored and condemned the war, failed too by a close vote of 647 to 611.

The shock to the antiwar group was that the opposition to the resolution was led by Genovese. The champion of a Vietcong victory now argued that since the majority of Americans supported the war, one could not argue against it by accusing his or her fellow citizens of being immoral. Adopting the resolution would mean that historians would have to teach the views it expressed, even if they disagreed. It would politicize the historical profession. The nonpolitical members of the association, who rejected the motion, would then have no choice but to resign from the organization. Genovese branded the New Left backers of the resolutions as "totalitarian," and he called on their professional colleagues to isolate them and "put them down, hard, once and for all." Conservative members of the profession cheered, and the radicals stood aghast.

We lost the vote, but ironically—almost twenty years later when the country found itself in a conservative mood—the leftists who had lost in the sixties enjoyed a belated victory. In the original debate, Professor John K. Fairbank had warned those gathered of the dangers of politicizing the professional association. Fairbank pointed out that such politicization could cut both ways; at a later time another political side could exploit the association "for an evil cause." New Left historian Howard Zinn dismissed Fairbank's concern: " 'pluralist' democracy is a facade for oligarchical rule," Zinn claimed. Today, radicals like Zinn are the dominant voice in the profession. A resolution recently passed by the Executive Board of the Organization of American Historians condemned apartheid and endorsed disinvestment; at the same time, the board tabled a resolution introduced by an old-fashioned mainstream historian opposing Soviet abuse of human rights as irrelevant to the concerns of American historians.

As the seventies began, I realized that for all my activity and revolutionary pretensions, I had not put my body where my mouth was; I had not even been arrested once. An action that seemed to offer such an opportunity was a citywide faculty action aimed at the Pupin Physics Lab of Columbia University. New York antiwar faculty were concerned about the dwindling of protest despite the horror of the Christmas 1972 bombing of Vietnam. We decided to hold a sit-in, in opposition to work on government contracts by Columbia physicists, whose research we believed was being used for the war effort.

Having learned its lesson in 1968, the Columbia administration never called in the police to arrest us. Finally, a small group broke into the offices, opened locked file cabinets, and took out the papers that provided the unknown details of the government contracts. As the group's most well-known historian, I was asked to go through the data, write it up, and issue a public statement on the involvement of the physicists in government research. We branded our revelations "Columbia's Pentagon Papers," held a televised press conference, and demanded an end to the research. Aside from the publicity, there was no concrete result of our efforts. Nor were we made to suffer any penalties for our break-in.

The swan song of the antiwar movement was a sit-in at the U.S. Mission to the United Nations. Held after the invasion of Cambodia, it may have been the very last action against the Vietnam effort held in the United States. A small group chained itself to seats in the United Nations, while the rest of us surprised the staff at the mission after pretending to be tourists and sat down in the center lobby. The action amounted to "criminal trespass." It was my last chance to be arrested, and I succeeded, but with somewhat comical results.

For some logistic reason, I was the first on line after the arrest to be told to enter a waiting paddy wagon. As I walked toward the truck, I noticed there was not a single police officer in the vicinity. Everyone else was still inside the mission arranging to get the other protesters out. It occurred me to that I could merely walk past the truck and go on home. I noticed, however, a solitary press photographer, who seemed to be engaged in taking my picture. Political duty called. The next day, the photo of my leisurely walk to the wagon, hand raised high in the official clenched fist of protest, appeared on the front page of *Newsday*, then a Long Island paper.

A few minutes after I entered the van, my fellow trespassers joined me. The cops treated us with kid gloves. It turned out that among those arrested were faculty members from the John Jay College of Criminal Justice, where more than a few of the arresting officers were students. The cops respectfully addressed us as "professor," and our wait in large coed cells at the local precinct was more of a social occasion than a criminal proceeding. When our court appearance finally took place a few weeks later, the judge threw the charges out and erased the arrest citation from our records. As long as we promised not to sit in again at the U.N. mission, he explained, we should not be penalized for our legitimate exercise of the right to protest. American democracy once again prevented us from gaining the martyrdom we sought.

Despite our best attempts at keeping Vietnam alive as an issue, the Nixon policy of "Vietnamization" was taking its political toll. Fewer students were in danger of being drafted, and the nation's attention had begun to shift away from the horrors of the war. For those of us on the left, the hope for revolution still lay in the Third World. And for those of us living in "the belly of the beast," as we called the United States, the greatest hope had been the Cuban revolution. Since 1959, Fidel Castro's success at "liberating" his small island from the grip of the world's greatest imperial power loomed as perhaps the greatest feat in the history of successful revolutionary efforts. It was Cuba more than any other event that helped create the New Left, and helped to create the myth that a similar revolution would be an actual possibility in the United States.

During the summer of 1973, I had been given the chance to travel to Cuba for a month with a small group put together by one of New York's most prominent radical chic personalities, Sandra Levinson. Once part of the New York *Ramparts* group, Levinson now headed a pro-Cuban support and research organization, the Center for Cuban Studies. Sandy, as we called her, lived half of each year in Cuba, and clearly saw herself as one who was dedicated to gaining support for the revolution in the U.S. The trip was to be a turning point in my education.

As I left for Cuba, I held the sentiment eloquently described in the early 1960s by the late C. Wright Mills, whose stance of hostility to academia and enthusiasm for the New Left was a model. Mills had said: "I am for the Cuban revolution. I do not worry about it. I worry for it and with it." The Cubans, for their part, wanted us to see their progress and to return with the same enthusiasm for the revolution as Mills.

It was quickly apparent that whatever one's intention, traveling to Cuba with Sandra Levinson inevitably made one a "tourist of the revolution"—one of those starry-eyed Western intellectuals who travel abroad to "socialist" countries and then report that they have seen utopia. The classic position of these tourists was described by Hans Magnus Enzensberger, who wrote that while he lived in Cuba among people in dire poverty, most of the "radical tourists" knew nothing of the real situation existing in the country. "I kept meeting Communists in the hotels for foreigners," he wrote, "who had no idea that the energy and water supply in the working quarters had broken down during the afternoon, that bread was rationed, and that the population had to stand in line two hours in line for a slice of pizza; meanwhile the tourists in their hotel rooms were arguing about Lukacs."

And so, while Cubans trying to get to work were squeezed into overcrowded buses in the August heat to ride to twelve-hours-a-day jobs, I sat at a lobster lunch in the refurbished Hilton on the Levinson tour, chatting with Regis Debray and Che Guevara's family, listening to their revolutionary political talk. It was there that I handed Debray a mildly critical piece about Stalinism and the New Left that had appeared in *Telos*. I remember the thrill I felt from the sense that I had acted on behalf of the libertarian anti-Stalinist left, and in revolutionary Cuba!

But even the Levinson tour had to leave the hotel, and when it did, the experience was sobering. We were taken to the refrigerator factory at Santa Clara, which produced 400 refrigerators per day. The air in the plant was fetid, stinking of fumes and chemicals. The appliances were being built with fiberglass insulation, and the workers had no masks or protective devices to stop them from inhaling the noxious fumes, which we knew could produce cancer. When we told the manager of our concern at the lack of protection for the workers, he told us: "If it were dangerous, Fidel would have told us. Masks would cut down on production, and we are certain that what we are doing is safe."

One of the stops we were taken to was the famed Havana General Psychiatric Hospital. The guides showed us before and after pictures. Once a classic "snake pit," the hospital was now a showcase—with Danish modern facilities for the patients, who were engaged in simple work and simple arts and crafts projects. It was not reassuring to us, however, to find that some of the patients obviously had nothing wrong with them, save that they were homosexual. The doctor in charge told us that homosexuality was a disease that justified commitment.

We were further disturbed by the glazed and drugged-out expressions of most of the inmates. When we asked about this, the head doctor told us that a large proportion of the patients had been lobotomized. The head doctor assured us that a lobotomy did wonders for behavior. When we left the hospital, a radical therapist in our group could contain himself no longer. "This stinks," he said. "Lobotomy is a horror; we have to do something to stop this. It's exactly the mentality we are working against at home." Another member of the group, a woman who later helped found the Committee in Solidarity with the People of El Salvador, looked gravely at the therapist and said, "We have to understand there are differences between capitalist lobotomies and socialist lobotomies."

As our tour progressed, the conflict in the group intensified. At one point, I criticized the Soviet invasion of Czechoslovakia in 1968. Castro's justification for that invasion, I said, was opportunistic and unconvincing. The response was heated: I was a counterrevolutionary, a reactionary, and, worst of all, a racist. "How could you care about the plight of white Czech workers," a black woman in the group said, "when U.S. imperialism is supporting the oppression of blacks in Portugal and Mozambique?"

I noticed how the egalitarian Cubans treated our guide like a queen. Sandy Levinson had her own permanent suite, received flowers and fresh rum each day, and had a car and driver at her disposal. More important, she had a supply of grass to smoke in her room, which she shared with well-known revolutionary Cuban intellectuals. This, as we knew, was illegal in Cuba and publicly condemned as evidence of counterrevolutionary and decadent bourgeois activity. Yet an official blind eye was turned when the decadence was engaged in by Levinson in her salon. The Cuban police state certainly knew how to pamper its Western apologists.

On my return home, I wrote up what I had seen in a report that appeared in Dave Dellinger's magazine *Liberation*. The magazine was flooded with more letters than it had ever received, and I learned that what I had meant to be a sympathetic but critical report on Cuba was intolerable to the left. "There is some good in everything," one reader commented: "the blockade [of Cuba] kept the intellectual paws of Professor Ronald Radosh off the Cuban people for fifteen years." And the Marxist historian Philip S. Foner declared that my report was valuable "only as demonstrating how a narrow prejudice against any form of Socialism which does not adhere to rituals of men like Radosh blinds such people to the realities of historical, revolutionary developments."

The others in my group responded with their own report, which they titled "Some of Us Had a Different Trip." They accused me of being arrogant for criticizing the "first Free Territory of America." Cuba, they claimed, had the values we North Americans lacked. "For all its flaws," they said, the revolution was "a profound and beautiful reality." Moreover, since Soviet aid had made the revolution possible, it was the duty of North Americans who supported the revolution not to criticize the Soviet Union. Such criticism, they said, detracted "from the fight against U.S. imperialism."

From the time of my Cuban experience, I gradually developed more and more doubts about my political "allies." In the late 1970s and early 1980s, I became involved once again in a movement against

U.S. intervention, this time in Central America. But after the Sandinista revolution in Nicaragua, I again saw the same betrayed hopes, the same shattered dreams—a repetition of the Cuban experience, as American leftists now proclaimed the Sandinistas as the practitioners of a new socialist model for the hemisphere. Ten years from the date of my Cuba trip, I went to Nicaragua, this time to report for *The New Republic*. I saw some developments that lent credibility to the radicals' enthusiasm, but more dominant ones that revealed the agenda of the Sandinista *commandantes* to create another Cuban-Soviet-style totalitarian state.

My criticism of the Sandinistas led to the breaking up of old friendships. James Weinstein, the former editor of *Studies on the Left*, became my sharpest critic. In a private letter to me, he explained that his new socialist newspaper *In These Times* could be critical of the Sandinistas, as long as what he printed was "constructively sympathetic," and was always put in the context of the U.S. war against the Revolution. Accusing me of a "vendetta" against both the Cuban and Nicaraguan revolution, Weinstein told me that my writing precluded the possibility that I really cared about helping "make either regime better." Moreover, he predicted accurately that I would "finish off whatever credentials [I had] on the left."

Weinstein was once a leader of the democratic left, but now even he could not tolerate fundamental criticism of Marxist revolutions. Once an anti-Stalinist New Leftist, Weinstein now insisted that the Soviet Union was a wayward friend. He was not deeply concerned about communism, he told me. On the contrary, "more often than not the Soviets were 'on the right side,'" while the U.S. "assumed world-wide responsibility for maintaining the neo-colonial status quo." Weinstein even resurrected the old smear tactics of the Communist Party, which he had been a member of in his youth, denouncing me as a "front for the CIA."

Despite such sharp attacks, I still clung to the hope of trying to build a genuine democratic socialist movement. Michael Harrington had split with his former comrades of the Socialist Party and formed a broad-based left coalition that he called the Democratic Socialist Organizing Committee. I had attended its first public conference in 1974. Still wary of Harrington because of my New Left prejudices, I waited two years before deciding to join DSOC. I then met with Harrington at a favorite Greenwich Village watering hole for artists and Old Leftists. "While I am committed to my own belief that the Soviet Union is bureaucratic collectivist," Harrington told me, "anyone is welcome to join in our organization. I'm sure some of our members even believe the Soviet Union is socialist." I understood that to mean that I would be more than welcome. Harrington made it clear that he was trying to make overtures toward the New Left and that he wished to avoid the mistake he made in the sixties, when he alienated the new radicals of SDS and forever gained their hostility, creating his own isolation from the "movement."

Irving Howe, who was also a leading member of DSOC, did not find my presence auspicious. I had immediately sought entrance at the top level, via election to the organization's National Board, but thanks to Howe's opposing me, I barely squeaked through. In opposing me, Howe quoted from passages of one of my books, in which I had taken potshots at Walter Reuther of the UAW. He did not have to worry. Within one or two years, my experience made me a strong democratic socialist, and I quickly saw the relevance of democratic politics, the shrewdness of building coalitions, and the destructive futility of revolutionary creeds.

As the seventies progressed, however, a current arose in DSOC that sought to merge with an obscure socialist group that had emerged from the ashes of the New Left, called the New American Movement. Composed of die-hard New Leftists who sought to build a revolutionary socialist party and thus rejected working in and with the Democratic Party, the group was led by an assortment of former sixties radicals and red-diaper babies who had come out of the old communist milieu. The left wing of DSOC favored the merger, and I presented many arguments in its favor. We prevailed, and eventually the merger took place.

The politics of the merged organization revealed that it was beginning to move further away from the sane type of democratic politics I had reluctantly come to appreciate. It spelled the end of DSOC as a group that worked, as Harrington used to put it, "for the left-wing of the possible," transforming it into yet another sectarian current. Those who always rejected Harrington as a hopeless social democrat flocked to the new group, while genuine anticommunist democrats stilled their voices or left the ranks. I now made known my strong feelings about the organization's leftward drift. DSOC members who once saw me as too left-wing now saw me as too far to the right.

One other event assumed major importance. In 1978, I began research for a book on the Rosenberg case. It was decades earlier, as a young high school student, that I stood amidst thousands of other New Yorkers who had gathered on East 17th Street off Union

Square in what was to be a deathwatch vigil for Ethel and Julius Rosenberg, the couple who had been convicted of conspiracy to commit espionage, and who were then executed. The futile campaign to save the Rosenbergs from death was the very beginning of my entrée into the world of the American left. For my whole generation, it seemed to me, the execution of the Rosenbergs on charges that they had given the "secret of the A-bomb" to the Russians was yet another proof that radicals in America were doomed to persecution. It never crossed my mind during those years that the Rosenbergs might be something other than martyred innocents.

As an adult, I continued to hold to my earnest belief in the Rosenbergs' total innocence, always thinking that in the future, new evidence would emerge to prove the complicity of the government in a frame-up. But after the Rosenbergs' sons, Michael and Robert Meeropol, won release of the FBI files, it became clear that instead of leading to the couple's final vindication, the files provided new and compelling evidence indicating Julius Rosenberg's involvement in espionage.

My research and subsequent publication, first aired in an article which appeared in 1979, summarized the material that led to my conclusions about the case. The article—coauthored with Sol Stern—concluded that Julius Rosenberg had been the central figure in a spy network, but that the government's actions against his wife Ethel were carried out exclusively for the purpose of breaking his will, and that the evidence of her involvement was flimsy. From the beginning, it was made clear to me by figures on the left that an honest reopening of the case was not welcome. One individual, a principal figure in the case, told me that historical truth was not a worthy goal if it did not serve to hurt the establishment. As a radical, he said, he understood that in the present epoch, it was best that such truth did not come out.

As a result of my article and book, people I had known for years stopped talking to me. Others suggested that I had become a traitor to the heritage of the left. "Why did you do it?" one friend asked. "You shouldn't have written that article." At that time, I certainly did not wish to provide ammunition for the new cold warriors. But as a historian committed to the truth, I believed that history also had its claims, even if the truth was unpleasant. I quickly learned that for most of the left, actual truth was not to be held a first priority. It was better to perpetuate a myth as long as it served the "correct" political position.

My judgment about the Rosenbergs' guilt was not viewed by my comrades in DSOC as a result of a historical search for truth, but, as one member put it, "a choice of research and topic that I should not have undertaken, since we are trying to recruit good Communists into our group and wean them away from the Party, and *they* believe the Rosenbergs were innocent." A leading member of the group, in arrogant tones, informed me that he "didn't understand why at this time I chose to engage in such scholarship, even though I always knew the Rosenbergs were not innocent. This isn't a matter of history," he put it, "but current politics." Harrington, who had promised to write a blurb for my book, was told by his comrades that he could not do so.

The Rosenberg File, which I had coauthored with writer Joyce Milton, appeared to rave reviews in the general press in 1983. The editors of the *New York Times Book Review* chose it as one of the ten best books of that year.

It had been made more than clear in the book that in our view the death sentence handed down against the Rosenbergs was itself a crime. Careful readers like Nathan Glazer, who reviewed the book for *Commentary*, noted in his essay that it was not until he read the volume that he came to understand that "the sentence was far too harsh, and that it was imposed and carried out at least in part because of the political temper of the times." That did not prevent Victor Navasky, editor of the left-wing *Nation*, from characterizing the book as a hideous defense of the death sentence against the Rosenbergs.

The leftist *Guardian*, which as the former *National Guardian* had printed the first defense of the couple in 1952, opined that the book's message lent itself "to the cause of cold war fascism." But the most extreme accusations came from a group calling itself The Fund for Open Information and Accountability, Inc., the very organization whose efforts brought about the release of the FBI files on the Rosenbergs, which made our research possible. In a special issue of the FOIA's magazine, *Right to Know*, a Communist professor, Norman Markowitz, accused us of perpetrating "age-old anti-Semitic stereotypes of Jews as disloyal and greedy" and of "apologizing for anti-Semitism that was central to the Rosenberg case." Markowitz justified these charges by explaining that "capitalism is both racist and anti-Semitic." Thus our book, in failing to use the Rosenberg case as a platform for denouncing capitalism, was ipso facto guilty.

If the charge of anti-Semitism was not serious enough, another article in the same magazine suggested that the book had "all the earmarks and objective consequences of an FBI Cointelpro operation." Exactly what these earmarks were the author, Ann Mari Buitrago, never explained. But she went on to argue that the "line" of the book (a telling phrase) supported "the kind of hysterical anti-Communism Reagan has employed in fashioning a dangerous foreign policy in Central America . . . and in mounting a campaign of repression against opposition to those policies at home." At the time Buitrago wrote these words, I considered myself an opponent of the Reagan administration's foreign policy in Central America. Indeed, I had just coedited a book on Central America that was designed to provide a critique of the Reagan policy. But to the mind of the neo-Stalinist left, to suggest that the Rosenbergs were guilty was to support the Reagan foreign policy. Even one of my coeditors on the book seconded the accusation. He told me that he knew I was a solid defender of the Reagan agenda, which I was not, because I had found the Rosenbergs to be guilty. During a break in the American Historical Association annual conference, he told me that "everything is related," and he knew that I had essentially joined the Reagan team.

Democratic Socialists of America, as the Democratic Socialist Organizing Committee was now called, also began to adopt the very left-wing stance that Michael Harrington and Irving Howe had rejected in the 1950s. The culmination came for me in 1985, when the group chose as keynote speaker for its convention the foreign minister of Nicaragua, Miguel D'Escoto. It was one thing to oppose U.S. foreign policy but another to announce your support of the totalitarian Leninists who were betraying the Nicaraguan revolution. It was as if Norman Thomas would have chosen Le Duc Tho, Ho Chi Minh's foreign minister, to convene a Socialist Party meeting in the 1960s. When it came time to renew my membership, I quietly let it lapse. I did not want to admit it, but even the concept of socialism had come to mean less and less. When I finally read an old debate between the Polish intellectual Leszek Kolakowski and E. P. Thompson, it struck a vital chord. In a nutshell, Kolakowski put his finger on the thought pattern of the man of the left: "all negative facts to be found in the non-socialist world," he wrote, ". . . are to be imputed to 'the system,' while similar facts occurring within the socialist world have to be accounted for by . . . the same capitalist system."

In the 1960s I considered myself a revolutionary socialist and looked upon the nascent New Left as a group of spirited young people who would see the need to develop a socialist ideology and who hopefully would turn to Marxism. I did not predict, as some did, that when they discovered Marxism, it would become the vehicle that would turn them toward nihilism and terrorism, and political fantasies that would culminate in the antics of the Weather Underground and the Brink's murderers.

In a criticism about my current politics, the left writer Paul Berman chastised me for having "lowered [my] old red flag," and for unashamedly "proclaiming that fact to the world." Berman was correct, and I have no apologies for that stance. The flag, I thought, was rightly colored red—dripping in the blood of its victims, shed in the name of an ideal that had never yet been realized. Communism had, as Kolakowski put it, become a "skull that will never smile again." Once having written for Paul Sweezy's Marxist journal *Monthly Review*, and then for *Studies on The Left*, I had begun the new year by appearing in the pages of the neoconservative journal of culture *The New Criterion*. In its pages I tried to reassess the meaning of the Spanish civil war, and the left's unfaltering treatment of that great divide as a simple issue of good guys (the Lincoln Brigade volunteers) versus bad guys (the Franco fascists). Written on the anniversary of that conflict, my article attempted to show that the issue was more complex than it once appeared.

In that article, I had written that for "most Left intellectuals, Spain in the Thirties is a cause to be reaffirmed rather than investigated." The civil war was not a simple fight between the forces of democracy and those of fascism. I argued, the closer one got to the reality of Spain, the more blurred became the morality. The reason the volunteers had fought was not to save an embattled democracy, but because Joseph Stalin sought some pawns with which to achieve his foreign policy goals: to give the republic limited help until Britain and France dropped their policy of nonintervention, and to secure a republic that would be under effective Russian control. Hence Stalin's agents in Spain did all they could to crush the actual revolution that had taken place. The Brigade volunteers, heroic as fighters, were a political, ideological, and propaganda instrument used by the Comintern for its own purposes. They formed an integral part of the Soviet-Comintern apparatus working in Spain. The Lincoln Brigade, as one heretic veteran of that battalion put it, was "inspired, organized, directed and completely dominated" by the Kremlin. "It created the Brigades for its own arcane strategic objectives—and got its money's worth." The 1931 republic had been reduced to ashes, I argued, and the Spanish Communists had succeeded in derailing a once popular revolution and transforming it into a totalitarian police state.

Although it occurred fifty years ago, the Spanish Civil War was still a watershed. To be on the left, even as its most honest component, one had to uncritically defend the republic and not face the bitter truth about its legacy. The fight, of course, was not about Spain, but—as Irving Howe seemed to realize in a bitter polemic against my piece—about Nicaragua and South Africa. Black liberation in South Africa, Howe wrote, must unreservedly be "our cause," even if it leads "to Communist domination." Howe, who once wrote that "it never was necessary to defend the Communist regime in Hanoi or the Vietcong guerrillas in order to oppose American intervention," now belonged to a political organization that supports the Marxist-Leninist regime that holds power in Managua. A man of the left had to stand with the Sandinistas and the African National Congress, the two forces current wisdom judges to be the inheritor of the mantle of freedom. If one raised the issue of the harshness and growing oppression within Nicaragua, the man of the left would reply, "The issue is U.S. support of the contras." If one dared to raise the issue of what kind of society would emerge in South Africa if the ANC became the only force leading the struggle against apartheid, one was condemned as a red-baiting tool of the South African regime. Nuance and distinction had disappeared from view, and the only response of leftists was that one had to make a choice: "Which side are you on?" Their demand was disingenuous. What they really meant was not that they opposed U.S. policy on this or that issue, but that they supported the enemies and opponents of the U.S. Their belief was clearly that "the enemy of my enemy is my friend." One did not feel surprised to find Jesse Jackson embracing Fidel Castro and Daniel Ortega. They were on *his* side, and he wanted the American people to join them.

As the 1980s progress, I find myself somewhere in limbo—chastened about the possibility of what I once thought would be the promise of socialism, but wary of those who believe that the United States has always stood unreservedly for freedom. Looking back now, it is clear to me that that early "defector" from the left, Sidney Hook, courageously understood the real struggle of our time when the rest of us were blind. Hook was right in defining the struggle as that of democracy versus totalitarianism and in arguing that despite all of its "failings, drawbacks, and limitations, the defense and survival of the West was the first priority." One had, in the last resort, no choice but to give critical support to American democracy.

I therefore thought it better to echo Dwight Macdonald's wise counsel in an earlier epoch, to "choose the West," although in making such a choice, one did not have to abandon opposition to incorrect, unwise, or even immoral policies that sometimes were pursued by elected leaders. But such opposition, when warranted, must be carried out by demanding that our elected leaders be held accountable to the standards of democracy. America's enemies hold to no such standard. "In the fight to the death between radically different cultures," as Macdonald put it, the humanist heritage of the West must be defended. That includes free and different political parties, free trade unions, and the protection of individual rights and civil liberties. Macdonald knew what my generation of the left had forgotten—that the Western democracies are living, developing societies open to change and responsive to popular pressure. By its very raison d'être, the left defines itself as standing on the other side of the barricades in the great battle of our time. Realizing this at last, I have said goodbye to the left and hung up the old red flag for good.

9

Errand into the Wilderness

Michael Novak

Since at least second grade, I have wanted to become a writer. From ages fourteen to twenty-six, I studied for the Roman Catholic priesthood until, six months before ordination, in 1960, I decided not to become a priest. Not long after I first began publishing in earnest, the Second Vatican Council (1962–1965) brought the Catholic Church to more favorable public attention than it had earlier received in America. From about 1967 until 1971, those who knew my writing had reason to describe me as a "progressive, left-of-center Catholic," and even as one who sided with the radical left, over against the "corporate liberalism" (as I then called it) of the mainline left. I liked being thought of in that way. Nonetheless, a left-wing friend described me to her colleagues in 1968 as one whose "temperament is conservative but who thinks himself into left-wing positions." (That taught me a new way of thinking about myself.) Slowly, though, I also thought my way *out of* left-wing positions.

My first published book was a novel, *The Tiber was Silver* (1961). I was long uncertain whether I wanted to be a scholar, a novelist, a social critic, or an engaged activist. The French tradition of Mauriac, Sartre, Camus, and others taught me that an intellectual could properly do all four, each in its season. Aristotle counseled that until he is at least fifty, a philosopher should engage in a broad range of activities at first hand. In my own poor way, I have given that a shot, more or less systematically involving myself in and reflecting upon various dimensions of American life.

During the three decades of my adulthood, political and cultural changes have occurred rapidly. "Movements" of many kinds have swept through the consciousness of readers and writers. On these changes swift judgments are often required. Making them, one can often lose old friends. Families—even spouses—have been driven apart by answering them in different ways. Those who were once allies often become, almost overnight, bitterly estranged. Too often these days, dinner parties erupt in loud and angry disagreement. All this happens because new forms of "consciousness"—concerning American "imperialism," détente, feminism, homosexuality, liberation theology, the rebels in Nicaragua—have confronted our generation with a relentless series of fundamental decisions. *What should we think? What should we hope for? What should we do?*

There is a "vulgar Marxist" way of answering these questions. There is a "line." In fact, other progressives often bully one into becoming "sophisticated." (There is in our society a deep, although disguised, hunger for orthodoxy, especially among persons who think of themselves as progressives. Most do not wish to appear to be orthodox, only sophisticated. It is the same thing.) With unprecedented speed, the literate are urged to adapt to new ideas, to new ways of thinking, and to new standards of judgment. Theology is done, again and yet again, "in a new key." I have come to call it *neodoxy:* obedience to the new.

At a certain point, one wants to get off the train; at least, *I* wanted to get off the train. The progressive "line" draws strength from many diverse cultural feeders but always runs in one direction. It is consistent in the disciplines and inhibitions it wishes to destroy, and in which direction it wants to move. (Near the top of the Book of Genesis, for example, we are told, "Man and woman He made them." *That* is one of the differentiations to be destroyed.) The climate becomes ever more utopian, ever more dreamy. The mildly Marxist analysis that is the vanguard of left-wing consciousness is not random or undirected. It is an analysis of a quite distinctive type. But this is to get too far ahead in the story.

———•———

I wrote some years ago that life is in some equal measure self-discovery and self-invention. In part we discover—over time and through much darkness—who we are. In part, through trial and error, we choose to be who we are; we give ourselves our own identity. In mobile and free societies such as ours, with access to an almost infinite range of experiences, books, and thoughts, it is not so easy as it once was to live a life of straight-line logic. Experiences occur that call into question earlier certitudes. Fresh insights and new paradigms allow us to break through earlier established horizons, sometimes from heights (or depths) that alter our vision of the entire landscape round about. In my case, I once had a vision of political economy that I have since come to discover was mistaken.

Like many young Catholics and Jews, I had imbibed from an early age a set of suspicions concerning big business, capitalism, Marlboro man individualism, and Anglo-Saxon ethnic superiority. While never seriously tempted to join a socialist party, I rather liked socialist analyses that attacked the complacency of America. The anticapitalism of such writers as R. H. Tawney on Protestantism and the acquisitive instinct appealed to me. One need not be a socialist or a Marxist to be fairly systematically anticapitalist (and radically critical of American society). For all practical purposes, though, one usually becomes thus the ally of socialists and Marxists.

Today, some of my best friends remain far to the left. *Remain* far to the left? During the past twenty years, by their own admission, they have moved ever farther left. Like me, they are voyagers. Their voyages in recent years have taken them into three specific desert fastnesses: that the United States is an imperialist nation oppressive to people in the Third World; that capitalism is an evil economic system, propelling imperialism abroad and multiple ills at home; and that the combination of imperialism and capitalism is fed by patriarchy, machismo, and male domination.

Although twenty years ago I was poised to journey into that wilderness myself, such friends now look around to find me not only absent from their caravan but among their nagging critics. Some have expressed hurt. Others find my own change of direction (even though it was not sudden, but protracted; and not secret, but argued out step-by-step in print) puzzling, troubling, and—when they are angry enough to say so—a mark of disloyalty, betrayal, and downright moral corruption. Their own deepening involvement with the left seems to them so correct, so commanded by the evidence, and so morally obligatory that it is truly difficult for them to understand my "defection." They know that their own views are moral. (I once thought so too, but no longer.) They feel themselves impelled by Christian faith and moral obligation. For them, it is a matter of *Saying Yes and Saying No* (the title of a book by one of my closest former colleagues, Robert McAfee Brown). If they say yes, while I say no, it is virtually impossible for them to allow that I am moral, or even to be open to argument that *their* position is immoral.

The opinion of me held by former comrades and readers occasionally arrives in unsigned hate mail (return address from some convent, religious house, or seminary), whose blunt message is that I have sold out. More often, it is expressed in person. In the spring of 1987, for example, an older rabbinic student accosted me at a meeting in Philadelphia: "You're Michael Novak? I used to admire what you wrote. You wrote some very good things. But now you've sold out to the business interests that run the American Enterprise Institute. I despise what you're doing now." He hadn't read any of my books of the past decade, of course. He didn't know anything about the AEI. He was repeating what others said. (I told him, "If that is your view, it's your problem.")

It's interesting to me that those who claim to represent the left as a humane alternative find it impossible to believe that their view is intellectually and morally dubious. And that their most commonly offered explanation for departures from their way of thinking is a crass one: money, power, fame. This suggests that they imagine themselves in a world abounding with temptations, which must be fiercely resisted, as if they themselves are in danger of selling out. This seems to leave intellectual inquiry with two outcomes only: either agree with them or be immoral. It also suggests awareness of their own precarious bad faith.

Thus, I worry about the self-ascribed morality of my former colleagues, although in a different way than they worry about mine. I fear that they have collapsed together two quite different spheres of discourse, the moral and the political. They have (purposefully) swept away the uncertainties of politics and of political reasoning, in order to enjoy the certainties of moral and religious passion. If anyone stands in their way, that alone is evidence of resistance to morality and true religion. It is to be, by definition, reactionary.

But something still deeper is at work. In the mental universe of those of my friends who have moved to the far left there appear to be only two types of persons: the oppressor and the oppressed. White males living in capitalist, democratic societies are oppressors by definition, unless they accept into their hearts all the pain of all the others, and unless they renounce who and what they are, confess their guilt, and humbly join in solidarity with the oppressed. This is the only narrow road to salvation. In this vision, there is much self-hatred and severe intellectual self-abnegation. Too painful to endure, this hatred is often diverted from the self and projected upon one's nation and one's people.

One other point. Many of my friends on the left would lose their identity, and their entire self-image would be shattered, if they should come to be thought of as "neoconservative." Then they would be vulnerable to the same sort of denunciations that they have seen showered upon me. To be thought to be conservative is a heavy weight to carry in the academy. Many mainline Protestants would rather die than be identified with the conservative evangelicals; many Catholics want desperately not to be identified with the conservatism of the immigrant church. Religious men who wish to be taken seriously in the world—and by their radical feminist colleagues—must be accepted as progressive and enlightened persons most of all. Who knows how many small deaths are undergone so that religious progressives will not be thought by others to be conservative?

Progressives protect their own. In a culture in which, as Alasdair MacIntyre writes in *After Virtue*, moral discourse is often reduced to boos and hurrahs, it is foolish not to recognize that being favored in the media enables the left to cheer the loudest and to enjoy the best protection. In intellectual circles, moderate leftists rule, and are easily intimidated by those lefter than they, to whom they unconsciously attribute moral superiority, feeling perhaps a little guilty about their own pragmatism.

Around them, socialist experiments crumble. The crown upon the heads of religious progressives, therefore, sits most uneasily. The most publicly uncelebrated fact of the late twentieth century is the death of the socialist idea, especially in economics. (Why, I often wonder, did it take me so long to discover this myself?) The 3 percent of the land allotted to private farming and to market transactions within the U.S.S.R. yields roughly 33 percent of the foodstuffs that reach the Soviet table, as Secretary General Gorbachev has been obliged to note—and to hold up as the standard for the "new" Soviet economy. Weary of being both socialist and poor, the Chinese have recently turned to private property, markets, and other capitalist techniques, thereby doubling their food production within two short years (an achievement which in a country of 1 billion citizens carries a certain clout).

Perhaps sensing the ground shift beneath their feet, my old colleagues on the left are most reluctant to enter into debate concerning the empirical record of the ideal they have made central to their moral vision: socialism as a means of liberating the poor. They are unwilling to point to any existing socialist society as the model toward which they aspire, or even to specify the institutions they believe essential to the socialism of their dreams. The dreamier, the better. I think they sense the verdict that history will pronounce upon them, for their tone is increasingly shrill and anxious. They have internalized the neo-Marxist analysis of oppression and dependency. Their paralysis springs from the shame they feel at being Americans. They have the right idea: to help the poor. But they have chosen methods bound to disappoint them. Slowly many will see that.

Not all, though. The older among them are fully grown adults who have formed their views deliberately, and are fully culpable or (as they think) praiseworthy on that account. Many of them believe that in international affairs, on balance, the United States is a force for evil. They oppose virtually every employment of U.S. force abroad. Some also hold that the American domestic system itself is either fundamentally evil or so radically corrupt as to be salvageable morally only through some unspecified restructuring, hazily described in the left-wing slogans of the last hundred years. It does not bother them that wherever such "restructurings" have been put into effect, they have created wastelands (especially for vast legions of peasants). They cheer such dismal failures as Yugoslavia or Cuba or Tanzania or North Vietnam or Nicaragua (only a few of them cheer the U.S.S.R. itself) as signs of the hopeful variety within communism. They come to the aid of those who seek to advance the purposes of such regimes and their allies, even when this means opposing the United States and its allies. They think capitalism is inherently evil, that business is based upon greed, and that Americans ought to live in shame for living as they do. They are alienated grown adults, who think that their alienation is a higher form of virtue, rather than a form of bad faith.

It is not they, then, who are likely to be persuaded through reason and an analysis of cases. They have made their commitment. It is, rather, the younger ones, still open-minded and searching, the questioning and the self-affirming, who know in the depths of their minds that self-hatred, alienation, and resentment are signs of an illness of the spirit, and that a falsely learned alienation is a lie. It is to the latter, not the former, that argument is usefully addressed. The former do not dialogue, I have sadly learned. They excommunicate. There is nothing to fear in that. It is a blessing.

— · —

In September 1947, I traveled by train to South Bend, Indiana, to begin my studies—a long course of studies—leading, I hoped, to ordination as a Catholic priest. I will never forget my first sight of the dome of Notre Dame or, once at the heart of the campus, of St. Mary's Lake, still and leaden in the hot late-summer air, and across it on a grassy mound the gray stones of Holy Cross Seminary, which was to be my home for four years. I was then just a few days short of my fourteenth birthday, about to become a high school freshman. I said a prayer of commitment. I would give it my best.

My parents had tried to dissuade me from entering the seminary. My father was in those days a touch anticlerical. "Remember, you're a Novak," he had said in our last embrace at the Pittsburgh train station, as if we were of noble lineage. He said one more time, "Don't let them put you on a pedestal." He had talked vividly about how lonely the life of a priest could be; he told me of a priest friend of his who had described how many achingly long evenings he had sat alone at the piano. My father had also described the many symbols—the cassock and collar, the being set apart, the eager deference of the people toward the clergy—that could relentlessly and steadily go to a young man's head. (I do not think now that he was right about that. In this generation, many priests are quite modest; a crisis in self-confidence is apparent now.)

A few weeks earlier, when I was out of earshot, my father had responded to my uncle, who strongly objected to my going to the seminary at such a young age, that I was unusually mature, that he had made his objections known, but that I had thought it out and was determined to go. "Besides," I heard him say, "the more I would say no, the more Mike would say yes."

I had long loved getting up early and walking a mile and a half across the iron-squeaking snow to serve the 7 A.M. mass, arriving early enough to kneel before the tabernacle in our parish church, with the red sanctuary candle flickering, where no one could observe me. I wasn't certain I would become a priest, but I was perfectly sure that I should try; the call was strong. At last giving up on his objections, my father said: "If you go, give it a good shot; stay at least a full year, don't give up easily. But when you want to come home, we want you here."

One afternoon, he and yet another uncle of mine had watched me play eighth-grade football (we had no league, nor any equipment but what we bought for ourselves). During the first half I scored five touchdowns, until I had to leave with my father. "Pretty good, Mike," Uncle Johnnie said at the car. "He's not well coordinated for this game," my father said matter-of-factly as he closed the car door on the other side. He had never said I should not play football in high school, although the local coach (famous in that area) had already stopped by to watch me play and to encourage me to come and see him. It is odd that part of me accepted my father's assessment of my abilities, although another part of me was exhilarated by the success on the field that I usually experienced.

There was no doubt in my mind, on arrival in South Bend, that I should enter the seminary *then, there*. I was not sure that I would manage to finish all four years in that gray building across the sky-reflecting lake. But I knew it was my inner destiny to try. I knew that if I did not try now, before high school, then football and girls—I was prematurely crazy about girls—would fatefully distract me. Now was the time, Notre Dame was the place. I had tried to enter the Jesuits and had inquired of several other communities. The Jesuits didn't take candidates until after high school, and the Holy Cross Fathers (who run Notre Dame) offered the broadest scope of priestly activities, from teaching and research, through television and journalism, to foreign and domestic missions. My eighth-grade yearbook suggested that I would be an anchorman or journalist (I wrote the prediction myself), but I was uncertain what I wanted to do, and wanted room to experiment. Holy Cross was perfect.

So it turned out to be. I loved my years of study, including Latin, Greek, French, and (much later) Hebrew and Italian. After graduating from high school, I chose to leave the Notre Dame province to join the newer and more pioneering venture of building up the new Stonehill College in Massachusetts. First, though, came a concentrated year of prayer and a more strictly monastic life in the novitiate at North Dartmouth, Massachusetts. The years at Stonehill were happy and fruitful (to my joy, our seminary team in the intramural football league lost only two games during four years). After graduation, my superiors selected me for study at the Gregorian University in Rome. I had been having doubts about becoming a priest. I wanted to do so many things that I didn't know how I could do them all, bound under obedience. I wanted and needed to be a free lance. But that conflict took a while to become intense.

Over the years, I had almost quit several times. (All one had to do was say the word and go; of the thirty-nine I started with in 1947, I was the last to go; none of the "original class" made it into the priesthood, although of course others who entered along the way did.) But I basically loved the study, the prayer, the atmosphere of charity and learning.

After two years in Rome, in 1958, I finally asked to leave. My superior back in Massachusetts, a marvelous priest (a missionary in Chile and Peru for many years), agreed that I should leave. "Still," he said, "you've put in so many years. Perhaps Rome got you down. Graduate studies in literature here may refresh you. Why don't you be a little more patient, make certain what you're doing, then decide? Either way, I'm with you."

It did seem reasonable to be certain that later I'd have no regrets. For another year and a half, I gave it all I had. Then I knew. Contrary to custom at the time, my superior allowed the whole seminary—in Washington, D.C., at Catholic University—to hold a good-bye party for me. That was a warming gesture. He also gave me money for a suit, my first in twelve years that wasn't clerical black. After a visit with my family, disappointed but supportive, I set off for New York City in January 1960 to make a career as a novelist, with a hundred dollars from my father. I found the garret of my dreams and worked hard.

By the time my first novel was accepted, late in the summer of that year, I had also won a fellowship in philosophy at Harvard. Not knowing better, I had applied only to Harvard and to Yale; Harvard offered more support. After having lived in Manhattan on $35 a week, earned by writing, I enjoyed the relative opulence of a Harvard dormitory and regular meals. But Harvard philosophy—heavy on logic and language analysis—was more narrow in its intellectual range than Stonehill or Rome had been, and it seemed to me terribly inadequate to the century of the Holocaust, to the turmoil in Europe (the Hungarian revolution of 1956 had occurred just as I arrived in Rome), and to the spiritual quest many had been experiencing in the late 1950s. *Harper's* asked me to do a piece for a special issue on the universities; it came out as "God in the Colleges," and was later reprinted in several anthologies of the New Left. Its basic theme was that behind the logic and the pragmatism, behind the cloverleafs and the swift, finned automobiles, there was growing a hunger to ask, "Who are we, under the stars, with the wind on our faces?"

—·—

In the seminary, I used to admire the intellectual leaders of the religious and philosophical left most of all. One of the first models around whom I wished to fashion my own career was the young

Michael Harrington, then of the Catholic Worker movement, who used to write in *The Commonweal* well before he became famous for *The Other America*. In the generation following Reinhold Niebuhr and John Bennett, Robert McAfee Brown and Harvey Cox were personal friends. In the mid-1960s, I was invited to serve as the first Roman Catholic on the editorial board of *The Christian Century*, and also on the board of *Christianity and Crisis*, Niebuhr's own journal. And, of course, I cherished my outlets in *The Commonweal* and the *National Catholic Reporter*, the two major lay Catholic journals. (There was a time, the joke went, that no religious magazine of the left could publish without Michael Novak on its board.) Gradually, I could no longer avoid seeming adversarial within these journals because they were moving leftward, while I no longer believed in left-wing visions.

How did that conversion happen? If I had been knocked from a horse by a blinding light on a single memorable day, it would be easier to say. Instead, it was quite gradual, through examining my own left-wing presuppositions one by one. Underneath this questioning, perhaps, lay a pursuit of self-knowledge, a drive to be faithful to my family and roots, to be myself.

Half of my grandfather's family remained behind in Slovakia when four brothers came to America just before the turn of the century. Part of our family still lives behind the Iron Curtain. Socialism to me was not, therefore, merely an intellectual symbol, but a family matter. Nonetheless, my education was as anticapitalist as that of any other liberal arts major who took seriously the anticapitalist reflections of English literary critics and of most literary giants in America and Britain. As a Catholic, I was perhaps somewhat more Euro-centered than my fellow students in my intellectual interests. I especially loved Albert Camus, but also read a great deal about the worker-priests of France and Catholic Action in Italy. I read the early (anticapitalist) writings of the Christian Democrats; Graham Greene, Heinrich Böll, Alberto Moravia, Ignazio Silone, and others. Following Michael Harrington (although suspicious of the scholasticism of his Marxism), I thought I could be a social democrat or democratic socialist—a democrat in politics, a mild socialist in economics, a blend of conservative and modernist in culture. It seemed there must be a "third way" between oppressive socialism and laissez-faire capitalism, probably something like democracy plus a cooperative economy gently directed in some new way.

— . —

It has never been difficult for me to identify with the poor. I was born among them. Johnstown, Pennsylvania, its steel mills strung out for a dozen miles along the valley floors of the Conemaugh and Stony Creek rivers, flanked by steep green hills, was a good place to grow up, among plain, solid people. The countryside is beautiful round about; deer are seen frequently, large bears occasionally, and ring-neck pheasants and rabbits are abundant. I used to marvel at the thick red smoke from the open hearth at Bethlehem steel, and the white-hot ingots brought out in toy-soldier rows to cool. Watching the thick clouds of smoke billow over the hilltops, I felt sorry for the almost naked Indians who once camped upon the Conemaugh, near the point where the two rivers join. (The Point Stadium still sits there, from which Babe Ruth once hit a home run 15 feet above the 406-foot mark in right field, my father says, and still climbing). The poor Indians had no industry, no heated homes, no wheels, no iron stoves. I was an admirer of Progress. It did not surprise me later to learn that the Germans sent the Graf Zeppelin over Johnstown, for espionage purposes, in about 1936, when I was three; and I think I faintly remember it. I certainly remember the vast formations of aircraft—especially the P-38s—winging overhead on their way to Europe from 1942 on, and the hulks of tanks, German and American, shipped back to the Johnstown mills for meltdown from the African campaign.

My father had had to leave school during the sixth grade to help support the family. His father had died when a carriage overturned on him at a funeral, when my father was two. His mother, who had been sent to America as a girl of sixteen with a sign "Passaic" around her neck, now supported six children by taking in washing and house-cleaning. They lived on Virginia Avenue, which clings to the side of a steep hill above the mills, its narrow frame houses almost two stories higher on the back side than on the street side; you have to see Virginia Avenue to believe it.

One uncle, on my mother's side, went to college, until the bank collapse in 1933 forced him to withdraw. Practically all the men went off to war. My father was all packed and ready for the Navy, when on the day before the train departed a telegram brought word of a new ruling exempting men of his age and number of children (then four). Later, in December 1944, another telegram announced the death of his best friend, Mickey Yuhas, in the Battle of the

Bulge. On the same day I was hit by a car while sledding and, the doctor said, came within an inch of having my skull crushed and an eye lost (my head smashed the headlight at its edge, and I went up over the fender). Three weeks later at midnight mass, marching in the choir in the darkened church with a candle in my hand, I was the eleven-year-old whose black eye made people in the pews cover smiles and whisper.

———.———

Marriage and a honeymoon in Rome in the fall of 1963, to cover the Second Vatican Council, interrupted my Harvard studies. The stunning new "openness" of the Catholic Church fulfilled many of my seminary dreams of what ought to happen. I was glad to be able to report on it, with all the freedom of a layman but with an insider's knowledge. Lord Acton's account of the First Vatican Council a century earlier was my model. From Stanford, Robert McAfee Brown came to Rome as a Protestant observer; soon enough, he proposed a teaching position at Stanford, where in 1965 I became the first Catholic in the religion department. It was there that my radical phase began.

Stanford in 1965 was just becoming alive with radical politics as Karen (big with our first child) and I arrived. Until early 1967, I was in favor of the Kennedy-Johnson commitment to South Vietnam, for Niebuhrian "realist" and anticommunist reasons. The cause was just. Gradually, though, I became convinced that the strategy and tactics of the conduct of the war were not likely to lead to success, and began to oppose it on just-war grounds.[1] This measured judgment did not satisfy the left, but did persuade many moderate people. I spent a month in Vietnam during the election period of August 1967, and came back with a sharper grasp of the concrete setting, a deeper appreciation of the complex antagonisms among the Vietnamese, and a confirmation of my modulated—but clearly antiwar—views. I was not, I could not be, an anti-American. "To love one's own country is not a sin," I used to paraphrase Camus. To stop the war was one aim; to negotiate a safe period during which to secure a free and mutual reunification of Vietnam over the long term was another, at once more complex and more honorable.

In the spring of 1968, after campaigning vigorously for Robert Kennedy and being devastated by his murder, I moved back east to the idyllic campus of Old Westbury, the newest branch of the State University of New York. Two things attracted me. First, Old Westbury was to be an experimental college, and educational reform was clearly a coming priority. Second, the president, Harris Wofford, had helped begin the Peace Corps, and his interests in Democratic Party politics and his enthusiasm for whatever he undertook were terribly winning. Given my seminary background, I felt I very much needed more experience of the world, especially in politics. At Old Westbury, we would be in the vanguard of educational reform, and I would learn a lot from the Peace Corps style of Wofford. My expectations were abundantly fulfilled, although as usual not in the way I expected.

So radical were the first hundred students admitted to Old Westbury for its first year in 1968–1969 that, in one survey, all students except one thought electoral politics was a bourgeois fraud and only that one planned to participate at all; he was for Eugene McCarthy. Both Harris and I went to the Chicago convention; that was a searing experience, amid stink bombs and tear gas, ignorant armies clashing by night.

Back on campus, the students soon turned against Harris; there were endless demonstrations, grievances, protests, and bizarre behaviors. The fact that the bookstore was open only during assigned hours was interpreted as "bourgeois"; one of the faculty members smashed the door down with his foot, and students took what they wanted. Another professor, to demonstrate a rigorously egalitarian atmosphere, met his seminar under the large classroom table, all squatting and ducking their heads at egalityrannical levels. Think of this as childish vulgar Marxism; the grown-up version has uncannily repeated itself in every Communist Party victory. At Stanford, the small proportion of radicals were (until violence erupted in the year following my departure) like a little salt sprinkled over a large roast. At Old Westbury, there was little else besides salt, and I very soon rebelled.

Most students wanted total liberty, meaning no standards, no restrictions, no differentiations, no authorities, no requirements. Against this, a few of us established a second college within the college, which quite deliberately we called the Disciplines College. Assignments, authorities, standards, requirements. We were said by some to be—what else?—fascists.

One of my favorite moments at Old Westbury was an invitation I extended to Herbert Marcuse to hold a seminar. Prussian to his fingertips, Marcuse said no student should feel competent to rebel against a teacher until he had mastered what his teacher knew; until then, revolution must mean discipline. *Delectatio morosa:* Marcuse plunged in the estimation of our most vocal radicals, and I enjoyed their discontent.

The very word "radical," of course, began to make me queasy. The entire vocabulary of the far left—which sounds the more plausible the less likely it is to be realized—assumes an entirely different significance when a dominant majority begins to act it out and to impose it. Some really *do* mean "paranoia is true perception." I began to understand the disbelief that many millions in this century have experienced when totalitarians actually began to put into practice the assault upon "bourgeois standards" that once sounded merely clever and literary. At Old Westbury, some really *did* mean that Shakespeare is "crap" and burned his books to dramatize their feelings. Someone even carefully placed human excrement on a piece of cardboard and put it in the desk drawer of a woman on the faculty. What some didn't like they simply disrupted. Anarchy and tyranny, contempt for disciplined intellect and a fascination with "the ferocious exercise of will"[2] are not so far buried in human consciousness that they cannot easily be released.

All the words of the far left began to sound new chords in my head. Like all words, each of them has an Orwellian double meaning. If one understands them in a decent, bourgeois liberal way, they have an attractive sound. (Who can be against freedom or equality?) If one grasps what these same words mean when they are acted out apart from the restraints of checks and balances, and through the coercions of a majority willing to throw tantrums in order to get its way, their true force is to dehumanize those who use them and to imperil any who get in the way. Played in the classic liberal key, words such as "freedom," "equality," "justice," and "the poor" have had a powerful meaning for my family and for many others. (The United States is like a Broadway hit, with immigrants lined up around the block by the millions waiting to get in.) Played in their naked vulgar Marxist key, the same words intend only one thing: a rationale for naked power. Wherever they are around the world, at the fringes of Britain's Labor Party or the German SDP, at feminist caucuses or among the Sandinista *turbas*, extreme leftists do whatever is necessary to get their way. My wife was told our house would be bombed; we took care to keep close track of both our children, then ages three and one.

The hard lessons learned from living in a "total community" with the fervent radicals of Old Westbury, who brooked no opposition and shouted down appeals to reason, were like a vaccination. What

Kolakowski wrote of the relation between Marx and the totalitarian U.S.S.R. might also be said of the relation between the ideas of the serious left and the infantile leftists of Old Westbury: while one could not predict from the words of the former what the latter would make of them, neither was there anything in the former that would prevent the worst from happening. And everything done by the new left could be justified by quoting amply from the old left.

At Stanford, the year after my departure, buildings were bombed. Elsewhere, the radical left turned to kidnappings, bombings, and bank robberies. The decline of the universities was in full swing. Many of my associates who had been hesitant were rapidly now becoming radicalized, just as I was moving in the opposite direction, becoming *de*radicalized. But disaffection with the left is not enough to constitute a true conversion.[3]

—— · ——

In 1975, American involvement in Vietnam ended with an irrational, irresponsible abruptness. The vision of hundreds of thousands of boat people, preyed upon by pirates who raped and looted and murdered, afflicted my conscience. As I read about the sufferings of the Vietnamese people left behind in Vietnam and (still later) of the systematic deceptions practiced by the North Vietnamese upon those of us in the antiwar movement, I dreamt at night of blood on my own hands. The situation in present-day Vietnam is a rebuke to the antiwar movement, as is the continuing expansion of Soviet air and naval power in the South Pacific.

More to the point, as I surveyed the economic record of the socialist nations of Eastern Europe, Asia, Africa, and Cuba, I could find none that I admired, or would choose as a model for the world. The socialist *economic* ideal clearly did not work in practice, not anywhere. Upon sustained reflection, it also became clear to me that its flaw lay not only in its practice, but in its fundamental ideas. Socialism as an economic ideal is not designed to create new wealth, but only to mobilize envy. Idealists say that its aim is to distribute wealth evenly. Realists must observe that socialist elites retain uncommon powers, privileges, and wealth. Socialist idealism is a deception.

The great advantage the socialist ideal brings to an intellectual, however, is difficult to do without. Socialism is essentially a vision for organizing history. Cosmic in its attraction, it offers security and solid footing. Through its gaze, we *know* that capitalist institutions are destined for the dustbin, that to favor freer markets is "ideological," and that the growth of collective power is inevitable in history.

Therefore, faced with any event or proposition, one must only analyze whether it furthers the collapse of capitalism or enhances the growth of collective power. If so, it belongs to the future, gains its *truth* from that, and ought to be applauded and supported. If not, we know that it is to be despised as out of date and doomed. Since the news industry is interested in the new, socialist imagery is the natural mental equipment of journalists. The inner radar of news judgment is a hidden, unconscious vision of what is coming to be and what is fading away. For this reason, virtually all communicators of the news are "vulgar Marxists." Those who are *not* infuriate their colleagues.

When I ceased relying upon socialist methods of analysis, therefore, I felt a significant inner emptiness. If one is not a card-carrying socialist, but a pragmatic leftist, one can of course employ many forms of socialist and Marxist analysis without being ideologically careful about the full sweep of their logic. Still, losing faith in socialist methods of analysis is like losing an inner compass, a chart, a vision. Fortunately, there fell into my hands, among other writings, some of the essays of Irving Kristol, recalling me to an intellectual tradition I had hitherto avoided: that of the American Framers and that of British and French liberals of the early nineteenth century. I trusted former persons of the left more than conservative intellectuals; the fact that others (soon to be labeled by Michael Harrington "neoconservatives") had doubts and questions similar to mine much strengthened me.

Both as a Slavic Catholic and by temperament, I am partial to thinkers who are somewhat skeptical of a merely geometric logic, of rationalism. I am attracted to thinkers who love the unpredictability of fact, who respect the ambiguity of history, and the concreteness of ethical reasoning and ethical perception—to Aristotle and Aquinas, for example, and to the Whig tradition. I respect those who give due weight to the ethical role of the family, to tradition, to religion, to the tacit wisdom built up through the social experience of the human race. For such reasons, the sheer individualism of some Anglo-American thinkers (from Bentham to Rawls) has always less than satisfied me. But such writers as Adam Smith, Edmund Burke, John Stuart Mill (despite my allergy to his socialist inclinations), Montesquieu, Bastiat, Lord Acton, and John Henry Newman awakened deeply responsive chords in me. When I read Hayek's postscript to *The Constitution of Liberty*, "Why I Am Not a Conservative," I responded as one who finally grasped a way of stating what I am. I belong to what used to be called the Whig tradition; its vision of progress is quite different from that of the "progressives"—a term captured by socialist ways of thought. In offering an alternative to the socialist dream of the future, it has captured the idea of the future. It is more realistic, more likely to work, proven in its successes. In these respects, this vision (for which I would have preferred the name "neoliberal") is a much greater threat to leftists than conservatives have ever been. That is why it infuriates leftists.

—— · ——

Meanwhile, on another front, another stage in my conversion began in 1970, continued through the process of writing *The Rise of the Unmeltable Ethnics* (1972), and culminated in my efforts on behalf of the McGovern campaign in 1972. In July 1970, just after I had set aside a report in the *New York Times* that Sargent Shriver, recently resigned as ambassador to France, was launching a national campaign to help elect Democrats to Congress, and just after telling my wife that I would love to be involved in that, my telephone rang. It was Mr. Shriver, telling me that he had just finished *The Experience of Nothingness*, and wanted me to write for him in his campaign. Could I come down to Washington? I didn't even shave my long beard.

There followed three splendid months of living with the Shrivers at their home in Rockville, Maryland, and flying out on fascinating campaign trips to some thirty states. We had a marvelous time. I don't think I have ever met a man with so much energy, so much enthusiasm, and such a serious practical interest in philosophical and religious ideas. We had so many good laughs, doing the zany things media campaigns force politicians to do (being pulled by speedboats on inflated tractor-tire inner tubes on a lake in South Dakota, for example), and so many long and happy conversations that those months are a kind of highlight in my memory.

Most of all, though, by election day in the congressional year 1970, I felt I had a far better grasp of the diverse neighborhoods of America than I had ever had before. I had seen at first hand the true significance of ethnicity and localism in American life. On the same day, we once met with black ministers for whom "quotas" mean being brought *in;* a Jewish women's group for whom "quotas" mean a history of being kept *out;* and an electrician's union (mostly Italian-Catholic) for whom "quotas" mean "they never include us." Political symbols have their own geography. A speechwriter needs to know which words mean what to whom, where, and when. Moreover, I learned to respect the great openness, yearning, generosity, and hope of all those ordinary people that we met along the way, hands rough or smooth, faces beautifully kept or weathered, speech cultivated or rough. Words that I had written about the American majority—complacently drinking beer in front of television—in *Toward a Theology of Radical Politics* now made shame color my cheeks. I met the American people in the flesh; my literary imagination had been calumnious. But this had not been my vision only. In rejecting it, I was rejecting the leftist vision of America (or Amerika), the anti-Americanism so common among my intellectual colleagues.

I noted, too, that the great political commentators often had things wrong. In poor black neighborhoods, we avoided speaking of crime, which we took to be a "code word"; but the local black politicians who spoke before Mr. Shriver attacked crime far more heatedly than anyone I had ever seen on television. In working-class neighborhoods, we often spoke in bars near factories or in union meeting halls that were far better integrated, whites and blacks in obvious camaraderie, than I had ever seen in any other social location. And why not? In major cities such as Philadelphia and Pittsburgh, Cleveland and Gary, Newark and Detroit, the great Democratic politicians such as Jack and Robert Kennedy, Lyndon Johnson and Hubert Humphrey, rang up great majorities among blacks and white ethnics alike. The more highly educated observers, I learned (most political journalists these days have graduate degrees), were nowadays less in touch with working-class America than I had imagined.

Ed Muskie was my candidate in 1972, but neither he nor his chief speechwriter, Robert Shrum, thought much of my thesis about whites and blacks together in *The Rise of the Unmeltable Ethnics*. Muskie struck me as an admirable man, as quick to irascibility as a Slav ought to be (I know it in myself), and genial and warm, too; but he seemed to think of himself as a Maine Yankee and patrician. In any case, McGovern won the nomination. And the instant Senator Eagleton pulled out, I *knew* Shriver would eventually be nominated for vice president, and began writing his acceptance speech. Without waiting to be invited, I showed up on his doorstep in Rockville the day the decision was announced. Although he already had a team of veteran Kennedy speechwriters hard at work, I labored quietly over my own draft of his acceptance speech. He slowly read all the drafts (unsigned), then accepted mine, and gave it hours later, on television, at the "miniconvention" hastily summoned to present him to the public.

There followed some ten or eleven hectic weeks on the Shriver campaign plane. We actually thought the crowds were getting bigger and more supportive toward the end; perhaps they were only compensating for being sorry they would not vote for us. In any case, as I saw more and more "sparklies" and "trendies" operating in the campaign—and heard the media appeals to the "new vote" of the blacks, the young, and women—I felt the Democratic Party changing its allegiance, away from working people and toward the symbol-making class around the universities, the news media, and the industries of culture. Partly as a consequence of their new class allegiances, since 1968 the Democrats have lost all but 21 percent of the electoral votes in the past five presidential elections.

Even before the campaign, I had begun to see that I was caught up in a new form of class warfare. During 1972, I published an essay in *Commentary*, "Needing Niebuhr Again," describing the "new class" of symbol makers who were wresting leadership within the Democratic Party from the labor unions, big-city mayors, and traditional politicians whose electoral base lay among the poor and working classes. This essay occasioned an editorial by Norman Podhoretz, the distinguished editor of *Commentary*, that led to a fresh burst of "new class" criticism chronicled by B. Bruce-Biggs in *The New Class* (1979). The more highly educated, more utopian "life-style" liberals were gaining salience throughout society, and the Democratic Party was quickly seduced by their glittery power. There was much evidence of this in the campaign of 1972. Mr. Shriver was greeted with scarcely veiled disdain, I thought, by workers at the gates of the Homestead Steel mills—my own kind of folks, who would normally be with us by upwards of 89 percent. In Joliet, Illinois, on a factory floor where I encountered dozens of Slovak faces that made me think of my cousins in Johnstown, workers did not want to shake McGovern-Shriver hands. Trying to find out why, I met with our "advance person"—a young woman wearing a miniskirt, high white boots, and a see-through blouse, with a large proabortion button on her collar. On that factory floor in 1972, the clash of social classes and cultural politics could scarcely have been more discordant.

After the campaign, I gladly joined with other traditional Democrats in founding the Coalition for a Democratic Majority, under the leadership of "Scoop" Jackson, Hubert Humphrey, Pat Moynihan, Tom Foley, and others. Foreign policy most worried me, but so did the efforts by upper-class liberals to separate blacks and Hispanics from white ethnics and from labor, discarding the latter (so blind they were) as reactionary and racist. I had requested a leave of absence from Old Westbury, precisely to campaign against Nixon in 1972 (a promise I had made myself when Humphrey lost in 1968). Fighting for the soul of the Democratic Party, I saw the other side gain control of it.

Now I understand that there are *two* "power elites" in this nation: (1) the "old elite," whose base lies in the business sector, and whose vision of what makes America great looks to her economic and political freedoms, and (2) the "new class," whose base lies in education and the new communications industries, and whose vision of what makes America great is a compassionate (therefore, large) government. (The so-called "Yuppies" of later years are divided between these two elites, trending now one way, now another.) Unknowingly, until now, I had been supporting the politics of the new class, out of an uncritical acceptance of "progressive" ideology. What would happen if I turned against the new class the same intensity of critical fire that I had earlier learned from my education to turn against the old elite? Didn't the new one deserve it more? The imbalance of criticism in the academy and among intellectuals is a scandal. The naked ambition of the new class for power, its self-interest, its lack of self-knowledge, and its moral arrogance are transparent. So are its resentments.

Even though I slowly was becoming deradicalized, the information in my head during these years was very often exclusively derived from writers of the far left. In *Ascent of the Mountain, Flight of the Dove* (1971), for example, I wrote that "a huge bureaucracy with an unparalleled budget has grown up around the Department of Defense." Again: "The economic, bureaucratic interests represented by that budget tend to govern the direction not only of American foreign policy but also of American domestic life. They determine what 'the realities' of American life are." The footnotes to such wildly exaggerated passages refer to such authors as Fred J. Cook, *The Warfare State*, Richard J. Barnet, *The Economy of Death*, a book of essays called *American Militarism 1970*, and Seymour Melman, *Pentagon Capitalism*. I had not been educated in the left-wing radical tradition, and I thought of myself here as being open-minded. What I did not do was to submit such partisans to rigorous cross-examination. As a percentage of gross national product, for example, military budgets in 1970 (not far above 5 percent) were a very small tail to be wagging a very large dog. Moreover, the relatively low spending on arms *qua* arms during the 1970s placed the nation in considerable peril, as even Jimmy Carter slowly realized. Far from being "militaris-

.tic," the American people were about to secure a long series of years of declining defense budgets. This was to happen just as the Soviets were rapidly expanding theirs. The new thrusts of Soviet expansion and the upsurge of terrorism were a vivid consequence. Less spending brought greater violence, not less.

For most of the 1970s, I was of two minds. Philosophically, I was slowly turning away from the radical left. Informationally, my mind was stuffed with uncritically accepted information from highly partisan sources. Furthermore, I was painfully eager to maintain my credentials on the left. I remembered Maritain writing (in defense of his support of liberal Christian Democratic movements) that he always wished to be "a man of the left." That seemed to me too, at that time, to be the only moral alternative. My *will* to be on the left was stronger than any intellectual reasons I could assemble for being there. What the heart wills the mind for a time finds reasons for. Until, one by one, those reasons turn to ash.

Yet even my first tentative criticisms of the left brought down upon my head passionate assaults, less given to answering my arguments than to questioning my morality. Some reviews of *The Rise of the Unmeltable Ethnics*, which I thought would help inspire the left to a base-broadening realism, were so unfair and so hostile to my person that, on at least one occasion (I was less thick-skinned then), I took to my bed until I could gain composure to get back to work. I had to call upon the intellectual guidance I had established for myself in *The Experience of Nothingness* (1970)—namely, the calm knowledge that one had to be prepared to go forward "with no supports," relying upon no one.

Reinhold Niebuhr had taught me to weigh powers, interests, and facts carefully *before* pronouncing moral judgment; so I knew I had to do some long rethinking. About all the left-wing information in my head, I began to ask, Is it actually well founded? No longer relying upon socialist forms of analysis (with their predetermined outcomes), I began to ask, What fair-minded evaluation can be made of capitalism? My first essay on this latter subject suggested that, at the very least, capitalism is among intellectuals "an underpraised and undervalued system." By contrast, I had learned that socialism, although highly praised for its "ideals," is quite disillusioning once the facts about any instances of its practice are examined. I backed into a more positive judgment of capitalism very, very slowly, having to fight against my broadly anticapitalist education.

On the theological side of the question, I found, one has to do most of the work oneself. Perhaps von Mises, Hayek, and others do persuade those who are already liberal (in the classical sense). But for those of us who were taught to think through anticapitalist analysis, such arguments can only be conducted in highly moral terms that present a comparable historical vision. Seven or eight new insights are necessary. It takes time and patience to achieve them. Cardinal Newman was correct: one can drive out a powerful idea only in the light of a still more powerful idea. It took me until 1982, with the completion of *The Spirit of Democratic Capitalism*, to begin to get that intellectually stronger set of ideas in my head. That vision remained critical of flaws in all three systems of American life—political, economic, moral-cultural—but in a systematic way I kept asking, *Compared to what?* At last, I was thinking empirically in a sustained way.

Slowly, I saw that being on the left had been a sort of "bad faith," a learned ideology that was false to my own experience, to that of my family, and indeed to that of millions of families all around the world. I had been teaching myself to debunk the American system, and by means of arguments whose plausibility lay, not in themselves, but in their conformity to a prearranged mental scheme: capitalism is of the past, immoral, and doomed, whereas steps toward a more socialist economy are "progressive," right, and predetermined by history to be victorious. Recently, I have encountered a slogan of the Sandinistas that shockingly expresses the relevant mental scheme, although in terms so gross that they would have repelled me even in my most progressive days: "To learn from the Soviet Union is to advance; to learn from the United States is to retreat." Supply "progressivism" for "Soviet Union," and "capitalism" for "the United States," and that is how I had earlier interpreted history. Reality does not support such blind faith.

The great and liberating interpretive idea, I have come to think, is Jefferson's: "The God who gave us life gave us liberty." Human beings are made in the image of God: creatures of insight and liberty, of intelligence and responsibility. The only social systems worthy of creatures of such gifted dignity are those that allow them to be relentlessly inquiring, creative, and responsible: a free polity, a relatively free economy, and a free moral-cultural order. All systems that secure such individual rights and that are now empirically available have predominantly capitalist economies.[4]

———·———

A story of this sort necessarily has two tracks, one consisting of a record of experiences, the other a record of newly acquired insights.

During my left-wing, or radical, period (1967–1971), bounded by the antiwar movement on the one end and the experience of "radical culture" at Old Westbury on the other, I had become adept at trying to explain my radical ideas in liberal terms. "Liberal" is the cover that most socialist-minded leftists employ to make their ideas seem continuous with those of the pragmatic, mainline left. I had to learn the hard way the discontinuity between "socialist" and "liberal," just as an earlier generation (Sidney Hook, for example) had learned to see the sharp divide between "communist" and "socialist." In that earlier generation, the dividing line had been commitment to democracy. Communists accepted Party discipline and were radically undemocratic. Democratic socialists and social democrats insisted upon the primacy of democracy and free personal inquiry. A generation later, the deplorable economic record of socialism since World War II is more in evidence; and the dependence of social democracy on capitalist institutions (markets, incentives, private property, and openness) is more transparent. In our generation, the dividing line between liberals and socialists is how much freedom to allow a free economy. "Socialists" (the word has lost much of its practical meaning) tend to favor greater political controls; liberals tend to favor greater economic liberties. At its best, this argument is pragmatic and experimental.

Some years after the fact, I have come to see the role played in my own thought by the gradual acceptance of several key ideas. As a matter of intellectual biography, it seems worthwhile to state a few of them, even without space to argue against the objections my earlier ways of thinking had employed to block them.

Utopianism Versus Realistic Morality

By nature, I tend to be idealistic and wholehearted; to respect ambiguity, irony, and tragedy is a tendency I have always wanted to strengthen in myself. But the discovery of the systematic biases of my own class, the new class, taught me that I must make a still sharper distinction between reasoning about moral ideals and reasoning about political realities. When I was on the left, I found myself looking *down* upon the American people, upon "vulgar" business activities, upon capitalism. I implicitly pictured my friends on the left and myself as more "pure" than all the others. In *Toward A Theology of Radical Politics* (1969), I had unmasked the "Myth of the Pure Protester," the contemporary version of Dostoyevsky's "Myth of the Grand Inquisitor." But it is one thing to detect a mythic structure in one's colleagues, and another to drive it out of one's own habitual practice. The Pure Protester loves his or her own moral purity, sacrificing all else to that. To overcome it, I learned, one has to distinguish more sharply between one's high moral claims and the actual effects of one's ideas and actions on the plain of battle.

To begin with, one must grant that others, too, make high moral claims. One must compare moral claims to moral claims. But one must also examine *what happens in history because of those moral claims:* one must compare *practice* to *practice.* Sometimes those who make high claims bring about results more evil than the results achieved by those whose moral claims have been more cautious. In practice, this meant for me that I must stop having contempt for those (to my right) with whom I was in moral disagreement. And I must take greater responsibility for the actual results of my own moral claims. For example, after the Democratic Convention of 1968, I was so hostile to Hubert Humphrey (because of a disgraceful speech he had made on the war at Stanford that spring) that I wrote in favor of abstaining from voting, even if Richard Nixon won the election. I added that those who followed such an injunction would incur an obligation to work that much harder to defeat Nixon in 1972—which explains my taking an unpaid leave of absence in the fall of 1972 to do so. This was moral purity masked as practical politics. I learned from such an error that I must never again seek moral purity at the expense of responsibility for the results.

As a result, I have striven to conduct argument with those with whom I disagree on two separate levels: to argue against their moral claims, on one level, and to argue against the probable practical consequences of their moral claims, on yet another. One effect of this resolution was to free me from the grip of the moral vision of the left, in the many forms in which I had encountered it. I began to examine its consequences more closely and to experiment with a better vision that might have better consequences. In short, consequences matter.

"Bad Faith"

One of the features of being on the left that most disquieted me was the "bad faith" in which it placed me. In arguing for left-wing positions, I found myself putting down other Americans, trying to shock "the complacent" (as I thought them) and writing of U.S. "militarism" and "imperialism." But who was I to be anything but grateful to this country that had taken in an impoverished and much oppressed family of former serfs from Slovakia, and that had given to me and countless others opportunities unprecedented in history? I had always tempered my radical criticism with explicit patriotism and gratitude, but still, I had conceded far too much to an unwarranted anti-Americanism. The more I examined the neo-Marxist analysis of oppression and dependency, the less tenable it was. Its main substance is emotional, not intellectual. It *begins* with feelings of guilt, awaits no evidence, and includes the final verdict in the method of analysis. Eventually, I could not stomach this bad faith. I understood the anger that union workers felt when they saw privileged university students burning American flags, for which so many in their own families (like Mickey Yuhas) had gladly given their lives. Working people shamed me into abandoning my bad faith.

Future as Truth

The first insinuation of a Marxist-Leninist way of thinking into one's mind is through epistemology: "The tide of history is on the side of revolution." Here is how it happens. The first temptation is to hold that "the correspondence theory of truth" is Aristotelian and old-fashioned. One should not examine claims to truth in the light of empirical evidence. Empiricism is static and reactionary. Instead, one must keep one's eye upon the goal of the future. Truth is what brings the revolution of the future into power. What helps the revolution belongs to the future and is true. What blocks the revolution is reactionary and against the stream of history, so it is false. The dynamic course of history has been scientifically discerned; history is driven forward both by the "contradictions of capitalism" and by the triumphant logic of egalitarianism, the end of alienation, and the common good, i.e., socialism. "To learn from socialism is to advance; to learn from capitalism is to retreat." Only "progressives" grasp the larger picture. Appeals to empirical fact regarding the failures of socialism are signs of bourgeois reasoning. To be a progressive is to be ennobled by an inner vision of a superior truth. It is to belong to a secular religion. If only one holds tightly to that shining vision, the imperfections of the present will be enveloped in the soft light of ideals that drive one onward. How much progress has been made already!

Having long fought against "cheap grace"—having been chastened by my own "dark night of the soul," as suggested in *The Experience of Nothingness* (1970)—I had long since fled from an adolescent Christian faith to an adult one. So I resisted the soft light of socialism.

No Robert Heilbroner or Irving Howe "visions" for me. I had Catholicism, a much tougher faith—tested by fire—and had no vacuum in the religious depths of my soul that socialism could possibly fill. If one doesn't need socialism as a religion, then it must stand or fall by its record in historical praxis. One advantage of a capitalist economy, indeed, is that it asks to be judged on no other than empirical and practical grounds. It is asymmetrical with socialism; it offers no comparable "vision."

Thus, as I mentally toured the horizon of the twentieth century, I could see less and less reason for any serious mind to believe— against the overpowering evidence—that actual socialism matches socialist claims. On the contrary, from the U.S.S.R. to communist Vietnam, from communist Albania to Cuba, socialism is a human wasteland. As for the "socialism" of Sweden, Israel, and France, many of their own socialists have come to see that what is most vital in such nations is their commitment to democracy, and what are most retardant are the state controls that drag down their market economies. In economics, democratic socialists are democratic capitalists who argue for slightly larger governmental initiatives and controls at the margin. In practice, democratic socialists and social democrats live as parasites upon democratic capitalist systems while claiming to have purer and larger hearts pulsing with "compassion." To some extent (when it works), this is a useful leaven and I sometimes support them. To a great extent, however, socialist visions serve the interests and ambitions of large segments of the educated class (who in Europe staff government-owned media, universities, and the massive welfare administrative apparatus) and paralyze the poor. In addition, many democratic socialists tend toward an unhealthy preference for the foreign policy of the U.S.S.R. over that of the U.S.A. in virtually every concrete circumstance. Most leftists are ritualistic anti-Stalinists. In practice, however, they nearly always oppose American policy. Sometimes they may be correct; the issue rests with exact judgment, case by case. Underlying ideological support for Cuba and Nicaragua, for example, is an epistemology that holds that socialism will prevail over capitalism, left-wing progressives over right-wing reactionaries, the vision of a shining future over the sad realities of Cuban prisons and fervent Sandinista Leninism. When one's vision is of paradise, the dungeons in which prisoners are tortured cannot be seen.

The Factual Record

Once one sets aside vulgar Marxist epistemology and tries to see the world whole and factual, one is free to judge socialism by its record—and to reexamine capitalism afresh. It is difficult to get socialists to name a socialist experiment on which they rest their case. Their touching faith in each successive project lasts only so long as the full story has not come out—in China before Westerners could freely visit it; in Albania before "socialist youth brigades" from Western Europe came home with shocking tales; in Cuba before Armando Valladares awakened the poets, essayists, and novelists of the outside world.

In Western Europe, socialists in power turn increasingly to capitalist techniques because they work better than socialist techniques. Once socialist economies are submitted to the same rigorous tests as capitalist economies, the jig is up. As an economic idea, socialism has died a thousand deaths by qualification. Markets, incentives, private property, and openness work better in the humble history of fact. Since it is basically an empirically derived set of techniques, one does not have to give capitalism even two cheers; still, in an imperfect world, it wins hands down. Chinese and Soviets pay it the sincerest form of flattery.

What Is Capitalism?

The liberal arts tradition of Britain and the United States owes much to the aristocratic traditions of the distant past, and keeps alive the resentment of aristocrats against the "philistinism" of the rising business class and the *nouveaux riches*. The social sciences are profoundly anti-individual, collectivist in spirit and in method, and often antithetical to the tacit wisdom of tradition and the indirect "spontaneous order" (Hayek) of many traditional social institutions, including markets. Thus, most of us grow up being taught to think ill of capitalists and capitalism. Some reasons are aesthetic. Some are class-based: aristocratic tastes preferred to business-inspired tastes. Some are radical. We may not hold that "property is theft" or fully accept the "labor theory of value," according to which all value derives from labor and any profit not distributed to labor is ill-gained. Nonetheless, socialists such as Tawney have taught us that capitalism is rooted in acquisitiveness, in selfish as opposed to public interests, and in vaguely tainted "profit." There are some on the left who regard capitalism as an essentially evil system that must be replaced. Perhaps a larger number have made peace with capitalism which, though vulgar and disreputable, is a necessary practicality. (Not even Adam Smith held actual businessmen in high regard.)

It took me a long while to recognize in myself just how much of this received wisdom I had uncritically received. Beyond that, there is also a taboo against assessing capitalism seriously and fairly. Within the horizon of progressivism, to approach the morality of capitalism as an open question is regarded as selling out. To render a favorable empirical verdict upon capitalism while recognizing its defects where they undeniably exist makes socialist analysis totter on its foundations. These foundations are mainly anticapitalist, negative rather than positive. (And insofar as they are positive, they are utopian.)

Those who remain attached to socialist methods of analysis, of course, do not give up even when they lose particular arguments.

Progressivism is a closed system. It has an answer to everything. It does not rest upon empirical verification; it does not employ the criterion of falsifiability. It insists upon "vision," upon "perspective," upon "point of view." Once one is within that horizon, nothing can penetrate it. It is reinforced by everything that happens. It is more like a religious faith than like a scientific theory subject to falsification. But it lacks one key constitutive element common to Jewish and Christian religious faith. Jewish and Christian faith hold each believer personally responsible for the reasonableness of the act of faith; both engage the unbeliever (present within every believer) in argument. The progressive never takes the doubter seriously; to doubt progressivism is considered to be not an intellectual but a moral act. For Jew and Christian, God is truth. For the progressive, history is a tale of irresistible power, to which truth is secondary. Progressives do not argue; they attack the *bona fides* of doubters.

That is why the first battle of the soul in rejecting the progressive horizon is to subject it to tests of empirical falsifiability. Since the first of all moral maxims is to think clearly, this struggle is a moral one. Does truth stand outside of history, as a judge upon it, or within it, as a subject judged by history? Some prefer to be "on the side of" history. Others choose to subject historical movements to the judgment of truth. Castro had Valladares under the thumb of history, naked in an unlit cell; but Valladares clung to a truth beyond the power of history.

Once one begins to examine the historical record of capitalist societies—the paradigm case is the United States—one learns that the received wisdom about the nature of capitalism is erroneous. Far from being theft, private property is (as even Leo XIII said) the necessary condition for individual freedom of action in history. The right to private property supplies the wherewithal for self-determination. This important empirical claim is subject to tests of falsifiability: An order that respects rights to private property is more likely to result in the improvement of nature, the advancing of the common good, superior creativity, and social vitality than any collectivist order. In the practical sphere, the proper question is, *compared to what?* Compared to traditionalist and socialist orders, the capitalist economic order has empirically shown superior results.

In my first ruminations, following Max Weber, I thought of capitalism as essentially consisting in a regime of private property, markets, incentives, and profits. But all traditional societies (such as Jerusalem in the biblical era, and most Third World regimes today) have had these. Still they were (or are) *pre*capitalist. Only slowly did I come to the precise capitalist insight: creativity is more productive than rote labor; therefore, the primary form of *capital* is mind. The cause of the wealth of nations is mind. Capitalism is not constituted solely by private property, incentives, markets, double-entry bookkeeping, or any other social techniques (though all these are necessary elements), but rather by a social order favorable to alertness, inventiveness, discovery, and creativity. This means a social order based upon education, research, the freedom to create, and the right to enjoy the fruits of one's own creativity. Thus, all the American steps to protect the rights of citizens to exercise their own practical judgments—i.e., Article I, Section 8, of the U.S. Constitution, asserting the rights of "authors and inventors"; the Homestead Act; the Land Grant College Act; and an immense national commitment to universal private and public education—were indispensable stages along the road to a civilization that favored invention and discovery more than any other in history. "The first developed nation" owes its development chiefly to the cultivation of intellect, both practical and theoretical.

The Nature of Communism

For intellectuals, the most divisive event of the twentieth century has been the rise of communism. How should communism be judged? For many intellectuals of a generation ago, communism was a profound temptation. Most attributed this to their own idealism, rather than to their lust for power or their envy of the business class. To others today, to seem friendly and unconcerned about the rise of communism seems to be more idealistic than to be anticommunist. Even before the era of Joseph McCarthy, to be anticommunist was thought to represent a failure of idealism, imagination, creative sympathy, and broad-mindedness. Besides, anticommunism seemed vulgar. It represented a middlebrow or lowbrow reflex, worthy perhaps of the *Reader's Digest* but scarcely of the academy. Thus, even today many who have refused to become communists would prefer not to be known as anticommunists—indeed, would prefer to be less anticommunist than anti-anticommunist.

This tendency has effects upon foreign policy debates. Many intellectuals today grasp the failure of the *Marxist* component of Marxism-Leninism—recognize, that is, the rebuff history has given to the nineteenth-century economics of Marx. But many of the same persons continue to accept, perhaps unconsciously, the *Leninist* doctrine that imperialism is the natural expression of capitalism. And they interpret American foreign policy (not Soviet foreign policy) accordingly. American foreign policy in Southeast Asia, in Central America, and elsewhere, they say, is driven by business interests. These consist either of malign multinational corporations or of the military-industrial complex. These accusations are fair enough; but it is only fair to hear the other side of the evidence, not merely to give in to reflexive feelings of guilt. The evidence does not support the accusations. Nonetheless, what is left of Marxism-Leninism is Leninism. The Leninist doctrine of imperialism satisfies deep anti-American longings.

There is no excuse for serious men and women not to have an exact and accurate picture of the power controlled by the Communist Party U.S.S.R.: in offensive nuclear might and strategic defense against nuclear attack; in naval power on (and under) every ocean surface; in conventional arms massed near the European frontier and along the borders separated from the Persian Gulf solely by Iran; in a covert intelligence force larger and more versatile than any in history; and in a capacity for ideological penetration, both in the West and in the Third World, unrivaled in human history. According to the Brezhnev Doctrine, where communism begins to govern it never surrenders. (The single minor roll-back has been Grenada.) By the end of the Carter administration, the boundaries defended by this doctrine had been extended far beyond those of 1945. Nicaragua, ripe as a plum, seems to be next in line. By 1998, if present trends continue, the boundaries protected by the Brezhnev Doctrine are quite likely to be more extensive than they are in 1988.

Pure Leninism is about power, naked power, brutal power, power through terror. To the dictator within a Leninist system, anything is permitted. To appeal to values beyond naked power in the hands of a Leninist vanguard, one must go outside of Leninism. Thus, belief in Marxism-Leninism as a set of substantive doctrines has waned, especially in communist nations. Ironically, though, utopian progressivism, the marshland in which communism incubates, thrives happily in the affluent West among the privileged. The resentments of intellectuals against the business class nourish it far more than any evidence warrants. Meanwhile, the naked military power of the U.S.S.R. is stronger than that of Adolf Hitler at the peak of his power. And Marxist-Leninist ideology, even in decline, still awakens an echoing resonance among intellectuals that the Nazi ideology, based upon race, never could.

The capacity of Western intellectuals to deny the reality of Soviet power, the scope of Soviet ambition, and the record of Soviet deception is one of the marvels of history. It represents a triumph of intellectual dishonesty and massive self-contempt. To refuse to take part in this "treason of the intellectuals" is said to be troglodytic, reactionary, the work of a cold warrior, bellicose, and a sign of reflexive anticommunism. It is none of these things. It is a refusal to go on being complicit in intellectual dishonesty and self-contempt. An exact and accurate picture must be argued out empirically. So also the strategic response. On concrete matters, honest persons may disagree. But resistance to communism, principled and militarily effective, is morally obligatory.

Openness

How can I explain to myself the attacks upon my own work by former colleagues on the left once I began to move from concentrating my criticism on the right to directing some of it onto the left? Persons who had written that I was brilliant began to find my work—which was far more penetrating than it had been—evidence of a bad character. No doubt, my positions of today have faults, which I would be glad to correct. Virtually never do my critics respond with argument, however. Only seldom have they met the case I have made head-on. Their main advice to their faithful flock is not to read my work. Their technique is ridicule in a falsetto voice; consult the reviews of *The Spirit of Democratic Capitalism* in religious left-wing journals. True, elsewhere the more open among them have accepted several basic points, and this process continues.

Knowing that I was wrong once, I would be glad to be shown again where now I am in error. I fear no arguments from the left. I welcome them eagerly. Having expanded my views before, to meet overpowering evidence, I would gladly do so again. To admit that one has been wrong is, after the first time or two, joyful work, because it demonstrates a willingness to follow inquiry where it leads.

I see, of course, that intellectual conversions, or "raisings of consciousness," still move some persons to the left. The left, given its epistemology, regards such conversions as signs of natural growth. Nonetheless, the numbers of those on the left who are embracing more and more of the "Whig" (realistic, democratic capitalist) analysis is growing yet more rapidly, for sound empirical reasons. In intellectual life, there is no determinism. Honest inquiry has its own power, its own laws, and its own respect for time.

The Ironic Law of Small Differences

It is an odd feature of arguments about political economy, I have found, that small differences in *the balance of judgment* have very large consequences for action. In the world of practice, judgments are necessarily probabilistic. Manicheanism is out. There are almost always *some* reasons for most (but not all) systemic positions. (Hitler's maniacal efforts to eradicate the Jews, like Stalin's earlier deliberate starvation of some 8 million Ukrainians, have come as close to pure and massive evil as the world has ever seen.) Thus, consider the judgment that, on balance, the United States is a force for good in the international arena. To interpret that judgment in numerical terms, one person may judge that by 51–49, or 55–45, it is correct; another, by 49–51, or 45–55, the other way. But this relatively small margin of difference between the acceptance and the rejection of that proposition may involve extremely large differences in further judgment and action. One may still wish to make judgments case by case. But one is *likely* to give the benefit of the doubt one way or the other: thumbs up or thumbs down. History demands action. Playing Hamlet is certain tragedy. Once a judgment is reached (by however small a margin), action must be wholehearted.

Moreover, judgment about political economy evokes high passion. Even if one disagrees with those on the other side of a question for action by only 2 or 5 or 25 percent, still, that difference has the effect that a civil war does in dividing the consciences of even close brothers within a family. At the extreme, killing one another may result (as in the American Civil War; among Vietnamese, Nicaraguans, and others). Far short of that, even in an argument over dinner, passions are likely to rise. The temptation of those on opposite sides to paint each other in extreme colors, to demonize one another, is extremely hard to resist.

In action in history, small differences in the balance of judgment often lead to dramatic, passionate, and life-and-death opposition. To recognize this helps to diminish fanaticism. But it does not alleviate the need to go into opposition. Civility is then an almost heroic achievement. Still, civility remains necessary.

Whether to the left or the right, in any case, those inquirers for whom I have the greatest admiration are willing to continue facing argument, to stay in dialogue, and to rethink things again. Surprisingly, one does not find in life many open minds. There are not multitudes whose drive to question is virtually unrestricted. When you find one whose views are radically different from yours but who is willing to discuss such differences openly and at length, you find a pearl of great price.

—— · ——

Where, then, am I today? As before, I remain both a Democrat and a member of the Democratic Party in politics ("republican" in the early American sense, a biblical or civic republican). In culture, I am, as Lord Acton was, that loneliest of breeds, a liberal Catholic; not a conservative one, because Catholicism is a living force, ever ancient and ever new. In economics, I am in favor of the mind-centered, creative, inventive system—in short, capitalism. I have come to see that these are the *three* liberations symbolized by the classic liberal tricolor: liberation from tyranny and torture, through *democracy;* the liberation of conscience, association, and expression, through *pluralism;* and liberation from poverty, through *capitalism*.

No one who holds faith with such commitments, Hayek wrote, is properly to be called a "conservative." For each of these three liberations names a *dynamic* principle as deep as human nature itself, the powerful propeller of history. These are the principles that will be decisive in the future, the principles at the heart of every form of progress. In practical cases, some will favor government intervention, others will favor a freer economy; in an open society, there is ample room for pragmatic argument and closely watched experimentation.

And yet, of course, to hold fast to such principles as these is not to have sprung as innocent and naked as Venus from the sea. It is to stand on principles one's forebears have wrested over centuries from the ambiguities and ironies of human history, and is, in that sense, conservative (a conservative is one who believes that his forebears were at least as intelligent as he). To hold to principles dynamic in their nature and yet ancient and traditional in their gradual elucidation is to be simultaneously a person of the future and of the past, a conservative and a progressive—in short, a Whig. Alas, that name seems no longer to be retrievable. But the principles it signals are everlastingly available, rooted as they are in the natural liberty (and its tendency toward historical progress) that our Creator has endowed in us.

And so I end my story. Having begun life in the bosom of a good family in an out-of-the-way steel town, best known for the tragedies it has endured by flood in 1889, 1936, and 1977; having had an excellent classical education in philosophy, literature, and theology; having from the start declared my intention to create a philosophy of the distinctively American experience; having begun by seeking a "third way" between capitalism and socialism, as a result of the typical anticapitalist biases of the humanities (not least in Catholic thought); having long looked for this "third way" in the direction of socialist thought and radical politics—after all this, during my forties, I came to find the socialist and radical paths destructive of truth, and signs of bad faith. And I came back to rediscover the power of the American idea, "man's best hope" as Jefferson called it in his First Inaugural. I came back, in short, to the tradition of Aristotle, Cicero, and Aquinas; of Madison, Hamilton, Jay, Jefferson, and Lincoln; of Montesquieu, Smith, Burke, and Acton—i.e., to the Whig tradition. Many call me a neoconservative. I prefer neoliberal. Yet the name matters less that the reality: a threefold commitment to democracy, capitalism, and pluralism, whose premise is liberation—from tyranny and torture, from poverty, and from oppression of intellect, art, and conscience. To be where I am, I judge, is a good place to be—for which thanksgiving be to my Creator, merciful to those who wander in the wilderness.

Notes

[1] Decisive in my thinking was Theodore Draper's article in *Commentary* in January 1967, which asserted that in December 1964, the North Vietnamese had moved 400 regular troops into South Vietnam—a tiny "invasion," it seemed to me then. We now know that many more troops than that had been coming south and from far earlier.

[2] Mussolini used this expression to define the essence of the new type of system in history, totalitarianism. In Mussolini is found the *locus classicus* of the "totalitarian/authoritarian" distinction.

[3] Political conversions are not as deep as religious conversions. Psychologically, as Gordon Allport once observed, they occur on different levels of the psyche. But they are deep enough, since they affect all one's judgment and actions as a citizen. Different visions of political economy embody different senses of reality, different views of human nature, different senses of historical narrative, and quite different forms of self-knowledge.

[4] Peter Berger's *The Capitalist Revolution* (Basic Books, 1986) assembles the empirical evidence in an easily accessible way, in the form of fifty falsifiable theses.

10

Why Did You Sign That Ad?

James Finn

"Dear Jim: Why Did You Sign?"

The open letter with this title was addressed to me by the editors of *Christianity and Crisis* in their issue of May 11, 1981. The ad they referred to, sponsored by the Committee for the Free World, had recently appeared in the *New York Times* over the signatures of a number of people. It began, "We—a group of intellectuals and religious leaders—applaud American policy in El Salvador," and ended "We applaud the determination of the United States government to assist the government of El Salvador which is working, against armed opposition, to build a more stable and equitable society and thereby add to the sum of freedom in the world." Sandwiched in between was a very brief argument, necessarily incomplete and unnecessarily strident, to support this position.

The editors of *C & C*, as the magazine was called, stated that "the gap between the views [many of] these people hold and our own is too great to permit useful exchange"—they named Elmo Zumwalt, Ray Cline, Eugene Rostow, Norman Podhoretz—"but we believe we share basic journalistic, political, ethical and religious values with you. . . . You have helped foster many several-sided exchanges on difficult issues. Your own books and articles reflect your own historical awareness and your ability to enter into viewpoints you do not share. You are not given to labeling others, and you are not easily labeled yourself. That's why we want to know: why did you sign that ad?"

On the basis of our personal histories, the question was entirely warranted. *C & C* had been started by the noted Protestant theologian Reinhold Niebuhr in the days preceding World War II when he feared that the near pacifism that permeated the Protestant churches and their major publications would leave this country and its allies defenseless against the threat of facism. Under his active guidance *C & C* had developed into a responsible voice of liberalism within the Protestant community. In the late fifties and the sixties I had shared with its editors and other like-minded people an active interest in, for example, ecumenism in religious affairs, advocacy of civil rights and racial justice in domestic affairs, and opposition to the Vietnam War in foreign affairs. We were not in lockstep agreement on every issue, but our differences were conducted within a common set of assumptions that we implicitly acknowledged, However, somewhere in our common efforts to promote understanding, equality, and justice, our paths diverged. For El Salvador was not to remain a lone or accidental point of difference. The issues on which I grew to anticipate significant differences with a number of friends and colleagues came to include Grenada, the threat of Soviet communism, the nuclear freeze, liberation theology, quotas, abortion, Central America, the Catholic bishops' pastoral letters on war and peace and on the U.S. economy, the strategic defense initiative (SDI), political prisoners in Cuba, Afghanistan, and—but the list grows dispiritingly long.

I wrote a several-page reply to the question of why I signed the ad, and the editors generously printed it, but that response was limited to the question of U.S. policies in El Salvador. To respond to the larger question of why the general divergence between my views and those of my interrogators took place, it is necessary to recall the battles in which we once joined forces and the principles we then shared.

The sixties were such a turbulent period in our national life and have become such a towering reference point that they have induced a partial amnesia in journalistic accounts of the preceding decade. The fifties were not, as they are sometimes portrayed, a time of Eisenhower slumbers and political complacency. As an associate editor of *Commonweal* during much of that period, I can testify that we had some thorny issues to contend with. The decade began with the United States engaging in a war in Korea. During those years there arose a man and a corrosive political movement associated with him that added to our political lexicon a still viable term—"McCarthyism." It was in 1955 that Mrs. Rosa Parks, a black woman, decided not to yield her seat on a bus to a white person—and set off the historic Montgomery bus boycott. In 1956, the Eisenhower administration released a copy of Khrushchev's secret speech to the Twentieth Party Congress in which he revealed and denounced Stalin's enormous reign of terror. In the late fifties, a young man with high political aspirations was required to pass through the strong but smudgy fires of religious prejudice before he could be elected the first Catholic President of the United States.

Not all of the issues that drew our attention were of such a high order, of course. For example, it is difficult to convince young people today that in those far-off years a movie could be condemned and stir up a ministorm because it contained the word "virgin." (So far have we traveled in our cultural liberation that for the price of a movie ticket preteenagers can now be educated in the language of Army barracks.) The intervening years have stamped finis on some of these debates, large and small, but amid the discontinuities some highly intractable issues remain, such as how to cope with communism, with nuclear weaponry, and with the relation of the haves and the have-nots in this country and in the world.

I regularly wrote about many of these issues for *Commonweal*. The weekly magazine described itself as a journal of opinion edited by Catholic laity, and in those years, the editors and devoted readers were frequently described as "Commonweal Catholics" or "liberal Catholics," the two terms being regarded as almost synonymous. In fact, the term "Commonweal Catholic" had been originally coined as a pejorative term by conservatives and then happily accepted as an accolade by—well, by Commonweal Catholics.

To be a liberal Catholic in those days was to be part of a necessarily self-conscious minority in both the church and in the liberal community, suspect by elements in each. It could not be otherwise. In the nineteenth century Pius IX had made a sweeping condemnation of philosophical liberalism, a relatively coherent theory that exalted individualism and taught the perfectability of man and an almost inevitable historical progress. Many Catholics too readily identified that condemned liberal philosophy with the pragmatic liberalism of contemporary United States. American liberals, frequently innocent of that philosophical background, felt uneasy with what they saw as an authoritarian, monolithic structure that could command the fealty of its members. During this period, *Commonweal* took upon itself the task of participating in and mediating between these two uneasy camps.

William Clancy, a colleague, wrote at that time "that it has been the high mission of liberalism to fight for much of what is right and true in the modern world, while those who should have aided, and even anticipated its battle, have stood aside, busy reviling 'Liberalism' for its philosophical errors. . . ." He went on to assert that what the "liberal Catholic" of our own time pleads for is that all Catholics become devoted to human dignity and freedom—as the liberal has been. If the liberal fought sound battles for inadequate reasons, Catholics should supply sound reasons and engage in the same battles. If the liberal advocated freedom of religion and the separation of civil and religious power because he was indifferent to or skeptical of absolute truth, Catholics should advocate these things on the basis of the inviolability of the human conscience and the necessary freedom of an act of faith. All of Clancy's fellow editors, I believe, shared these attitudes. I know that I did.

——·——

Because of the constant, recurring need to address the large issues that both joined and separated liberals and Catholics, *Commonweal* invoked, more frequently than most other journals of opinion, first principles of political behavior, most often implicitly, sometimes explicitly. We frequently examined such concepts as the relation of church and state, religion and society, morality and politics, ends and means, rights and responsibilities, the person and the common good. The most notable philosophical influences were decidedly Aristotelian/Thomistic, particularly as their relevance to contemporary political affairs was clarified by such modern writers as Etienne Gilson, Jacques Maritain, and the American theologian of religious liberty John Courtney Murray, S.J.

Although many of the discussions and debates that took place in the pages of the journal would be cast in different terms today, I believe that the principles on which they turned are still illuminating and relevant—and were during the sixties and later when they were largely abandoned by many who had once supported them, and brushed aside by those who wanted simpler approaches to our societal problems. This group included, notably, religious leaders who gave advice to the young during the Vietnam War, some of whom continue to dispense their advice very generously today.

Among these principles are the following:

• Politics, at its best, deals with penultimate questions, religion with the ultimate. It is an intellectual error and a political danger to confuse them.

- Politics cannot be separated from moral considerations. Politics makes choices among possible courses of action that affect the citizens' welfare. These choices are necessarily—but not always easily—subject to moral judgment.

- Politics sometimes forces choices between unpalatable alternatives. To choose the lesser of the evils is a moral act.

- Politics, being concerned with public affairs, should be informed by a morality appropriate to society and the state. That morality is not to be equated with the morality appropriate to the individual person.

- Politics, properly understood, assigns primacy not to the subjective intention of the actor, but to the objective end of the act.

- Politics *is* the art of the possible. Ideals hold up what, ideally, should be done; political action operates within limiting conditions that circumscribe what can be done. Utopia is not political.

We invoked these and related principles in many of the controversies in which we joined. For example, to ask whether Catholicism was compatible with American democracy was once considered a sound and lively question. (Maybe it still is in some quarters.) But that question, we pointed out, is itself confused, betraying a lack of understanding not only of religion but of democracy. The proper question is whether democracy is compatible with Catholicism (or with any other widely held belief, including atheism). Since no political system, including democracy, is fit to pass on ultimate questions—although totalitarianisms try—it must necessarily be subordinate to that which speaks directly to our conscience, to which we must be faithful. When claims come into conflict, as they inevitably will, the rational being will try, by persuasion, to induce agreement. In doing this we are not abandoning our principles, our belief in our own claims. We are acting on the principle, the basic truth, that people have a right to self-government. It is with this understanding that, as citizens, we are free and privileged to be Americans.

Not all readers will accept these formulations as their own, I fully realize, for they have been developed within a tradition that is alien to many Americans. But they are the principles that informed my thinking then, and which continue to.

Learning a number of these principles even as I employed them, I became embroiled in a wide range of issues, both in my own name and in the more august role of the anonymous editorial writer. Reviewing a historically distorted TV program on Martin Luther, I provoked a slew of written responses that confirmed—if such confirmation were needed—that the Reformation and Counter-Reformation were alive and vibrant in America, but also that the necessary work of reconcilation was under way. During a heated and bitter dispute over a policy that would allow the prescription of contraception devices in city hospitals, I argued in the pages of the magazine that the Catholic Church could uphold its own principled teaching on birth control and attempt to extend that teaching while the Catholic citizen could—and in this case, should—refrain from attempting to impose a particular policy on the larger community. (It was a measure of the journal's influence that, as I later learned, my article had a significant influence on the subsequent policy of allowing city hospitals to prescribe contraceptive devices.) I wrote about McCarthyism and, when the Senator died, wrote our editorial obituary. I recalled that McCarthy, while he was a political power, created a cleavage in our society that divided people who were otherwise united by earlier commitments to party, country, or religion. While he was a power to contend with, I went on, there were too few articulate voices to oppose him. I mentioned, in contrast, the journal's own role:

> *Commonweal* early opposed McCarthyism because the editors believed that it embodied a simplistic approach to ethics and politics. Truth and falsehood, good and evil, are not so neatly divided and measured as McCarthyism implied. The evil of Communism can not justify every action nor determine every attitude of its adversaries. Differences in prudential political judgments are inevitable; they are not sufficient to justify charges of treason. . . .

Although the specter of McCarthyism had faded, we do it less than justice, I argued editorially, if we forget that it once swayed the highest offices in the land and made light of checks and balances and, even more important, that such a movement is a political possibility that is never finally exorcised. Under other guises, it can return.

Because the journal opposed McCarthyism, it was criticized for not being sufficiently anticommunist. The criticism was unjustified. There was an overall *Commonweal* policy on communism that I inherited with my office as editor and which remained virtually unchanged when I left. It was neither simple nor simpleminded, but it was direct and clear. The magazine had many occasions to revert to that policy and the analysis of communism that undergirded it, but it will suffice to mention only one such occasion—in which some readers may detect overtones of more current debate on U.S.-U.S.S.R. relations. In his first term as President, Dwight Eisenhower said, before his departure for an international conference, that he was going to try to change the spirit that had reigned in such conferences during the preceding ten years. He was going to try to introduce an ingredient that had so far been missing, "an honest attempt to conciliate, to understand, to be tolerant, to try to see the other fellow's viewpoint as well as our own."

Reflecting on the President's declared intention, the magazine reiterated its stand that diplomacy must remain the major instrument in the cold war. But it also stated that in the present world situation, the United States "had no choice but to maintain a large military establishment as a deterrent to Soviet aggression." And it continued: "[I]n some things the crusading anti-Communists are profoundly right. We can never be 'tolerant' of a system which enslaves millions of human beings; we can never 'understand' regimes which practice calculated deceit; we cannot 'try to see' the viewpoint of those who have made systematic murder a cornerstone of their policy and totalitarian terror their pattern for domination of the world. . . ."

To speak of negotiating with the Soviet Union when it has proved its sincerity, the journal continued, is to be a captive of a fraudulent illusion. The Soviet Union could prove its sincerity "only by ceasing to be, in any recognizable form, the Soviet Union." When terror and labor camps are done away with and the satellites are free, then it will be time to talk of sincerity. In the meantime, even though the mask of the enemy be friendly, one must negotiate from strength. Only there lies a chance for peace and justice.

It was out of this matrix of explicit principles, assumptions, interests, and debates that emerged what my *C & C* friends termed our shared "basic journalistic, political, ethical and religious values." I also shared with these people a number of feelings that pulsed through our country in the early sixties. With his election John Kennedy not only broke through already weakened religious prejudices but, as the first President to be born in this century, promised a new and exhilarating future. (I had wanted *Commonweal* to endorse John Kennedy editorially but, losing that argument with the other editors, I contented myself with writing an article, "The Difference to Me," in which I gave reasons for supporting his campaign for the presidency.) Pope John XXIII threw aside the counsels of those he called the "prophets of doom" and, with his 1963 encyclical *Pacem in*

Terris, issued to all people a call to peace on earth. In this same period, Martin Luther King spoke of an impossible dream that began to seem possible, of a loving community of black and white together. And we produced in this country a generation of young people whom a host of observers discovered to be, *mirabile dictu,* the most intelligent, the most informed, the most open and free, the most honest, the most beautiful in American history. It was the dawning of a new time, signaled by new kinds of music, new styles of dress, new highs.

—— . ——

It was not long, of course, before these high hopes were humbled and the dream began to take on the unsettling quality of a nightmare. The assassination of President Kennedy led to the confrontation of Lyndon Johnson and Barry Goldwater in the elections of 1964. Writing in a special election issue of *C & C,* I said of the Republican candidate, whom I regarded as a pleasant but politically simpleminded person, that it was necessary not only that he lose but that he "lose by a great margin." He did, but the massive defeat did nothing to shift the national course on which we were, apparently, set. It was during the subsequent period, as we approached the critical year of 1968, that—although I did not realize it at the time—there began a distancing between my views and those of many of my friends. There was no Damascus experience, no single incident, no sudden insight that triggered the changes, for we continued to attend similar meetings, go on the same antiwar marches, be outraged by the same political blunders. It was rather the accumulation of a number of incidents.

During those years my work for an organization then named the Council on Religion and International Affairs (CRIA) brought me into contact with a wide range of people: officials who were shaping our war plans, generals who were carrying them out, academics who were government consultants, initiators of and participants in the student teach-ins, soldiers who were soon to embark for Vietnam, protestors, conscientious objectors, people high in church bureaucracies, and leaders of antiwar organizations and movements. In my travels around the country I took the opportunity to produce a book, *Protest: Pacifism and Politics,* based on conversations principally but not entirely with those who opposed U.S. policies in Vietnam—Dorothy Day, Daniel and Philip Berrigan, Julian Bond, John Lewis, Joan Baez, Richard John Neuhaus, Bayard Rustin, Denise Levertov, Abraham Joshua Heschel, Paul Ramsey, Staughton Lynd, and about two dozen more. I also served on the board of the World Without War

Council and that of Clergy and Laity Concerned About Vietnam, organizations that came to develop significantly different political positions, those of the council being thoughtful and sound.

It took no special perspicacity to perceive that the people I talked with had no common vocabulary. They often used the same words, of course, but they did not intend the same meaning. That failure to communicate was, however, merely a symptom of a deeper flaw in our societal approach to broad political policies. That flaw remains.

The political archaeologist who digs around in the sixties will find that an almost unprecedented amount of verbal attention was paid to morality, a number of people discovering, as if for the first time, its role in political discourse and behavior. Too often, alas, what they turned up was the moral equivalent of fool's gold or a gold of such unalloyed purity that it could not withstand the stress and weight of political action.

Some examples: Attempting to seize the high ground of debate, the *National Catholic Reporter*, an influential weekly newspaper, asserted that the war in Vietnam was no longer a political issue, that it had now become a moral issue. The implication, of course, was that the war had moved somehow from one realm of human action to another and that having failed to find a political solution we could now resolve the issue by making a moral choice. And, of course, the moral choice was clear. This is not an unfair extrapolation. When Bishop Fulton J. Sheen appeared on CBS-TV's "60 Minutes" in 1969, he was the first major U.S. Catholic leader to advocate unilateral troop withdrawal from Vietnam. Responding to a question from Mike Wallace, he said that such a withdrawal would be "a moral action," not a political one. As others were to show, this separation of morality from politics could lead to different but equally odd conclusions. In the first serious speech he made about the war, Senator Eugene McCarthy said he wasn't going to argue about the legality or the morality of the war, that he just thought there was no proportion between our proposed military action and any possible good that would result from it. But in talking about the proportion of our military efforts to the consequences, he was invoking, apparently unwittingly, a major tenet of just-war doctrine, the principle of proportionality, which is intended to define moral and political limits of action.

These examples would be easy to multiply. What they did, in short-circuiting the relation between morality and politics, was to diminish, to demean, the hard political thinking that was necessary to drive to any adequate solution. Such reaction put a premium on a politically uninformed moralism. It is one side of a coin, the other side of which is a *realpolitik* that would discard considerations of morality for other than rhetorical and cosmetic purposes. It invited mutual disdain rather than dialogue between decision makers and citizen-critics. (Dean Acheson, a former secretary of state, expressed such disdain pungently in late 1969: "The intellectual, strictly channeled into one discipline, wants to run them all. This is why Dr. Spock gives me a pain, why Bill Coffin [the Reverend William Sloan Coffin, then chaplain at Yale]—a hell of a nice fellow—by being a Protestant clergyman knows everything about international affairs. He doesn't. When I was a trustee at Yale I wanted to give him a hemlock cocktail to relieve him of his responsibilities.")

Much of the explosive violence and intense despair of the late sixties came to a high point of concentration as we approached the presidential elections of 1968. It was a time when—to appropriate a phrase of Kipling—many people seemed to act on the principle that "if you can keep your head when all about you are losing theirs," you don't know what's going on. It was a time of deep social disruption, accompanied and intensified by swings of moods that are now difficult to recall with accuracy. Many activists found the atmosphere of intense rebellion and a mindless nihilism to be exhilarating. Others knew we were living through dark days.

I expressed my own feelings in something I wrote for *The New Republic* about the Catholic Worker at that time. I had long admired the Worker movement and many of the people associated with it including its cofounder, Dorothy Day. Living always on the edge of poverty itself, the Worker sheltered, clothed, and fed as many of society's outcasts and derelicts as it could, seeing in each of them the spark of divinity. The organization was destined, however, to remain on the fringe of social and political life, since, according to Dorothy Day, it was founded as a Catholic, anarchistic, pacifistic organization. Most quixotically, it took the Sermon on the Mount as a practical guide to political and social action.

Writing of that organization as we approached elections that were to give U.S. citizens a choice between Richard Nixon and Hubert Humphrey—the latter an honorable man who had, by then, been politically eviscerated by Lyndon Johnson—I said that in the dark days we were living through the only consolation for many citizens was that at least one of the leading candidates must lose. It is in such times that movements such as the Catholic Worker assert their relevance. "For when what seems possible is so clearly inadequate and what is impossible seems necessary, the radical and the utopian become increasingly attractive. I have neither faith nor hope that the ideals of the Catholic Worker will soon prevail in this world. It is their fate to be the leaven, the salt of the earth. But if we are not nourished with their impossible ideals we will die."

—— · ——

It did not occur to me when I wrote these words that activists would soon take the leaven for the whole, attempt to nourish themselves and others on salt alone, and attempt to press impossible ideals into almost immediate political practice. Yet that is what happened when an intemperate infatuation with radicalism swept across the country.

And as radicalism came in, liberalism began to crumble. The label "liberal," long an honorific, became a smear term, used to suggest a flabby middle position clung to by those who did not have the intellectual or moral integrity to move toward either the radical left or the conservative right. The Vietnam War was described as a liberal war, begun under a liberal administration, defended by liberal statesmen and theorists, and carried out under liberal political principles. In their open letter to me the editors of *C & C* had said, "You are not given to labeling others, and you are not easily labeled yourself." I believe both assertions to be accurate, and I would add that I do not usually label myself. But during those days, when most of my friends were rapidly making their passage from liberalism to "radicalism," I asserted—with what I knew at the time to be a degree of perversity—that I was a liberal. Although I was skeptical of the depth of the mass political conversion I saw taking place, I was nevertheless fearful of where it might take us. Asserting a liberal identity was a frail act of resistance.

Those who lived through and participated in the events of those now fabled days will recall the major organizations, marches, milestones, and each will have his or her very particular memories. I recall a number of small incidents in which I discovered that some of my activist friends held views that I could not possibly share. I remember when a friend told me that given the grievous injustices of our society, the days of reform, amelioration, and Martin Luther King were gone; down with Band-aids, up with radical surgery; only revolution—an actual American revolution—would do the necessary, and we should be midwifes to its birth. Another friend defended the arbitrary killing of an American sailor by a nationalist group in Puerto Rico because "the legitimate ways for the citizens of that colony to revolt are closed to them." On another occasion, expecting ready agreement, I launched an attack on "radicals" who defended a black man sniping at a white New York cop from an apartment roof only to be told by an academic liberal, "But surely you can understand that a racist society drove him to such a desperate act." Her alleged profound understanding led this sophisticated lady—I intend no irony—to proffer both moral and legal forgiveness for a clearly murderous act.

When, in a board meeting of Clergy and Laity Concerned About Vietnam, I demurred at some of the outrages committed by student protesters on college campuses, a fellow board member enlightened me about the proper view to take of such antics: "Protect the universities! For God's sake, don't you realize, they're part of the problem. They educated these guys [our then political leaders]. They deserve to be shut down. We should start over."

All of these persons are still active in various organizations, with varying degrees of influence, one now described as a neoconservative, the others self-defined as liberals.

A final example of a somewhat different order. It was very difficult in those days to get a sympathetic and reasoned hearing on college campuses. I was surprised, therefore, when a close friend of mine, someone from whom I had learned much about politics, its great value and its definite limitations, returned from addressing a large group of college students flushed with excited pleasure. "I think I'm onto something," he said. More than politely interested, I asked him what he had said to arouse what must have been a warm response. He had told them, he reported, that he and many of his friends had supported the U.S. role in Vietnam because the specter of a communist victory seemed even more evil. But "maybe we've accepted too easily the choice of the lesser of two evils. Maybe we should reject them both, and just work for what's right." That brought large applause, and at the end of his talk one of the students yelled out, "Welcome to our generation." "And you *liked* that?" I impolitically blurted out. His swift glance dismissed my question, any further discussion, and me. But I believed then as I do now that this thoughtful man, whom I had seen acting with high courage under great pressure, had capitulated to the pressures of the time. He did not lack for company.

The accumulation of such incidents—and I could easily add to the list—increased my skepticism about the direction many of my liberal friends were going. I can name three major constellations of incidents that helped anneal that skepticism and kept me from joining the growing caravan headed far left. The first encompassed the multifarious antiwar activities of the Catholic left, which projected a world view that I found skewed and unsavory. The second was the series of self-serving, irrational campus disruptions, followed by the squalid collapse of the "responsible" academic authorities. The third was the reaction of many antiwar activists to postwar human rights issues. These reactions ranged from the self-flagellant to an ostrichlike approach. I will consider each of these three constellations in turn.

Among the phenomena that blossomed amid the diverse antiwar protests there was one that was termed, not wholly inaccurately, the birth of the Catholic left. There were always, of course, some Catholics on the left in this country. They held out the faint promise that they were harbingers of forces yet unmobilized. In fact, at a time when I was quite susceptible to the attractions of socialism, I had written an article for *Dissent* that anticipated favorably the possibility of a true Catholic left's coming into existence in this country. When that left did arrive, it was not what we had expected, but a changeling. It had little to do with the Old Left in this country, little to do with liberal Catholics. It had, however, a close resemblance to the nonreligious New Left. The mix of radicalism, pacifism, religious symbolism, nonviolent protest, and civil defiance that this new Catholic left introduced into the antiwar movement was novel. Again, my reaction was somewhat different from that of many of my colleagues. We had our usual share of differences and agreements about the efficacy and political legitimacy of breaking into government offices, destroying draft cards, and spilling blood around. I, however, became increasingly concerned about the appropriation of religious symbols, meanings, references, and values for political purposes.

The introduction of religious themes, religious values, into social action is time-honored, of course, and Martin Luther King had provided a recent example of how potent they could be. Those people who maintain that religion and politics should be kept in separate compartments, never to mix, are simply confused. Such a separation is not theoretically desirable in our society or practically possible. All depends upon how they are related. In the late sixties, I began to perceive that many protesters were abusing that relation, to the detriment both of religion and politics. I came to this realization slowly and reluctantly because many of the people involved were friends and acquaintances of mine.

I tested my growing uneasiness against the perceptions of a number of people. One of them, Norman Podhoretz, who was sympathetic to my views, suggested that I write an article for *Commentary* describing this phenomenon. "Just let yourself go," he advised. "Spell out what you see and what you think about it." His invitation was generous and timely, coming as it did when the activist Catholic left was coming into full prominence. I started the article several times but never completed it. I simply could not bring myself to criticize as harshly as I believed they deserved, the ways in which the members of the radical Catholic left joined their religious beliefs, their political judgments, and their methods of protesting. I reminded myself of Aristotle's statement that "I love Plato, but I love truth more." I also held as a conscious principle that in political matters one should look first, not at the intentions of the actors, but at the objective results—the consequences of their acts. Nevertheless, aware that my friends on the Catholic left were running various personal risks, I did not overcome my reluctance to criticize them publicly when they seemed most vulnerable. I have not, however, become less critical of their stance and their subsequent influence, attenuated as it may have become, on moral-political debate and discourse, particularly among young religious activists.

All who lived through the sixties or who have read about the most dramatic antiwar activities must have a clear image of blood being poured over draft records, draft cards being collected and burned in church-related services, prayers of exorcism, prayers of penance—those acts often being led by ordained clergy. Many of these acts were, of course, deliberate attempts to parallel religious services, religious symbols, religious values. The propriety and effectiveness of such behavior are still open, I believe, to analyses and judgment. I was and am less concerned with these acts in themselves than with the surreptitious importation of religious principles into policy questions, the collapse of the transcendent into the historical, the equation of the ultimate with the penultimate. To make this criticism is not to exclude religion and religious values from our society and its governance. It is to say that, like all other values and principles, those derived from religion must enter the arena of political determination on the basis of evidence, reason, and persuasion. However convinced one may be of gospel truths, one cannot apply them directly to political problems and expect political solutions. The mustard-plaster approach is not appropriate to the treatment of societal ills.

Permit a slight excursus here. In attempting to take religious values that governed their personal lives and transfer them directly to societal issues—as many on the Catholic left attempted to do—these protesters were tapping into a deep American strain of ill-considered political theory and practice.

Consider three superficially different observations:

1. American political theory texts frequently quote the nineteenth-century Italian nationalist Camillo Cavour as saying, "If we had done for ourselves what we have done for Italy, what scoundrels we would have been."

2. The late Hans Morgenthau, a leading political theorist in this country for many years, once wrote: "No compromise is possible between the great commandment of Christian ethics, 'Love Thy Neighbor As Thyself,' and the great commandment of politics, 'Use Thy Neighbor To The Ends Of Thy Power.' It is *a priori* impossible for political man to be at the same time a good politician—complying with the rules of political conduct—and to be a good Christian—complying with the demands of Christian ethics. In the measure that he tries tries to be the one he must cease to be the other."

3. This slogan was made familiar in the sixties: "Make love, not war."

As different as these three comments appear to be, they have one thing in common: they assert or imply a closer relation between individual morality and social morality than political life can possibly sustain—or should try to accommodate. They fail to recognize that politics has an autonomy proper to itself that differs from that proper to personal relations.

Cavour's observation implies that one can use the same standards to judge actions appropriate to the state and those appropriate to the individual person but then make different moral judgments, the acts of a scoundrel being, apparently, appropriate to the state. But the comparison of the two kinds of actions is misguided to begin with. This becomes more evident when we consider Morgenthau's statement. I admired Hans Morgenthau and his writings, but I believe his analyses of the relation between individual morality and collective power to be deeply flawed. There are Christians, some pacifists, for example, who would accept as valid the statement that I quoted from Morgenthau, but they remain sectarians—they do not represent the great mainstream of Christian political thought in the West. That theory posits as natural the political community and asserts as proper and good the responsibility of maintaining that community and ensuring its welfare. Only within the terms of that understanding can one make the moral politico-moral discriminations that our social life demands. The Christian statesman or politician who does his best to make those discriminations is acting properly both as politician and as Christian. He will then be judged, as all politicians properly are, on his competence. Morgenthau's error is to take an injunction applicable to the individual person—"Love thy neighbor . . ."—and then assert that the state, in the person of the politician, cannot act upon that injunction. But the observation is totally irrelevant. Taken seriously, it inevitably leads, as it led Morgenthau, to a narrowly sectarian view of Christian morality and to a belief that, tragically but necessarily, politics is immoral.

The same error in all its crudity is encapsulated in the antiwar slogan "Make love, not war." The flaw should be immediately evident when we ask to whom this injunction is directed. Can we tell the state to make love? The idea is preposterous. It is an activity proper only to persons. Can we tell the individual person to make war, or not to make war? Again, outside of Ramboesque fantasies, the idea is preposterous. The citizen can, of course, either support or reject the country's policy on a particular conflict, and we have institutionalized procedures for such actions. As concerned citizens, the pacifist and the selective conscientious objector have their own roles within these procedures, but in a legitimate democracy such as ours they must function within the institution, they cannot transcend it.

These three observations—the evaluation of the statesman, the teaching of the political scientist, and the injunction of the antiwar activist—all confuse the relations between individual and political morality, and it is this confused understanding which informed, or misinformed, much of the message of the radical Catholic left.

Never developed and articulated in a single document, the political world view of many on the Catholic left paralleled or mirrored traditional religious views. It was comprehensive. It posited an overall System in terms of which all issues could be located and judged. Within that System good and evil contended, temptation was everywhere evident, and compromise with the powers of darkness was a sign of weakness. While some maintained a principled pacifism, others thought that the path to political salvation led through the fires of revolution. On the way there were false idols to be encountered and overcome (variously named as the concept of national security, capitalism, transnational corporations, the military-industrial complex, and so forth). Inevitably there would be martyrs who would form a pantheon of moral heroes. In many of their expressions, the certitude proper to religious truths was transferred to the contingencies of particular national policies.

Some particular examples will illuminate the various ways in which this world view found expression. On May 17, 1968, a group that came to be known as the Catonsville Nine burned Selective Service records, an act for which they were duly tried, convicted, and sentenced. According to one report, Daniel Berrigan, who participated with his brother Philip at Catonsville, said of their actions: "Since politics weren't working anyway, one had to find an act beyond politics: a religious act, a liturgical act, an act of witness. If only a small number of men could offer this kind of witness, it would purify the world." Possibly despairing that even that small number of men could be found in this country, Father Berrigan later observed that America was so riddled with corruption that it didn't need to be overturned, it would collapse from within. America was, apparently, beyond redemption.

Two other participants, Thomas and Marjorie Melville, had served, before their marriage, as Maryknoll missionaries in Latin America. On their own testimony, they were poorly prepared in religious, political, or social terms. One of them, for example, initially believed and acted upon the belief that the salvation of the Guatemalan Indians they instructed, even those who participated in Catholic services, depended on their learning a Catholic catechism. Their crash, education-by-experience course in Latin America overturned such primitive views and led them to see the world in a quite different perspective. They now grasped the cause of the undeniable oppression and ongoing political struggle in Latin America. The United States had long kept the countries of Latin America in imperial bondage, and the Catholic Church had served the cause of that imperialism. They also recognized that the rights and wrongs of the struggle did not present themselves in simple black-and-white terms. It was their luminous insight that "many hues of gray" were involved. Yet, in their experience, "the Catholic church and the United States government have *inevitably* failed to recognize this." Since that was the case, they had lost faith both in the hierarchy of the Catholic Church and in the government of the United States. "We feel that both *only exacerbate* the struggle and hinder the quest for human dignity in so many parts of the world" (emphasis added).

—— · ——

Well, so much for hues of gray. Though they left the Maryknoll missionary order, these two people had remained missionaries, simply transferring their severe and simple judgments from the spiritual realm to the social—"Is there a difference?" Tom asked rhetorically. Although it has not completely vanished from present religious-political discussion, the intellectual crudity of such expressions has usually been supplanted by other more attractive and sophisticated versions of the same message. But it *is* the same message.

The impact that the Catholic left had in this country was due to the novel tactics it employed and the rhetorical strength and grace of its most articulate participants, but even more to the fact that the novel tactics were employed by Catholics. I, and many others, had grown accustomed to the "radical" activities and judgments of various speakers within the Protestant community, including leaders at posts of high responsibility. To offer one telling example: The World Council of Churches (WCC) is made up of 300 member churches representing Orthodox, Anglican, Old Catholic, Pentecostal, and Protestant traditions. (The Catholic Church is not a member.) These churches, in turn, have hundreds of millions of adherents around the world. In a conference preparing for one of regular, major assemblies of the WCC, the director of the Commission on the Church's Participation in Development spoke. This man, who was responsible for formulating the ways in which development, including economic development, should serve the poor of the world, made a grand assertion. He said that "Christians should note that protest against the church's defense of the poor and exploited comes not in religious, but in political pages. The idols never want to be removed." He then went on to say that the idols against which Christians must struggle today include racism and the transnational corporations.

It had come to this: the director of development equating the undeniable evil of racism with transnational corporations, the latter an idol to be removed! With a little imagination—or memory—the reader will recognize the direction of this typical argument. The home base of many of the large transnational enterprises is the United States; the United States is the strongest defender of capitalism and free enterprise; the evils perpetrated by these capitalist entities are, therefore, supported by the United States; the United States is, therefore, . . . and so forth.

No entity with the power of the large transnational corporations is going to be entirely free of corruption, coercion, and the occasional misuse of that power. But these are flaws that call for continual vigilance and correction, not the overthrow of what are almost inevitable corporate developments in an interdependent, international economy. But such a sober and realistic assessment was not enough for the WCC director. Where others saw—and still see—only flaws, however great, he perceived evil. And what is evil must be condemned and totally rejected. These transnationals had met their judgment. Such views dovetailed smoothly with those of the new Catholic left.

—— . ——

There were others outside of the religious community who were attracted to the Catholic left. The confluence of the antiwar movement in the United States, the revolutionary ferment in Latin America, and the aggiornamento of the Vatican Council (1960–1965) had real force in the United States. Many outside any religious community saw how the Catholic left might further their own political purposes. By violently yoking religious fervor to revolutionary commitment, Camilo Torres was one of the first to provide the entry for some of these people. Torres was a priest-sociologist, born into a upper-middle-class family in Colombia. On becoming intensely aware of the oppression of the peasants and the oligarchic structure of most societies in Latin America, he came gradually to believe that only violence would break through the constraining force of that system. ("The Catholic who is not a revolutionary is living in mortal sin," he wrote.) He joined guerrillas fighting against the Colombian establishment and was killed in an encounter with the regular army in 1966. He became an early moral hero in the growing pantheon of the religious left. In the book of Torres's writings that he edited in 1971, John Gerassi—a leftist, political scientist, and definitely not religious—found it apropos to say that the peasant in Latin America identifies the source of all violence and injustice more and more with the United States. "Quite rightly so." The formal freedoms of speech and press and all that is encompassed in the term "democracy" are, he went on, part of a society that is based on competition, greed, and oppression. Because of its inherent violence, that society must be destroyed.

And, with an eye cocked to the religious community, the following:

> A new one *will* replace it [our present society]. It will be done through violence, because those who will build the new society must use violence to destroy the old. Those who destroy today will be building tomorrow, or in twenty years. By destroying today, they will learn better how to build tomorrow. In politics, we call them "the vanguard." In ethics, they call them "the moralists." In religion, you call them "God's children."[1]

If John Gerassi were the only one to develop—in my terms, exploit—the passions and politics of the religious left, he would scarcely be worth mentioning. But the nonreligious radical left has made a sound evaluation of the political resources of the religious community, and of its real and potential strength. That community includes many people, dedicated idealistic people; it can command allegiance, time, money; it has many channels of communication, from pulpits to schools to various media; it is transnational; it can transcend petty political considerations to speak of deep moral responsibilities. Further, the radical religious left is increasingly critical of capitalism, multinational enterprises, U.S. foreign policy, U.S. military expenditures, and U.S. deterrence policies. It is increasingly favorable to greater government intervention in economic matters, to socialism, socialist countries, Third World declaratory policies, unilateral arms control measures, liberation by revolution. Just as in past decades many liberals said they could buy Reinhold Niebuhr's social ethics without his theology, so now many leftists can buy the policies of the religious left without its religion. Some of the ties between the religious and nonreligious left were forged during the passionate days of the antiwar protest. They have since become almost regularized. ("The Religious Left is the only Left we have," wrote a fervent writer for *The Nation*.)

I watched as the left in this country shifted the political center of gravity within the institutional structure of the Catholic Church and that institution seemed poised to emulate some of the least desirable policies of the National Council of Churches and some of its mainline Protestant constituent churches. The Catholic Church in this country has strong institutional moorings and a highly developed social doctrine, and has not been given to sudden and frivolous shifts. But it has not proved impervious to the effects of a knee-jerk radicalism. Item: I participated in "Call to Action," a program initiated by the bishops in the late seventies. Carefully developed over a period of years, it was a well-financed, nationwide attempt to make audible within the church the voices of all Catholics, including especially those whose voices are often muted or unheard. The intentions were admirable and the aspirations high. Yet in the plenary session of that program the delegates voted for a resolution that was almost pacifist and that, if put into practice, would make it practically impossible for the United States to provide military aid for its allies. The noted sociologist Father Andrew Greeley dismissed the Call to Action participants as a bunch of kooks. Too easy a dismissal. They were and are the social activists who help shape the social attitudes of other Catholics—and they share many of the traits of the radical left.

The reader will have noted by now that I have criticized a number of organizations and activities in which I participated. My criticism is not, however, entirely hindsight, after the fact. I made many of these criticisms at the time, sometimes only quietly to colleagues but more often within the organizations or in my journalistic accounts. It was, in part, this constant resistance to and questioning of various programs and policies that kept me from moving further to the left with a number of my friends and which led, gradually, to a recognizable rupture with their political views.

The second large constellation of incidents that changed my political perspective took place on the campuses of this country. I now read accounts of teenagers who look back nostalgically to a past they never knew and in which they think they would like to have participated. "It was an extremely interesting culture," said one teenager about the sixties. "People did what they wanted to do. They had values and they went for them. Things were so different then." Indeed! Among the things that took place on campuses as people "did what they wanted to do" was the loss of free speech. Those who held the "wrong" opinions were not allowed to express them, even if they were duly elected, dedicated government officials. Students decided that they should have a greater voice in determining what requirements, if any, their particular course of study should entail. Faculty authorities capitulated. Faculty offices were ransacked and the offenders went unpunished, often uncriticized. "Radical" students "radicalized" faculty members who eagerly sought their approval. (The president of Yale, for example, felt called upon to say that he was skeptical of the ability of a black revolutionary to achieve a fair trial anywhere in the United States.) There were, of course, a number of principled and courageous teachers and administrators who withstood the barrage of criticism that was the lot of those who resisted the pressures of social conformity, but there was widespread failure among university representatives to uphold the liberal principles to which their declared educational values committed them. These educational leaders had mouthed such values for years, their rhetorical embroidery of these values being part of their academic apparel. But when the principles were sharply challenged, behold, their putative adherents were scarcely to be seen. If there is one thing more ridiculous than an emperor without clothes, it is a set of clothes, in a position of authority, without the emperor. And that proved to be what one saw on campus after campus during the testing time. Liberal principles continued to be pronounced even as they were being betrayed. Liberalism, as it was nourished in the academic community during those years, proved too frail for the battle. In these events I was less an actor than an interested spectator, observing my academic friends respond in various ways. Some found ingenious ways to show that suppression of free speech was liberation and that capitulation to student pressure manifested flexibility; others built solitary ivory towers; and some of the most dedicated grew weary with the quotidian battle to be true to their professional responsibilities.

That failure in and of the academy marked, for me, the partial collapse of a community with which I implicitly allied myself—the world of the liberal, academic intellectual. One was not part of it but many of one's friends were, and one could have a general trust in its purpose and its integrity. That trust proved to have been unduly sanguine.

—— . ——

The third constellation of events that caused me to shift my political perspective was the postwar reactions of those who were fellow activists in opposing the war in Vietnam. The first issue in which I found myself in deep disagreement with many of my friends concerned how this country should treat draft resisters, draft evaders, and exiles. These resisters had only exhibited premature morality, said some people who had acted as draft advisers. They should be welcomed home in honor, with no penalty for acting against the laws of the land.

I was struck that this argument was advanced by many who had for years preached the social gospel, social justice, social responsibility. Suddenly the individual conscience was to be the supreme arbiter. The argument was not whether the evaders had acted out of moral conviction—that was assumed. It was over the responsibilities that attached to such actions when they came into conflict with the laws and regulations of a legitimate government. I argued for amnesty with alternative service on the basis that if a citizen holds and acts on principles that put him or her at odds with the laws of the community, he or she should be expected to pay the costs of such opposition. It is a proper function of the government so to legislate when conscientious claims are in conflict. (My disagreement with some people on this issue deepened when, in judging the acts of Lieutenant Calley, who was accused of deliberately killing civilians during the war, they wished to relieve him of any personal responsibility. "If he is guilty, we are more guilty." Suddenly the individual conscience disappeared and the guilt or responsibility for his acts was displaced onto the entire society.)

"There will always be people to minimize violations of human rights and to justify those they acknowledge. This is happening now in Vietnam." Thus the opening sentences in "Fighting Among the Doves," an article in which I examined the response of antiwar activists to the abuse of human rights in Vietnam after the war. During the war I had argued, futilely it seems, that there was no peace movement in this country; there was only an antiwar movement composed of people with quite different agendas, and it would break up when the war was over. This it did, sharply and dramatically, on the issue of human rights.

When the war ended in April 1975, there was no immediate bloodbath, as those most antagonistic to North Vietnam had predicted. Americans, weary and relieved, let their attention be drawn to other areas, other problems. But then there began to issue from Vietnam rivulets of disturbing rumors, then small streams of information regarding political prisoners. If true, the news was very bad. A small group of people drafted an "Appeal to the Government of Vietnam Regarding Human Rights." Before releasing this appeal publicly, one of the drafters, Jim Forest, a Catholic pacifist with the Fellowship of Reconciliation, sent highly respectful letters to the Vietnamese Observer at the UN recounting the reports that had been received and asking for some response. (Over twenty congressmen and the director of SANE also sent letters.) They went unanswered until the International League for Human Rights held a well-publicized press conference at which it expressed the same concerns. Soon after that conference I received, as I presume all who signed our appeal received, a rather sketchy, quite inadequate and unconvincing response from Ambassador Dinh Ba Thi. Subsequently our appeal was released publicly, signed by over 100 people. (These included Joan Baez, Roger Baldwin, Malcolm Boyd, Roberta Cohen, Dorothy Day, James Douglass, Allen Ginsberg, Bishop Thomas Gumbleton, Ken Kesey, Aryeh Neier, Richard John Neuhaus, Gordon Zahn, and Howard Zinn.) That carefully constructed appeal was rejectly, vigorously, by others in the peace movement, some of whom slandered and abused those who composed it. One common item in the notes of rejection was the replacement of the United States for Vietnam as the fit object of censure. As one longtime participant in the movement wrote to Jim Forest, "If the Vietnamese *had* chosen the course of mass executions and plunder, of political prisoners and torture, it would have been our own strategies of terror and brutality which drove them to it." Another group of activists countered the appeal with an open statement of their own entitled "Vietnam: A Time for Healing and Compassion." This statement reads in part:

> The present government of Vietnam should be hailed for its modera-
> tion and for its extraordinary effort to achieve reconciliation among
> all of its people. We share the view that American citizens should
> be gravely concerned about abuses of human rights, whether they
> occur in our country or abroad. This concern is especially appropriate
> where our government supports a foreign regime that is engaged
> in flagrant abuse of its own people—abuses including systematic
> torture. But Vietnam presents a different case. The present suffering
> of the Vietnamese people is largely a consequence of the war itself
> for which the United States bears a continuing responsibility.

The tactic employed here is by now drearily familiar. Turn aside the charge that is made, avoid discussing the evidence on its own merits, turn the criticism back upon the United States. Among the signers who subscribed to this statement, and their then affiliations, were James Armstrong, Bishop, United Methodist Church; Richard Barnet, Institute for Policy Studies; Robert McAfee Brown, Union Theological Seminary; Richard A. Falk, Princeton University; Don Luce, Clergy and Laity Concerned; Paul F. McCleary, National Council of Churches; Cora Weiss, National Coordinator, Friendshipment; Corliss Lamont, Coordinator (of the statement group).

The trust these people placed in the new government of Vietnam was rudely abused, as was soon made clear by the testimony of the boat people who, at great risk to their lives, began to stream out. The scale of the brutality inflicted by the victorious Vietnamese government remains an uncompleted story even today. But has that brutality, severe even by the high standards set in this century, shattered the illusions, shaken the confidence of those who so misread the nature of the Vietnamese revolutionaries and the socialist society they were to build? Has it given them pause about the nature of Castro's regime or that of the Sandinistas? Not so one could notice.

These, then, are some of the events that caused me to become gradually disenchanted with the political configurations that were once mine. As I have been recounting these somewhat scattered fragments of recent history I have been vaguely aware of a presence, as of the spirit of some friendly interlocutors hovering over my shoulder. "Dear Jim, haven't you presented a distorted picture, given only extreme examples from a time now past? After all, that radical infatuation you mentioned did not lead to a permanent union. Liberals *have* come home."

Well, dear shades, during the crisis of the sixties the liberal community did not prove entirely trustworthy, witness the widespread desertion of its best principles. The possibility of a similar infatuation is still there. As for the examples, they may be extreme. I think they are. But they are not uncommon or untypical. I can readily offer a number of current examples. Second, that moderate left is all too sensitive to the radical left. It gets pulled in that direction.

"Pulled in the wrong direction? Not trustworthy? Those are strong words. Can you back them up?"

Nothing could be easier. Let us consider Central America, and let us begin by agreeing that the issues are complicated, have deep historical and cultural roots, derive from indigenous conditions, and involve great-power interests. Let us also agree that we cannot address the problems there in any useful way unless we understand what has happened in recent years. Then let us ask where the sympathies of the liberal left will lie. How will it interpret the nature of the Sandinista leadership? Well, those questions have, of course, already been answered. Early on, an official for the National Council of Churches talked blithely—though formally—about eliminating the center in El Salvador so that the necessary choice of supporting the leftist guerrillas would then become clear. And even though Napoléon Duarte had the strong support of highly influential Catholics in the United States, spokesmen for the Catholic hierarchy testified before Congress that they opposed military aid to El Salvador from any source. Well and good. But could they think that the Soviets would be as attentive to their advice as some members of Congress? The appearance of reasoned balance in such statements is fraudulent.

As for the nature of the Sandinista regime, I think the evidence that it is consciously Marxist-Leninist is irrefutable and readily available. (Douglas Payne, a colleague at Freedom House, which is fiercely independent in its political advocacy, has provided documentary evidence in his monograph *The Democratic Mask*.) Nor were the Sandinistas pushed in that direction by the United States. Within months after coming to power, they eagerly established connections with the Communist Party of the Soviet Union. This evidence is either ignored or belittled by many on the left. (I presume we need not dwell overlong on those who positively welcome such collaboration.) I do not suggest that the recognition of these facts leads to an immediately desirable policy, only that we will not have such policy without that recognition.

I recognize that a number of people are bemused and sometimes impressed by the presence of priests in highly visible positions in Nicaragua—even though they cannot function as priests, since the Vatican has suspended their priestly faculties. Our friends at *America* magazine printed an interview with their fellow Jesuit father Miguel D'Escoto, Nicaragua's foreign minister, in which he slandered a number of people, including Nicaragua's Cardinal Obando y Bravo. The magazine offered no editorial explanation or apology. Since the magazine is not politically radical or strident, its premise, I presume, is that it's all good clean political fun on issues about which reasonable people can disagree. Since D'Escoto also abused the Institute on Religion and Democracy, of which I'm a member, I replied to him in an open letter *America* was good enough to publish. I was particularly distressed by what I regarded as a most blatant distortion and exploitation of religious values. He had, after all, said that the church had betrayed the people and then had placed the people in opposition to the church; he had said that he respected canon law and had then rejected its application to him; he had said that he respected and would remain faithful to his superiors and the Pope and had then rejected their direction. "How is it," I asked, "that you, your priestly faculties suspended, assuming a highly political position, making highly political judgments, are fulfilling a priestly function [as he had claimed], and the Cardinal, as he fulfills his narrowly defined priestly functions, is being political?" Surprise! No answer to me or to the editors of *America,* which he undoubtedly reads.

—— . ——

Since that time this man has received the Lenin peace prize. On accepting it he found it in his heart and mind to say:

> I believe that the Soviet Union is a great torch which emits hope for the preservation of peace on our planet. Always in the vanguard of the overall struggle for peace, the Soviet Union has become the personification of ethical and moral norms in international relations. I admire the revolutionary principles and consistency of the foreign policy of the Communist Party of the fraternal Soviet Union.

However, I do not expect the accumulation of mere evidence to change the judgments of those who wish to align themselves with socialist countries or socialist causes. (I use the term "socialist" here with the meaning that the countries of the Soviet bloc normally assign to it.) Recent case in point: After the truly harrowing accounts of life and death in Castro's prison provided by Armando Valladares, Jorge Valls and others who have spent more than twenty years there, one would have thought that the romantic adulation some have lavished on Castro in the past would have been curbed. Not so. In a recent issue of *America* Castro was described in the most glowing terms as a great crusader who now strives to overcome "the profoundly immoral political and economic structure that is squeezing the life-blood out of third-world nations." And the writer then pondered, "Where in the world may we find so Christian a head of state?" We have here descended into a valley fogged with madness. Such responses are beyond caricature. And you will recognize that I have drawn them not from radical sources, but from those that are usually described as liberal or moderate.

"We're unlikely to come to perfect agreement on these issues. But two questions, please. You seem to have stuck almost entirely to foreign policy issues. Do you have the same general attitudes on domestic issues? And if the responses provided by the left are inadequate, where do you look for greater enlightenment?"

I would on another occasion be pleased to address domestic issues more fully. But before we leave foreign policy issues, I would add that on questions such as the nature of the Soviet threat and how to counter it, on the relation between the U.S. and Third World countries, on the role of transnational enterprises and economic growth in underdeveloped countries, on the evaluation of the overall performance of America in the world today—on these and related issues I find the responses that moderates and conservatives have offered in recent years are more nearly adequate, more useful, more suggestive than those offered by the left. (Distinctions, as always, are in order. *Commonweal* accepted, quite correctly, President Reagan's description of the Soviet Union as an "evil empire" and rejected, quite correctly, his attribution of all the world's ills to that evil empire. But when it offered a soundly argued editorial analyzing the benefits and dangers of deterrence, its readers criticized it for not being more prophetic, more moral, more courageous and for not calling for the dismantling of the deterrents.)

"We see. You've joined the party of reaction, dangerous deficits, greed, and international adventurism."

We seem to have left the arena of rational discourse. Allow me, then, to respond to your charge with a peroration. Charles Peguy once said that "it is impossible to know how many acts of cowardice have been committed out of fear of not appearing progressive." That's still true. I do not believe that conservatives have the solution to all our problems, even in theoretical terms. We are operating in the realm of relative merits, relative advantages. The great deficits we have accumulated are a problem we have yet to cope with. Our policies in Central America are sadly muddled, but those opposed to these policies do not offer persuasive assurance that they will do better. Quite the reverse. As for liberals being the party of compassion and conservatives the party of hard-hearted greed, I think that's pure malarkey. ("They may have won the war," said La Passionara after Franco's victory, "but we had the best songs." The left wing of the Democratic Party seems bent on emulating her, substituting compassionate slogans for songs.) There has been an element of adventurism in the politico-military policies of the Reagan administration—as there was in those of its predecessors. But this administration is more ephemeral than the attitudes and principles we are discussing.

If I were to try to encapsulate my attitudes, the grounds of my own political stance, I would not initially invoke the usual terms. Like most Americans, liberal or conservative, left or right, I would like to see the extension of democracy and freedom in countries around the world. As always, the problem is how to effect such an extension. And, as is most common, it is presented to us in its political and economic dimensions. I tend to remain skeptical of those who are confident that their vision totally encompasses these dimensions. Such people are too readily tempted to reach for apocalyptic solutions, and if they are not to be found at one extreme of the political spectrum, they will be sought at the other extreme.

I believe, further, that before the problems that beset us are economic or political or military or technological, they are spiritual. To put that in other terms, I look back on the sixties as a time when some new and valuable things were released into our culture, but even more as a time when values on which much of our national confidence rested suddenly collapsed—or were unaccountably deserted. I do not mean to overdramatize. I do not foresee a rising tide of barbarianism beneath which we will be submerged. But I believe that there is a general moral disarray in our society. The lust for constant distraction among the affluent, the lust for revolution, apocalyptic solutions, and utopias among political activists, and for drugs throughout all levels of our society are symptoms of that disarray.

We are being challenged in many ways to answer basic questions: What does it mean to be human? How do we live in community? What are the values worth dying for? What is it that we can hope for? These are, admittedly, not questions that we can expect politics to answer. But it is on the answer to such questions that our politics must ultimately rest.

Note

[1] *Revolutionary Priest: The Complete Writings and Messages of Camilo Torres*, edited and with an introduction by John Gerassi (New York: Vintage Books, 1971), p. 460.

11

The Wide and Crooked Path

Carol Iannone

What the sixties were to become for me, although I did not recognize it at first, was an intense internal struggle to possess my own soul against the traps of pseudothought. Mine was more a contest of thoughts than of actions, an embattled sentimental education in which I discovered a crowded marketplace of cheap ideas to distract me from the task of facing myself, and in which I eventually had to pay the consequences of surrender to the rampant half-truths, self-deceptions, self-justifications, and outright lies that are certainly not peculiar to any age but to which some ages, like the sixties, offer less resistance.

The whole process did not begin in my experience with picketing, marching, sitting down, or demonstrating; in fact, it never included those things, although I was to buy most of the political package soon enough. No, the sixties—that chronologically misnamed era, as someone has observed—began for me sometime toward the end of the decade in a theology class at Jesuit Fordham University in which I learned that the God of my childhood was dead. I too had chuckled in the irreverent atmosphere of post-Vatican II at the downfall of the old bearded man in the sky and the collapse of the triangle with the eye in its center. I suddenly sensed in that class, however, some serious withdrawal of foundations. Naively, considering the adolescent cynicism of those around me, I asked the teacher if I could continue to pray for the grace to study. I don't know why my query took that particular form; I was not a natural student and had little real personal discipline despite (or perhaps because) of years in Catholic schools. But I guess now that I was angling for something deeper than just a study aid.

Amid the smirks and chortles, the teacher told me briskly and with some condescension that such an idea was stupid; instead of praying to God to help me study, I should just sit down and study. (But that was the whole point of grace, I thought, a point that would seen recede from my grasp: "The good that I would, I do not"!) Suddenly, the ground gave way and the world opened up as a cold and hostile place. I stood squarely alone, devoid of the lightness of grace, relying on the chancy forces of willpower and the troubling inconsistencies of rationalism, with no way to transcend the gap between the me I was and the me I hoped to become.

That was it. I didn't realize it fully until much later, but at that moment, for all practical purposes, my faith was gone. I had lost any concept of a God at hand, a present help in trouble, and from then on I was on my own, open and vulnerable to the aggressive shifts and turns that were rapidly to follow.

The Church meantime had become a place of ecstasy. A lot of sublimated sexuality seemed to bubble to the surface and to prompt a good deal of the exuberance of those times, I came to see. Boys and girls began to write long letters to each other testifying to the fervor of their renewed religion. Nuns and priests defected to get married, often to each other. Masses were held in people's apartments, on lawns, in gardens, the officiating priests often clad in T-shirts and chinos. There was singing, dancing, music. Someone was always thrusting a cup of wine at you, offering you a piece of bread, clasping your hand or hovering near you for the kiss of peace. It seemed you could never be alone with God anymore. Everyone seemed more in love with each other than with Him—not surprising, since He had become something of a formality. Out of my experience went the darkened churches I could slip into on Saturday afternoons to unburden my heart.

What was there anymore to unburden? The concept of sin had shriveled; it was no longer important to follow the teachings of Christ so much as the "example of his life," i.e., "love." Love and do what you will, Paul was supposed to have said, although I've never been able to find the exact quote and, in any event, had he been able to see how his words would be used, he might well have unsaid them. The appalling trivialization of the meaning and essence of love was one of the chief barbarisms of the sixties. (Its residue persists to this day in the poorly focused talk of compassion and brotherhood, but even more in the stunning superficiality of sexual relationships.) The new morality was guided not by an expanded sense of love, but by impulse—by what it felt right to do in the moment, with the frequently and sanctimoniously reiterated proviso that it not hurt anyone else (also only in the moment).

No one talked about the contexts, the consequences, the responsibilities, the limitations, the contradictions that can occur even between competing goods, let alone good and evil (a word that dropped out of the lexicon), and that far from inhibiting love, define it. No one talked about the disorganization of character that results from petty indulgence and how hard it is to establish internal order afterwards. These things you had to discover for yourself; with all the cultural cheerleading you heard going into the new "life-styles," you were entirely alone in finding your way back.

Nevertheless, it seems clear now that I cannot blame my loss of faith on the upheavals of the times. Despite years of catechism, masses, communions, confessions, benedictions, and so forth, my house had been built on sand and great was the fall of it. Then too, for a sensitive, scrupulous child, the pre-Vatican II Church was in many ways a house of horrors, as dark and cheerless as anything that Calvinism had devised. My moments of grace had often been achieved outside of the rituals and sacraments to which I was nevertheless bound by fear. (Missing the nine o'clock children's mass was one of my chief anxiety dreams well into adulthood.) Later in my life, I was able to discern how different the more Old World Catholicism of my mother was from mine. When she retreated with her novenas, rosaries, and candles, it was to enter a world of unconditional peace, solace, and comfort. But many of us who came up under the American Church had become acquainted with guilt, terror, self-condemnation, a false concept of self-sacrifice, and an abiding sense of our own worthlessness.

Those who tried to destroy the spurious conceptions of God that had produced this cruelty weren't wrong, but they had nothing substantial to put in their place. The superficial freedom they advanced was too much the reverse image of the bondage they thought they were escaping. And they underestimated how excruciatingly difficult it would be to find a genuine release from what enslaved us. (It seems logical now that this lack of understanding of true spiritual freedom, combined with the loss of real faith in God's power to aid

His creation, should have culminated in a political response—"liberation" theology—in which working out one's own salvation is replaced by material advocacy for the poor.)

A great flood of unhappiness and confusion was to issue from my collapse of faith when it finally caught up with me. But in the iconoclastic air of the sixties it was possible to avoid its implications and even make light of it. The problem went underground, so to speak, appearing as a general disaffection (possible to mistake in those days for a legitimate response to cultural ills) or in an intensification of my occasional bouts of melancholy. My first job out of college was as a substitute teacher in a Catholic grammar school. During the interview, the more traditional-minded sister-principal asked me if I believed in the Real Presence, i.e., that Christ is really present at the moment of consecration in the mass. I probably should have been ashamed to say it, but I told her yes, and at that point I saw no contradiction since I had not really troubled to think things through. He was really there, I thought, He just didn't matter to me. But I was never to know a solid moment of peace or joy until I had found my way back to Him, years later and in terrible pain.

——·——

I grew up in an extended family that started out in the Italian section of East Harlem, and a large part of our identity was rooted in the idyll of the immigrant culture of those streets. For those of us too young to have experienced much of it firsthand it was almost as real as for those who did, because we never tired of hearing the stories of the older folks, who never tired of telling them. The community was tightly knit, consisting of many large and interlocking families and little enclaves of "paesani." There was always a hand for those in need, often extended surreptitiously for those too proud to admit their trouble. When a boy returned from the war or a bride descended from her home on her way to church, the entire block turned out to greet them. (A wonderful wide-angle photograph preserves this moment on my mother's wedding day.) On Saturday nights, people would visit each others' houses until four in the morning and then continue talking by the door until the arrival of the milkman. There were the feasts, the weddings (children always invited), the splendid, emotion-wracked funerals, the Italian theater, and concerts on summer nights in the park along the river. And, we were told, when the voice of Caruso was heard wafting across East Harlem some decades before, it was liable to be not just a recording, but Caruso himself, paying a visit to friends.

It was largely a working-class and small-business community, but there was considerable prosperity. There was a classy dress shop at 125th Street and Fifth Avenue, and dressmakers, milliners, and music teachers had plenty of employment. Between First and Third Avenues, 116th Street was lined with brownstones inhabited by the professionals—the judges, doctors, lawyers who seemed to feel no need to leave the old culture behind despite their upward mobility (something that would later perplex me), but who continued to enjoy the life of the neighborhood—the boccie games, the long Sunday dinners, and the frequent parties with mandolins and accordions.

But other stories troubled me, like that of the young doctor who had left Italy and journeyed to Harlem to seek his future. Even from across the Atlantic, his family managed to constrain him from marrying the woman with whom he fell in love because his mother didn't want him to remain in America. I came to conjecture when I started to feel the tension myself that his capitulation to his mother had derived from the confusion of identity that such an ultracohesive culture can produce: where was the boundary between oneself and others? Blessed were you if there was no conflict, but if there was, it was liable to be sore and sharp; and if you would come to feel at times that you couldn't live within the family, neither could you live without it. Thus the young doctor eventually left Harlem, as his mother had wanted, to return to his hometown in Italy. But by that time he *had* married, very inappropriately—"out of spite," it was said—and was to live out an unhappy, lonely life, according to reports. Refusing to go to his mother's deathbed many years later, he turned his face to the wall when his brothers came to implore him to come. The young woman he hadn't married, my great-aunt, refused all other suitors and never recovered from her early bitterness. Left to care for her parents, she remained deeply emotionally dependent on the family all her life, and often raged against its strictures.

I lived only a little scrap of my childhood in the neighborhood before the various families began their treks into the boroughs and suburbs. But the core of the culture went with us—above all, the absolute and peremptory centrality of the family life. This was bound to cause conflict as the American century progressed, probably even without the special pressures of the sixties, but my search for a separate identity was exacerbated by the extreme version of an unconditioned individuality beyond circumscription that was borne of the sixties. I felt an enormous strain between the gospel of feelings and impulses advanced by the changing times—the imperatives to find myself, to live for now, to try it if it felt good, and so forth—and the sublime, self-abnegating images of the family myth, in which grown children cared for sick parents, went to work to help out their brothers and sisters, and came home on Friday nights with a treat for the family. At family gatherings, particularly in the presence of the men, I would long, for the moment, to be the woman they thought I was or thought I would become.

My faith in family solidarity did not erode as quickly as my faith in God. It gradually diminished, until at my grandmother's deathbed, some half dozen years after college, I realized that it had been something of a deception. The intensity of the extended family life can be wonderful, exhilarating, almost magical, but it can exact a great price of selfhood (something clearly not recognized by those who began recommending the extended family as an "alternative" to the restrictions of the insular nuclear American model).

It may seem odd that someone from a working-class Italian immigrant background would succumb to the upper-middle-class luxury of countercultural thinking (and, indeed, my one attempt to join an antiwar rally in Central Park was frustrated when my mother implored me not to go because the night before she'd dreamt of a bullet in the head), but there was an underlying continuity. Having grown up under two ideologies of self-denial, I was susceptible to an ideology of self-fulfillment, especially one advanced, like the former ones, for the greater good. Ironically, the philosophies of the new age turned out to be another form of perverse self-denial, as one surrendered the precious concreteness of one's own reality (however difficult) on the altar of ephemeral dreams and promises. But the notion that individual liberation was leading to a collective regeneration of society prevented me from seeing this clearly at the time.

For all my commonsense skepticism, I came to support and even admire the radicalism, or at least the ideas I took to be behind it. Up close it was possible to see that the activists were often spoiled, infantile, self-consumed, full of resentment and free-floating, generalized rage. (The anti-Americanism that could seem so righteous at the time now seems a transparency for hatred of authority, of country, of parents, and finally of self.) As for their heroism, if you've read the stories of a few martyrs, it's hard to be really impressed by a bus trip to Washington and an overnight arrest. And I had my doubts about the professor who encouraged the students to demonstrate against the false hierarchies of privilege but wouldn't risk sitting down himself because he was untenured.

I gradually came to hate the war, and I probably did believe that America was too materialistic (since I believe it now), but I doubt the political issues were really the bottom line. I think now that I was drawn to the messianic dimension of the radicalism, the (deceptive) promise of the grace that I had lost. I wanted it to be true that there were whole other and better ways to live, not just for me, but for everyone—that life could be freer, easier, purer if only one could throw off the artificial restraints. Echoes of these longings for a better world could surely be heard in the folk music we listened to at the time, music as emotionally unsettling as the rock music kids listen to today.

Many have attributed this kind of aspiration to a Howdy Doody, Lone Ranger generation brought up in peace and prosperity devoid of a tragic sense. It's possible. But at the same time, we were a generation that learned about torture, brainwashing, and concentration camps as children and practiced air raid drills in grammar school. When I was a young girl, a series ran in the *Post* in which concentration camp survivors told of various tortures they had undergone. One man, for example, had been suspended for days from his hands tied behind his back, the ground beneath him hollowed out just enough to be beyond the reach of his toes. In sixth grade we were told of an incident in which Chinese communist soldiers had invaded a school in the countryside, lashed the children's hands behind their backs, and hammered chopsticks into their ears. How many adolescent discussions sputtered out into " 'But what would you do if you were in a concentration camp? Would you be able to stick to the moral rules if your survival was at stake?" Or, "What would you do if the Communists tortured you? Would you be able to resist betraying your friends?" Perhaps the sense of suffering was too great to be properly absorbed.

Be that as it may, with the loss of my faith and the confusion about my family identity (both felt and never acknowledged), reality sometimes weighed very heavily on me, along with the ominously impending demands of adulthood; I wanted there to be a way in which I wouldn't have to face the difficult day-to-dayness and the "load of my own unhappiness" which, like St. Augustine, I had begun to drag around with me. And the thought that somehow a collective salvation could be achieved—that the social structure could change so radically that what I dreaded facing could be dissolved into some newer order of priorities, some purer hierarchy of values— was irresistible and compelling beyond words. I can almost remember the morning, a good decade or so after it all began, that I woke up and realized that no such changes would occur—that I would have to face, alone, all that I had hoped to evade, now only the more difficult to deal with because so long postponed.

Of course I wouldn't have recognized such deep-seated evasions at that time if they had come up and hit me on the head, and if anyone had tried to make me see them, I would probably have laughed him to scorn. But then again, no one did try, at least not to my memory. Educated people among the older generations seemed simply unprepared for the sixties, and were probably in many cases themselves compromised by its false hopes and tinny promises of personal and sexual freedom. It was years before I met anyone who understood the new thought and could challenge it effectively. (Family resistance was pretty much dismissed, of course.) Rejoinders that almost seem obvious now were hard to come by at first. But truth to tell, I wonder if any reasonable rejoinders would have been effective at the time. The call of the counterculture was not an appeal to reason, to say the least, but a very aggressive defiance of it.

The counterculture was able to gain so much ground because it insisted that any resistance to its blandishments was attributable to "uptight," middle-class morality—for example, to the frantic effort to preserve privilege, to the fear of the hidden homosexual in all of us, or to some other remote, shifting, and poorly understood motivation. This way of discrediting counterarguments has dealt a great and lasting blow to reasoned discourse that allows for motivations without letting them destroy all opposition.

At one point when I was still resisting the new thought, I tried to get a more traditional professor to deplore the use of Hamlet's remark, "Nothing's either good or bad but thinking makes it so," in a popular song of the day. I was frightened enough of such relativism to want him to reject it outright. After all, that remark is uttered by the early Hamlet; the later Hamlet arrives at greater certainty (as another professor had noted in Shakespeare class—why didn't I ask *him* to repudiate the lyrics of the song?) The professor would not give me the straightforward reassurance I wanted, and in a way he was right not to, since there is truth in Hamlet's earlier remark. Therein lay another lesson that I can see now. It is very hard to counter the simpleminded assertions of the left (or in this case the simpleminded distorted way a truth was being used) if you don't want to fall into simpleminded assertions of your own. And simple new ideas can seem more compelling than complicated old ones.

Thus, even though I'd joined a Young Conservative Club in high school, I eventually found that the conservative movement of that time, the esteemed William Buckley notwithstanding, couldn't compete with the instant excitement generated by the New Left.

The understanding of poverty furnishes an example. Anyone who made even the most modest effort to perform some kind of social service in those days, in my case in a day camp and foster home, could see how complex a picture poverty presented up close: how some poor people have a surprisingly buoyant sense of life; how some contribute miserably to their own difficulties; how frequent were the failures of even one's best efforts in working with them; how unglamorous and small were one's successes, at least when considered against the vaunting idealism of the age. How much easier it became to blame the system entirely and to demand large-scale solutions to eradicate the problem together with its troubling reminder of the tragic dimension of human life. ("The poor ye have always with ye," said Jesus in a statement seldom quoted by Christians today.) It became necessary to judge severely anyone who didn't agree with such solutions, because to acknowledge the possibility of disagreement, I see now, meant to acknowledge the possibility of mortal life as inherently imperfect, to lose the sense of burning righteousness, and to be returned to the dry quotidian with a crash.

This kind of doublethink applied to a lot of things at the time. I guess we believed the publicity about being idealistic, and we were perhaps also flattered by certain older people with their own agendas into believing it about ourselves. Hadn't Robert Kennedy told my older brother's class at commencement that they were the best-fed, the best-educated, the best this, the best that generation in American history and that they were to go out and do great things? So we obliged by denying the implications of what in our experience contradicted the golden view.

But once in a while something would happen to pierce the glow of beatitude. I was at a party one night when the wife of one of the young men announced that he'd just been rejected for the service because of overweight. One of the other women phoned the news to her boyfriend and conveyed his comment to us all: "Congratulations on being a fat unpatriotic slob." The boyfriend had intended the remark to be entirely ironic, we knew, a mocking send-up of the hawkish crew-cut mentality, but perhaps because of being relayed secondhand, the remark fell flat. A moment of embarrassment ensued, and for that moment at any rate a lot of the pretense was suddenly stripped away.

The draft provided many opportunities for phony idealism and self-deception. There was some genuinely principled draft resistance, but the term was a misnomer in many cases. It is certainly a human enough impulse to want to avoid combat, and if the country allows it through various deferments, I suppose you can expect young men to take advantage of them. But this could hardly be construed as idealism, and yet we often did so construe it, remembering to rehearse the injustices and atrocities of the war every time someone reported on his various maneuvers to obtain a deferment. I sometimes wondered secretly if it was true that these men would gladly fight in a just cause, as they often said. Many young men were genuinely opposed to the war, but it was never easy to know how much of their behavior was based on principle and how much on simple self-preservation. Not having to make the distinction with any care was one of the cheap "luxuries" available in the thought of the time; and being female made you equally anxious not to do so, since you felt a little guilty about not being directly on the line.

This kind of thinking made it possible to become a modern liberal without much effort, without real examination of the issues, and without knowing anything about the history of radical politics. (For a long time I didn't even know why it was called the *New* Left.) With an extra access of doublethink it was even possible to become a proponent of the new ideas and yet still fancy that you were above their worst excesses. Then too, as an immigrant's daughter who had paid many bright-eyed visits to the Statue of Liberty with her father, I kind of knew somewhere that I didn't really believe all the Amerika rhetoric. Yet, with existential inexorability the ideas to which I was giving lip service were affecting me more deeply than I realized.

If I seemed to become a liberal within weeks, my best friend managed to become a radical overnight, more proof, I see now, that the countercultural appeal was not to reason—hers was a really startling transformation that eventually tore us apart. She was beautiful, bright, creative, athletic, funny, a wonderful friend, and full of promise which had begun to blossom in college. We had been close from freshman year in high school, and it was she in fact who had introduced me to the *National Review* and influenced me to join a Young Conservative Club. Then suddenly she was into everything—drugs, sex (with an attendant bout of gonorrhea), a sort of communal living arrangement, demonstrations, open hostility to her parents, nude parties, minor skirmishes with the law, and so forth. Her transformation was so dramatic and was so obviously built at least in good measure on the eruption of unsavory traits of temperament that I should have been tipped off. Up close I could see that her new life was disheveled and even sordid; but in theory I somehow found it enviable, even romantic. She was breaking all the shackles, she was finding herself, she was free.

Her boyfriend treated her with a jealous, domineering, sexual possessiveness that sometimes tipped over into sadism—another contradiction that I could not quite fathom at the time. None of the nonradical men I knew would have dared to treat a woman that way—putting his hand down her blouse in public to show proof of ownership. We are accustomed to hearing that modern feminism was born when women in the movement woke up to the shock of how conventionally the radical men behaved toward them. But I wonder how much of the impulse toward feminism arose in opposition to the masculine brutality specifically unleashed by countercultural dictates to overthrow the norms, including some types of deference to women.

I tried at one late point, I thought for her own good, to confront her with the deterioration of her life. She countered cuttingly, and correctly, with the dry misery of my own and brought me to tears. Not knowing enough about the sources of your own unhappiness makes you very vulnerable to radical assaults.

—·—

The considerable confusion I was experiencing in all areas of life might actually have led to some sort of self-confrontation had not the atmosphere been so full of the "hot winds of change," as playwright August Wilson appreciatively calls them. There were so many means of evasion one could explore in the name of finding oneself—taking a trip, changing jobs, starting a romance, or living with someone instead of marrying him, so you wouldn't have to make up your mind whether you loved him enough to commit your life to him. Kicking and screaming we are dragged into adulthood, I heard someone say years after these events, but my time was not yet.

I wandered into publishing, where I was positioned as an editorial assistant, one of those low-level "glamour" jobs that were perfect breeding grounds for the female discontent that we were then hearing so much about (and have been hearing ever since). I felt encouraged to view my dissatisfaction as not peculiar to me, but typical of women's lot in patriarchy, and I jumped at the chance. I announced that I was quitting my job and shaded my decision with political dimensions—could females only type and fetch coffee? I asked by implication in my resignation notice. Actually, I didn't only type and fetch coffee, and, moreover, several of the editors, including my own, were women. I was really announcing my failure to stick to something until I had gained the knowledge, ability, and temperamental capacity to advance. Some years later, forced to do temporary secretarial work to help support myself, I realized I was being made to learn the lessons I had refused the first time around.

Not surprisingly, my next "decision" was to go to graduate school, where I suppose I hoped to escape from the real world a bit longer (but where it finally caught up with me). Truth to tell, however, in returning to school to study literature I was returning to something I really loved. I had felt a genuine excitement in learning at college, and literature had opened up to me the fierce and subtle world of ideas and feelings the way Chapman's Homer had opened up the ancient world to Keats. Thankfully, Fordham had by no means been in the vanguard of the various reforms of the day, and my education had been basically in the classical style, not least in its overall structure, give or take a few radical-minded younger professors. My teachers, perhaps because they hadn't as yet succumbed to the insistence to think otherwise, saw me, as far as I could tell, as an individual with potential, not as a member of some marginal group needing special treatment.

Still, without knowing it, I had already begun to experience in college, to some degree, the enlistment of literature in the radical cause, something that I was to see much more of in graduate school at Stony Brook (where I was attracted by the unstructured, innovative curriculum and implicit promise of revelation). It wasn't until I started teaching and hearing myself talk about the corruption of civilization, the superiority of outsidedness, the inevitable alienation of the sensitive soul, and so forth—long after I had stopped believing in these things, at least in their simpler versions—that I realized how deeply such ideas had taken root in me. It took a long time for me to see that if Conrad is exposing the hypocrisy of civilization in *Heart of Darkness*, for example, he is not also implying that primitivism is better, or that civilization is dispensable, disposable, or even readily alterable. And if *Huckleberry Finn* is about rebellion against civilized restraints, it does not follow that civilized restraints should be discarded.

One professor had used literature to illustrate how the person of superior insight must sometimes lie to protect the harsh truths of life from corruption and distortion by society. This kind of lying occurs in both of the works just mentioned, in fact. There is a shred of veracity in this idea—Jesus spoke in parables, for example, and told his disciples not to cast their pearls before swine, although he never licensed actual lying. But it is also the kind of idea that, without a proper disciplining context (such as Jesus supplied), easily lends itself to misapplication—to gain a false sense of superiority over the ordinary run of humanity, or to justify lying or withholding the truth when revealing it might simply be unpleasant (something I frequently did to protect the "truth" of my new "life-style" experiences from my family).

But I was eventually to see as well that there had been a certain unsustainable idolatry implicit in the way literature had been treated in the classical humanist tradition of the literary generations before the sixties. This may well have accounted for the weariness I began to sense in some professors in graduate school who were defecting from a worn-out faith. Indeed, one eminent literary critic announced that the study of literature had become "moribund." But, more important, the idolatry may also have had the result, I see now, of preparing the way for the incorporation of modern literature into the service of the counterculture. To question the truths of the texts, to counter the alienation, outsidedness, disaffection, and rebellion one often found in post-Enlightenment literature, would have been considered almost sacrilegious. Norman Mailer's frenzied orgiastic ideas received the enthusiastic support of the literary establishment of the fifties because they were seen as part of the sacrosanct process of artistic exploration. There was a time, and some people imagine we are still in it, when the educated liberal felt he could welcome the literary assault against ordinary decencies, fully confident that the center would always hold.

At any rate, probably due to a combination of two factors, disaffection from the previous sacred trust, and the growing urgency to radicalize literature, all sorts of foreign elements were introduced into the curriculum during the seventies—structuralism, deconstruction, Marxism, and, the one most important for me, feminism. A couple of years into my studies, I was invited to team-teach a course in women and literature.

At first I experienced some discomfort over the content of the course, which seemed to be more about the women in the class than about the literature. But I soon came around. The female voice had been silenced throughout history (!), and consciousness raising was necessary in order to bring to the surface the long-suppressed truths. Instead of literature being dead on the page (but literature had always been alive for me!), we were making it kindle in our experience.

I began to enjoy and even revel in the utterly systematic although utterly spurious property feminism takes on when it is used as a tool of analysis, especially to the exclusion of all others. Like Marxism, feminism follows a single thread, the exploitation of women, to explain everything from advertising to religion. How comprehensible everything became. All injustice and evil were caused by patriarchy; dismantle patriarchy and we would have the brave new world of feminism, humane, generous, peaceful, good. Women had been defined by men; let women define themselves and thereby change the world.

Until I perceived this messianic dimension fully, my interest in feminism had been spasmodic. Even though I'd had access to it in quitting my job in publishing, for example, I had always been a little sceptical. The women in my family wielded enormous domestic power (too much as far as I was concerned), and even in later moments of utmost ideological fatuity I could not pretend that they wielded this power out of frustration in not having careers. And in the family of a factory worker who labored long and hard to keep his wife at home with the children, it was difficult to make a case for the exploitation of women. Then too, if I often professed to be disappointed when men resisted feminism, I secretly found it even more disappointing when they succumbed to it. But what were reservations like these in the face of the "dream of a world in which things would be different," to quote Theodor Adorno? I remember earnestly insisting to one sympathetic young man that all of civilization had been distorted due to the exclusion of the feminine principle and that once this was restored, we would think and feel and act in totally and unimaginably different ways. The female perspective was to be the means of perfecting all things, bringing the hope of salvation and yes, dear reader, the promise of grace.

I insisted to one doubtful professor that the women and literature class was not reductive, as he suspected, but expansive. We were gentle and subtle, I explained, not aggressive or strident. We were simply examining how the literature dealt with women, how we all responded to that, and how it illuminated our own lives. What could be wrong with that? Of course, there were ideologues who would reduce it all to propaganda, but we were above that; there were vulgar feminists as there were vulgar Marxists, but not us. We were being sophisticated, detached, disinterested.

I realize this may sound somewhat disingenuous now, since I was also utterly convinced of the rightness of the cause, but I was basically sincere (if a little cunning in not always revealing the extent to which the course had become consciousness raising). I could not be accused of bias, as I saw it, because what others were calling bias I saw as the truth.

But another openly critical professor gradually managed to unsettle me enough to make me uneasy teaching the course a second time. I've been unable to remember what sorts of things he used to say to me, except that I was constantly exclaiming "What a terrible thing to say!" This was a typical female reaction to resisted truths, he answered. I was even further shocked by this assertion, since no one was permitted at that time to characterize female behavior for good or ill, except of course the feminists. Nevertheless, I listened distractedly. I also sketched out an idea for a dissertation—a feminist analysis of Nathaniel Hawthorne, Henry James, and Virginia Woolf— that I somehow knew I would never really write, because I was suffering a writer's block and moreover had no real ideas, not necessarily in that order. At about this time too, I had a dream that I would one day write for *Commentary*. I continued along in this confused fashion until at last life intervened to bring me to my Kronstadt experience.

My chairman arranged for me to have a job interview at one of the upstate state colleges. The position entailed teaching three courses in the English department. On the ride up, the train stalled several times, and I kept popping the tranquilizers that I had come to rely on in stressful situations. They made me appear subdued during the interview, but that still can't explain everything that ensued.

Although only one of the three courses I would teach was in women's studies, I was met at the railroad station by the department's two feminists, who were allowed to question me alone at a nearby Howard Johnson's while consuming huge quantities of ice cream. (My own chairman later expressed surprise at this—at my being questioned alone, not at the ice cream. At Stony Brook, he said, a "control" person was always present for interviews of this kind, to prevent politics from overtaking other considerations.) These two laid the ax to my ideal of a subtle, intellectually disinterested feminism. They had no patience with any ambiguity or hesitation of any kind, and when I told them I was a feminist "in a state of evolving definitions" there was a conflagration.

They were radical lesbian man-hating feminists, and they raked my fastidious liberalism over the coals (their lesbianism could be readily established from their published writings, I learned later, not that I needed any additional proof). Literature was to be taught for its negative female stereotypes, to show women students "what the culture thinks of them." Male writers like Hawthorne and James were sexists and chauvinists whose main object in creating women characters was to detail their punishment for transgressing the limits of the female role. These two feminists practiced a very one-dimensional literary criticism that seemed to allow nothing for irony, ambiguity, tone, layers of characterization, narrative complexity, and so forth. One of them displayed direct, personal hostility. The milder one admitted to me in the ladies' room after it was over that it was unusual to be anything less than polite to a candidate. That was as much of an apology as I would get.

The inquisition over, they deposited me at the English department, signaling to their chairman that I was unacceptable. I underwent the formality of an interview with the chairman, who was clearly just a rubber stamp. Later he wrote my chairman that the two had sent him a letter characterizing me as "incompetent in women's studies" and "hostile" and "dull" besides. (Dull maybe, due to the tranquilizers, but hostile impossible, at least partly for the same reason.)

I was stunned. It was bad enough to have been treated so poorly, and to have found such simpleminded vulgar hate-filled ideologues pushing their wares in college classrooms, apparently with the blessing of their wimpy chairman, but even worse, the nature of this kind of assault was entirely new and utterly appalling to me. I naively persisted in believing that we'd had, basically, an intellectual disagreement. I had foolishly sent them a letter, right after the interview and before hearing from my chairman, to explain my position better. But they had attacked my professional competence and even, in a way, my character, and they had done so behind my back and with intent to harm.

I may have wished that my conversion experience had involved something more noble and expansive than just getting kicked in the rear end, but be that as it may, I could no longer evade the implications of the way I'd been traveling. It was some time before I took my official leave of feminism and the left (in fact, I had another broadly similar if less important run-in with two other lesbians in a women's studies class I taught at another college). But the heart and soul were out of it for me after that humiliation.

Everywhere I looked I began to see the cracks in the theory and the gaps between theory and practice. Feminism was a legitimate academic and literary approach, but could not be judged by ordinary academic and literary standards. Wrongfully excluded from the mainstream tradition, women writers had also been wrongfully seen outside of their separate "female tradition." Women were the same as men, women were different from men, according to ideological need. Women were angry and rebellious but also loving and tender. Women were the humane and nurturant sex, but they could leave their children in day care centers ten hours a day. Feminism sponsored choice for women, but not the choice of the domestic role. Feminism would better all of society, even though so much of its advocacy was, like affirmative action, obviously narrow and self-interested. Feminism was for the social good even though it openly advocated dismantling the entire social order. (Suppose some people liked things as they were?) I began to wonder, feminism might indeed change the world, or at least our part of it, but into what would it change it?

It didn't matter that I was reassured repeatedly that my interviewers were the extremes, the exceptions; I had glimpsed something of the ruthlessness of ideological commitment, at odds with its purportedly humane objectives. What good did it do to insist that they were only the exceptions when "exceptions" like that had muscled their way into power? Liberal feminism of my type and the genteel liberalism of the chairman, for that matter, had no defense against aggression like that, much in the way the milder forms of socialism had no protection against the more ruthless. In fact, I was beginning to see that liberal feminism had helped call this kind of thing into being. A typical academic feminist, I had observed the customary separation between my ideas and the extremes they permitted and even encouraged. But now I would be forced to see the continuum.

My way of approaching literature had been to see Hawthorne and James, for example, not as simple purveyors of oppressive patriarchal values, but as implicit critics of such values, sometimes even when they might seem to be explicitly upholding them. But although this represented a slightly more generous attitude toward the writer and made better use, I thought, of literary subtleties like irony, ambiguity, and tone, it still imposed a scheme upon the literature that was not legitimate. A writer has the right to criticize society or not, without various partisans rushing forward to claim his or her effort for some ideological framework. Whether imposed from within or without, ideology destroys literature and its life-generating possibili-

ties, which sometimes conflict with preconceived ideas, as life-generating possibilities have a way of doing.

I could see too that although I'd been gentler about it than some
teachers probably were, I had also encouraged women to look at
their experience only within feminist terms. Consciousness raising
inflames the discontent that is bound to be present in every woman's
life and then in the ensuing disarray invites her to see it as the
result of oppression, and to look to alleviate it in political terms.

To the extent that the personal becomes political, the woman
loses contact with herself. She is constrained from seeing how many
"feminine" problems are moral and characterological more than social
or political, and are problems that, regardless of origin, only the
individual can overcome—the inclination to vanity, self-centeredness,
and sensuality; the longing to idolize men; even the tendency to
surrender to emotional weakness. Then there is the hidden destruc-
tiveness in the various female poses and postures of helplessness
and dependency women have always been loath to acknowledge,
and which feminism has helped them avoid acknowledging too. When
Susan Brownmiller argues that "while the extremes of masculinity
can harm others (rape, wife beating, street crime, warfare . . .),
the extremes of femininity are harmful only . . . to women themselves
in the form of self-imposed masochism," she is revealing a terrible
ignorance of human nature. "Self-imposed masochism" is selfish and
hurtful to others as well as self.

The preliminary result of the politicization of the internal life
may seem liberating, but the end result is enslavement, since politicization diminishes the individual's sense of control over her own destiny
and weakens her self-discipline by encouraging her to blame others.
(How much manipulation of men became possible through excuses
supplied by feminism?) Much New Left thought began with the
demand for greater individual freedom, but the real demands of freedom then led to a rush into collective, prefabricated identities, with
feelings, thoughts, and ideas dictated by ideology. Feminism has
enabled women to behave childishly—to demand equality and independence, but also preferential treatment and special protection as
a group.

Feminism has also made many things worse by preventing women
from seeing their experience clearly, as in the unspeakably dishonest
comparison of women with blacks, or in the pretense, upheld by
almost everyone, it seems, that women have never really wanted to
stay home with children, but have always wanted the careers denied

them by society which must now pay compensation. Feminism refuses to see how much of a hand women have had in creating the system as it now stands, and how much it has served women's needs as well as men's. Feminism also joins the rest of the New Left in disdain for the Western tradition, although it is only on the basis of this tradition that a campaign for greater freedom for women could even have been mounted. On the other hand, with all its faulty but rigidly held convictions about certain matters, feminism is utterly and foolishly amoral about a whole host of issues—unable, for example, to decide if prostitution is exploitation of women or a praiseworthy example of women controlling their own sexuality in patriarchy. Similar debates go on over pornography, surrogate motherhood, and so on.

I was ready to listen more carefully to the skeptical professor. He became a generous and superlatively insightful mentor, and he supplied the historical context of what had been happening to me. I finally learned something about the Old Left and the disillusionment it had produced. Somewhere into this time I tucked a breathless, riveting, eye-popping few weeks of reading Alexander Solzhenitsyn for the first time. I was staggered. We began to hear, also at about this time, of the aftermath of the war in Vietnam—the boat people, the Vietnamese gulags, the Cambodian genocide, the fall of Laos. I could hardly believe that the ideas I had so "innocently," in some cases almost absentmindedly held were complicit in all that, but it was so. Nothing could be worse for the people of Southeast Asia, I had avowed in my ignorance of communism (forgetting what lessons the Church had tried to teach us) than our lethal presence there. But there was something worse, much worse.

I began to see the devastating effects of the counterculture in all areas of our lives. I have already implied some of these in passing—the deterioration of the relationship between the sexes, due to feminism and the sexual revolution; the appalling diminishment of the moral life (for the left morality is reduced to having the correct view on its roster of issues—nuclear war, the poor, the homeless, race, and so forth); the cynical disparagement of our country and its institutions and history; the decline and fragmentation of the educational experience; the dissolution of the structures of reasoned discourse; and the loss of the sense of individual responsibility in favor of blaming society.

I decided that I for one couldn't afford the luxury of the left. Many promoters of its unworkable ideals seemed to fare well enough, denouncing the rampant injustice and corruption of our society at every turn while advancing their careers and pursuing lives of comfort, complete with dinner parties and summers in the country. If so many were suffering so unjustly, what right had I to a good life? Looking for something to live by, I thus found myself truly disorganized by the contradictions and inadequacies of New Left thought. Soon after these events, I met a young man, also a graduate student, in a sunny-side-up self-help program that the two of us would have been ashamed to join previously. We realized that because we both had consciously or unconsciously agreed that "gloom and doom" were the only proper response to the world's inequities, we had added two more people to the load of the world's problems. Change was possible without destroying the whole system. I dreamt of a better world, but the present one was savaged in the name of principles I endorsed.

I'd love to be able to say that this was the end of the follies, but there was still one more necessary, painful detour I took. Some time before, the increasing chaos of my personal life had landed me in a therapist's office during a seizure of desperation. (Far from realizing my internal disarray, I had first thought I was physically ill, and it took several doctors to convince me otherwise.) I became very involved through this therapist with the work of Wilhelm Reich. Eventually I underwent orgone therapy and took courses and seminars on Reich's work.

Despite the fact that Reich is usually associated with the radical/liberal left, the group that I joined was politically conservative, and the members maintained, with considerable proof, that Reich had become conservative later in his life. They were strongly anticommunist and professed a brilliant critique of the modern liberal character that in my disaffection I rejoiced to read. They insisted that Reich's orgasm theories had been distorted and misunderstood. These theories did not imply or endorse license, or four-lettering, as Reich scornfully called it, and there was nothing in them that was incompatible with a humane, loving, rational way of life. Achieving "orgastic potency"—not to be reduced to having simple ordinary orgasms—was the path to joyful, neurosis-free fulfillment for the individual and to a just, well-functioning order for society.

There is much in Reich's work that is valid and important, but overall it is another failed utopianism, wielding the usual argument of failed utopian ideologies—they do not fail, their application has been incorrect or insufficient, their theory remains pristinely valid. I see now that I was looking in Reich's work for things to be both ways—a more conservative, cautious approach to social change combined with the salvific dimension, both individual and collective, that I had always sought.

I had to learn after my disgust with the left that conservative politics are not ipso facto a sign of inner light. And I had to discover the pervasive influence of Marx on so much contemporary thought. Since Reich had renounced communism as "red fascism," I thought I was safe, and I was utterly shocked to be brought to see how close Reich's ideas were to those of Marx—the claim to science, the absolute materialism, the insistence on explaining all phenomena by a single factor, the hope, however remote, not just for amelioration but for a complete transformation of society. I'd been led and misled by ideas whose origins I knew little about. Again, I was amazed. Then too, if Reich did renounce the Soviet state, he was mainly an anti-Stalinist, holding on to his faith in Lenin until the end—a distinction I learned from Solzhenitsyn.

My own therapy, which involved screaming, kicking, biting, and so forth, was causing enormous upheaval, but to little effect that I could discern. Many people also in orgone therapy were trying Actualizations, a spin-off of EST, on the recommendation of their therapists. I tried it too and soon decided that the therapists' recommendation of this crude mass behavioral modification program that should have been anathema to anyone seriously committed to Reich's work was a tacit, inadvertent admission that the therapy was not working to effect personal change, or not working in the way Reich had described. I tried to participate as best I could, but credulity was wearing thin. I sat there one day in the workshop watching a young woman practically go into a primal in order to satisfy the conductor's demand that she feel her feelings and I pondered. It was the beginning of the eighties and I wondered if I was ever again to inhabit a world of sanity.

All occasions began to conspire against me, or perhaps for me. I chanced to come upon a celebrity who had undergone orgone therapy some years before and had written a book about its marvelous results in his life and the splendid marriage it had led him to. I had heard that he was now separated from his wife, and in the glimpse I caught of him, walking about the streets of New York, he seemed older and less exuberant than the person who'd written the book, an ordinary mortal, not the "new man" I foolishly expected. The sight of him made me come face-to-face with the fatuity of my own expectations.

Then facts, public facts, took a hand. It suddenly came to light that the doctor-therapist chiefly responsible for carrying on Reich's work after his death had had a second "wife" for seventeen years that he had never told anyone about, even (or I suppose especially) his real wife. He lived with the second "wife" every weekend when he was supposed to be at his laboratory. He had even had a child by her, who was about ten years old at the time of the discovery, while the doctor was nearly eighty. Many defended his behavior, some declaring, in effect, that sometimes a lie is necessary to protect the truth. (Where had I heard that before?) In addition, a biography of Reich himself published about that time revealed that Reich had forced two of his wives to have abortions, and had had an affair while one wife was in the hospital for treatment of cancer.[1]

It was hard to avoid the conclusion that the kind of personal sexual fulfillment Reich preached might indeed conflict with basic decencies and higher values, as is always the case with utopian theories. While sexual weakness could scarcely be unknown to someone who had matured in the counterculture, this was the first time it really sank in that an *ideology* of sexual freedom could prompt ruthless behavior and *justify* it. In the face of the revelations about Reich and the doctor, I heard people say, more than once, that the healthy, orgastically potent man cannot submit to social restraints. It also occurred to me for the first time that sexual liberation had been especially hard on women. I decided that I didn't need to analyze anything any further. I could take Jesus's advice and know them by their fruits. Then, after a few more shifts and lurches in my own therapy and a brief switch to another doctor, I could see quite clearly that apart from outside events, orgone therapy could never solve my problems.

——·——

The illusions were gone at last. I was forced to face myself. I had been a coward—in running panic-stricken both from the challenges of life and from the spiritual demands of my own nature. I had allowed myself to be unfortunately and needlessly affected by the general antipathy to God and religion in our intellectual life. All the professors with whom I had studied T. S. Eliot, for example, had always prefaced explication of his later work with the insistence that we would examine it as poetry and not take seriously its content. (And this was the figure who had ruled our culture for decades.) I had decided that I too would repudiate the foolishness of religion, the refuge of losers and rejects who could not take life as it is. But then of course I exhausted myself chasing after nearly every false god the sixties could devise. I saw that I had to have the courage of my own experience, and the salvation I couldn't live without could be found nowhere but in Him. (For that matter too, it has gradually become clear to me that it is no accident that our secularized, classical-humanist-rationalist-positivist tradition was unable to defend itself against the countercultural assault.)

The understanding that I couldn't live without God flashed over me while I was reading *The Courage to Be,* in which Paul Tillich makes a crucial distinction between fear and anxiety. He argues that while normal fear is fear of some specific evil, anxiety is fear at the vulnerability of the human condition itself. Such fear can obviously find no remedy within human experience, and to live— as opposed to merely exist—with such fear is utterly impossible. Escapes can be had of course, in drugs, alcohol, sex, money; and even more sophisticated escapes are available in work, art, intellection, or ideology; but there is no final remedy within mortal existence to the problem of being implicit in this anxiety.

It was really quite simple, but not painless, after that. Once the resistance was gone and I was forced to open up my heart, I found Him, or He found me. He had been right there all the time, in fact. In a way, the wide and crooked path had been straight and narrow all along, leading to Him, the God of love and principle, giver of all the grace that I could possibly want.

What does salvation mean to me, some might ask. Not something in far-off eternity, any more than it was that day in theology class when I struggled to hold on to a sense of the nearness of God. It means to be conscious here and now of having a place, being connected, feeling at peace, regardless of circumstances. It means not having to believe in the power or reality of fear or envy or any other sin, or of sickness or death or accident or error, for myself or anyone else. It means not having to accept as a finality this vast chaotic farce of material existence and then, paradoxically, being able to see it illumined and transformed beyond any expectation. It means not being destroyed by its pain or deceived by its ephemeral pleasures, but abiding serenely, knowing that no situation, no matter how severe, is beyond His healing love. It means not having to define oneself and one's prospects by the thousand worthless gauges of mortal existence and not having to be led about by the fads, clichés, and self-deceptions that can substitute for thought in our time. It means knowing that God's plan is unfolding for man even here and now and despite the material picture. It means to be able to experience a love that transcends contingencies and to see one's besetting demons dissolve again and again before a courageous heart.

I am supremely grateful that I was forced to take this journey, because what I have found is greater than anything I could even have dreamed of before.

Note

[1] Myron Sharaf, *Fury on Earth* (New York: St. Martin's Press, 1983).

12

Irish Catholic

Richard Rodriguez

DISCONTINUITY

There is a crucifix over my bed. I am in bed, my eyes are open. I am waiting for the sound of midnight—a burst of horns, a fire whistle, a woman's scream.

A car passes on the wet pavement outside. My room revolves on a rail of light. And then it is dark. January 1, 1960. The new decade has come to Sacramento, California. It is no longer Christmas. In the morning there will be a cold mass at church, then the Rose Parade on TV. And the long gray afternoon will pass away through a series of black-and-white football games; in a few days I will be back at school.

I am fifteen years old, old enough to be dating. I am not dating. I am brown. I envy my older brother's cool, his way with girls. My brother's bed is empty. My brother is out at a party. I am bookish and witty, though I don't have such maypole words for myself. I write the gossip column ("The Watchful Eye") in the *Gael*, the school paper. I am much more than the class clown; I am the leveler, caustic enough to force my male classmates to a truce. I am bright, a straight line. I am ambitious for college—some school that is hard to get into—a brick castle filled with rich kids where I will clean up, because I want more than they do. I want to be a college professor. I will have run out of things to read. I want to be a journalist on a train far, far away, hurtling toward the present age of my parents. Thirty-six. Thirty-six.

My family has moved three times in Sacramento, each time to a larger house than before. We live in a two-story house. We have two televisions. Two cars. I am not unconscious; I cherish our fabulous mythology: My father makes false teeth. My father received three years of a Mexican grammar school education. My mother has a high school diploma. My mother types eighty words per minute. My mother works in the governor's office where the walls are green. Edmund G. Brown is the governor. Famous people walk by my mother's desk. The other day Chief Justice Earl Warren said hi to my mother.

Every New Year's Eve my mother cries in front of the TV when Guy Lombardo marks auld lang syne. "It's so sad," my mother says. The crowd in Times Square cheers. This year, however, we have gone to bed early. The back-porch light is on for my brother. I have stayed awake in the dark to feel the difference of a new decade.

There is no difference. It is the unexpected that my life is protected against. Inevitability is what my parents have bought me with their ascent into the American middle class. My ambition will match their desire. I will go to college in the sixties. I will not be the first in my family to attend college, but I will be the first to leave home for college. I will go to Stanford in the sixties. Four years later I will take my first plane trip—TWA's Royal Ambassador Service—to New York. I will go to graduate school at Columbia, then Berkeley.

Ten years from tonight, I will be a graduate student at Berkeley. I will expect to be a college teacher. I will be spending the Christmas break in my apartment on College Way, writing a paper on Henry James's *The American*. I will be composing elaborate opinions about the naive and the worldly, about the Protestant American and the cynical Catholic orders. Over my bed will be a blowup of Marlene Dietrich.

Sacramento, the first minutes of 1960: The ectoplasmic corpus of the crucifix glows with confidence. Awake on my bed, I am inclined forward: I want the years coming to improve me, to make my hand a man's hand and my soul a man's soul.

The sixties will be my sacramental confirmation. The fifties already have defined my life. As 1949 became 1950, we lived in a one-story house on 39th Street, a few blocks closer to Mexico. There were no faces like ours on the block. Nor were there voices like ours on the block. When I began school, my classmates seemed of one blank face and of one emotion, which was cheerful. The majority of the class carried lunch boxes full of snowballs of frosted pastry. It was an American classroom. And yet we were a dominion of Ireland, the Emerald Isle, the darling land. "Our lovely Ireland," the nuns always called her.

The conclusion of my education will be at secular universities where the majority of my teachers will be Jews—many of them only a generation from working-class memories. But the Sisters of Mercy will remain the most influential. They will claim me for Ireland.

What was my initial resistance? When I came to the classroom unable, unwilling to speak English, the nuns methodically elected me. They picked on me. They would not let me be but I must speak louder, Richard, and louder, Richard. I think of those women now, towers, linen-draped silos inclining this way and that, and only their faces showing; themselves country lasses, the daughters of immigrants. They served as my link between Mexico and America, between my father's dark Latin skepticism and the Edenic cherry tree of Protestant imagining. Pulling ears, straightening collars, blushing, strong-arming, my nuns ushered their students in straight lines toward an American future none of us could conceive. Years after, the nuns would leave me a skeptical figure within tall library windows, regarding the swirling chaos on the quad below.

From its influence on my life I should have imagined Ireland to be much larger than its picayune place on the map. During the hot Sacramento summers I'd pass afternoons in the long reading gallery of nineteenth-century English fiction. I gathered a not inaccurate picture of London and of the English landscape. Ireland had no comparable place in my literary imagination. As a Catholic schoolboy I had to learn to put on the brogue in order to tell Catholic jokes, of gravediggers and drunkards and priests. Ireland sprang from the tongue. Ireland set the towering stalks of the litanies of the church to clanging by its inflection. Ireland was the omniscient whisper from a confessional box.

Did your mother come from Ireland? Around March 17th, a Catholic holiday, my mother—that free-floating patriot—my mother would begin to bristle. "If it's so wonderful, why did they all leave?" But it was her joke sometimes, too, that we were Irish. My mother's surname is Moran, her father a black Irishman? She laughed. Her father was dark and tall, with eyes as green as leaves. There were Irish in nineteenth-century Mexico, my mother said. But there was no family tree to blow one way or the other. The other way would lead to Spain. For Moran is a common enough name in Spain as through Latin America. Could it have been taken, not from Ireland, but *to* Ireland by the Spanish—Spanish sailors shipwrecked by Elizabeth's navy?

My younger sister asked me to help her with an essay for school. The subject was Ireland. I dictated a mouthful of clover about Dublin's Jewish mayor and some American celebrities and politicians, Ed Sullivan, Dennis Day, Mayor Daley, Carmel Quinn. "Ireland, mother of us all. . . ." The essay won for my sister an award from the local Hibernian Society. I taunted her the night she had to dress up for the awards banquet. My mother, though, returned from the banquet full of humor. They had all trooped into the hall behind the Irish flag—my sister, my mother, my father, an assortment of old ladies, and some white-haired priests.

When Father O'Neil came back from his first trip home to Ireland, I was in third or fourth grade. There was a general assembly at school so we could see his slides, rectangles of an impossible green bisected by the plane's wing. Dublin gray, stone and sky. The relations lined up in front of white houses, waving to us or just standing there. There was something so sad about Father then, behind the cone of light from the projector, in Sacramento, at Sacred Heart School, so far from the faces of home and those faces so sad.

Ireland was where old priests returned to live with their widowed sisters and (one never said it) to die. So it was a big white cake and off you go. Ireland was our heart's home. I imagined the place from St. Patrick's Day cards, a cheerful Catholic place—a cottage, a bell on the breeze, and that breeze at your back, through quilted meadows and over the winding road. Sacramento, my Sacramento, then, must seem to Father O'Neil as flat, as far away as Africa in the Maryknoll missionary movies. Life was the journey far from home, or so I decided as I watched Father O'Neil popping squares of memory upside down into a projector.

Fading Ireland. . . . The American experience of Catholicism as an immigrant faith, a ghetto contest of them against us, was coming to an end in America. In the colored pages of *Life* magazine the old dead Pope with his purple face and his hooked nose was borne aloft through St. Peter's. My generation would be the last to be raised with so powerful a sense of the ghetto church. An American of Irish descent and athletic good looks would soon be elected President, our first Catholic President, of the United States. As the old Pope passed through the doors of death, American Catholics were entering the gates of the city. A fat, expressive Italian Pope would soon call his church to "aggiornamento," a new rapprochement with the non-Catholic world. As the fifties passed, however, the nuns went on neatly dividing the world, as if they remained the Fates they had always been. We were the Catholics and all others, alas, were defined by the fact of their difference from us.

By the time many of us got to college the temptation would be to turn back embarrassed by the parochialism of our Catholic schooling. The gothic habits, the very names, Sister Mary Damien, Sister Mary Aquin, the prohibitions, the virtues would seem, from a distance of modernity, funny. There was no other word for it.

But then that was the general tone of the sixties, an irreverent laugh-in—for the theme of the sixties was the theme of discontinuity. As higher education became mass education, a generation of Americans, many the children of parents who did not make it to college, found themselves living a new future. We were not fated to become like our parents; we should not have to submit ourselves to compromise, to memory. We would therefore believe we were freed from history. History was evil because it hadn't, after all, worked. Look at the wars, look at the poverty. We were innocent. We were at the edge of an Aquarian Age, or so the lyrics of the sixties hustled us to believe.

"The sixties were about mommy and daddy, a family affair," says a friend of mine who ran off with a soldier. It has become the fashion appropriate to an age of individualism to date the start and the end of the era according to private calendars. Another friend, a woman who became a nationally known antiwar activist, says the sixties began with her divorce in 1962.

Shall I say the sixties began for me in 1963 when my parents drove me to Stanford University? My sixties began in the 1950s. In the fifties, billboards appeared on the horizons which beckoned restless Americans toward California. If you asked, people in Sacramento in the fifties said they were from Alabama or from Portugal. Somewhere else. Sacramento of the 1950s was the end of the Middle Ages and Sacramento growing was the beginning of London. In those days people were leaving their villages and their mothers' maiden names to live among strangers in tract houses. Highways swelled into freeways. People didn't need anyone else to tell them how to behave on K Street. And God spoke to each ambition through the G.I. Bill.

I should say that my sixties began in the sixteenth century with the Protestant Reformation. For the sixties were a Protestant flowering. The famous activists of the decade were secular Jews who heralded a messianic future. But the true fathers of Woodstock, of sit-ins, and of rock pastoral were the dark-robed Puritan fathers.

In the early 1950s, Sacramento, California, was a city of over 100,000 people, a river town, the "Camellia Capital of the World." Sacramento was the great city of the Central Valley, the state capital. As the fifties advanced, people arrived by the hundreds, then thousands each month. Downtown Sacramento began to skid with the building of Country Club Shopping Center. The city was growing north and south.

A statewide university system was created on an economic paradigm of supply and demand to accommodate middle-class ambition. Dr. Clark Kerr named it a "multiversity." The problem was numbers. Mass education caused the market value of the diploma to decline and so did the glamour of undergraduate living. It was a dilemma peculiar to American ambition and one Henry James might have understood.

In the fall of 1963, President Kennedy was assassinated in Dallas. *Life* magazine printed a eulogy that said, "When you're Irish what you know is that life will break your heart." The next year, on a spring afternoon, when windows were open and radios were up, my roommate at Stanford walked in to announce, with the smile he usually reserved for pictures of naked women, that they were busting heads at Berkeley. In the papers the next day students at Berkeley, using insect words, complained of the impersonality of the multiversity, of being reduced to IBM numbers.

The sixties should have been my time. I was the son of Mexican immigrant parents. I was the nonwhite American who was to be given full access to American life. If it had all gone as planned for me—the radical politics become bureaucratic affirmative action policy—I should have ended up teaching *Hamlet* at some vast Arizona or Ohio state university, liberal, discontent, tenured. But the romanticism of the sixties never took. Blame it on Ireland. I never bought into the idea that I could be free of the past, except in obvious ways. Oh, I had become free of Mexico—no longer spoke Spanish, no longer cared to or could. People at Stanford thought I was Pakistani. Ireland still clung to my heart in the sixties. The nuns' lessons—of sin, of historical skepticism—were real lessons. They were not offered as metaphor and I never took them as such. And my best friends in high school and college, as today, carried names that came from the trusted Old Sod—Murray, O'Donnell, Keating, Faherty.

Larry Faherty is my best friend in high school. Larry Faherty wears a ducktail sealed with emerald green Stay-Set. He gets kicked out of Brother Michael's English class all the time for having long hair, which is an impertinence. Larry Faherty is rich. His parents have moved to a new house on a new street on the new south side of town. Larry Faherty loves Mexico, he has been there on vacation every summer since his freshman year and he speaks Spanish to me. Though I answer in English. My mother worries about my association with Larry Faherty. He and I go to San Francisco on the Greyhound and eat French dinners. We'd go anywhere to see *Black Orpheus*.

Larry Faherty is in New Orleans with his family for Christmas, so we have not spent New Year's Eve together going to the movies. He will send me a postcard written in Spanish.

It must be around two in the morning when my brother's blue Plymouth pulls into the driveway. The car door slams.

He comes in the back door, he opens the refrigerator and the bottles rattle. My mother calls out to him. Did you turn off the light? Yeah. His voice is thick with American disrespect.

His foot is on the stairs. I close my eyes. He turns on the light for a moment, he turns it off. He fumbles around in the dark. He falls into bed. January 1960, at the edge of my adolescence, in the first hours of the new decade, amid the warmth and the smells of all that is now lost to me, I put away my ambitions and fall asleep.

PROTESTANTS

One weekday in summer I am riding my bicycle past the Fremont Presbyterian Church. The door is wide open. So I stop to look. Painters on scaffolds are painting the walls white. I walk in. The room glows with daylight drawn through yellow pebbled glass windows. There are no side altars, no statues. There is a wooden pulpit and a table on which stands a gold-painted cross. There are no kneelers in the pews. Don't the Protestants pray on their knees? This is only a room—a place of assembly—now empty but for its heavy golden light and its painters. Whereas my church is never empty so long as the ruby burns in the sanctuary lamp; my church is filled with all times and all places. All the same, I like this plain room, this empty Protestant shell. I ponder it as I ride away.

It is 1956. It is summer and already, though it is not yet noon, the dry heat of Sacramento promises to rise above the fat dusty leaves to a hundred degrees. I hate the summer of Sacramento. It is flat and it is dull. And yet something about summer is elemental to me and I move easily through it.

America happens in summer. At school, during the rest of the year, America is an abstraction—an anthem or a concept for the civics class. It is easier to see what is meant by the Soviet Union. At church, at the end of the mass, the priest prays for "the conversion of Russia," for it is Our Lady of Fatima's special request. Russia is not an abstraction, it is evil and has the fat red face of evil or the gummy-eyed stare of people who ladle watery soup from huge cauldrons. Russia bears the weight of history, of people on the move, people forced from their villages. America is unencumbered by history and rises even as the grasses, even as the heat, even as planes rise. America opens like a sprinkler's fan, or like a book in summer. At the Clunie Library in McKinley Park, the books which please me most are books about boyhood and summer.

My Sacramento becomes America. America is the quiet of a summer morning, the cantaloupe-colored light, the puddles of shade on the street as I bicycle through. There is a scent of lawn. Think of America and you'll think of lawns, force-fed, prickling rectangles of green, our pastures, our playgrounds, our commons, our graves.

On Saturdays I cut the front lawn. On my knees I trim the edges. Afterwards, I take off my shoes to water down the sidewalk. Around noontime as I finish, the old ladies of America who have powdered under their arms and tied on their summer straw hats walk by and congratulate me for "keeping your house so pretty and clean. Whyn't you come over to my house now . . . ?"

I smile because I know it matters in America to keep your lawn trim and green. It matters to me that my lawn is as nice as the other lawns on the block. On those Saturday mornings, Sacramento is busy painting and hammering, washing the car. I feel happy to be part of the activity. I cannot explain it—I am twelve years old— I have no way of discerning a theological aspect to what I sense about Sacramento on Saturday mornings. I do not know that the busyness is Protestantism.

Behind the Protestant facade of our house, the problem is Mexico. The problem is Ireland, the problem is Rome. I love the Latin mass and trust the questions and the answers. I feel the assurance of belonging to an institution that stretches over all time. But at home there is always something to pray for. Somebody's sick or somebody's out of a job. At night the family prays the rosary, five sets of ten Hail Marys. Asking for favors.

Catholicism at home, our Mexican faith, centers on Our Lady of Guadalupe. It is the image of Our Lady of Guadalupe, her downcast girl's face, which hangs over my parents' intimate bed. The Virgin is "ours," my mother says. In the sixteenth century, shortly after the Spaniards had overtaken Mexico and left the Indians demoralized, the Virgin Mary came on a cloud of birdsong to a Mexican peasant named Juan Diego. The new thing for the New World was that Christian Mary appeared in the God-joke guise of an Indian princess.

The problem is that Sister Mary Celestine decides to have our sixth-grade class reenact the story of Guadalupe and she does not chose me to play the part of Juan Diego.

"Why not?" my mother wants to know at dinner.

Sister Mary Celestine has assigned the role of Juan Diego to Peter Veglia. "The Veglias aren't Mexican," my mother says, lining up her knife and her spoon, "they are Spanish." Sister Mary Celestine has missed the point. (Peter Veglia is cute. My mother has missed the point.) My mother says she is going to speak to the nuns.

"Don't," I say.

So I play an astounded Indian in a crowd scene. Offstage I listen as the Guadalupe, with spikes of tinfoil stapled onto her cape, speaks tenderness to the upturned face of Peter Veglia. She says that she wants the Indians to come to her in their suffering. She does not promise to end human pain. She promises that she will share the Indians' suffering, which is our cue to shuffle onstage and fall to our knees. The curtain closes as irresolutely as it has parted.

What had Mexico taught my parents? They had come to America; they had broken with the past. My parents were hardworking. My parents were doing well. We had just bought our secondhand but very beautiful DeSoto. "Nothing lasts a hundred years," my father says, regarding the blue DeSoto. He says it all the time; his counsel. I am sitting fat and comfortable in front of the TV, reading my *Time* magazine. My mother calls for me to take out the garbage. "Now!" My father looks over the edge of the newspaper and he says it: Nothing lasts a hundred years.

I think I might want to be an architect. I sketch the plans for vast amusement parks to make Sacramento beautiful. I am pleased by the new twelve-story El Mirador Hotel downtown. Sacramento meets my optimism. There is a new mall planned over by Sears.

Sacramento is annexing to itself miles of vacant land. United Airlines has announced direct service to New York City. All of it matters to me. I figure that I am at the very center of the world. The United States is the best country, California has just become the most populous state, and Sacramento is its state capital.

It becomes a sort of joke between my father and me. "Life is harder than you think, boy." You're thinking of Mexico, papa (while I fold the newspapers for my route). "You'll see," he says.

One of my aunts goes back to Mexico to visit, and she returns and tells my mother that the wooden step—the bottom step—of their old house near Guadalajara is still needing a nail. Thirty years later! They laugh. My father is attentive to the way Sacramento repairs itself. The streetlight burns out, a pothole opens on the asphalt, a tree limb cracks, and someone comes from "the city" within a day. My father shakes his head. It is as close as he comes to praising America.

Like the Irish nuns, my father is always remembering. He remembers the political turmoil of Mexico. He grumbles about the intrigues of Masonic lodges in Mexico. My father talks about how America stole the Southwest from Mexico. (And how Mexicans could never forget it.) Americans died at the Alamo to make Texas a slave state. And what does *puta* history do? She gives Texas to the gringo.

America has a different version, the ballad of Davy Crockett. On television Walt Disney Mexicans at the battle of the Alamo are dressed in French-style uniforms—white suspenders crossed over their bellies. I watch with my family downstairs. And for the first time I want the Americans—those greasy, buckskin Texans—to lose and die.

At a time when most boys in Sacramento are sporting coonskin caps, my father teaches me the story of the St. Patrick's Brigade. In the nineteenth century, there were Irish immigrants to the United States, most of them teenagers, who enlisted to fight in the Mexican-American War. They ended up in Mexico and when they saw how the gringos behaved in Catholic churches and when they saw how the gringos treated women, the Irishmen changed their flags, my father said. So the Americans hung them as traitors one afternoon in Mexico City.

Mexico was a place of memory. America was the beginning of the future.

Ireland became the mediating island. I grew up in Ireland. The priests and the nuns seemed to believe in America. Priests were optimists. They were builders and golfers. They bellowed their Latin. They drove fast in dark-colored cars. They wore Hawaiian shirts. They played hard at being regular guys, and they told jokes to cover any embarrassment when they collected money for new hospitals or new high schools.

The nuns made me learn the preamble to the Constitution. The nuns taught me confidence. There was no question about my belonging in America. I mean that literally. There was no question. There was no question about English being my language. The nuns were as unsentimental as the priests were sentimental. But they all assumed my American success.

The only exception to the rule of confidence at school came with religion class. At the start of each school day, after the "Morning Offering," after the pledge of allegiance to the flag of the United States of America, our young hearts were plunged in the cold bath of Ireland. For fifty minutes life turned salt, a vale of tears. Our gallery—our history, our geography, our arithmetic—was Ireland. The story of man was the story of sin which could not be overcome with any such thing as a Declaration of Independence. Earth was clocks and bottles and heavy weights. Earth was wheels and rattles and sighs and death. We all must die. Heaven was bliss eternal, heaven was a reign of grace bursting over the high city and over the mansions of that city. Earth was Ireland and heaven was Ireland. The dagger in Mary's heart was sorrow for man's sins. The bleeding heart of Jesus was sorrow for man's sins. Our consolation alone was Our Redeemer, our precious Lord. Man needed Christ's intervention—His death on the cross. God the Father had given His only begotten Son. *That cross you wear isn't a pretty bauble, Patsy, it's like wearing a little electric chair around your neck.* Christ had instituted a church—a priesthood, sacraments, the mass—and man required all the constant intercession of the saints and the church and the special help of Mother Mary to keep the high road. All alone man would wander and err like pagan Caesar or like Henry VIII.

At nine-thirty the subject changed. The class turned to the exercises of worldly ambition—spelling, writing, reading—in preparation for adulthood in comic America. The nuns never reconciled the faces of comedy and tragedy, and they never saw the need.

While I was in high school, the swarming magnetic dots of the television screen began to compose themselves into black faces during the nightly news; the civil rights movement was gaining national attention. Black Protestantism had until then seemed to me a puzzling exhibition of perspiring women and wet-voiced men chained to a rhythm that was foreign to me. Suddenly on the nightly news there appeared Dr. Martin Luther King, Jr., and everything I thought I knew about saints began to change as I contemplated that face, as I listened to that voice. I began to believe in heroes.

By the time I got to Stanford I believed in man-made history. I tutored ghetto children. I paraded through downtown Palo Alto toward my first antiwar rally. I was an English major at Stanford; increasingly, though, I began taking courses in religion, mainly Protestantism. I took on a new hero—a Protestant theologian named Robert McAfee Brown. These were the years of ecumenism, and I had outgrown any caution regarding contact with non-Catholics. I eagerly bit into the Protestant apple the nuns had warned me against, and I admitted its sweetness. When my mother learned that I was taking a course from a Protestant minister, she made me promise that I would ask the Catholic chaplain at Stanford for permission. I didn't, though I told her I did.

So began my Protestant years. I was attracted to the modesty of style, the unencumbered voices of Luther and Calvin, free of the trinketed cynicism of Mexico and the nagging poetry of Ireland. And there was a masculine call to action. One week Dr. McAfee Brown was flying to Rome to serve as an official Protestant delegate to the Vatican Council. All the while he was writing books; he knew more about Catholicism than the nuns could have told me. He would be off the next week to Selma.

I entered a master's program in religious studies at Columbia University; I took most of my courses across the street at Union Theological Seminary. When Columbia was closed by sit-ins and police riots, I sat in the library of Union Seminary reading eighteenth-century Puritan autobiographies—books of people who had learned to read late in their lives. They spoke from their pine houses and from within the rings of their candles about personal confrontations with God.

Were these the renowned dour Puritans? But here were people who believed in the possibility of change, sudden conversion. One could be born again, sin could be overturned like a wooden table, like a bucket of water. With God's help one could stand on one's own feet. There was no necessary tragedy. Was there a need, then, for angels and priests?

It was thus in the late sixties, in a neogothic library in New York City, that I found a theology to escape my father's skepticism and my mother's famous intimacy with the Virgin Mary.

As I read, I remembered the close-cut lawns of Sacramento, I saw the face of the Puritan. It was an old lady's face I saw; she wore a yellow dress with sunflowers on the pockets, she wore a sun hat. She stopped to congratulate me for keeping my lawn so pretty. She was smiling.

EVIL

On my part it is less a decision to get to know Larry Faherty than a fascination I decide not to deny myself.

"Faherty, take off those stupid sunglasses," Brother Michael interjects into the *Iliad*.

Skinny, pale, slouching, yesterday Larry Faherty won the essay contest I had expected and wanted desperately to win.

"Faherty, I'll give you three to take them off. ONE . . ."

Our courtship: Larry and I are sitting at the far end of the football field during the lunch hour, a blurry distance from the school-yard monitor. Larry saves his milk cartons to use as ashtrays. Larry has been reading a book by James Baldwin about negroes in Harlem. Larry Faherty has been to New York. Larry Faherty calls Sacramento "Sacramenty." Larry Faherty writes poetry. I have been to Mexico with my parents to visit relatives. Larry went to summer schools in Mexico to learn Spanish. Larry is not afraid of Mexico. Sometimes he makes it sound male. "We all went down to the whorehouse," he says, flicking an ash. Sometimes he tells Mexico as a woman. No one there asks if he is gringo. The Mexicans speak to him only in Spanish, with *cortesia*—it's in the language, he says.

Larry Faherty protests the smallness of the island.

Peter Raderman—of the duckling yellow crew cut and the school sweater—warns me in confidence (and for my own good) that Larry Faherty will ruin me . . . "socially." So Larry is jeopardizing my tenuous ties with circles of athletic glamour and social celebrity at school. My mother worries. My parents are in awe of his parents. Larry's mother is a teacher; his father works for the government. My sister Sylvia says look at his hair as Larry rides up on his bicycle.

Larry Faherty's hair: It is long and it is greasy. Every four weeks or so, Larry's hair descends to his collar. There is a ritual confrontation in Brother Michael's English class.

"TWO . . ."

Brother Michael is late in his twenties, passionate, athletic, sarcastic, the stuff of crushes. Not only does he understand the classics, he plays the lead role. All the boys think he is their favorite teacher. But he is mine. I have managed to become his pet. After school, Brother Michael encourages me, he spends time with me, he gets me to write for the school paper. In class I am careful not to act kissy. I told you, I am the class wit. Like Falstaff, I take hits and then I hit back. I am as ready to laugh at your humiliation as you are to laugh at mine.

Larry Faherty sits silent, he judges me when I make the class laugh, even at the expense of Brother Michael, which I figure Larry ought to enjoy.

Larry Faherty is the one kid in class I regard as brighter than me. His essays, done the night before, have big words stuck in like cherries. When Larry gets kicked out of class, he is not allowed to come back until he has gone to the barber. Because I am the obedient Catholic schoolboy, because I never get in trouble, I am fascinated by Larry Faherty's defiance.

"THREE." A rustle of black serge, the little wind of starch and sweat as Brother Michael rushes past; a furious slap knocks the sunglasses clattering across the floor.

I too laugh when the pneumatic hinge has finally jerked the door shut against Larry. My mother has no reason to fear. I will always be attracted for the same reason that I will never become. Because I am a Catholic.

The Christian Brothers traditionally have been teachers of the poor. There is talk of the Jesuits coming to town to build a rich school in the suburbs. In Sacramento, Christian Brothers High School teaches the middle class. But the governing male ethos is tough. There will be order in the classroom because there is order in the cosmos—marches, genuflections, reverend address. I am indebted to my elders, the scholars, the theologians who preceded me. My teacher, by definition, assumes authority.

During a high school religious retreat, the traveling Redemptorist priest with a crucifix slung in his sash like a musket brays counsel to the assembly of 500 boys. There is the one about the boy who went away to a non-Catholic college and lost his faith because he was encouraged to think he knew all the answers by himself, fool. The sin of pride. Pride is not submitting to authority. Pride is insisting on one's own way. Pride is lonely, men, lonely as hell.

The purpose of Catholic education was not "originality." At Christian Brothers we read Aquinas and we read Shakespeare. At Christian Brothers, having a mind of one's own was a problem. Like Larry

Faherty. We were trained to keep order. From my class at Christian Brothers would come yet another Catholic generation of policemen and FBI agents and firemen, even a White House Secret Serviceman.

An Irish kid named Denny who sat in front of me in French class and who this morning wears a checkered shirt will become a cop. He will be driving after midnight down a rainy street and he will be killed by a rifle shot through the passenger window. In 1961, in Brother Paul's French class, Larry Faherty drums his pencil eraser against his closed French grammar. Oh God he is bored with Brother Paul, with French, with Sacramento. It is Mexico Larry loves, not France. Spanish.

Larry Faherty scolds me for not speaking Spanish. He calls me affectionately—the insulting word for the son who pretends to be a gringo—*pocho*. We are the odd couple, Larry is 6 feet tall, fair, Spanish-speaking. I answer in English. We spend a summer working for John F. Kennedy's election. We go to movies. He tells me what I should have known about sex, about girls, letting his line down tenderly, a little at a time, into the clear pool of my imagination. We talk about politics and about Mexico and about the young man Larry saw shot down to a pool of blood on a street in Mexico City. On Friday nights he honks for me in his father's Chrysler, the cigarette dangling from his lip. "Salutti Beulah Mumm," he calls out to the window of Beulah Mumm, the librarian who lives next door to us. "Salutti Cerrutti," he honks at the house of Mrs. Cerrutti. "There's something funny about that kid," my father says. We go to a jazz coffee house. We order espressos. I never finish mine. Black musicians with preoccupied red eyes play for dulling hours. It amuses Larry to overtip the waitress—sometimes two or three times the amount of the bill—"to see what she will do." She keeps the money, of course, and with a poker face.

Larry scorns me for not taking chances. I refuse to hitchhike. I refuse to smoke cigarettes. I refuse Spanish. And yet, I think, Larry senses Mexico in me, I am his way of escaping Sacramento. But if I am his negro, he is mine too. His casual relationship to money, his house with a swimming pool, these I take as ethnic traits. What dooms our friendship is that we stare past one another. What he sees in me is innocence, an inferiority complex, Mexico. He is all casualness about the things I intend to have. I want what he claims to discard. I ingratiate myself to Larry Faherty's parents and I get invited down to Southern California beach towns where they spend the summers.

And so for two or three years we know each other better than we know anyone else in the world. But then we graduate and I am to go to Stanford—"Stahnnn-ford," Larry says with a plummy cartoon voice, disapproving my choice. Larry goes off to college too. There is some kind of trouble. (Larry is vague on the phone.) He transfers to another college in the Midwest. We exchange letters. We see each other at Christmas. He is becoming sadder, handsome.

One summer Larry Faherty joins the Peace Corps, a fine young Kennedy cadet. There is a war in Vietnam and Lyndon Johnson is President. Larry writes from Africa. Then there is trouble again. Larry has been kicked out of the Peace Corps—"for not wearing pyjamas," Larry is quoted as saying in the Sacramento papers, which headline the story. The Peace Corps official is vague in response.

1968. We are, both of us, deep in the sixties now. But Larry Faherty has nowhere to go when the sixties become the sixties. From Africa he quotes Ayn Rand; he grumbles about the uniform answers of the newly fashionable left. His mood passes. His liberal heart cannot justify America's war in Vietnam, and his next letter says so.

The letters become less frequent. I am living in New York. I hear he is living in Paris. I have no address for him there. In New York, at Columbia, student demonstrations in April close down the university. Politically, I still think of myself as of the left. I write letters to congressmen. I march in antiwar demonstrations up Fifth Avenue. But I cannot follow the decade all the way down the line. Date my defection with the murder of Dr. Martin Luther King, Jr. After his death, the Pauline vision of a society united is undermined by hack radicals like Stokley Carmichael, proclaiming a protestant separatist line. The virtue of the sixties moves from integration to defiance. The posture of the outsider is perceived as glamorous. Students at Columbia are reading *The Student as Nigger* in order to justify their privilege, a version of noblesse oblige which puts me in mind of the rah-rah twits in a Wodehouse comedy.

I do not believe in sudden protestant changes, reformations, so much as I believe in fade-outs and soft loosenings. My friendship with Larry Faherty has no denouement.

There is a vacuity, an abeyance, an alignment to the spring afternoon as I walk defiantly toward the library between jeering students and silent policemen. The protest is all about me—about the need for more "minority students" and the "racist" university. Rocks and bottles are thrown and the horses charge in my wake.

For religious as well as for temperamental reasons, it is impossible for me to imagine a propriety which will justify the seizure of an office of authority. I will never be a hero of the sixties brand. I will go to the library to confront the Protestant Reformation.

A manufactured sign in somebody's dormitory window urges passersby to "Question Authority." Why (me with my Samsonite briefcase) should one simply, as a matter of reflex, question authority?

An august historian of Protestant history lectures on Galileo—the inevitable example—as I sit in the classroom and I am silent, though I would protest to him that, if the church was wrong, it was possibly wrong for a valid reason. For the church sought to protect the communal vision, the Catholic world—a rounded, weighted, lovely thing—against an anarchy implicit in the admission of novelty. Novelty should only come from within the church; a question not of facts but of authority.

America is the fruit of a Northern European idea of freedom. How should I protest? America has justified modernity. How much can America hear from the Catholic schoolboy who defends the medieval Catholic dream? Of what value to America are notions of authority, communality, continuity? Tolerance is the noble Protestant virtue to replace Catholic orthodoxy. But, lacking a Catholic longing for union, what could America's protestant sixties lend to the Protestant enterprise beyond flea-bitten utopias—reversions to an arcadian world—nomadic trappings, natural religion, mushrooms, sitars, incense?

The sixties offered assurance that middle-class Americans, even Americans among the upper classes who yearned for purity, could disenfranchise themselves, see themselves, by virtue of their era, as orphans of authority and that way achieve ultimate identification with "the people." All you had to do was leave home.

His head bandaged after a student–police riot in the university president's office, a friend at Columbia tells me that only during the sit-in had he come to understand the meaning of "community."

Many of the hundreds of riot policemen on campus at Columbia eat in John Jay Hall. They eat, most of them, on one side of the cafeteria; most of the students eat on the other. I make it a practice, a theatrical point, of sitting on the blue side, among what Catholic intuition teaches me to recognize as the righteous angels.

It was not then nor is it now a matter of divorcing myself from the opinions of the left. In the contest of politics, I was of the left. But in the overarching debate, I took the Catholic side, even if I saw the Protestant necessity clearly. The era's individualism seemed to me to stray too far from the communal need, an exploration of limits I privately called by its Catholic name: error.

What happened to the boys I grew up with at Christian Brothers? What happened to my teachers? What happened to the church? We were educated in the sixteenth century and then set loose in the modern city.

A mile from where I live now, an ex-cop, an ex-boxer named Dan White was elected to the Board of Supervisors of San Francisco— the city of gays, of drugs, of violence, of rock. Dan White remembered the neighborhoods as villages. He had never really been to the city before. He went mad. He crawled through a window of city hall with a loaded gun in his pocket. He murdered the mayor and the homosexual member of the Board of Supervisors. Newspaper accounts described Dan White's house. There were maps of Ireland on the walls and there were holy pictures and there were phonograph records of Irish ballads, sentimental and stirring.

It is possible to recognize the stuff of ballads in the life of Dan White, to recognize in the story of a dishonored man the American Catholic dilemma carried to an impossible conclusion.

In the 1840s, the nativist argument against accepting the Irish in the U.S. was Mexico. The fear was that the Irish would conspire with their fellow papists to overturn Protestant America. The truth of my education was that Catholicism made Irish immigrants, as it made me, into the sort of Americans who upheld the collective idea of America, even more perhaps than did the Puritan fathers for whom this country was an escape.

Something is now clear about Larry and that is my betrayal of him. The last time I saw Larry Faherty, he was ducking down in the backseat of his father's Chrysler in the parking lot of the Greyhound station. Larry had wanted to see me. Our meeting was rushed, nervous, but lacking the fervor demanded of it. Larry was on the lam, he was sure the cops were looking for him because he was in trouble with the draft board. He wasn't supposed to be in the country.

"Salutti Beulah Mumm . . . ?" He hoisted a duffel bag onto his shoulder.

Just go, I thought.

Then the dusty Greyhound carried my blessed hero away. The last I heard he was in Mexico, where I imagine his rebellious soul lapped by corrupt, warm waters.

In 1973, I went to England to pursue a study of puritanism and the rise of the novel. I sat in the darkening library of the Warburg Institute reading *Paradise Lost*. Even as I became fascinated with the glamour of Milton's Satan, I saw the absolute necessity to avert my soul's eye from a logic that would make mere individualism a virtue. The logic of Milton's faith made Satan the hero of man's creation.

ENVOI

"Personal essays," the editor writes—not theory, autobiography. He says he is compiling a book of them, points of view. "Describe the odyssey you took through the sixties, how your life was changed. . . ."

The sixties never happened to me. I didn't get a divorce. I never took drugs. I didn't schoon the desert in a VW van. I wasn't packed off to Saigon or chased up into Canada. "I don't even listen to rock music," I answered him.

The sixties were gringo time. White-middle-class crisis! The white middle class decided it no longer wanted the diploma, the seals, the ribbons and the stole I had cherished from boyhood. The white middle class pretended to be poor. I took the prizes, as many as I could get, but I had no competition.

The man who lives across the hall tells me that he is interested in studying Hinduism. He grew up an Irish-Catholic.

The prescription of the sixties was for cutting loose. But I believe in continuous time, as I believe in God. I believe that the boy of ten relentlessly dogs the man of forty. Four blocks from where I live today, in St. Dominic's Church, my parents were married. I have, in forty years, traveled and lived in several cities and countries, have gone to universities and met people. And I have ended up four blocks from the apartment house where my mother lived when she first came to America.

I would have liked you to believe that I strode through the protestant sixties purblind as Brideshead. As a Catholic schoolboy, I had been taught, if I had been taught nothing else, that we lived in a group. Ironically, this lesson implicates me in the sixties. Though I remain a Catholic I did not evade the sixties, nor did my church evade the sixties.

I live alone. I have no children. I read at night. I jog at noon. I live in an apartment in a four-story Victorian which was designed to house an optimistic nineteenth-century family of many polite children. There are no children in my neighborhood. Most of the people I know best are living lives changed from the lives of our parents.

"Go on back to the safe world of your Irish nunnies who praised you for being so obedient," one friend of mine says. Jewish. He doesn't go to temple, though, he prowls the public toilets of city parks, looking for sex. My friend says he is careful. He says I am sentimental.

St. Dominic's, down the block, is dark and sparsely attended. Most of the people in church who are my age sit alone, hugging their shriveling souls or else they sit staring through the bland recitation of vulgarized mysteries, and then they stand up and go home.

It is a liturgy meant to assure those of us who live in the city, alone in what we rather hesitate to call our faith. The Catholic Church insists that we are still a community, notwithstanding the evidence of the empty pews. The lector announces the Proclamation of Faith through her microphone: "Letter B. Page 36 in your missalettes. 'When we eat this bread and drink this cup. . . .'" Proclaiming the death of the heart.

Most Sundays I cross town to attend mass in the Hispanic part of the city at St. Peter's, a nineteenth-century Irish church. It is dark and of an opulent vulgarity, with squeaky floors, a gallery of painted statues susceptible to candlelight and roses. A virile St. Patrick occupies a little gothic pavilion to the right of the main altar. The church is now filled with Spanish, with dark-eyed children and teen-aged parents, and with waves of the sound of wailing babies which puts one in mind of the souls in purgatory, and with the off-key, full-throated singing of the women of Mexico.

During the sermon I study the stained glass windows to the blessed memories of Mary Anns and Patricks. The Irish have left the city for suburbs. I expect this Hispanic generation sitting around me to make a similar journey toward the middle class and away from this village church in the heart of the city.

There comes a moment in *Hamlet* which seems to me one of the saddest moments in the world. *Hamlet* stops, literally Hamlet steps out of his play to address the audience. Hamlet stands alone and apart; Shakespeare no longer believes with Catholic assurance. The traditional faith of the playwright is that we are social creatures; all that is most essential to know about ourselves and about each other we know in communion, in conversation. The play tells all.

Hamlet becomes a modern man when he speaks his true heart

to the void. He leaves the play behind him—a contraption, a booth—his father's Chrysler. *Hamlet* becomes a novel, which is the genre that Protestantism gave literature.

Four blocks from my house is a gym where men with pale thin legs sit harnessed to bucking Nautilus machines like victims of polio. I pay money to hang upside down on a bar listening to Vivaldi on earphones. My guru, my coach, is a twenty-four-year-old man from Dublin who is training to compete next year in the Mr. Ireland contest.

Another teacher, before she died, sent me a card, a confident florid verse. Sister Mary Regis (she also signs herself in the post–Vatican Council style with her family name—Sister Mary Downey) tells me that she will not be able to come to the lecture I am going to give in Sacramento as she has a "chronic illness." (She is dying of cancer.) "Keep me in your prayers and I do you."

"When the nuns die, they die alone," Father O'Neil (he of the slides of Ireland) says to me a few months later. We are walking in the school yard of Sacred Heart; we are followed by a photographer who is shooting a going-home-again-article for *People* magazine, because my book has just been published. The photographer encourages Father O'Neil to "act normal."

I remember when Father O'Neil arrived from Ireland. His hair was black. He was handsome. He was shy. He apologized for his Irish, then. In this pause I am facing a man with gold teeth and gray hair. But the accent endures as a hint of youth clinging to him.

"None of their students ever come back. . . ." He is talking of Sister Mary Regis. I ask him how many nuns are left teaching at Sacred Heart School. There are two.

Sister Mary Regis writes: "Yes, I have fond memories of you and your days at Sacred Heart. Do you remember that you carried a notebook and asked millions of questions?"

I want to praise them. They deserve better than the ridicule the sixties heaped at their feet. I did not learn from any other of my teachers as I learned from my nuns that teaching is a vocation, a holy life, selfless, complete.

At Berkeley, in 1975, my sixties came to an end. The popular press discovered what it called the "me generation" on campus. No more warm-weather revolutions. I taught Freshman English while the Asian students at the back of my classroom studied biochemistry behind propped-up Shakespeares. I lectured on *Hamlet*.

One yellow day in April revolution came to me. It was time for me to graduate to a full-time teaching position. I'd had offers. That day—the day I had to make a choice—I decided to turn down all offers by way of rejecting the romantic label the sixties had pinned on me: "Minority Student." I just didn't want it. I moved across the Bay to San Francisco. I publicly scorned the sixties and became entangled in the memory of the era as a critic.

Which is how you find me now, on a Sunday morning in 1987. Over my desk is an etching by David Hockney from a suite of etchings suggested by the fairy tales of Grimm: A reading chair, empty, by a tall window. Outside the leafed trees. Titled *The Boy Who Left Home.*

In a few minutes I will be leaving for the church across town, the Mexican church I told you about, where still I search for home.

"Keep me in your prayers," the nun would write to her third-grade student, remembering him as a boy on her deathbed. And I do you. Oh Ireland, Ireland.

Index

Abel, Lionel, 12
Abortion, 26
Abrams, Elliott, 214
Abrams, Jacob, 213
Acheson, Dean, 282
Acton, Lord, 250, 254, 271
Actualizations, 322
Adorno, Theodor, 18, 108, 315
Affirmative action, 95
Africa, black identification with, 69
African National Congress, 237
Afro-American culture, 95
Afro-American studies, 54
After Virtue (MacIntyre), 243
AIDS, 184, 185
Alcatraz, 176
Allen, James, 10
America, 298, 299
American Civil Liberties Union, 147, 153
American Federation of Teachers, 138–141,
  143, 148, 152
American Historical Association, 223, 225
American Militarism 1970, 258
Americanization, 157, 158
Antinomianism, 14–23, 25–29
Anti-Semitism, 39, 43, 123, 234
Aquinas, Thomas, 254
Arendt, Hannah, 108
Aristotle, 254
Armstrong, James, 296
Aron, Raymond, 125
Arts in Society, 75
Ascent of the Mountain, Flight of the Dove (No-
  vak), 258
Auerbach, Solomon, 10
Ayres, Billy, 177

Baez, Joan, 37, 181, 280, 295
Bagdikian, Ben, 184
Bakunin, Mikhail Aleksandrovich, 57
Baldwin, James, 171
Baldwin, Roger, 295
Balzac, Honoré de, 48
Baraldini, Sylvia, 117
Baran, Paul, 17, 108
Barnet, Richard, 258, 296

Bastiat, 254
Beat Generation, 64
Beauvoir, Simone de, 108
Bedacht, Max, 7
Bell, Daniel, 125, 154
Bellow, Saul, 12
Benjamin, Walter, 108
Bennett, John, 248
Bentham, Jeremy, 57
Berkeley, California, 13, 47, 164–166, 174,
  175, 221
Berman, Paul, 236
Bernstein, Eduard, 9
Bernstein, Leonard, 48
Berrigan, Daniel, 20, 280, 289
Berrigan, Philip, 280, 289
Besig, Ernest, 147
Best, George, 81–82
Bierce, Ambrose, 56
Bilingual education, 157–158
Bill of Rights, 86
Bittner, Egon, 122
Black consciousness movement, 35, 69
Black Muslims, 78, 218
Black Panthers, 35, 47, 48, 78, 79, 83, 84,
  117–119, 170, 174, 200–202, 203
  in 1970s, 178–179
Black power movement, 19, 69, 70, 218
Black Students Union, 133, 136, 137, 138
Black studies, 137
Blacks
  civil rights movement, 19
  communists and, 10
Bloch, Ernst, 110
Boat people, 120
Bohemianism, 16, 28
Boll, Heinrich, 248
Bolsheviks, 6, 9
Bond, Julian, 280
Book of Laughter and Forgetting, The (Kundera),
  187
Boudin, Cathy, 214
Bourne, Randolph, 108
Boyd, Malcolm, 295
Brandeis University, 122
Brandes, Georg, 10

Bravo, Obando y, 298
Brink's robbery, 117, 220, 236
Browder, Earl, 7
Brown, H. Rap, 47
Brown, Norman, 18
Brown, Robert McAfee, 242, 248, 250, 296, 337
Brownmiller, Susan, 319
Bruce-Biggs, B., 257
Brzezinski, Zbigniew, 141
Budapest School, 123
Buitrago, Ann Mari, 235
Bukharin, Nikolay, 6
Bunche, Ralph, 4
Burgess, Ernest, 14
Burke, Edmund, 254
Burton, Philip, 153

Call to Action, 292
Calley, Lieutenant, 294
Cambodia, 35, 117, 120, 200, 221
Cambridge, Massachusetts, 3
Camus, Albert, 108, 248, 250
Cannon, James, 7
Capitalism, 44, 58, 241, 244, 272
  freedom and, 123–124, 125
  redefining, 265–267
Carlson, Anton, 14
Carmichael, Stokely, 47, 70, 71, 72–73, 74, 145, 218, 341
Carr, E. H., 108
Carter, Amy, 86
Carter, Jimmy, 155, 183, 258
Castro, Fidel, 73, 74, 228, 230, 237, 299
Catholic left, 285, 286, 288, 291
Catholic Worker, 282–283
Catholicism, 271
  liberalism and, 275–276
Catonsville Nine, 289
Cavour, Camillo, 287
Center for Advanced Study in the Behavioral Sciences, 154
Center for Cuban Studies, 228
Center for European Studies, 126
Central America, 231, 235, 297–298, 300
Century of the Child (Key), 21
Chaney, James, 66
Chessman, Caryl, 165
Chicago, Democratic Convention in, 36–37, 173–174
Chomsky, Noam, 26, 50, 108
Christianity and Crisis, 273, 274, 280, 283
CIA, 74, 86, 87, 169
City College of New York, 13
City University of New York, 221–223
Civil Rights Act of 1964, 69
Civil Rights Bill, 68
Civil rights movement, 19, 46–47, 60, 61, 64, 65, 69, 89, 96, 97, 167–168, 175, 217
Clancy, William, 275–276
Cleaver, Eldridge, 78, 170–171, 174
Cleaver, Kathleen, 78–79
Clergy and Laity Concerned About Vietnam, 281, 284
Cline, Ray, 273
Coalition for a Democratic Majority, 155, 257
Coffin, William Sloane, 19

Cohelan, Jeffrey, 169
Cohen, Roberta, 295
Cold War, 215, 219
Collectivistic liberalism, 28–31
Columbia University, 114
Commentary, 41, 234, 257
Commission on the Church's Participation in Development, 290
Committee on Degrees in Social Studies, Harvard, 124
Committee for the Free World, 273
Committee in Support of Central America, 185
Commonweal, 248, 274, 275, 278, 299
Communism, 8, 128, 194, 236
  nature of, 267–269
Communist Party, 2, 15, 16, 28, 29, 112, 185, 193, 209–211, 231
  in 1970s, 177–178
  Soviet, 297
Communists, 8, 9, 11–12, 13, 14, 216
  blacks and, 10
Connections, 108
Connor, Bull, 167
Conrad, Joseph, 41, 48, 313
Conservatism, 208
Conservatives, advantages over liberals, 45–46
Constitutional liberalism, 15, 16, 29
Cook, Fred J., 258
Coover, Robert, 44
CORE (Congress of Racial Equality), 62, 166, 217
Cornell University, 22
Corporate liberalism, 215, 239
Council on Religion and International Affairs, 280
Courage to Be, The (Tillich), 324
Cox, Harvey, 248
Cronkite, Walter, 173
Cuba, 74, 228–230, 244
Cuomo, Mario, 44

Dahl, Robert, 145
Daley, Richard, 173
Davis, Angela, 213
Day, Dorothy, 280, 282, 295
Debray, Regis, 229
December 4th Movement, 117
Decter, Midge, 55
Dellinger, Dave, 83, 85, 218–219, 230
Democracy vs. totalitarianism, 237
Democratic Convention
  Chicago, 1968, 36–37, 173–174
  1984, 44
Democratic Mask, The (Payne), 297
Democratic Socialist Organizing Committee, 231–232, 234, 235
Democratic Socialists of America, 235
Der proletarische Sozialismus (Sombart), 9
D'Escoto, Miguel, 235, 298
Desegregation, 63
Deutscher, Isaac, 108, 166, 199, 215, 224, 225
Dewey, John, 21
Dissent, 41, 51, 285

Divestment, 26, 54, 56
Dixon, Marlene, 22–23, 24
Doctorow, E. L., 44, 57
Dohrn, Bernadine, 175, 177
Doors, the, 175
Dornbusch, Sanford, 158
Douglass, James, 295
Downriver (Collier), 182
Draft, 49
Drugs, 48
Du Bois, W. E. B., 214
Du Bois Clubs, 216
Duarte, Napoleon, 297
Dunn, Robert, 7
Durkheim, Emile, 125
Dynamics of Faith (Tillich), 64

Economy of Death, The (Barnet), 258
Eisenhower, David, 40
Eisenhower, Dwight, 279
El Salvador, 273, 274, 297
Eliot, T. S., 323
Ellison, Ralph, 167
Ellsberg, Daniel, 86
Empire and Revolution (Horowitz), 199
Encounter, 41
Engels, Friedrich, 11
Enzensberger, Hans Magnus, 228
Esquire, 26
Euromissile controversy, 126, 127–129
Experience of Nothingness, The (Novak), 259,
    263

Fair Play for Cuba Committee, 35–36
Fairbank, John, 226
Falk, Richard, 296
Fanon, Franz, 108, 174
Farakhan, Louis, 55
Farmer, James, 217
Fellowship of Reconciliation, 295
Feminism, 55, 129–130, 312, 314–320
Feuer, Lewis, 163
Finnegan's Rainbow (Joyce), 62
Fisk University, 61–62
Fitzgerald, Frances, 19
Foley, Tom, 257
Fonda, Jane, 175–176, 181
Foner, Philip, 230
Foner, Laura, 220
Ford, Henry, 57
Ford, James, 10
Forest, Jim, 295
Forster, E. M., 43
Foster, W. Z., 7
Frank, Gunder, 17
Frankfurt Institut fuer Sozialforschung, 18
Frankfurt School, 110, 122
Franklin, Bruce, 185–186
Free love, 28
Free Speech Movement, 35, 47, 166
Free University, 218
Freedom Rides, 88, 89
Freud, Sigmund, 125
Friedan, Betty, 172
Fund for Open Information and Accountabil-
    ity, Inc., 234

Geertz, Clifford, 109
Genet, Jean, 36
Genovese, Eugene, 223, 225, 226
Gerassi, John, 291
German Communist Party, 8
Gerth, Hans, 108
Gilbert, David, 220
Gilson, Etienne, 276
Ginsberg, Allen, 37, 64, 165, 295
Gitlow, Benjamin, 7
Glazer, Nathan, 51–52, 234
Goldwater, Barry, 280
Goodman, Andrew, 66
Goodman, Paul, 18, 19, 37, 43, 108
Gorbachev, Mikhail, 129, 243
Great Britain, 129
Greeley, Andrew, 158, 292
Green, Edith, 153
Greene, Graham, 248
Grinnell College, 106
Guardian, 77–83, 234
Guevara, Che, 74, 229
Gumbleton, Thomas, 295
Gurian, Waldemar, 8

Habermas, Jurgen, 18
Haight-Ashbury, 32–34, 172
Halberstein, Seymour Bob, 35
Handlin, Oscar, 157
Hare, Nathan, 137, 149
Harrington, Michael, 216, 231–232, 234, 235,
    248, 254
Harris, Abram, 4
Harvard, 13, 55, 93, 114, 123–125, 221
Havana General Psychiatric Hospital, 229
Hayakawa, S. I., 135, 139
Hayden, Tom, 165, 173–175, 181, 199, 216
Hayek, Friedrich, 254, 260, 265
Haywood, Harry, 10
Heart of Darkness (Conrad), 313
Heilbroner, Robert, 264
Heller, Joseph, 220
Hentoff, Nat, 216
Heschel, Abraham Joshua, 280
Hilliard, David, 174
Hinckle, Warren, 169
Hiss, Alger, 21, 31
Hiss-Chambers trial, 50–51
Historical Materialism (Bukharin), 6
Hitler, Adolph, 8, 195, 270
Ho Chi Minh, 80, 81, 90, 116
Hoffer, Eric, 172
Hoffman, Abbie, 37, 86, 87, 224
Hoffmann, Stanley, 125
Hofstadter, Richard, 140
Hollywood, 3
Holmes, John Clellon, 64
Holmes, Oliver Wendell, 58, 213
Holocaust, 123, 124
Homosexuality, 26
Hook, Sidney, 237, 261
Hope Against Hope (Mandelstam), 42
Horkheimer, Max, 18, 108, 123
Horowitz, David, 175, 176, 178, 182, 183,
    185
House Committee on Un-American Activities,
    214

House Subcommittee on Education, 153
Howard University, 4
Howe, Irving, 38, 216, 222, 232, 235, 237, 264
Hubbard, Ron, 14
Hume, Britt, 170
Humphrey, Hubert, 36, 37, 154, 174, 256, 257, 261, 282
Huntington, Samuel, 125
Huntley-Brinkley, 70

Idealism, 58
In These Times, 223, 231
Independent Committees to End the War, 219, 220
Individualistic liberalism, 15, 16
Industrial Party, 7
Industrial Workers of the World, 28
Institute on Religion and Democracy, 298
Intellectuals, 53–54, 118–119
  nature of, 40–41
Intellectuals and the Powers and Other Essays (Shils), 53
International League for Human Rights, 295
Interracial relationships, 76–77
Invisible Man (Ellison), 167
Israel, 124

Jackson, George, 183–184
Jackson, Henry ("Scoop"), 174, 257
Jackson, Jesse, 58, 237
Jackson State, 117
James, Henry, 48, 56, 59
James, William, 156
Jaspers, Karl, 46
Jefferson, John, 167, 168
Jefferson, Thomas, 260
Jefferson Airplane, 222
Jet, 72
Jews, 48, 106, 124
  politics and, 38–39
Jews in the Russian Revolutionary Movement (Schapiro), 39
John Birch Society, 149
John XXIII, Pope, 279–280
Johnson, Lyndon, 36, 72, 172, 219, 256, 280, 282
Joyce, James, 62

Kaplan, Harold, 12
Keniston, Kenneth, 91
Kennedy, John, 165–166, 256, 279, 280, 331
Kennedy, Robert, 172, 250, 256
Kent State, 117, 221, 222
Kerouac, Jack, 64, 165
Kesey, Ken, 295
Key, Ellen, 20–21
Keynes, John Maynard, 43
Khmer Rouge, 120–121
Khrushchev, Nikita, 122, 165, 211, 275
"Khrushchev divorces," 188, 189, 191
Kimbro, Warren, 83, 84
King, Martin Luther Jr., 47, 48, 58, 89, 156, 167, 172, 218, 280, 285, 337, 341
Kirkpatrick, Jeane, 110
Kissinger, Henry, 121
Knight, Frank, 10, 13

Koestler, Arthur, 163
Kolakowski, Leszek, 108, 205–207, 235, 236, 253
Kopkind, Andrew, 48
Kristol, Irving, 41, 51, 53, 172, 254
Krueger, Maynard, 10
Ku Klux Klan, 167
Kundera, Milan, 182, 187

Lamont, Corliss, 296
Landes, David, 125–126
Laos, 200
Lasch, Christopher, 223
Latin America, 289
Lawrence, T. E., 42
Le Proces de Socrate (Sorel), 9
League for Industrial Democracy, 216
Leary, Timothy, 225
Leftism, 48, 51, 56–58
  See also New Left
Leites, Nathan, 12
Lenin, Vladimir, 9, 11, 37, 57
Leninism, 268–269
Lester, Julius, 79
Levertov, Denise, 280
Levi, Edward, 23, 24
Levine, David, 220
Levinson, Sandra, 228, 230
Lewis, John, 280
Liberal, defined, 40
Liberalism, 15, 16, 47, 55, 57, 155, 157, 283, 293
  Catholicism and, 275–276
  collectivistic, 28–31
  constitutional, 29
  corporate, 215, 239
Liberals, conservatives and, 45–46
Liberation, 83, 85–86, 219, 230
Lichtheim, George, 108
Little Rock, Arkansas, 47
Look Out, Whitey! Black Power's Gon' Get Your Mama! (Lester), 60, 76
Los Angeles Times, 134
Lovestone, Jay, 7
LSD, 225
Luce, Don, 296
Luce, Henry, 44, 171
Lukacs, Georg, 108, 110, 123, 128
Luxemburg, Rosa, 221
Lynd, Robert, 145
Lynd, Staughton, 216, 218, 225, 280

McCarthy, Eugene, 281
McCarthy, Joseph, 21, 31, 149, 165, 278
McCarthy, Mary, 50
McCleary, Paul, 296
Macdonald, Dwight, 108, 237–238
McGovern, George, 154, 174, 256
MacIntyre, Alasdair, 243
McLucas, Lonnie, 83, 84, 85
McNamara, Robert, 50, 87
Mage, Shane, 224–225
Mailer, Norman, 36–37, 104, 314
Main Currents of European Literature in the Nineteenth Century (Brandes), 10
Malcolm X, 108, 218
Malraux, André, 42

Man, Henry de, 9
Mandelstam, Nadezhda, 42
Mao Tsetung, 8
Maoist Progressive Labor Party, 112
Marcuse, Herbert, 108, 109, 117, 119, 125, 149, 224, 251–252
Maritain, Jacques, 276
Markowitz, Norman, 234
Marx, Karl, 11, 48, 57, 125, 322
Marxism, 9, 13, 17, 25, 54, 55, 124, 128, 198–199, 205, 235–236
Marxist Perspectives, 223
Meeropol, Michael, 214, 233
Meeropol, Robert, 214, 233
Melman, Seymour, 258
Melville, Marjorie, 289
Melville, Thomas, 289, 290
Mencken, H. L., 7, 46, 58, 171
Menshevism, 224
Metro-Vickers trial, 7
Meyer, Frank, 11–12, 14
Mezvinsky, Ed, 215
Michels, Robert, 9
Miliband, Ralph, 206, 207
Mill, John Stuart, 57, 125, 254
Miller, Arthur, 214
Mills, C. Wright, 17, 26, 43, 108, 145, 228
Milton, Joyce, 234
Minerva, 20
Minor, Robert, 7
Mississippi, 67, 69
Mississippi Freedom Democratic Party, 61
Mississippi Summer Project, 61, 67
Mitford, Jessica, 184
Montesquieu, 254
Monthly Review, 236
Moravia, Alberto, 248
Morgenthau, Hans, 287, 288
Mosse, George, 108
Moynihan, Daniel Patrick ("Pat"), 51, 257
Mumford, Lewis, 43, 48
Murray, John Courtney, 276
Muskie, Ed, 256

Nation, The, 11, 234, 292
National Catholic Reporter, 248, 281
National Council of Churches, 292, 297
National Guardian, 234
National Security Agency, 176–177
National Welfare Rights Organization, 78
NATO, 127, 128, 129
Navasky, Victor, 214, 234
Nazism, 122, 123, 124
Nearing, Scott, 7
Negotiations Now, 219
Neier, Aryeh, 295
Nessen, Charles, 177
Neuhaus, Richard, 280, 295
Neumann, Franz, 108
New American Movement, 232
New Class, The, 257
New Criterion, The, 236
New German Critique, 123
New Haven Seven, 83–85
New Left, 16, 17, 106, 107, 112–114, 116, 117, 119–123, 127–130, 162, 163, 165, 169–175, 178, 183, 185, 186, 189, 195, 197–200,

202, 205, 206, 213, 215–220, 226, 229, 231, 232, 235, 247, 285, 310, 311, 320, 321
New Republic, 11, 231, 282
New University Conference, 221
New York City, 3
New York Review of Books, 26, 48
New York Times, 11, 134, 177, 273
New York Times Book Review, 234
New Yorker, The, 48
Newfield, Jack, 216
Newman, Cardinal, 260
Newman, John Henry, 254
Newport Folk Foundation, 69
Newton, Huey, 78, 116, 145, 174, 178
Nicaragua, 231, 235, 237, 244, 268, 298
Niebuhr, Reinhold, 248, 259, 274, 292
Nixon, Richard, 21, 35, 36, 37, 48, 154, 155, 173, 221, 225, 258, 261, 282
Nonconformity, 41
Nonviolence, 65

O'Brien, Conor Cruise, 224
Oglesby, Carl, 107
Old Left, 16, 17
Old Westbury, State University of New York at, 250–253
One-Dimensional Man (Marcuse), 109, 117, 119
OPEC, 124
Open marriage, 35
Organization of Latin-American Solidarity, 72
Orgone therapy, 321, 322, 323
Ortega, Daniel, 237
Orwell, George, 58, 181
Other America, The (Harrington), 248
Oxford University conference, 1973, 205

Pareto, Vilfredo, 9
Park, Robert, 8
Partisan Review, 41, 44, 128
Passin, Herbert, 12
Payne, Douglas, 297
Peace movements, 126–127, 128, 129
Peguy, Charles, 299
Pentagon Capitalism (Melman), 258
Peretz, Marty, 126
Perkins, James, 22
Philadelphia, 6–7
Piccone, Paul, 128
Pitts, Elijah, 167
Plamenatz, John, 159
Podhoretz, Norman, 51, 257, 273, 286
Poland, Jefferson, 136
Political Parties (Michels), 9
Political Passages, 20
Pool, Ithiel, 12
Princess Casamassima, The (James), 56
Private ownership, 15
Progressive Labor Party, 216, 220
Progressivism, 266
Protest: Pacifism and Politics (Finn), 280

Queensborough Community College, 220

Rackley, Alex, 83, 84, 85
Radical Caucus of Historians, 225
Radosh, Ronald, 126, 230

Ramparts, 169–172, 175, 176, 182, 183, 215, 228
Ramsey, Paul, 280
Randolph, A. Philip, 218
Reagan, Ronald, 55, 129, 155, 184–185, 189, 196, 207, 221, 235, 299
Red Family, 175
Reich, Wilhelm, 321–323
Reisman, David, 42, 140
Republic of New Africa, 78
Reuther, Walter, 232
Revolutionary Notes (Lester), 77
Revolutionary Youth Movement I, 112
Revolutionary Youth Movement II, 112
Right to Know, 234
Rise of the Unmeltable Ethnics, The (Novak), 255, 256, 259
Robinson, Hyacinth, 56
Rockefeller, John D., 57
Rockefellers, 182
Rolling Stone, 170
Roman Catholic. *See* Catholicism
Rosenberg, Arthur, 8
Rosenberg, Ethel, 31, 50–51, 214, 233, 234, 235
Rosenberg, Harold, 41
Rosenberg, Julius, 31, 50–51, 214, 233, 234, 235
Rosenberg File, The (Radosh), 234
Rosenfeld, Isaac, 12
Rostow, Eugene, 273
Rubin, Jerry, 172, 173
Rusk, Dean, 50
Russell, Bertrand, 8
Russian Revolution, 42
Rustin, Bayard, 218, 280

Sacco-Vanzetti trial, 50–51
Sahl, Mort, 40
Sams, George, 83, 84
San Francisco State College, 132, 135–137, 139, 141, 142, 151, 153, 154, 155, 159
Sandinistas, 231, 237, 260, 297
SANE Nuclear Policy Committee, 219
Santayana, George, 45, 48
Sartre, Jean-Paul, 108
Saying Yes and Saying No (Brown), 241–242
Schachtman, Max, 7
Schapiro, Leonard, 39
Scheer, Robert, 169, 175
Schmidt, Helmut, 129
Schneider, Bert, 178
Schuman, Frederick, 14
Schwerner, Michael, 66, 67
SDS (Students for a Democratic Society), 106, 107, 113, 114, 116, 118, 122, 133, 148, 150, 154, 175, 215, 216, 220, 232
Seale, Bobby, 84, 174
Second Vatican Council, 250
Secret Agent, The (Conrad), 41
Segregation, 63
Sex, 48
Sexual freedom, 28
Shaw, Bernard, 48
Sheen, Fulton J., 281
Shils, Edward, 53, 54
Shriver, Sargent, 255–257

Shrum, Robert, 256
Silone, Ignazio, 248
Silverman, Don, 220
Sit-ins, 64
  University of Chicago, 23–24
Slippery-slope argument, 51
Smith, Adam, 125, 254, 265
SNCC (Student Non-Violent Coordinating Committee), 60, 62, 65, 69, 70, 71, 76, 78, 79, 81, 82, 167, 218
Social democracy, 9, 17, 28, 130
Social fascism, 8
Socialism, 9–10, 16, 43, 58, 206, 235, 244, 253–254, 263–265, 272
Socialist Review, 223
Socialist Revolution, 223
Socialist Scholars Conference, 224, 225
Socialist Workers Party, 219
Solidarity, 123
Solidarity Left, 181, 185
Solzhenitsyn, Alexander, 123, 320, 322
Sombart, Werner, 6, 9
Sontag, Susan, 20, 26, 50
Sorel, Georges, 9
Sorensen, Theodore, 220
Soul On Ice (Cleaver), 170
South Africa, 54, 237
Southern, Terry, 36
Southern Christian Leadership Conference, 78
Soviet Union, 7, 9, 110, 120, 126–129, 193, 198, 231, 232, 243, 260, 269, 279, 299
  antinomianism and, 17, 18, 27–28
Spanish Civil War, 236–237
Spartacist League, 224
Spirit of Democratic Capitalism, The (Novak), 260, 269
Spock, Dr. Benjamin, 19
Stalin, Joseph, 171, 194, 195, 270
Steffens, Lincoln, 6
Steinbeck, John, 172
Stender, Fay, 183, 184
Stendhal, 48
Stern, Sol, 215, 233
Stevenson, Adlai, 40, 45
Stokes, Louis, 153, 154
Stone, I. F., 166–167
Strategic Defense Initiative, 26
Students for a Democratic Society. *See* SDS
Studies on the Left, 215–217, 223, 231, 236
Sufrin, Sidney, 9–10
Summerskill, John, 137
Sunday Ramparts, 170
Sunnyside, Queens, 188, 190–191
Sussman, Warren, 223
Sweezy, Paul, 17, 108, 236
Swift, Jonathan, 38
Synanon, 172
Systèmes socialistes (Pareto), 9

Tawney, R. H., 6, 241
Telos, 123, 128, 229
Teresa, Mother, 46
Theory and Practice of Bolshevism (Russell), 8
"Third of September, The" (Lester), 80–81
Third World, 58, 113, 124, 228, 241, 292, 299

Third World Liberation Front, 133, 135, 137, 138
Thomas, Norman, 217, 218–219
Thompson, E. P., 108, 235
Thompson, Hunter, 170
Thucydides, 141–142
Tiber was Silver, The (Novak), 239
Tillich, Paul, 64, 324
Time, 79
Tocqueville, Alexis de, 125
Tolstoy, Leo, 77
Torres, Camilo, 291
Totalitarianism, 12, 14–18, 25–28, 130, 193, 194, 196, 197, 237
Toward a Theology of Radical Politics (Novak), 256, 261
Travers, Mary, 214
Treutlein, Theodore, 147
Troeltsch, Ernst, 6
Trotsky, Leon, 7, 8, 42, 57, 142, 171
Trotskyists, 12
  in Socialist Workers Party, 219–220
Truman Doctrine, 171

Ulysses (Joyce), 62
United Nations, 124
  sit-in at, 227
Universities
  antinomian activity in, 21–22
  attacks against, 20
  liberalism in, 55–56
  violence at, 47
University of Chicago, 10–13, 20, 22–25, 39, 40
University of Wisconsin, 3, 13, 107–109, 111, 214

Valladares, Armando, 299
Valls, Jorge, 299
Van Patter, Betty, 178–179, 183, 202
Vietnam, 35
Vietnam War, 19, 36, 49, 50, 107, 110, 112, 118, 119–121, 127, 130, 155, 173, 181, 199–200, 215–221, 225–226, 228, 250, 253, 281, 283, 284, 294–296
Vonnegut, Kurt, 44
Voting Rights Act of 1964, 69

Walgreen, Albert, 11
Walker, Alice, 89
Wallace, George, 149
Wallace, Mike, 281
Warfare State, The (Cook), 258
Warhol, Andy, 36
Washington *Post*, 184
Waskow, Arthur, 225
Watergate, 35
Weather sisters, 130
Weather Underground, 220, 236
Weatherman, 35, 112, 114–117, 119, 175, 177, 184
Weber, Max, 6, 125, 267
Weinstein, James, 223, 231
Weiss, Cora, 296
Wenner, Jann, 170
West Germany, 124, 126, 127, 129
Westmoreland, General, 50
White, Dan, 343
Williams, Raymond, 108
Williams, William A., 108, 215
Wilson, August, 312
Wirth, Louis, 11
Wofford, Harris, 251
Wolfe, Bertram, 7
Wolfe, Tom, 48
Wolff, Kurt, 122
Women's movement, 172
Women's Studies, 54
Wordsworth, William, 166
World Council of Churches, 290
World Marxist Review, 215
World of Our Fathers (Howe), 38
World Without War Council, 280–281
Wright, Richard, 171

Yom Kippur War of 1973, 124
Yugoslavia, 244
Yuppies, 258

Zahm, Gordon, 295
Zinn, Howard, 226, 295
Zionism, 124
Zumwalt, Elmo, 273
Zur Psychology des Marxismus (de Man), 9
Zwerdling, Daniel, 170